Neutrality in International Law

Neutrality is a legal relationship between a belligerent State and a State not participating in a war, namely a neutral State. The law of neutrality is a body of rules and principles that regulates the legal relations of neutrality. The law of neutrality obliges neutral States to treat all belligerent States impartially and to abstain from providing military and other assistance to belligerents. The law of neutrality is a branch of international law that developed in the nineteenth century, when international law allowed unlimited freedom of sovereign States to resort to war. Thus, there has been much debate as to whether such a branch of law remains valid in modern international law, which generally prohibits war and the use of force by States.

While there has been much debate regarding the current status of neutrality in modern international law, there is a general agreement among scholars as to the basic features of the traditional law of neutrality. Wani challenges the conventional understanding of the traditional neutrality by re-examining the historical development of the law of neutrality from the sixteenth century to 1945. The modification of the conventional understanding will provide a fundamentally new framework for discussing the current status of neutrality in modern international law.

Kentaro Wani is Associate Professor at the Osaka School of International Public Policy, Osaka University, Japan.

Routledge Advances in International Relations and Global Politics

121 **Regional Integration and Democratic Conditionality**
How democracy clauses help democratic consolidation and deepening
Gaspare M. Genna and Taeko Hiroi

122 **Profits, Security and Human Rights in Developing Countries**
Global lessons from Canada's extractive sector in Colombia
Edited by James Rochlin

123 **The Politics of Place and the Limits to Redistribution**
Melissa Ziegler Rogers

124 **Apology and Reconciliation in International Relations**
The importance of being sorry
Edited by Christopher Daase, Stefan Engert, Michel-André Horelt, Judith Renner, Renate Strassner

125 **The United States and Turkey's Path to Europe**
Hands across the table
Armağan Emre Çakır

126 **Western Muslim Reactions to Conflicts Abroad**
Conflict spillovers to diasporas
Juris Pupcenoks

127 **U.S. Security Cooperation with Africa**
Political and policy challenges
Robert J. Griffiths

128 **Russia's Relations with Kazakhstan**
Rethinking post-communist transitions in the emerging world system
Yelena Nikolayevna Zabortseva

129 **Reinventing Regional Security Institutions in Asia and Africa**
Power shifts, ideas, and institutional change
Kei Koga

130 **Sincerity in Politics and International Relations**
Edited by Sorin Baiasu and Sylvie Loriaux

131 **Neutrality in International Law**
From the sixteenth century to 1945
Kentaro Wani

Neutrality in International Law
From the sixteenth century to 1945

Kentaro Wani

LONDON AND NEW YORK

First published 2017
by Routledge

2 Park Square, Milton Park, Abingdon, Oxfordshire OX14 4RN
711 Third Avenue, New York, NY 10017

Routledge is an imprint of the Taylor & Francis Group, an informa business

First issued in paperback 2018

Copyright © 2017 Kentaro Wani

The right of Kentaro Wani to be identified as author of this work has been
asserted by him in accordance with sections 77 and 78 of the Copyright,
Designs and Patents Act 1988.

All rights reserved. No part of this book may be reprinted or reproduced or
utilised in any form or by any electronic, mechanical, or other means, now
known or hereafter invented, including photocopying and recording, or in
any information storage or retrieval system, without permission in writing
from the publishers.

Notice:
Product or corporate names may be trademarks or registered trademarks,
and are used only for identification and explanation without intent to infringe.

British Library Cataloguing in Publication Data
A catalogue record for this book is available from the British Library

Library of Congress Cataloging in Publication Data
Names: Wani, Kentarảo, 1977– author.
Title: Neutrality in international law : from the sixteenth century to 1945
/ Kentaro Wani.
Other titles: Dentảoteki chảuritsu seido no hảoteki seikaku. English
Description: Abingdon, Oxon ; New York, NY : Routledge is an imprint of
the Taylor & Francis Group, an Informa Business, [2017] |
Series: Routledge advances in international relations and global politics |
Includes bibliographical references and index.
Identifiers: LCCN 2016035214| ISBN 9781138284777 (hbk) |
ISBN 9781315269276 (ebk)Subjects: LCSH: Neutrality–History.
Classification: LCC KZ6422 .W3613 2017 | DDC 341.6/4–dc23
LC record available at https://lccn.loc.gov/2016035214

ISBN: 978-1-138-28477-7 (hbk)
ISBN: 978-1-138-36603-9 (pbk)

Typeset in Galliard
by Wearset Ltd, Boldon, Tyne and Wear

Contents

List of abbreviations	vii
Table of treaties	ix
Table of cases	xiv
Table of national legislations	xv
Acknowledgements	xviii

Introduction   1

    1 Conflicting views on the current status of the law of neutrality 2

    2 Generally accepted assumptions about the traditional law of neutrality 5

    3 Perspectives, objectives and the structure of the book 7

1 Origins of the concept of neutrality: neutrality from the sixteenth to eighteenth centuries   17

    1 Neutrality treaties: neutrality in State practice from the sixteenth to eighteenth centuries 18

    2 "Institutionalisation" of neutrality: the theory of neutrality presented by eighteenth-century scholars 26

    3 The place of the so-called "neutral commerce" in the historical development of the law of neutrality 39

2 The law of neutrality as an institution of general international law: 1793–1918   55

    1 The emergence of the law of neutrality as an institution of general international law 56

    2 The right to remain neutral and its conditions 102

vi *Contents*

**3 The development of the law of neutrality in the period
1919–45**   141

*1 Reliance and non-reliance on the law of neutrality during the
interwar period and the Second World War 142*
*2 A new conception of neutrality as presented by writers in the
interwar period: origins of the confusion that currently exists 164*

Conclusion   188

1 Conclusion of this book 188
2 Issues for further research 189

Bibliography   193
Index   223

Abbreviations

ADAP	*Akten zur Deutschen Auswärtigen Politik 1918–1945*
AJIL	*American Journal of International Law*
Argument of the United States	Argument of the United States, Delivered to the Tribunal of Arbitration at Geneva, 15 June 1872, in *PRTW* 3:1–258
BDFA	*British Documents on Foreign Affairs: Reports and Papers from the Foreign Office Confidential Print*
BFSP	*British and Foreign State Papers*
BYIL	*British Year Book of International Law*
Case of Great Britain	Case on the Part of the Government of Her Britannic Majesty to the Tribunal, in *PRTW* 1:205–413
Case of the United States	Case of the United States laid before the Tribunal of Arbitration at Geneva, in *PRTW* 1:1–204
Counter Case of Great Britain	Counter Case of Her Britannic Majesty's Government, in *PRTW* 2:197–410
Counter Case of the United States	Counter Case of the United States Presented to the Tribunal, in *PRTW* 1:414–856, and *PRTW* 2:1–196
CTS	Clive Parry, ed., *Consolidated Treaty Series*
DDB	*Documents diplomatiques belges, 1920–1940*
DDS	*Documents diplomatiques suisses: 1848–1945*
FRUS	*Foreign Relations of the United States*
LNTS	League of Nations, *Treaty Series*
PRTW	*Papers Relating to the Treaty of Washington*
RCADI	*Recueil des Cours de l'Academie de Droit International*
RDILC	*Revue de Droit International et de Législation Comparée*

viii *Abbreviations*

RGDIP	*Revue Générale de Droit International Public*
TNA: PRO	The National Archives (Public Record Office), London
UNTS	United Nations, *Treaty Series*
ZaöRV	*Zeitschrift für ausländisches öffentliches Recht und Völkerrecht*

For other abbreviations which are used in this book, see *The Bluebook: A Uniform System of Citation*, 20th ed. (Cambridge, Massachusetts: Harvard Law Review Association, 2015).

Table of treaties

1351
Treaty between England and Castile, signed at London, 1 August 1351   40

1353
Treaty of Commerce between England and Portugal, singed at London, 20 October 1353   40

1522
Neutrality Treaty between Burgundy and France, signed at Saint-Jean-de-Luz, 8 July 1522   19

1595
Treaty between France, Spain and the Swiss Confederation regarding the neutrality of Burgundy, singed at Lyon, 22 September 1595   19

1596
Letters of Neutrality Accorded to Lorraine by France, done at Abbeville, 19 June 1596   19, 21, 22, 26

1632
Neutrality treaty between Sweden and the Catholic German States, singed at Mainz, 29 January 1632   19–20, 26
Neutrality treaty between Trier and Sweden, singed at Mainz, 12 April 1632   19, 20, 21

1634
Treaty of Confederation and Alliance between France and Christian States of Circle and Franconia-Rhine, singed at Frankfurt, 20 September 1634   24–25

1646
Neutrality Treaty between France and Tuscany, signed at Florence, 11 May 1646   19, 21

1647
Neutrality Treaty between Mainz and France, signed at Frankfurt am Main, 9 May 1647   19

x *Table of treaties*

Neutrality Treaty between Sweden and Courland, signed at Holmiæ, 4 June 1647 19

1658

Neutrality Treaty between France and Mantua (Articles by which France Accords Neutrality to Mantua), signed at Modena, 9 July 1658 19

1661

Treaty of Peace and Alliance between Portugal and the Netherlands, signed at The Hague, 6 August 1661 53

1663

Treaty of Alliance between France and Denmark, signed at Paris, 3 August 1663 52–53

1670

Articles of Alliance and Commerce between Great Britain and Denmark, signed at Copenhagen, 11 July 1670 52, 53

1672

Renewal, Prolongation, and Explanation of Alliance between France and Sweden, signed at Stockholm, 14 April 1672 52, 53

1675

Neutrality Treaty between Denmark, the Electorate of Brandenburg, Münster, and Brunswick-Lüneburg-Hannover, 11 (21) September 1675 19
Neutrality Treaty between France and Brunswick-Lüneburg, 18 October 1675 19

1689

The Neutrality Treaty between France and the Swiss Confederation, 7 May 1689 19

1733

The Neutrality Treaty between France and the Netherlands, 24 November 1733 19, 21

1756

The neutrality treaty between Austria-Hungary and France, 1 May 1756 19, 20, 21

1800

Treaty of Peace and Neutrality between France and Solms, sighed at Offenbach, 19 October 1800 121
Treaty of Peace and Neutrality between France and Wied, signed at Offenbach, 22 October 1800 121
Treaty of Peace and Neutrality between France and Hesse-Homburg, signed at Offenbach, 23 October 1800 121
Convention of Peace and Neutrality between Erbach and France, signed at Offenbach, 20 November 1800 121

Table of treaties xi

1803

Convention of Neutrality and Subsidy between France and Spain, signed at Paris, 19 October 1803   121

1804

Convention respecting Neutrality and Subsidies between France and Portugal, signed at Lisbon, 19 March 1804   121

1805

Treaty of Neutrality between France and the Two Sicilies, signed at Paris, 21 September 1805   121

1839

Treaty between Austria, France, Great Britain, Prussia and Russia, and the Netherlands, signed at London, 19 April 1839   9

Treaty between Austria, France, Great Britain, Prussia and Russia, and Belgium, signed at London, 19 April 1839   9

Treaty between Belgium and the Netherlands relative to the Separation of their Respective Territories, signed at London, 19 April 1839   9, 16

1856

Declaration respecting Maritime Law (The Declaration of Paris), signed at Paris, 16 April 1856   6, 14, 42, 52, 122

1871

Treaty between Great Britain and the United States for the Amicable Settlement of All Causes of Difference between the Two Countries, signed at Washington, 8 May 1871 (Washington Treaty)   80, 83

1874

Project of an International Declaration concerning the Laws and Customs of War (The Brussels Declaration)   90–91, 95, 96

1899

Convention (II) with Respect to the Laws and Customs of War on Land, signed at The Hague, 29 July 1899

Annex (The 1899 Hague Regulations)   96, 131

Article 54   95, 97, 131

Article 57   91, 131

Article 58   131

Article 59   91, 131

Article 69   131

1907

Convention (III) relative to the Opening of Hostilities, signed at The Hague, 18 October 1907   135

Convention (IV) respecting the Laws and Customs of War on Land, signed at The Hague, 18 October 1907   1

xii *Table of treaties*

Convention (V) respecting the Rights and Duties of Neutral Powers and Persons in Case of War on Land, signed at The Hague, 18 October 1907 1, 94–97, 100–102

Article 1   9, 94
Article 2   94, 95
Article 3   94, 95
Article 4   94, 95
Article 5   95
Article 6   94
Article 7   87, 95
Article 8   95
Article 9   95, 177
Article 10   101
Article 11   95
Article 12   95
Article 13   96
Article 14   95
Article 15   95
Article 16   96–97
Article 17   96–97
Article 18   96–97
Article 19   97

Convention (XIII) concerning the Rights and Duties of Neutral Powers in Naval War, signed at The Hague, 18 October 1907   1, 97–102

Article 1   97–98
Article 2   98, 151
Article 3   98
Article 4   98
Article 5   98, 180
Article 6   98, 160, 183
Article 7   87
Article 8   60, 83, 98, 132, 182
Article 10   99, 132, 151
Article 12   99, 131, 151
Article 13   96, 131
Article 14   99, 131
Article 15   99, 131
Article 16   99
Article 17   99
Article 18   99
Article 19   99–100
Article 21   100
Article 23   100

Table of treaties xiii

1909

The London Declaration (Déclaration relative au Droit de la Guerre Maritime), signed at London, 26 February 1909   15

1919

The Covenant of the League of Nations (Part I of the Versailles Treaty)   1, 11, 12, 141
Article 12   142, 144, 148
Article 13   142, 144
Article 15   142, 144
Article 16   141, 143–144, 145–148, 149, 150, 177

1925

Locarno Treaties (Treaty of Mutual Guarantee between Germany, Belgium, France, Great Britain and Italy, done at Locarno, 16 October 1925)   141

1928

General Treaty for the Renunciation of War as an Instrument of National Policy (The Pact of Paris; The Kellogg–Briand Pact)   3, 12, 154, 156, 157–158, 170–171,177–178, 181, 183, 184, 192

1945

Charter of the United Nations   1, 3, 11, 12
Chapter 7   2
Article 25   2
Article 41   13
Article 43   13
Article 51   13, 184, 191
Article 103   2

1949

Geneva Convention for the Amelioration of the Condition of the Wounded and Sick in Armed Forces in the Field of August 12, 1949   1
Geneva Convention for the Amelioration of the Condition of Wounded, Sick and Shipwrecked Members of Armed Forces at Sea of August 12, 1949   1
Geneva Convention relative to the Treatment of Prisoners of War of August 12, 1949   1
Geneva Convention relative to the Protection of Civilian Persons in Time of War of August 12, 1949   1

1977

Protocol Additional to the Geneva Conventions of 12 August 1949, and relating to the Protection of Victims of International Armed Conflicts (Protocol I), adopted at Geneva, 8 June 1977   1
Protocol Additional to the Geneva Conventions of 12 August 1949, and relating to the Protection of Victims of Non-International Armed Conflicts (Protocol II), adopted at Geneva, 8 June 1977   1

Table of cases

International Arbitration
Alabama claims arbitration   64, 74, 79–83, 84, 98, 103, 105, 107, 111, 122, 128, 132

International Military Tribunal at Nuremberg
In re Goering, 1 October 1946   181

Germany
Marietta Nomikos, Prize Court of Hamburg, February 16, 1940   185

Great Britain
Ex parte Chavasse, (1865) 4 De G.J. & S. 655   87

United States
The Big Alerta, 13 U.S. (9 Cranch) 359 (1815)   127
The Commercen 14 U.S. (1 Wheat.) 382 (1816)   129
The Conserva, 38 F. 431 (E.D.N.Y. 1889)   124
The Estrella, 17 U.S. (4 Wheat.) 298 (1819)   127
The Itata, 56 F. 505 (9th Cir. 1893)   142
Gelston v. Hoyt, 16 U.S. (3 Wheat.) 246 (1818)   59
The Gran Para, 20 U.S. (7 Wheat.) 471 (1822)   75–76, 77, 134
Henfield's Case, 11 F. Cas. 1099 (C.C.D. Pa. 1793)   57–58
L'Invincible, 14 U.S. (1 Wheat.) 238 (1816)   127
The Laurada, 85 F. 760 (D.Del. 1898)   73, 129
Richardson v. Maine Fire and Marine Insurance Company, 6 Mass. 102 (1809)   89
The Santissima Trinidad, 20 U.S. (7 Wheat.) 283 (1822)   75–76, 87
Seton, Maitland & Co. v. Low, 1 Johns. Cas 1 (N.Y. 1799)   89
Talbot v. Janson, 3 U.S. (3 Dall.) 133 (1975)   127
The Three Friends, 166 U.S. 1 (1896)   127
United States v. Murphy, 84 F. 609 (D.Del. 1898)   125
United States v. O'Sullivan, 27 F. Cas. 367 (S.D.N.Y. 1851) (No. 15,974)   132
United States v. Quincy, 31 U.S. (6 Pet.) 445 (1832)   75–77, 79
Wiborg v. United States, 163 U.S. 632 (1895)   73

Table of national legislations

Argentine
Declaration of Neutrality in the Bolivian-Paraguayan War, May 13, 1933   178
Decree concerning Argentine Neutrality in the Crimean War, June 16, 1854   126

Belgium
Declaration of Neutrality (1939)   154
Penal Code (1867)   63

Bolivia
Penal Code (1834)   63

Brazil
Ordering the Observance of Complete Neutrality in the War between Bolivia and Paraguay, May 23, 1933   178
Penal Code (1890)   63

Chile
Declaring the Neutrality of Chile in the War between Bolivia and Paraguay, May 13, 1933   178

Dominican Republic
Penal Code (1884)   63

Great Britain
The Foreign Enlistment Act (1819)   60–63, 64, 68, 74, 79, 80, 98, 125, 128
The Foreign Enlistment Act (1870)   125
Order in Council as to Enemy Goods in Friends' Ships, and Friends' Goods in Enemy Ships (1557)   24, 41, 43
Order in Council Permitting British Subjects to Engage in the Military and Naval Service of Spain, June 10, 1835   123
Proclamation of the Prince Regent Prohibiting British Subjects from Taking Part in the Contest between Spain and the Spanish-American Provinces, November 27, 1817   61, 123
Proclamation Prohibiting the Trade with Spain or Portugal (1601)   41

xvi *Table of national legislations*

France
Declaration of Neutrality in the American Civil War, June 10, 1861   63
Declaration of Neutrality in the Russo-Turkish War, May 6, 1877   126
Edit sur l'admirauté (1584)   24, 41, 43
Ordonnance touchant la marine (1681)   52
Penal Code (1810)   63

Italian States before unification
Genoa
Edito della Republica di Gênova toccante la navigazione e il commercio in tempo di guerra del 1. Juill. 1779   122
Papal States
Edito del Papa toccante la navigazione e il commercio in tempo di guerra d. 4. Mars 1779   121–122

Sardinia
Penal Code (1859)   63

Tuscany
Regolamento fatto per il Gran Duca di Toscana toccante la navigazione e il commercio in tempo di guerra del 1. Agosto 1778   121

Venice
Edito della republica di Venezia toccante la navigazione e il commercio in tempo di guerra del 9. Sept. 1779   122

Italy (after unification)
Penal Code   63

Japan
The Act on Measures to Ensure the Peace and Security of Japan in Perilous Situations in Areas Surrounding Japan (1999)   2
The Act on Restriction of Maritime Transportation of Foreign Military Supplies, etc. in Armed Attack Situations (2004)   2

The Netherlands
Ordonnance des Etats Généraux des PROVINCES-UNIES, qui défend tout commerce avec l'ANGLETERRE. Faite à la Haye, le 5. Decembre, 1652
Penal Code   63
Declaration of Neutrality (1939)   154

Norway
Declaration of Neutrality (1939)   150

Peru
Proclamation of Neutrality in the Bolivian-Paraguayan War, May 13, 1933   178
Proclamation of Neutrality in the Franco–Prussian War, 24 October 1870   126

Portugal

Decree of the King-Regent of Portugal, Declaring the Neutrality of Portugal in the Crimean War, May 5, 1854   126

Penal Code   63

Royal Decree regarding Neutrality in the American Civil War, July 29, 1861   126

Royal Decree regarding Portuguese Neutrality in the War between Austria, etc., and Prussia and Italy, July 2, 1866   126

Spain

Declaration of Neutrality (1939)   163

Decree concerning Neutrality in the Franco-Prussian War, June 26, 1870   126

Penal Code   63, 64

Royal Decree concerning Neutrality in the Crimean War, April 12, 1854   126

Royal Decree concerning Neutrality in the American Civil War, June 17, 1861   126

The United States

The Lend-Lease Act (1941)   159, 160, 182

The Neutrality Act of 1794   57, 58–59, 72, 74, 98

The Neutrality Act of 1817   59

The Neutrality Act of 1818   73, 75, 76, 77, 78, 79, 127

The Neutrality Act of 1935   181

The Neutrality Act of 1936   181

The Neutrality Act of 1937   158–159, 181

The Neutrality Act of 1939   159, 160, 181–182

Proclamation Enjoining Neutrality as to Canada, January 5, 1838   125

Proclamation of Neutrality (1939)   158

Uruguay

Decree Proclaiming Neutrality in the War between Bolivia and Paraguay, May 12, 1933   178

Acknowledgements

This book is an English translation of *Dentoteki churitsu-seido no hoteki-seikaku*, which was published in Japanese by the University of Tokyo Press in 2010. The original Japanese version is an expanded version of the PhD thesis defended at the University of Tokyo in 2007. In addition to translating the original Japanese version into English, I have made a number of revisions on it and updated some information; thus, this book is the newest version of my work on neutrality in international law.

I am most grateful to my supervisor, Professor Akira Kotera, for his constant support and advice, without which I could not have completed this research project. He passed away in 2014, at the age of 61. I am deeply grieved by his sudden death. This book is dedicated to Professor Kotera.

Introduction

One of the most important roles of law is to regulate the use of violence and physical force among members of society. Since the early period of the development of international law, many efforts have been made to regulate war, that is, physical violence among the members of international society. Methods for regulating war in international law include (a) the rules regulating the resort to war itself (the so-called *jus ad bellum*), (b) the rules governing relations between belligerent States (the so-called *jus in bello* in the narrow sense) and (c) the rules governing relations between belligerent States and third States (the law of neutrality). With regard to (a), the prohibition of war and the use of force by States has become a principle of general international law brought about by the developments from the Covenant of the League of Nations (1919)[1] to the United Nations Charter (1945).[2] A number of treaties have been adopted with regard to (b), which is often referred to as international humanitarian law, such as the 1907 Hague Convention respecting the Laws and Customs of War on Land and its annexed Regulations, and the four Geneva Conventions of 1949 and their Additional Protocols of 1977.[3] In addition, in recent times, a permanent international criminal court (the International Criminal Court) has been established to impose criminal responsibility upon individuals who violate these conventions. In comparison to these developments, there has been insufficient development of international law and international law research in connection to (c). Following the two conventions adopted at the Second Hague Peace Conference in 1907 (Convention (V) respecting the Rights and Duties of Neutral Powers and Persons in Case of War on Land and Convention (XIII) concerning the Rights and Duties of Neutral Powers in Naval War),[4] no further treaty has been adopted in relation to this issue, and the quality and quantity of research in comparison to that of (a) and (b) is relatively meagre.

Nevertheless, since the reality is that war and armed conflict continue to occur even under modern international law, which in principle prohibits war and the use of force by States, rules governing the relation between a belligerent State (a State party to a war or international armed conflict) and a third State (a State not party to a war or international armed conflict) are still necessary. There has been much debate as to the current status of the law of neutrality,[5] which once regulated the relations between a belligerent and a third State: whether the

2 *Introduction*

law of neutrality is still legally valid in modern international law, and whether the principle of the non-use of force requires some kind of revision to that law. Relatively recently, the applicability of the law of neutrality to the Iran–Iraq War (1980–88) and the NATO bombing against Yugoslavia (1999) has been a subject of controversy.[6] The applicability of the law of neutrality to cyber warfare is also debated in recent years.[7] In Japan, the issue of neutrality has been debated in relation to the Act on Measures to Ensure the Peace and Security of Japan in Perilous Situations in Areas Surrounding Japan (1999),[8] and the Act on Restriction of Maritime Transportation of Foreign Military Supplies, etc. in Armed Attack Situations (2004).[9, 10]

As discussed below, there are conflicting views regarding the current status of the law of neutrality, and numerous uncertainties continue to exist. However, there is a general agreement among scholars as to the basic features of the traditional law of neutrality. Section 3 elucidates the reasons for the need to reconsider the assumptions about the traditional law of neutrality that have been generally shared by contemporary writers. The modification of these assumptions will provide a completely new framework in which we discuss the current relevance of neutrality in modern international law. The purpose of this book is to identify the legal characteristics of the traditional law of neutrality by re-examining its historical development, and through that, to posit a perspective that will resolve the various issues regarding the current status of the law of neutrality.

After overviewing the content and structure of the debate regarding the current status of the law of neutrality (section 1) and identifying the details of the generally accepted assumptions about the traditional law of neutrality (section 2), we will explain the reasons why we must reconsider these assumptions (section 3).

1 Conflicting views on the current status of the law of neutrality

Among the issues concerning the current status of the law of neutrality, the resolution is relatively simple in cases where the Security Council of the United Nations decides to take enforcement measures under Chapter VII of the United Nations Charter.[11] Since the decisions of the Security Council are legally binding on member States of the United States (Article 25 of the United Nations Charter),[12] and the obligation to abide by those decisions takes precedence over other obligations of international law (Article 103 of the UN Charter), the member States shall abide by those decisions, and in doing so, they are not regarded as violating the other obligations of international law.[13]

On the other hand, solutions are much more difficult when the Security Council does not take any measures. In such instances, where Articles 25 and 103 of the United Nations Charter do not apply, the issue to be considered is what attitude, under general international law, a States not participating in a war or international armed conflict should take.[14] More specifically, the issue is whether it is permissible for a third State[15] to take an attitude of "non-belligerency" ("non-belligérance"; "Nichtkriegführung"). Non-belligerency is "the situation of those States which, while not wishing to enter the conflict on the side of one belligerent, do not, at the same time, choose to be bound by traditional neutrality obligations".[16] In other words, in modern international law, the issue is whether it is lawful for a State that does not take part in a war or international armed conflict to assist a belligerent State by choosing an attitude of non-belligerency, as opposed to strict neutrality.

Many writers affirm the legality of an attitude of non-belligerency in present international law, that is to say, the legality for a third State to assist a belligerent State.[17] There are mainly two grounds for this view.[18] The first ground is the change in the legal status of war brought about by the outlawry of war. According to these writers, "the duty of impartiality",[19] which formed the central part of the traditional law of neutrality, was a collorary of the freedom of States to resort to war and the equality of belligerents in traditional international law (so-called the "non-discriminatory conception of war"[20]): As all belligerents were equal, it was not permissible for a third State to discriminate between belligerents by assisting one party. However, since the freedom of States to resort to war has been denied by the Pact of Paris and the United Nations Charter, the traditional law of neutrality, the historical foundation of which was the freedom of States to resort to war, has lost its validity. Since belligerents are distinguished between a lawful party and an unlawful party in modern international law, it is legal for a third State to provide assistance to a lawful belligerent. The second ground for the view affirming the legality of an attitude of non-belligerency is that, since the Second World War, third States have supplied belligerent States with military assistance in wars and armed conflicts, and new rules of customary international law that permit an attitude of non-belligerency have been established. Such practices includes assistance from the United States to Great Britain in the early part of Second World War (1939–41), assistance from the United States to Great Britain in the Falklands/Malvinas Conflict (1982) and the provision of weapons by France to Iraq in the Iran–Iraq War (1980–88), among other examples.[21]

According to those writers who affirm the legality of attitudes of non-belligerency, it is also permissible for a third State to voluntarily choose the status of neutrality. In other words, a State has the following three choices in a war or international armed conflict under modern international law: (1) a belligerent State (a State party to an international armed conflict), (2) a neutral State and (3) a non-belligerent State. Although many writers affirm the legality of attitudes of non-belligerency, there still remains many uncertainties, such as the legal advantages for a State to choose a neutral status, or in other words, the differences in the rights accorded to a neutral State and a non-belligerent State. More specifically, it is still uncertain whether equal protection accorded to a neutral State, such as the right of territorial inviolability and freedom of maritime commerce, is also accorded to a non-belligerent State as well, or whether a non-belligerent State is to receive less favourable treatment than a neutral State

4   *Introduction*

in these matters. In this regard, Schindler, for example, observes that "the present international law only admits the intermediate attitudes [the attitudes of non-belligerency], but it does not clarify their legal consequences".[22] Gioia and Ronzitti also states that the issue of whether non-belligerents and neutrals are to be treated equally in prize law "is still not clear", and that "it is still necessary to clarify what, if any, are the legal consequences of an attitude of 'non-belligerency', as apposed to strict neutrality".[23]

On the other hand, there are writers who argue that attitudes of non-belligerency are internationally wrongful acts.[24] The ground for this view is the continuing validity of the traditional law of neutrality in modern international law. According to those writers, under the traditional law of neutrality, a State that did not take part in a war between other States automatically became a neutral State and was bound by the duty of impartiality; the situation is no different under modern international law. In the following way, those writers repudiate the two grounds for the view that affirms the legality of attitudes of non-belligerency, which are mentioned above. With regard to the first ground, they argue that an existing rule of customary international law may be modified or abolished only by a new rule of customary international law, which are formed by State practice accompanied by *opinio juris*. The traditional law of neutrality, which was developed as a body of principles and rules of customary international law, cannot be modified or abolished merely as a logical consequence of the change in the legal status of war under international law. It can be modified or abolished only when new rules of customary international law that modify or abolish it are established. Therefore, the next issue concerns the second ground for the view that affirms the legality of attitudes of non-belligerency: whether new rules of customary international law have been established that modify or abolish the traditional law of neutrality. According to those writers who deny the legality of attitudes of non-belligerency, the practice of assistance given by third States to belligerents is nothing more than an internationally wrongful act, and new rules for customary international law have not been established.

As we have seen, the views of contemporary writers regarding the current status of the law of neutrality differ on two points: (1) the influence of the change in the legal status of war upon the traditional law of neutrality and (2) the evaluation of State practice since the Second World War. However, there is general agreement among those writers as to the basic features of the traditional law of neutrality. The first ground for the view that affirms the legality of attitudes of non-belligerency is that the historical foundation of the traditional law of neutrality was the freedom of States to wage war in traditional international law, which itself is not denied by writers who deny the legality of attitudes of non-belligerency. According to them, the traditional law of neutrality does not lose its validity merely because its historical foundation has disappeared: the traditional law of neutrality, which was formed as a body of rules of customary international law, can be changed or modified only by new rules of customary international law. On the other hand, the ground for the view denying the

legality of attitudes of non-belligerency is the continuing validity of the traditional law of neutrality, under which all States that did not take part in a war
automatically became neutrals and were bound by the duty of impartiality. This
assumption about the traditional law of neutrality is also shared by those writers
who affirm the legality of attitudes of non-belligerency in modern international
law; however, according to them, the traditional law of neutrality has lost its
validity as a logical consequence of the change in the legal status of war and by
new rules of customary international law.

In sum, the conflicting views on the current status of the law of neutrality
have shared some basic assumptions about the traditional law of neutrality.
However, if these assumptions, upon which writers have debated about the
current status of the law of neutrality, were incorrect, debates about the current
status of the law of neutrality would have to be reconstructed. We will show in
section 3 that these assumptions need to be reconsidered. However, prior to
that, let us look in more detail at those assumptions shared by contemporary
writers.

2 Generally accepted assumptions about the traditional law of neutrality

Among the assumptions about the traditional law of neutrality that have been
generally shared by contemporary writers, the following two are of particular
importance: (1) that the right to remain neutral did not exist in the traditional
law of neutrality, and (2) that the historical foundation of the traditional law of
neutrality was the unlimited freedom of States to resort to war and the equality
of belligerents in traditional international law (the so-called "non-discriminatory
conception of war").

2.1 Non-existence of the right to remain neutral

It has been generally assumed by contemporary writers that in traditional international law, "States in wartime were only entitled to choose between the status
of neutrality on the one hand and that of belligerents on the other."[25] In other
words, a State that chose not to participate in a war automatically became a
neutral. This means that, conversely, a State was free to participate in a war
between other States by becoming a belligerent State. Apart from States that
were obliged to remain neutral by special treaties (such as permanently neutral
States), the *duty* of States to remain neutral in time of war did not exist in
general international law. Regarding this point, there is an agreement among
writers.[26]

On the other hand, did a State have the *right* to remain neutral?; that is to
say, if a State wished to remain neutral in time of war, should the belligerent
States have respected that wish? In other words, the issue is whether a belligerent State was not allowed to force a State that wished to remain neutral into
becoming a belligerent State by waging war on it – in which case, to remain

6 Introduction

neutral is the right of the State – or whether the belligerent State could force a State that wished to remain neutral into becoming a belligerent State by waging war on it – in which case, to remain neutral is not the right of the State.

It has been generally assumed that States did not have the right to remain neutral in the traditional law of neutrality.[27] For example, Erik Castrén states: "[i]n a subjective sense, the right of neutrality would be the right to remain outside a war; general international law does not, however, grant this right".[28] Yasuo Ishimoto also observes: "in classical international law, belligerent States were permitted at any time to declare war on third States. Thus, the position of neutral States to remain outside a war was not ultimately under the legal protection".[29]

The basis of such an assumption is that, in international law prior to the First World War which recognised the unlimited freedom of States to wage war, belligerent States, as a matter of course, should have had the freedom to declare war on neutral States, which has not necessarily been proven by State practice or the literature prior to the First World War.[30] It has been considered almost as self-evident that the right to remain neutral did not exist in the traditional law of neutrality.

2.2 Historical foundation of the traditional law of neutrality: the equality of belligerents

As noted in section 2.1, it has been generally assumed that, in traditional international law, a belligerent State was free at any time to make war on a State that wished to remain neutral, thereby making such a State a belligerent. From this perspective, the law of neutrality is considered not as an institution that provides rules as to whether a State is a neutral or a belligerent (rules as to when a State acquires and loses the neutral status), but as an institution that defines the rights and duties of a neutral State in relation to belligerents, *as far as* it remains a neutral State.

The content of the law of neutrality that defines such rights and duties is largely explained not in terms of the rights of a neutral State but by its duties. That is because the so-called "rights of neutral States" (such as the territorial inviolability and freedom of maritime commerce) are not rights that are newly and specially afforded by the law of neutrality but nothing more than rights which all States have under the law of peace.[31]

The duties of neutral States are categorised into "the duty of acquiescence" and "the duty of impartiality".[32] The duty of acquiescence refers to the duty of a neutral State to tolerate the lawful exercise of belligerent rights by belligerent States towards neutral nationals.[33] Among the belligerent rights that may be exercised by belligerent States, what have been of particular importance are prize measures.[34] According to the principles established by the 1856 Declaration of Paris,[35] a belligerent State may, on the high seas and in the territorial waters of belligerent States, seize and confiscate: (1) enemy ships and enemy cargoes on board enemy ships, (2) contraband cargoes on enemy ships,

(3) contraband cargoes on neutral ships (in certain circumstances, neutral ships transporting contraband of war and non-contraband cargoes may also be confiscated), (4) neutral ships that have violated the blockade and their cargoes and (5) neutral ships engaging in unneutral service (hostile assistance) and their cargoes.[36] On the other hand, the duty of impartiality refers to the duty of a neutral State to treat belligerent States impartially without providing military assistance or convenience. The duty of impartiality is further divided into the duty of abstention (the duty to abstain from providing belligerent States with military assistance), the duty of prevention (the duty to prevent the military use of its territories by belligerent States or private individuals) and the duty of non-discrimination (the duty to treat all belligerents equally in matters that are not covered by the duties of abstention or prevention).

According to contemporary writers who have studied the law of neutrality, the historical foundation of the traditional law of neutrality, the "core content" of which was the duty of impartiality,[37] was the unrestricted freedom of States to resort to war and the equality of belligerents (so-called the "non-discriminatory conception of war"). For example, Hearsch Lauterpacht states that "[t]he historical foundation which underlay the modern formulation of the doctrine of absolute neutrality was the absolute right of States to resort to war",[38] and states more specifically in another article that "until the First World War, the right to wage war was an unlimited prirogative right of sovereign States; no neutral States, therefore, could arrogate to itself the right to pass judgment on the legality of a war and to shape its conduct accordingly".[39] Shigejiro Tabata also observes: The introduction of the concept of neutrality "was a corollary to the introduction of the non-discriminatory conception of war, according to which belligerents could not be viewed as right and wrong. In other words, during a war, third States could not make a judgment on the right or wrong of the belligerents. Therefore, it was inappropriate to provide special assistance to one party, and the third State had to be impartial towards both parties, which is the point of such a conception [of neutrality]".[40] In sum, the traditional law of neutrality, which obliged third States to treat all belligerent States impartially and to abstain from providing assistance to any belligerent, was not established on the basis of the just war doctrine, according to which belligerents were divided into right and wrong, rather it was first established in international law from the late eighteenth to nineteenth centuries, in which States had the unrestricted freedom to wage war, and therefore, all belligerent States were viewed as equal. Such a view is taken not only by Lauterpacht and Tabata, but is also shared by many other writers.[41]

3 Perspectives, objectives and the structure of the book

3.1 Doubts about existing studies

A doubt immediately arises with regard to the generally accepted assumption about the traditional law of neutrality. As we have seen in section 2.2, it has

8 Introduction

been generally assumed that third States were prohibited from discriminating between belligerents in traditional international law, which recognised the unlimited freedom of States to resort to war and viewed all belligerents as equal. Until the First World War, however, it was completely lawful for a hitherto neutral State to assist one of the belligerents *after* entering the war and becoming itself a belligerent.[42] This being so, why should a State not assist one of the belligerents *before* entering the war, that is, as a neutral State?

If such a doubt is correct, there should be another basis for the duty of impartiality in the traditional law of neutrality. A possible explanation is that a neutral State was required to observe the duty of impartiality as a condition of not being involved in a war. In fact, some writers do explain the basis for the duty of impartiality in this way. For example, Heintschel von Heinegg states, "until the beginning of the twentieth century, it was legally self-evident that the strict duty of impartiality was imposed on *third States that did not want to be involved in a war*".[43] Also, according to Henry Meyrowitz, providing assistance to one belligerent is "an act of war" against the other belligerent,[44] and the latter State may involve the State that provides assistance to the enemy in the war:[45] The risk of getting involved in a war by discriminating between belligerents is not simply a factual risk (risque de fait) but also a legal risk (risque en droit).[46] Therefore, "impartiality constitutes ... an indispensable element of the status of neutrality",[47] and in order to remain neutral and not get involved in the war, a third State had to take an attitude of impartiality towards belligerents.

However, if we explain that a neutral State was required to observe the duty of impartiality *as a condition* of not being involved in a war, conversely, it must be the case that the status of a neutral State of not being involved in a war was *legally protected* as long as it observed the duty of impartiality. We cannot maintain this explanation if a belligerent State was legally free to wage war at any time on a neutral State, regardless of whether the neutral State observed the duty of impartiality. However, as shown above, it has been generally assumed and even considered to be self-evident that the traditional law of neutrality did not afford neutral States the right not to be involved in a war, or in other words, that belligerent States were free to wage war on neutral States at any time. This has been considered as self-evident because it has been assumed that in international law prior to the First World War, which recognised the unlimited freedom of States to wage war, belligerent States should certainly be free to wage war on neutral States. Such an assumption has not been denied by Heintschel von Heinegg or Meyrowitz.[48]

However, this assumption itself, which has been regarded as self-evident by most writers, must be reconsidered. It is because, in former times, whether a belligerent State was free to wage war on a neutral State at any time was by no means a self-evident matter. This is illustrated by the controversy that arose among international lawyers over the German violation of Belgian neutrality in 1914.

Introduction 9

3.2 *Controversy over the German violation of Belgian neutrality in 1914*

In the First World War, Germany, which was at war with France, in order not to lose time by breaking through the heavily guarded German–French national border to attack France, devised a military operation (the famous "Schlieffen Plan") to break through to the northern part of France via Belgium, which was lacking in defence. In carrying out this military operation, the German government made a demand to the Belgian government for the German army to be permitted to pass through Belgian territory (Notification of 2 August 1914). As the Belgian government refused this demand (3 August 1914), the German army invaded Belgian territory without the permission of the Belgian government (4 August 1914).[49]

At the time, Belgium was a permanently neutral State. As one of the State parties to the 1839 London Treaties concerning the permanent neutrality of Belgium,[50] Germany (as the successor of Prussia) was obliged to respect the neutrality of Belgium on the basis of those treaties. This obligation included both (1) the duty to refrain from infringing the territory of Belgium and (2) the duty to refrain from making war on Belgium.[51] Therefore, there could be no objection to the fact that the aforementioned actions of Germany in relation to Belgium violated the London Treaties, unless justified by some grounds such as legitimate defence (*Notwehr*), which was asserted by the German government. Besides the issue of permanent neutrality, it was debated whether the actions taken by Germany against Belgium were lawful under general international law.

As regards this issue, there were writers who took a view that the actions of Germany in this case were lawful under general international law. For example, an editorial comment published in 1915 in the *American Journal of International Law* took such a view. It acknowledged that Article 1 of the 1907 Hague Convention (V) respecting the Rights and Duties of Neutral Powers and Persons in Case of War on Land provided that "[t]he territory of neutral Powers is to be inviolable". However, it argued that the aforementioned notification sent by the German government to the Belgian government on 2 August 1914 was an ultimatum, and therefore, war broke out between Germany and Belgium due to the Belgian government's refusal on 3 August 1914 to accept the ultimatum. Thus, when the German army invaded the territory of Belgium (4 August 1914), Belgium was *not a neutral* but *a belligerent*, and Article 1 of the Hague Convention did not apply to Belgium.[52] Furthermore, according to this editorial comment, the act on the part of Germany of making war on Belgium as a neutral State did not in itself violate any rules of general international law. This was because "international law in its present development apparently allows nations to go to war whenever they please".[53] In sum, the position of this editorial comment is that a belligerent State is free to wage war on a neutral State, and by doing so the belligerent can at any time change the neutral State to a belligerent State; and the protection provided to a neutral State by the law of neutrality (such as the right of territorial inviolability) can be legally taken away at any time.

10 Introduction

On the other hand, there were writers who argued that the actions of Germany in this case were illegal under general international law. For example, in his articles published in 1916 and 1917, Charles de Visscher criticised the aforementioned editorial comment published in the *American Journal of International Law* and regarded the actions of Germany in this case as "a violation of the rules of positive international law".[54] This is because, according to de Visscher, the law of neutrality "protects the right of a *third State* not to be involved in the war (de protegér le droit d'une *troisième Puissance* de n'être pas impliquée dans la guerre)".[55] If a belligerent can freely take away from a neutral State at any time the protection afforded by the law of neutrality (such as the right of territorial inviolability), by waging war on the neutral State, thereby changing a neutral State to a belligerent State, both the practical value and the legal value of the law of neutrality would be lost.[56] In other words, it is de Visscher's view that the law of neutrality prohibits belligerent States not only from violating the territory of a neutral State but also from changing a neutral State to a belligerent by waging war on the neutral State.

In sum, if we go back to the time of the First World War, there were clearly conflicting views as to whether a belligerent State was free to wage war on a neutral State at any time; in other words, whether a neutral State was guaranteed the right not to be involved in a war.

3.3 The structure and scope of this book

Did the traditional law of neutrality, as de Visscher argues, protect the right of third States not to be involved in a war? This book tries to answer this question by re-examining the historical development of the law of neutrality from the sixteenth century to 1945, and thereby to identify the legal characteristics of the traditional law of neutrality.

This book is structured as follows.

Chapter 1 goes back to the two origins of the conception of neutrality in international law: the practice of concluding neutrality treaties since the sixteenth century and the literature of eighteenth-century international law scholars. Section 1 of this chapter examines neutrality treaties concluded between several States in Europe since the sixteenth century. Neutrality treaties are taken as the starting-point for the inquiry in this book for the following reasons. As has already been pointed out by some writers, such as Wilhelm G. Grewe, Alberto Miele, and Stefan Oeter, the word "neutrality" was first used as a concept of international law in neutrality treaties concluded between several States in Europe since the sixteenth century. In State practice between the sixteenth and eighteenth centuries, neutrality was not a legal status automatically established at the outbreak of war, rather it was a legal status *contractually* created by a neutrality treaty concluded between a belligerent and a third State.[57] Therefore, in order to clarify the concept of neutrality in State practice during this period, the content of neutrality treaties should be examined, rather than considering the relation between belligerent States and third States in

Introduction 11

general. Next, section 2 of this chapter examines the theory of neutrality as presented by eighteenth-century scholars such as Bynkershoek, Wolff, Vattel and Hübner. In contrast to the State practice at that time, eighteenth-century scholars argued that a third State could become a neutral, even if it did not conclude neutrality treaties with belligerents, and this theory became the basis for the law of neutrality as an institution of general international law that was established in the nineteenth century.

Chapter 2, which provides the core content for this book, considers the process in which the law of neutrality was established as an institution of general international law in the period from the end of the eighteenth century to the early twentieth century. The theory of neutrality presented by eighteenth-century scholars, according to which a State could become a neutral even if it had not concluded neutrality treaties, came to be supported by the State practice after the late eighteenth century, and the law of neutrality was established as an institution of positive general international law.

Chapter 3 demonstrates the continuing validity of the traditional law of neutrality during the interwar period and during the Second World War. Specifically, this chapter will show that, although neutrality appeared to be temporarily disappeared as an institution of international law following the introduction of the collective security system in the Covenant of the League of Nations, a variety of States once again came to rely on the law of neutrality in the late 1930s and thereafter, when the collective security system of the League of Nations was not effectively functioning and that in the Second World War, the law of neutrality functioned in the same way that it had been prior to the First Word War.

The objective of this book is to identify the essential character of the traditional law of neutrality, as a preliminary work to resolving the various issues regarding the status of the law of neutrality in modern international law, examining which is not in itself the objective of this book. Therefore, the scope of this book is confined to the period immediately before the conclusion of the United Nations Charter; that is, up to 1945. The status of the law of neutrality after the conclusion of the United Nations Charter is an issue to be studied in the future.

Notes

1 The Covenant of the League of Nations (Part I of the Versailles Treaty), *CTS* 225:188–205.
2 Charter of the United Nations, 26 June 1945, in *Documents of the United Nations Conference on International Organization San Francisco, 1945* (London: United Nations Information Organizations, 1945), 15:335–553.
3 Convention (IV) respecting the Laws and Customs of War on Land, signed at the Hague, 18 October 1907, *CTS* 205:277–298; Geneva Convention for the Amelioration of the Condition of the Wounded and Sick in Armed Forces in the Field of 12 August 1949, *UNTS* 75 (1950): 31–83; Geneva Convention for the Amelioration of the Condition of Wounded, Sick and Shipwrecked Members of Armed Forces at Sea of 12 August 1949, *UNTS* 75 (1950): 85–132; Geneva Convention relative to the

12 Introduction

Treatment of Prisoners of War of 12 August 1949, *UNTS* 75 (1950): 135–285; Geneva Convention relative to the Protection of Civilian Persons in Time of War of 12 August 1949, *UNTS* 75 (1950): 287–417; Protocol Additional to the Geneva Conventions of 12 August 1949, and relating to the Protection of Victims of International Armed Conflicts (Protocol I), adopted at Geneva, 8 June 1977, *UNTS* 1125 (1979): 3–608; Protocol Additional to the Geneva Conventions of 12 August 1949, and relating to the Protection of Victims of Non-International Armed Conflicts (Protocol II), adopted at Geneva, 8 June 1977, *UNTS* 1125 (1979): 609–699.

4 Convention (V) respecting the Rights and Duties of Neutral Powers and Persons in Case of War on Land, signed at the Hague, 18 October 1907, *CTS* 205:299–304; Convention (XIII) concerning the Rights and Duties of Neutral Powers in Naval War, signed at the Hague, 18 October 1907, ibid. 395–402. The authentic text of these conventions is French. The English translation of these conventions is printed in Schindler and Toman, *Laws of Armed Conflicts*, 1399–1430.

5 In this book, the terms "traditional law of neutrality" and "traditional international law" are referred to as the law of neutrality and international law before the First World War and the terms "modern law of neutrality" and "modern international law" as the law of neutrality and international law after the Second World War. One of the essential differences between "traditional international law" and "modern international law" is the legal status of war and the use of force in these laws. While States had unlimited freedom to resort to war in international law before the First World War, after the First World War, war and the use of force by States were gradually prohibited by treaties such as the Covenant of the League of Nations (1919), the Pact of Paris (1928) and the Charter of the United Nations (1945). The interwar period and the period during the Second World War, which are often regarded as transitional periods from "traditional international law" to "modern international law", shall be included in this book's research object, which is a preliminary work to resolving various issues regarding the current status of the law of neutrality. On the "structural change" from "traditional law of neutrality" to "modern international law", see e.g. Ishimoto, *Changing Structure of International Law*, 1–32 [in Japanese]; Matsui *et al.*, *International Law*, 4–10 [in Japanese].

6 On the issue of neutrality in the Iran–Iraq War, see e.g. Bothe, "Neutrality at Sea", 205–211; Gioia and Ronzitti, "Law of Neutrality", 221–242; McNeil, "Neutral Rights and Maritime Sanctions", 631–643; Mehr, "Neutrality in the Gulf War", 105–106; Russo, "Neutrality at Sea", 381–399. On the issue of the applicability of the law of neutrality to the NATO's bombing campaign against Yugoslavia, see e.g. Gabriel, "Die Gegenläufigkeit", 219–236; Greenwood, "Kosovo Campaign", 111–144; Michel, "Le statut juridique de la neutralité", 197–218.

7 See e.g. Kastenberg, "Non-Intervention and Neutrality in Cyberspace", 43–64; Kelsey, "Hacking into International Humanitarian Law", 1427–1451; Heintschel von Heinegg, "Neutrality in Cyberspace", 35–46; Heintschel von Heinegg, "Territorial Sovereignty and Neutrality in Cyberspace", 141–156.

8 The Act on Measures to Ensure the Peace and Security of Japan in Perilous Situations in Areas Surrounding Japan, Act No. 60 of 28 May 1999.

9 The Act on Restriction of Maritime Transportation of Foreign Military Supplies, etc. in Armed Attack Situations, Act No. 116 of 18 June 2004.

10 See e.g. Mayama, "Guidelines for U.S.-Japan Defence Cooperation and Inspection of Ships", 109–137 [in Japanese]; Mayama, "Maritime Neutrality and Logistic Support", 20–30 [in Japanese]; Matsuda, "New Guidelines", 46–50 [in Japanese]; Morikawa, "Acts concerning Japan-US Defence Cooperation", 44–52 [in Japanese]; Morikawa, "Maritime Transportation Act", 11–19 [in Japanese].

11 See Schindler, "Probleme des humanitären Völkerrechts", 21. On the relationship between neutrality and the collective security system of the United Nations, see also, Schaub, *Neutralität und Kollektive Sicherheit*, 81–138.

Introduction 13

12 A member State is not obliged to provide armed forces used for military enforcement measures unless it has concluded a special agreement with the United Nations pursuant to Article 43 of the United Nations Charter.

13 There appears to be room for member States of the United Nations to remain neutral while implementing the enforcement measures decided by the Security Council. It would depend on the content of the decided enforcement measures. This relates to the issue of what acts a State needs to perform or abstain from in order to remain neutral, which is one of the very issues that this book attempts to resolve. In this regard, if we consider, as Chaumont does, the abstention from military activities as the essence of neutrality, it would be possible for a member State implementing non-military enforcement measures (Article 41 of the United Nations Charter) to claim the neutral status. See Chaumont, "Nations Unies et neutralité", 1–59. A question naturally arises as to what legal advantages accrue to the State claiming the status of neutrality in such a case, which also composes the very issues that this book attempts to resolve.

14 If the law of neutrality is still valid as a legal institution in modern international law, another issue that arises is whether it applies only to a war in the legal sense or also to an armed conflict other than a war. On this issue see e.g. Greenwood, "Concept of War", 283–306; Petrochilos, "Relevance of the Concepts of War", 575–615; Schindler, "'Kriegszustand'", 568–571; Schindler, "State of War", 3–20. It is still unclear whether the concept of "war" is legally relevant in modern international law, and, if it is, what legal effects are produced by "war", as compared with the legal effects attached to the "use of force" or "armed conflict". As Tadashi Tanaka observes, "the solution to those issues is the most difficult issue concerning the legal regulation of the use of force in international law". See Tanaka, "Basic Structure of International Law Governing the Use of Force", 271 [in Japanese]. Since definitely resolving such difficult issues is far beyond the scope of the present work, we provisionally use the expression "war or armed conflict" as a term indicating situations to which the law of neutrality *might apply*.

15 In this book, the term "third State" is referred to as a State not participating in and de facto remaining outside a war or armed conflict, regardless of whether the State's status to remain outside a war or armed conflict is *legally* guaranteed. In contrast, the term "neutral State", the meaning of which is what this book attempts to clarify, anticipating the conclusion, is a State that is *legally guaranteed* to remain outside a war. Historically, while all third States were entitled to be neutral States under general international law since the end of the eighteenth century, in the preceding period only third States that concluded neutrality treaties with the belligerents could become neutral States. Therefore, this book distinguishes between the terms "neutral State" and "third State".

16 Gioia, "Neutrality and Non-Belligerency", 76.

17 See e.g. Chadwick, *Traditional Neutrality*, 199–200; Gioia, "Neutrality and Non-Belligerency", 76–80; Greenwood, "*Jus ad bellum* and *jus in bello*", 230; Ishimoto, *Historical Study on the Law of Neutrality*, 209, 225–226 [in Japanese]; Komarnicki, "Place of Neutrality", 419–502; Oeter, *Neutralität und Waffenhandel*, 135–146; Schindler, "Aspects contemporains de la neutralité", 261–277; Schindler, "Transformations in the Law of Neutrality", 373–381; Skubiszewski, "Use of Force", 840–841; Tabata, *New Lecture on International Law*, 2:294–295 [in Japanese].

18 In addition to the two grounds mentioned in the main text, some writers refer to the right of collective self-defence (Article 51 of the United Nations Charter) as a ground for the legality of attitudes of non-belligerency. According to them, as a State may assist the victim of aggression by using armed force, assistance not involving the use of armed force would *a fortiori* be lawful. See e.g. Schindler, "Transformations in the Law of Neutrality", 373.

19 The author will argue in this book that the so-called "duty of impartiality" or "duties of neutral States" in the traditional law of neutrality, which is enclosed within

14 Introduction

quotation marks in this book, was not *duties*, but rather a set of *conditions* that a State was required to fulfil *if* it wished to remain neutral. See below, Chapter 2, section 2.2.

20 The term "non-discriminatory conception of war", commonly used in Japan, is seldom used outside Japan. See Yanagihara, "Idea of Non-Discriminating War", 4 [in Japanese].

21 On the practice of assistance provided by third States to belligerents in armed conflicts since the Second World War, see Oeter, *Neutralität und Waffenhandel*, 87–128.

22 Schindler, "Aspects contemporains de la neutralité", 275.

23 Gioia and Ronzitti, "Law of Neutrality", 242. Under the traditional law of prize, neutral vessels and cargoes were accorded more favourable treatment than that accorded to enemy vessels and cargoes. According to the principles established by the 1856 Declaration of Paris, while belligerents may seize and condemn all enemy merchant vessels and enemy cargoes on board, they may condemn neutral merchant vessels and cargoes on board and neutral cargoes on enemy vessels only when the cargoes are contraband of war or when the vessels have breached the blockade or engaged in unneutral service (hostile assistance). If the traditional law of prize, which distinguishes neutral vessels and cargoes from enemy vessels and cargoes, is still valid in contemporary international law, a question arises as to whether vessels and cargoes of a "non-belligerent" State are accorded the same treatment as that accorded to neutral vessels and cargoes, or the same treatment as that accorded to enemy vessels and cargoes or the treatment that is more favourable than enemy vessels and cargoes but less favourable than neutral vessels or cargoes. On this issue, for example, the "San Remo Manual on International Law Applicable to Armed Conflicts at Sea" (1994) and the International Law Association's "Helsinki Principles on Maritime Neutrality" (1996) define "neutral States" as all States not participating in an armed conflict and consider that the same rules regarding contraband of war and blockade apply to all "neutral States" so defined. In other words, they take a view that vessels and cargoes of so-called "non-belligerent States" are accorded the same treatment as that accorded to vessels and cargoes of strictly neutral States. See International Institute of Humanitarian Law, *San Remo Manual*, 68, 87–88, 189–190; International Law Association, *Report of the Sixty-Seventh Conference*, 372, 374.

24 See e.g. Bindschedler, "Neutrality, Concept and General Rules", 553; Bindschedler, "Die Neutralität im modernen Völkerrecht", 26; Bothe, "Neutrality at Sea", 206–207; Bothe, "Neutrality in Naval Warfare", 391; Köpfer, *Die Neutralität*, 157; Pieper, *Neutralität von Staaten*, 279–282.

25 Heintschel von Heinegg, *Seekriegsrecht und Neutralität im Seekrieg*, 100.

26 See e.g. Castrén, *Present Law of War and Neutrality*, 423; Ishimoto, *Historical Study on the Law of Neutrality*, 18–20 [in Japanese]; Tucker, *Law of War and Neutrality at Sea*, 165. From the perspective of those who support the just war doctrine, it is not permissible for a State to participate in a war on the side of the belligerent waging an unjust war, and the State's freedom to participate in a war is limited to that extent. See Kelsen, *Principles of International Law*, 84–85.

27 Apart from the literature cited in notes 28 and 29, see also, Balladore-Pallieri, *Diritto bellico*, 382; Gioia, "Neutrality and Non-Belligerency", 78; Tucker, *Law of War and Neutrality at Sea*, 165, 202.

28 Castrén, *Present Law of War and Neutrality*, 422–423.

29 Ishimoto, "International Organization and Neutrality", 31 [in Japanese].

30 For example, Ishimoto criticises McNair's view, according to which "a belligerent [ought not] to draw the neutral into the war" (Oppenheim (McNair ed.), *International Law*, 4th ed., 2:493), by only citing Kunz's view, according to which "under general international law there exist neither *the duty to remain neutral* nor *the right to remain neutral*" (Kunz, *Kriegsrecht und Neutralitätsrecht*, 215 [italics in the original]), without further substantially refuting it. Ishimoto, *Historical Study on the Law of Neutrality*, 19–20 [in Japanese]. McNair's view that Ishimoto criticises is in reality

Introduction 15

a view originally advanced by Oppenheim in the third edition of his *International Law* (1921), which was later maintained in the fourth edition of the same book (1928) edited by McNair. On Oppenheim's view regarding the right to remain neutral, see Chapter 3, section 2.1.

31 In this regard, see in particular Ishimoto, *Historical Study on the Law of Neutrality*, 20–21 [in Japanese].

32 On the classification of the "duties of neutral States", see Gioia, "Neutrality and Non-Belligerency", 80, 85.

33 However, although it is often stated that a neutral State is *obliged to acquiese or tolerate* the lawful exercise of belligerent rights by a belligerent State, the real meaning of such a statement is unclear. This point shall be examined in Chapter 2, section 1.4.3.

34 Belligerent rights exercised against neutral nationals are not limited to prize measures. For example, when a belligerent bombards or attacks enemy towns, it is not prohibited to kill and damage collaterally neutral nationals and properties that exist there. Moreover, a belligerent may requisition not only enemy properties but also neutral properties in occupied territories. Furthermore, a belligerent is, under certain conditions, entitled to requisition or utilise means of transport (such as merchant vessels, aircrafts, motor vehicles and railway materials) that have temporarily come from the neutral territory to the belligerent's territory or occupied territories (*jus agnariae*; the right of angary). See Takano, *Outline of International Law*, 2:483 [in Japanese].

35 Declaration respecting Maritime Law between Austria, France, Great Britain, Prussia, Russia, Sardinia, and Turkey, signed at Paris, 16 April 1856, *CTS* 115:1–3.

36 In prize law, the enemy or neutral character of a vessel is determined by the flag that the vessel is entitled to fly. In contrast, although it is recognised that the enemy or neutral character of goods is determined by the enemy or neutral character of its owner, States have differed in the tests for determining the owners' enemy or neutral character. While States such as Great Britain and the United States have determined it by the owners' domicile (the so-called Anglo-American doctrine), States such as France, Italy, Germany and Russia have determined it by the owners' nationality (the so-called continental doctrine). The London Conference held in 1908–09 failed to resolve this divergence in State practice. The London Declaration of 1909, which provides that the neutral or enemy character of goods found on board an enemy vessel is determined by the neutral or enemy character of the owner (Article 58), does not contain any provisions for the determination of the neutral or enemy character of the owner. Final Protocol of the Naval Conference between Austria–Hungary, France, Germany, Great Britain, Italy, Japan, the Netherlands, Russia, Spain and the United States, signed at London, 26 February 1909, Annex: Déclaration relative au Droit de la Guerre Maritime, *CTS* 208:338–354. On the problem of the enemy or neutral character in prize law, see e.g. Colombos, *Treatise on the Law of Prize*, 67–120; Brown, *Der neutrale Charakter*, 29–124; Tucker, *Law of War and Neutrality at Sea*, 76–86.

37 Tabata, *New Lecture on International Law*, 2:291 [in Japanese]. The place of the duty of acquiescence in the traditional law of neutrality and the relationship between the duty of acquiescence and the duty of impartiality shall be discussed in Chapter 2, section 1.4.3.

38 Oppenheim (Lauterpacht ed.), *International Law*, 7th ed., 2:639.

39 Lauterpacht, "Limits of the Operation of the Law of War", 237.

40 Tabata, *New Lecture on International Law*, 2:291–292 [in Japanese].

41 See the literature cited in notes 136 and 151 of Chapter 3.

42 As stated in section 2.1, there is a general consensus among writers regarding this point.

43 Heintschel von Heinegg, *Seekriegsrecht und Neutralität im Seekrieg*, 143 [italics added].

44 Meyrowitz, *Le principe de l'égalité des belligérants*, 374.

16   Introduction

45 Ibid., 334, 398.

46 Ibid., 398.

47 Ibid., 383.

48 If one challenges such an assumption, one has to prove that there existed the right of a neutral State not to be involved in a war under the traditional law of neutrality, namely that a belligerent was in principle prohibited from resorting to war against a neutral State and to identify the legal basis for such prohibition. However, no scholar has ever proved and clarified these points.

49 On the German violation of Belgian neutrality in 1914, see Taoka, *Right of Self-defence*, 51–60.

50 Treaty between Austria, France, Great Britain, Prussia and Russia, and the Netherlands, signed at London, 19 April 1839, *CTS* 88:411–420; Treaty between Austria, France, Great Britain, Prussia and Russia, and Belgium, signed at London, 19 April 1839, ibid., 421–426; Treaty between Belgium and the Netherlands relative to the Separation of their Respective Territories, signed at London, 19 April 1839, ibid., 427–443.

51 As to the duties arising from permanent neutrality treaties, see Taoka, *Permanent Neutrality and Japan's Security*, 210–213 [in Japanese].

52 "The Hague Conventions and the Neutrality of Belgium", 961. The author of this Editorial Comment is unknown since Editorial Comments published in the *American Journal of International Law* at that time did not include authors' name, in contrast to Editorial Comments published in that Journal in recent years.

53 Ibid., 959. As an example of other writers who adopted the same view as that adopted in this Editorial Comment, see Falconbridge, "Right of a Belligerent to Make War upon a Neutral", 204–212.

54 De Visscher, "La théorie de la nécessité", 79.

55 De Visscher, "De la belligérance", 99 [italics in the original].

56 Ibid., 100. As an example of other writers who adopted the same perspective as that of De Visscher, see Garner, *International Law and the World War*, 2:214–217.

57 See Grewe, *Epochen der Völkerrechtsgeschichte*, 433–461, 629–637; Miele, *L'estraneità ai conflitti armati*, 1:96–214; Oeter, "Ursprünge der Neutralität", 447–488; Oeter, *Neutralität und Waffenhandel*, 9–34.

1 Origins of the concept of neutrality

Neutrality from the sixteenth to eighteenth centuries

As stated in the Introduction, some scholars such as Grewe, Miele and Oeter have pointed out the fact that treaties called "neutrality treaties" were concluded between States in Europe from the sixteenth to eighteenth centuries, and in State practice during this period, the status of neutrality was not a status *automatically* established as a result of the outbreak of war: rather, it was a status *contractually* and *individually* created by a neutrality treaty concluded between a belligerent and a third State, i.e. a State not participating in the war. The studies by these scholars should be highly regarded for focusing on neutrality treaties, which have been overlooked by most other scholars, and for identifying the significance of such treaties in the historical development of the law of neutrality.[1]

However, there are some inadequacies in those studies by Grewe, Miele and Oeter.

First, there are differences of opinions among them as to the content and legal character of a neutrality treaty, or in other words, as to what legal relation was established by a neutrality treaty. To state in advance the conclusion of section 1 of this chapter, a neutrality treaty was a treaty in which a contracting State not participating in a war promised not to assist the enemy of the other contracting State, and the latter contracting State promised not to involve the former State in the war. This conclusion is the same as that held by Miele. In contrast, Grewe only focuses on the fact that, in a neutrality treaty, a contracting State not participating in a war promised not to assist the enemy of the other contracting State, and he overlooks the fact that the latter contracting State promised not to involve the former contracting State in a war.[2] In view of these differences of opinions among scholars, we need to reconsider the provisions of neutrality treaties and to clarify the character of such treaties. Section 1 of this chapter will discuss these points.

Second, Grewe, Miele and Oeter have not identified the theoretical basis of the theory of neutrality as presented by eighteenth-century scholars. According to them, while a neutrality treaty concluded between a belligerent and a third State had been considered as a precondition for the legal status of neutrality in State practice between the sixteenth and the eighteenth centuries, eighteenth-century scholars *institutionalised* the conception of neutrality ("eine rechtliche

18 *Origins of the concept of neutrality*

Institutionalisierung" of the conception of neutrality[3]), in that the legal status of neutrality became to be established without concluding neutrality treaties. As there are differences of opinions among scholars regarding the character of neutrality treaties, it is quite natural that there are also differences of opinions regarding the nature of the theory of neutrality presented by eighteenth-century scholars, which *institutionalised* the conception of neutrality on the basis of the practice of neutrality treaties. However, Miele, who came to the same conclusion as taken by this book with regard to the character of neutrality treaties, has not clarified how the conception of neutrality could be *institutionalised*. In other words, a neutrality treaty was an agreement between a belligerent and a third State by which the former promised not to involve the latter in a war. Miele has not clarified why belligerent States should not involve a third State in a war when such an agreement does not exist. Section 2 of this chapter considers the theory of neutrality as presented by eighteenth-century writers, especially its theoretical basis.

Section 3 will consider the issue of third States' maritime commerce with belligerents in wartime (the so-called "neutral commerce"), which has been emphasised in descriptions of the historical development of the law of neutrality in existing studies, and its relationship with the conception of neutrality as clarified in sections 1 and 2 of this chapter.

1 Neutrality treaties: neutrality in State practice from the sixteenth to eighteenth centuries

1.1 Origins of the concept of neutrality in international law

The Latin word *neutralitas*, which is the basis of words meaning neutrality in several European languages (neutrality, Neutralität, neutralité, neutralità, etc.), was formed in the Middle Ages from the Classical Latin word *neuter*. *Neuter* is an adjective that corresponds to the English word "neither" and the word *neutralis*, meaning a "neutral State", as well as the word *neutralitas*, meaning the status of neutrality, were established on the basis of the word *neuter*. Although the word *neuter* appears in dictionaries of Classical Latin, the words *neutralitas* and *neutralis* did not exist in Classical Latin and only appeared in the Middle Ages as Vulgar Latin.[4]

The process how the words *neutralitas* and *neutralis* derived from the word *neuter* is explained by Christian Wolff (1679–1754):

> In war those are called middle parties (*In bello Medii*) who are attached to neither belligerent party (neutri belligerantium parti adhærent), consequently do not involve themselves in the war. They are commonly called neutrals (*Neutrales*) because, for the purpose of the war, they favour neither party (neutri parti belli causa favent), and the condition of the nations which follow neither of the belligerent parties in war is called neutrality (*Neutralitas*), and their lands are called neutral lands (*Terræ neutræ*).[5]

The word *neutralis* is used because these States support neither (*neuter*) of the belligerents as allies, and its status is referred to as *neutralitas*. The word *neutralitas*, which had at first been used as a medical term,[6] came to be used as a concept of international law in the sixteenth century in treaties called "neutrality treaties" (*pacta neutralitatis*; traités de neutralité). Within the range of available primary historical resources, the oldest neutrality treaty is a neutrality treaty concluded between Burgundy and France in 1522,[7] and many neutrality treaties were concluded until the eighteenth century.

The chronological order of published neutrality treaties as found in Du Mont's *Corps universels du droits des gens* and Parry's *Consolidated Treaty Series* is as follows: (1) the neutrality treaty between Burgundy and France (8 July 1522),[8] (2) the treaty between France, Spain and the Swiss Confederation regarding the neutrality of Burgundy (22 September 1595),[9] (3) the letters of neutrality accorded to Lorraine by France (19 June 1596),[10] (4) the neutrality treaty between Sweden and the Catholic German States (29 January 1632),[11] (5) the neutrality treaty between Trier and Sweden (12 April 1632),[12] (6) the neutrality treaty between France and Tuscany (11 May 1646),[13] (7) the neutrality treaty between Mainz and France (9 May 1647),[14] (8) the neutrality treaty between Sweden and Courland (4 June 1647),[15] (9) the neutrality treaty between France and Mantua (9 July 1658),[16] (10) the neutrality treaty between Denmark, Brandenburg, Münster, and Brunswick–Lüneburg–Hannover (11(21) September 1675),[17] (11) the neutrality treaty between France and Brunswick–Lüneburg (18 October 1675),[18] (12) the neutrality treaty between France and the Swiss Confederation (7 May 1689),[19] (13) the neutrality treaty between France and the Netherlands (24 November 1733)[20] and (14) the neutrality treaty between Austria–Hungary and France (1 May 1756).[21]

We will first examine the content of these treaties, that is to say, the content and character of legal relation established by a neutrality treaty between a belligerent and a third State (section 1.2), and then will consider the background to the practice of concluding neutrality treaties during this period (section 1.3).

1.2 Content of neutrality treaties

1.2.1 Reciprocal relationship between a belligerent and a third State in a neutrality treaty

A neutrality treaty is a treaty concluded during a war (or immediately before the outbreak of war) between a belligerent and a third State, in which they exchange certain promises.[22] The neutrality treaty that most clearly shows the reciprocal relationship between the promise on the part of a belligerent and the promise on the part of a third State is the neutrality treaty between Sweden and the Catholic German States in 1632, which was concluded during the Thirty Years' War. This treaty, after providing in the preamble that "the King of Sweden, in consideration of the desire of the Duke of Bavaria and the Catholic League to acquire neutrality (aiant égard au désir que le Duc de Bavieres, & la Ligue

20 *Origins of the concept of neutrality*

Catolique ont d'obtenir la Neutralité) ... will accord the neutrality on the following conditions (accordera la Neutralité aux conditions suivants)", and provides, as one of the "following conditions", that Bavaria and the Catholic League shall "faithfully and sincerely observe neutrality (observeront la Neutralité inviolablement & sincerement)" (Article 7).[23] In short, in this treaty, Sweden, a belligerent in the war, promised to accord neutrality to Bavaria and the Catholic League (third States in the war) on the conditions that the latter States promised to observe neutrality in the war.

What does it mean for a third State to "observe neutrality", and what does it mean for a belligerent State to "accord neutrality" to the third State? In other words, what were the promises made by each contracting State in a neutrality treaty? We shall answer these questions by analysing the provisions of neutrality treaties.

1.2.2 *"Observe neutrality": promise on the part of a third State in a neutrality treaty*

A direct definition of the meaning of the term "observe neutrality" is not found in the provisions of neutrality treaties, but the meaning of this term can be clarified by examining the way it is used in each treaty.

Some neutrality treaties provide that a contracting State shall not assist the enemies of the other contracting State and shall, "*on the contrary*", "observe neutrality". For example, Article 7 of the 1632 neutrality treaty between Sweden and the Catholic German States, provides that the Catholic German States shall not permit the enemies of Sweden to enlist or assemble soldiers, purchase or transport weapons or to carry out any other preparations for war within their territory, and "*on the contrary (au contraire)*", shall "faithfully and sincerely observe neutrality".[24] Also, Article 6 of the 1632 neutrality treaty between Trier and Sweden, provides that the former shall not permit the enemies of Sweden to enlist or organise soldiers, etc. in its territory, and "*on the contrary (sed)*", shall "observe neutrality faithfully and sincerely wherever".[25] The 1756 neutrality treaty between Austria–Hungary and France provides that Austria–Hungary agreed not only to "abstain from direct or indirect involvement" in the war between France and Great Britain over America (the Seven Years' War) but also that, "*on the contrary (au contraire)*, Austria–Hungary shall maintain complete and strict neutrality".[26]

Also, there are neutrality treaties which provide that a contracting State shall, "*in accordance with neutrality*", abstain from giving assistance to the enemies of the other contracting State. For example, Article 2 of the 1675 neutrality treaty between France and Brunswick–Lüneburg provides that "*in accordance with this neutrality (Conformement à cette Neutralité)*", Brunswick–Lüneburg shall not directly or indirectly assist the enemy of France or its allies in any area.[27]

These provisions of neutrality treaties show that direct or indirect involvement in a war, or the provision of assistance to the enemies of the other contracting State are considered to be "contrary" to observing neutrality, and that abstaining from assisting the enemies of the other contracting State is considered to be "in accordance with" neutrality. In sum, in neutrality treaties, to "observe neutrality" means not to involve in the war and to abstain from assisting the enemies of the other contracting State.

1.2.3 "Accord neutrality": promise on the part of a belligerent in a neutrality treaty

Next, what was the promise on the part of a belligerent State in a neutrality treaty? What does it mean for a belligerent State to "accord neutrality" to the other contracting State?[28]

By examining the provisions of neutrality treaties, we can find that the content of promise on the part of a belligerent State in a neutrality treaty was to abstain from attacking and from involving the other contracting State in the war. For example, the letters of neutrality accorded by France to Lorraine in 1596 "by the grace of the Holy King of France (par la grace de Dieu Roi de France)", provides that the country and territory of Lorraine "remain completely free from all aggressions and acts of hostility (demeurent du tout libres de toutes invasions, & actes d'hostilité)".[29] Also, in the 1646 neutrality treaty between France and Tuscany, France promises that, "in accordance with the neutrality (Conformement à la neutralité)", the armed forces of France, when attacking Siena, shall not damage in any way the territory or property of Tuscany.[30] The 1733 neutrality treaty between France and the Netherlands provides that the Austrian Netherlands shall "not to be involved in the war over the Poland issue", and France shall "not attack the Austrian Netherlands".[31] Furthermore, in the 1756 neutrality treaty between Austria–Hungary and France, Austria–Hungary promises to maintain neutrality, and, "reciprocally (reciproquement)", France "declares and promises that it shall abstain from attacking or carrying out aggression against the Netherlands region under the rule of the Queen of Austria, or to other kingdoms, regions and territories".[32]

The meaning of the term "accord neutrality" becomes clearer when observing the 1632 neutrality treaty between Trier and Sweden. This treaty, after providing for the promise on the part of Trier as a neutral in Articles 1 to 7, provides in Article 8 that "Sacred Royal Majesty [the King of Sweden] shall not strike in a hostile manner (hostiliter offendet) at us [Trier], the territories of the Archbishop or Bishop or any hereditary territories, and shall not impose any kind of military burden upon us, and rather, *on the contrary (sed)* ... shall respect and observe the neutrality (colet & observabit Neutralitatem)".[33] In this provision, to "strike in a hostile manner (hostiliter offendet)" at Trier is contrasted with to "respect the neutrality (colet ... Neutralitatem)" of Trier. In other words, in this neutrality treaty, respecting the neutrality of the contracting State means abstaining from striking in a hostile manner at that State.

Scholars during this period also understood that the promise on the part of a belligerent in a neutrality treaty was to abstain from attacking and waging war on the other contracting State (a neutral). For example, Wolff, in his book

22 *Origins of the concept of neutrality*

published in 1764, states that "[b]elligerents entering into a treaty of neutrality bind themselves to the one who is the adherent of neither party, that they will not bring hostile force (*vim hostilem*) against him and his property", and "[a]gainst those who are neutrals in war the belligerents have no right of war (jus belli)".[34]

In sum, for a contracting State to "accord neutrality" or to "respect neutrality" of the other contracting State means that the former State abstains from attacks, aggression and hostility, in relation to the other contracting State (a neutral), and do not involve it in a war, which was the promise on the part of a belligerent States in a neutrality treaty.

1.2.4 *Legal nature of neutrality treaties*

As discussed in the preceding sections, a neutrality treaty is a treaty in which a contracting State promises to *observe neutrality* (to abstain from providing assistance to the enemies of the other contracting State), and, *reciprocally*, the other contracting State (a belligerent in the war) promises to *respect the neutrality* of the former State (not to involve that State in the war). In other words, a neutrality treaty is not a treaty which only provides that a neutral State should not assist the enemies of the other contracting State – Grewe understands the character of a neutrality treaty in this way[35] – but, as understood by Miele, it is a treaty where a neutral State is guaranteed to "remain *de jure* outside the conflict" on the conditions that it does not provide assistance to the enemies of the other contracting State.[36] As stated at the beginning of this chapter, while there have been differences of opinions among scholars with regard to the legal nature of neutrality treaties, as a result of a reconsideration of the provisions of neutrality treaties, we can conclude that the view of Miele is correct.

1.3 *Function of neutrality treaties in State practice*

1.3.1 *A neutrality treaty as a precondition for the legal status of neutrality*

As observed in section 1.2, neutrality treaties often provide that a contracting State (a belligerent in a war) *accords* (accorder; indulgerer) or *grants* (octroyer) neutrality to the other contracting State. Also, the letters of neutrality accorded by France to Lorraine provides that the neutrality was accorded "*by the grace of* the Holy King of France (*par la grace de* Dieu Roi de France)".[37]

It becomes clear from such provisions that neutrality was the legal status accorded or granted by neutrality treaties and that a neutrality treaty was a precondition for the legal status of neutrality. In other words, in State practice between the sixteenth and eighteenth centuries, neutrality was neither a status that a third State could unilaterally select, nor a status that was automatically established as a result of the outbreak of war. Some writers have already pointed out this. For example, Oeter, discussing neutrality during this period, observes:

Origins of the concept of neutrality 23

"Neutrality was understood as a definitely special status, to grant which was left to the discretion of the Powers concerned. There was no right for third States to demand respect for the status of neutrality".[38] Miele also states that "conventional neutrality, deriving from the intentions of the Parties,... can in no way be considered as the 'necessary' juridical condition for international subjects remaining outside a conflict".[39] There were also some contemporary writers who took the view that neutrality was the status contractually created by neutrality treaties. For example, Johann Wolfgang Textor (1638–1701), in his book of 1680, wrote: "Neutrality ... is ... constituted from consent or agreement (consensu vel pacto)", and "it is necessary, as regards the efficient cause of neutrality, that the belligerents on each side must unanimously consent to give this neutrality...". Therefore, according to Textor, "[a] belligerent that does not give this consent is not bound to recognize the neutrality...".[40]

In a neutrality treaty, which was considered to be a preconditon for the legal status of neutrality, a belligerent *accorded* neutrality to the other contracting State and promised not to involve that State in the war. This means that a belligerent was free to attack or involve in the war with any State with which it had not concluded a neutrality treaty. The practice of States during this period confirms this. For example, in the Thirty Years' War (1618–48), despite their demands for neutrality to be respected, the neutrality of several third States that had not concluded neutrality treaties was not recognised by belligerents, and they were invaded or attacked by the belligerents.[41] In the Seven Years' War (1756–63), the Netherlands – while it had concluded a neutrality treaty with France in the War of the Polish Succession (1733–38), no such treaty had been concluded with the belligerents in this war – was invaded and occupied by the French army.[42] Contemporary writers at the time also realised such realities. For example, Wolff, in his book of 1764, while not normatively justifying, realised the fact that belligerents often committed many things by which wrong is done to neighbouring States with which they had not concluded neutrality treaties.[43]

According to the prevailing view today, there has been a transition in the legal status of war in international law from (1) the period in which the just war doctrine was supported (before the mid-eighteenth century), to (2) the period in which the unlimited freedom of States to resort to war was recognised (from the latter half of eighteenth century to the early twentieth century), and to (3) the period in which war and the use of force by States have been in principle prohibited (after the First World War).[44] However, as we have seen, in State practice before the eighteenth century, it was considered to be lawful for a belligerent to resort to war against a third State with which they had not concluded a neutrality treaty. Then, how can we explain this, in relation to the prevailing view today that the just war doctrine was supported before the mid-eighteenth century? Regarding this question, it might be possible to explain as follows: When it is said that the just war doctrine was supported before the mid-eighteenth century, reference is made solely to the literature of writers such as Vitoria, Suárez and Grotius, and it has not been proven that the just war doctrine was supported by the practice of States. Rather, it seems to be that the just

24 *Origins of the concept of neutrality*

war doctrine was not supported by the practice of States at that time.[45] Proving that the just war doctrine was not supported by State practice goes far beyond the scope of this book, and there are no studies that have conclusively proven this point. However, based on what has been clarified by the existing studies to date, it is reasonable to suppose that the just war doctrine was not supported by State practice before the eighteenth century.[46] In other words, the just war doctrine was a doctrine that was only supported by scholars, and the practice of States during this period admitted the freedom of States to resort to war against other States with which they had not concluded neutrality treaties.

1.3.2 States that do not take part in a war but are not neutrals: allies and other States

As we have seen, since a neutrality treaty was considered to be a precondition for the legal status of neutrality in State practice from the sixteenth to eighteenth centuries, a State that had not concluded a neutrality treaty with belligerents was not considered as a neutral even if it did not take part in the war as a belligerent. Textor, who considered that the status of neutrality was constituted by an agreement between a belligerent and a third State and supported the same approach as adopted in State practice, wrote in his book published in 1680: "[F]or example, in the recent Germano-Gallic War, the King of Poland, the Grand Duchy of Muscovy, and other princes might in this sense called as neutrals (neutrales), in that they were not the ally (socii) of either belligerent – yet, strictly speaking and in the usage the Law of Nations, those only are neutrals who derive their middle position (media) from consent or agreement".[47]

As indicated here by Textor, in State practice from the sixteenth to eighteenth centuries, there were two categories of States that did not take part in a war but were not considered as neutrals: (1) allies (*socius*) of either belligerent, which provided some kind of assistance to the belligerent and (2) other States that did not provide assistance to any belligerent but were not to be regarded as neutrals as they had not concluded neutrality treaties.[48] The municipal laws of several States relating to prize law, as a term meaning States that were not enemies (enemyes; ennemis; Vyanden), used various terms such as, "our allies, confederates and friend States" (the 1557 Order in Council of England),[49] "our allies, confederates or friend States (nos alliez, confederez ou amis)" (the 1584 edict of France),[50] "our allies, friend States and neutral States (Onse Geallieerden, Vrunden ende Neutralen)" (the 1652 ordinance of the Netherlands).[51] This fact also confirms the conclusion that not all States that did not take part in a war were regarded as neutral States.

Allies are States assisting either belligerent. While there were cases where such assistance was given by participating in a war and becoming itself a belligerent, there were also cases where assistance was given without participating in a war. For example, Article 12 of the alliance treaty concluded between France and several German States in 1634 provides that "*in the case that His Majesty [the King of France] has difficulty to declare war or make war* on her own initiative for any reason, she [the King of France] shall assist the confederates with personnel and monies".[52] This article clearly shows that there may be cases in which a State assists belligerents without becoming itself a belligerent. There were many other alliance treaties that provided that contracting States not participating in the war to provide military assistance to belligerents, and there were cases where such assistance was actually provided.[53] States that provided such assistance were not neutrals and were not guaranteed the legal status of not being involved in the war. However, States that did not wish to enjoy such a legal status might provide assistance to a belligerent. While there might be cases where such States were not involved in the war due to the situation of the other belligerent, this did not mean that such States were *legally guaranteed* to remain outside the war, but it simply meant that they de facto remained outside the war.

1.3.3 Political background to the practice of concluding neutrality treaties

As has been discussed in the preceding sections, a neutrality treaty is a treaty in which the contracting State (State A: a belligerent State) agrees to respect the neutrality of the other contracting State (State B: a neutral State) and not to involve State B in the war, on the condition that State B does not to assist the enemies of State A. The neutral status of State B, that is, the legal status of not being involved in the war was, in State practice before the eighteenth century, constituted by a treaty of neutrality. A neutrality treaty was advantageous for the security of State B, which wished to remain outside the war. If State B did not (or could not) conclude neutrality treaties with belligerents, it was not legally guaranteed to remain outside the war. On the other hand, from the perspective of belligerents, as a neutrality treaty was considered to be a precondition for the legal status of neutrality, belligerents could choose either to conclude neutrality treaties with States against which they did not need to make war, or not to conclude neutrality treaties with States against which they needed to make war. Neutrality treaties were concluded when there were a community of interests between a belligerent and a third State. The political background to this community of interests can be summarised as follows.

The practice of concluding neutrality treaties emerged in the sixteenth century. In this period, France and the Holly Roman Empire (the House of Habsburg) began a struggle over the rule of the Italian Peninsula. In this struggle, the security of the central European States geographically located between the two States, as well as the security of States in north and central Italy, became an issue, and they adopted a policy of concluding neutrality treaties with the belligerents.[54] In the Thirty Years' War (1618–48) – which can be seen from the perspective of international relations in Europe as a continuation of the conflict between France and the Holly Roman Empire, and from the perspective of North European history as a conflict between Sweden, Denmark, Poland and the Holy Roman Empire to gain control over the Baltic Sea[55]

26 *Origins of the concept of neutrality*

– several German and Italian States attempted to ensure their security by concluding neutrality treaties with the belligerents (France and Sweden). After the peace of Westphalia (1648), States that desired to secure their own security concluded neutrality treaties with France, which had the superior position in Europe and repeatedly waged war in this period.[56]

Neutrality treaties were means of guaranteeing security for small States surrounded by larger belligerent States (France, Sweden, Spain and Austria, etc.)[57] and were concluded on the basis of the wishes of those small States.[58] This can be understood, for example, from the 1632 neutrality treaty between Sweden and the German Catholic States, which was concluded in view of the "*desire of Bavaria and the Catholic League to acquire neutrality*"[59] and from the letters of neutrality accorded to Lorraine by the King of France in 1596, in which "neutrality was recognised by France *for the sake of [Lorraine] (en sa faveur)*".[60]

However, neutrality treaties were concluded only when they were also profitable for the belligerents. As seen from the perspective of belligerents, there are cases in which it is profitable to prevent third States from taking part in a war on the side of the enemy, even by expending cost for recognising the neutrality of third States, that is, making recompense for promising not to attack or involve the third States in the war. The belligerents, by doing so, can avoid an unreasonable increase in the number of enemies and can concentrate their limited military resources upon the original enemies.[61] On the contrary, in cases where it is not profitable for belligerents to conclude neutrality treaties, they do not conclude neutrality treaties and do not respect the neutrality of the third States.

2 "Institutionalisation" of neutrality: the theory of neutrality presented by eighteenth-century scholars

As discussed in the previous section, in State practice from the sixteenth to eighteenth centuries, the legal status of neutrality was considered to be a status created by a neutrality treaty concluded between a belligerent and a third State. In contrast, eighteenth-century scholars such as Cornelius van Bynkershoek (1673–1743), Christian Wolff (1679–1754), Emer de Vattel (1714–67) and Martin Hübner (1723–95) presented the theory according to which even States that had not concluded neutrality treaties with belligerents could become neutrals. As will be seen later, the legal effects of neutrality established in this way are the same as those of neutrality established on the basis of neutrality treaties: the legal effects of creating the duty of the belligerent States to abstain from waging war on neutral States. Thus, eighteenth-century scholars generalised and expanded the circumstances in which the legal status of neutrality was created, by denying the need of concluding a neutrality treaty, which had been regarded as a precondition for the status of neutrality in State practice. That is why some writers such as Oeter have observed that eighteenth-century scholars *institutionalised* the conception of neutrality.[62] We will consider how such institutionalisation was possible (section 2.2), but before that, it is necessary to confirm the existing theories before the seventeenth century (section 2.1).

2.1 Existing theories

2.1.1 The just war doctrine

A BASIC DETAILS OF THE JUST WAR DOCTRINE

International law scholars prior to the seventeenth century supported the just war doctrine. The just war (*bellum justum*) doctrine was advocated long before by Cicero, which was later taught by St. Augustine (AD 354–430) and Isidore of Seville (*c.*AD 570–636) in the Middle Ages, and developed as a theory by theologians and canon law scholars in the Middle Ages, who then passed it down to modern theologians (Vitoria, Suárez, etc.) and legal scholars (Ayala, Gentilis, Grotius, etc.).[63] According to St. Thomas Aquinas (*c.*1225–74), who played a central role in the formation of the just war doctrine, there are three conditions for a war to be just: (1) the supreme authority (*auctoritas principis*), (2) a just cause (*causa iusta*) and (3) a rightful intention of belligerents (*intentio bellantium recta*).[64] Later scholars developed their arguments on the basis of these three conditions. Certainly, there were some discrepancies among scholars as to the detailed conditions for a war to be just, and the order of priority of these conditions. However, there was a general agreement among scholars that a just cause was necessary for a war to be just, and the central issue of the just war doctrine was consistently the issue of just causes.

According to the just war doctrine, a just cause of war exists only when an injury (*injuria*) is inflicted upon oneself. For example, Vitoria states that "[t]here is a single and only just cause for commencing a war, namely, a wrong received".[65] Suárez states that "just and sufficient reason for war is the infliction of a grave injustice which cannot be avenged or repaired in any other war".[66] Grotius also states that "[n]o other just cause for undertaking war can there be excepting injury received".[67]

According to the just war doctrine, war is a means of remedy for violations caused by injuries inflicted and therefore resembles a lawsuit.[68] For example, Suárez, whose theories regarding the traditional Scholastic doctrine of just war are regarded to be the most detailed, holds that, even between States, there is a need for punishment for injury, but as there are no judicial systems with a higher authority than that of the State, war is conducted on the basis of a kind of "power of jurisdiction (*potestas jurisdictionis*)" of the State itself.[69] Grotius also argues in his *De jure belli ac pacis*, that "[i]t is evident that the sources from which wars arise are as numerous as those from which lawsuits spring; for where judicial settlement fails, war begins",[70] also likening war to lawsuits, and in Chapters 2 to 19 of Book 2 of the same book he discusses the sources from which wars arise, that is, the specific details of the rights and the legal relations that should be protected by a just war.

28 Origins of the concept of neutrality

B THE OBLIGATION TO ASSIST A BELLIGERENT WAGING A JUST WAR

In the just war doctrine, it is just for a State to assist another State waging a just war, which is even an obligation under the law of nature.[71] For example, according to Gentilis, it is just not only to defend oneself but also to defend the cause of others (honourable defence (*defensio honesta*)). According to Gentilis, in universal human society, as all people are related by blood (*cognatio*), and people are born for the sake of society, it is obligation (*officium*) to help others.[72] According to Grotius, "by nature every one is the defender of his own rights", but "to render service to another, so far as we can, is not only permissible (licetum), it is also honourable (honestum)".[73] Also for Grotius, justness of a war to help others is based on "the mutual tie of kinship among men (hominum inter se conjunctio)".[74]

However, a State is not always obliged to assist another State carrying out a just war. For example, according to Gentilis, "honourable defence" becomes an obligation only when such a defence does not present a risk to the one carrying it out.[75] Grotius, discussing whether a person or State is bound to undertake war to help others, argues that, "if danger is evident, it is certain that a man is not so bound, for he may prefer his own life and interests to those of others".[76]

In sum, to assist a belligerent carrying out a just war is an obligation only when it does not present a risk to oneself. As Fujio Ito points out, the obligation to assist a State carrying on a just war is, "despite being called an obligation at its root, is actually closer to a right or a liberty".[77] Therefore, even in the just war doctrine, it is assumed that there exist States that remain outside a war by abstaining from assisting any belligerent, considering the possibility of risk to themselves. The next issue is whether the legal status of such States remaining outside a war was understood to be that of neutrality by pre-seventeenth century scholars.

2.1.2 Absence of the conception of neutrality

The Latin words *neutralitas* (neutrality) and *neutralis* (neutral) had been already used in treaties and other official documents since the sixteenth century,[78] but these words were rarely used in legal literature until the eighteenth century. In pre-seventeenth-century legal literature, words such as "a common friend (*amicum communem*)",[79] "those who are of neither side in war (*his qui in bello medii sunt*)",[80] "those who are not involved in war (*his qui extra bellum sunt*)"[81] and "those who keep out of a war (*eorum qui à bello abstinent*)"[82] were used to denote States other than belligerents.[83]

However, that the words *neutralitas* and *neutralis* were not used does not necessarily mean that the *conception* of neutrality or the *idea* that formed the basis of the theory of neutrality in the later period was absent in the literature before the seventeenth century. As stated above, the words *neutralitas* and *neutralis* did not exist in Classical Latin but appeared as Vulgar Latin in the Middle Ages. As pointed out by Ryoichi Taoka, the reason why the words *neutralitas*

Origins of the concept of neutrality 29

and *neutralis* were not used in the pre-seventeenth century by scholars is thought to be due to the fact that scholars at the time who were influenced by the Renaissance used as little as possible any Vulgar Latin that did not exist in Classical Latin.[84] The Renaissance took as its ideal the cultures of Classical Greece and Rome, and the culture of the Middle Ages was despised; thus Vulgar Latin words that did not exist in Classical Latin were seen as incorrect.

Then, did the *conception* or *idea* of neutrality exist in the literature before the seventeenth century?

First, in this period, there were writers who mainly discussed the legal relations between belligerents and scarcely discussed the legal relations between belligerents and third States. For example, Vitoria and Suárez, apart from stating that belligerents should not kill or take the things of foreigners (*peregrinos*) and travellers (*hospites*) within the territories of the enemies, made almost no arguments regarding the relations between belligerents and third States.[85]

From the basic logic behind the just war doctrine, this was rather natural. As stated above, in the just war doctrine, war is seen as a means of punishing a party that has inflicted an injury and of recovering one's rights. When carrying out war, in order to punish a party that has inflicted an injury and to recover one's rights, it is permissible to kill or injure persons belonging to the enemy and to take their property. However, it is self-evident according to the just war doctrine that war is not to be carried out against States that have not inflicted any injury, that is to say, States other than the enemy, and it is not permissible to kill or injure persons belonging to those States and to take their property. In this sense, it was very natural that scholars who supported the just war doctrine scarcely discussed the legal relations between third States and belligerents.

However, even before the seventeenth century, there were scholars who supported the just war doctrine and at the same time discussed in relative detail the legal relations between belligerents and third States. For example, Grotius, as Vitoria and Suárez did, affirms that from the basic logic behind the just war doctrine, there is no need to discuss the legal status of parties other than belligerents, by stating that "[i]t might seem superfluous for us to speak of those who are not involved in war (extra bellum sunt), since it is quite clear that no right of war (jus bellicum) is valid against them".[86] However, Grotius points out that "in time of war on the pretext of necessity (necessitate) many things are done at the expense of those who are at peace, especially if they are neighbours", and, on the basis of this reason, discusses the relations between belligerents and third States in the chapter entitled "Those who of are neither side in war (De his qui in bello medii sunt)".[87] In this chapter, Grotius observes that the "duty (officium) of those who keep out of a war (eorum qui à bello abstinent)" is to "do nothing whereby he who supports a wicked cause may be rendered more powerful, or whereby the movements of him who wages a just war may be hampered", and, "[i]n a doubtful matter, however, those at peace should show themselves impartial to either side in permitting transit, in furnishing supplies to troops, and in not assisting those under siege (æquos se præbere utrisque in permittendo transitu, in commeatu præbendo legionibus, in obsessis non

30 Origins of the concept of neutrality

sublevandis)". Furthermore, in terms of those who keep out of war, he states that "[i]t will even be of advantage to make a treaty (fœdus) with either party that is waging war, in order that it may be permissible to abstain from war while retaining the goodwill of either (bona voluntate), and to render to each the common duties of humanity (communia humanitatis officia)".

Were those arguments of Grotius, who did not use the very terms neutrality (*neutralitas*) or neutral (*neutralis*), in substance, the conception or idea of neutrality? Opinions may be divided with regard to this question.[88] In particular, the passage "[i]n a doubtful matter, however, those at peace should show themselves *impartial* to either side in permitting transit, in furnishing supplies to troops, and in not assisting those under siege" [italics added] can be seen as substantially the same idea as the theory of neutrality presented by eighteenth-century scholars, the basic principle of which is the impartiality towards belligerents. However, Grotius does not state anything about why third States should show themselves *impartial* to belligerents in a doubtful matter. The reason for this may be either to avoid being involved in war, or to avoid supporting an unjust belligerent, which is contrary to the law of nature, based on an incorrect judgement of the justice or injustice of the war. It is not clear which is the real intention of Grotius. If it is the former, it is possible to reason that Grotius' argument is substantially the same idea as the theory of neutrality, but as Grotius does not state anything about this point, the possibility of the latter intention cannot be excluded. Hence, it is safe to conclude that Grotius did not have a clear conception or idea of neutrality.

2.2 The theory of neutrality as presented by eighteenth-century writers

As shown in the previous section, pre-seventeenth century scholars did not have, at the very least, any clear conception or idea of neutrality. In contrast, eighteenth-century scholars, who also adopted the just war doctrine in the same way as prior scholars, began to discuss the issue of neutrality in a clear manner.

2.2.1 The just war doctrine

Eighteen-century scholars generally supported the just war doctrine. For example, Hübner, in his book of 1759, clearly adopted the just war doctrine, by stating: "All the just causes of war relate to either of the following two causes: 1 *offence in its real meaning*, that is, offences regarded as such by the law of nations; 2 *positive refusal* ... of an unquestionable *perfect right* (*un Droit parfait*). All wars carried out for reasons other than these may be called unjust."[89]

Wolff and Vattel also supported the just war doctrine in saying that, based on the principles of the natural law of nations (*jus gentium naturale*; Droit des Gens Naturel), a just cause was necessary in order for a war to be just and that the just causes of war refer to injuries (*injuria*; injure) already inflicted on oneself or that may be inflicted.[90] According to them, since injury refers to an

Origins of the concept of neutrality 31

attack or an infringement on one's "perfect rights (*jura perfecta*; droits parfaits)", "[t]he right to use force, or to make war, is given to Nations only for their defense and for the maintenance of their rights".[91] However, while adopting the just war doctrine based on the principles of the natural law of nations, Wolff and Vattel presented a theory that mitigates the strictness of the natural law of nations, based on the voluntary law of nations (*jus gentium voluntarium*; Droit des Gens Volontaire).[92] In other words, in the natural law of nations, various rights are recognised for States carrying out a just war, such as the right to kill enemies, the right to take prisoners of war and the right to destroy and confiscate the property of enemies. Such rights are not recognised for States carrying out an unjust war. However, according to this principle, both States carrying out war would assert that the other party is unjust, which would brutalise the war, making it difficult to bring the war to an end. To avoid such disorder and to mitigate the strictness of the natural law of nations, certain principles are introduced under the voluntary law of nations: (1) War, as regards its effects, must be regarded as just for both belligerents and (2) what is permissible for one belligerent is also permissible for the other. In other words, rights granted to a just belligerent are also recognised for States carrying out an unjust war, such as the right to kill the enemies, the right to take prisoners of war and the right to destroy and confiscate the property of the enemies.[93]

Bynkershoek is often viewed as a scholar who denied the just war doctrine.[94] However, it seems reasonable to understand that he implicitly adopted the just war doctrine. Bynkershoek, in his *Questions of Public Law* of 1737, states that "the only correct ground for war is the defence or recovery of one's own (nostri defendendi vel recuperandi causa, sola belli ratio est)" and that "[w]e make war because we think that our enemy, by the injury (injuriam) done us, he merited the destruction of himself and his people".[95] This is the same idea as the traditional doctrine of just war, according to which war is viewed as being carried out against the State that has inflicted injury, for the "defence or recovery" of its own rights. Bynkershoek discusses the cases in which a State has concluded alliance treaties with two States that make war against each other, and argues that such a State should assist "one which has *the juster cause* (*justiorem causam* habet)".[96] This also shows that Bynkershoek adopted the just war doctrine, according to which a just cause is necessary to wage war. Certainly, Bynkershoek does not discuss in any systematic manner the conditions for which a war is just, and the crucial point in his arguments in *Questions of Public Law* is the issue of the means and methods of warfare that may be exercised by belligerents during war rather than the just war doctrine itself.[97] But we cannot deny that Bynkershoek's basic idea was the just war doctrine.

In sum, the just war doctrine was in principle supported by eighteenth-century scholars, though some revisions were made to the doctrine by Wolff's and Vattel's voluntary law of nations, and was not systematically discussed by Bynkershoek. As stated previously, from the basic logic behind the just war doctrine, it is self-evident that war may not be carried out against third States, that is, the States that have not inflicted an injury, and it is unnecessary to discuss the

32   *Origins of the concept of neutrality*

legal status of third States. Nevertheless, as we shall see below, eighteenth-century writers discussed the legal status of third States in detail by using the concept of neutrality.

2.2.2 *The theory of neutrality*

A THE STATUS OF NEUTRALITY CREATED INDEPENDENTLY OF
NEUTRALITY TREATIES

Eighteenth-century writers clearly realised the practice of States of concluding neutrality treaties between belligerents and third States. For example, Wolff states that "since it is frequently to the advantage of one of the belligerent parties, that one may not perchance enter into a treaty of war with the opposite party, or even in the absence of a treaty give aid to it in case of necessity, consequently that one may remain neutral, a treaty of neutrality (fœdus neutralitatis) is usually made".[98] Vattel also observes that "[a] Nation which is carrying on war, or is about to carry on war, frequently takes the step of proposing a treaty of neutrality (un Traité de Neutralité) to a sovereign of whom it is suspicious".[99]

Those writers are of the opinion that the conclusion of neutrality treaties is beneficial not only to belligerents but also to third States. For example, Wolff writes that "if they [belligerents] would obey this law [law of nature] in the present case, there would certainly be no need of a treaty of neutrality".[100] As discussed later, according to Wolff, belligerents are prohibited by the law of nature from waging war on States that do not provide assistance to the enemies. However, according to him,

> belligerents, although they ought not to do so, nevertheless in spite of natural obligation (naturali ... obligatione) do commit many things by which wrong is done to neighbouring nations. Therefore, it is not superfluous that treaties of neutrality should be contracted, since a sense of shame is usually more efficacious than natural obligation.[101]

Vattel also states: "Treaties of neutrality are useful, and even necessary, for another reason. The Nation which wishes to secure its own peace when the flames of war are burning in its neighbors' territories can not do better than conclude with the two belligerents treaties in which it is expressly agreed what each party may do, or require, in virtue of the neutrality."[102]

While neutrality treaties were often concluded between belligerents and third States that wished to secure their own peace, eighteenth-century writers argued, from the theoretical viewpoint, that it was not necessary for States to conclude neutrality treaties in order to remain neutral. For example, Wolff states that "[a]ny nation, indeed, *without a treaty itself being made, can be a neutral,* in so far as it furnishes to neither of the belligerent parties the things which can be useful to it in war, which are usually furnished by allies, or furnishes to each party those things which nation owes to nation by nature independently of war".[103] Also, Hübner observes that neutrality treaties "are created from an excess of precaution and fear" and are "not significant in universal international law".[104] Furthermore, Vattel states that "[w]hen a war breaks out between two Nations, *all the others* who are not bound by treaties *are free to remain neutral*".[105]

According to those writers, the legal effects of neutrality created independently of neutrality treaties are the same as those of neutrality created by neutrality treaties. Wolff makes this abundantly clear by stating that "the belligerents, when they contract a treaty of neutrality, bind themselves *by force of the treaty* (*vi fœderis* se obligant) to that which is already due by nature".[106] In other words, concluding a neutrality treaty is to restate in the form of a treaty the duty originally borne by belligerents in the law of nature, and neutrality based on a neutrality treaty as well as neutrality not based on a neutrality treaty are equal in terms of their legal effects. Therefore, according to Wolff, belligerents "ought to refrain from all hostile violence against him [a neutral]", and "[a]gainst those who are neutrals in war the belligerents have no right of war".[107] Also, according to Vattel, the benefit for States of becoming neutrals is that the States are not regarded as enemies by belligerents,[108] and that belligerents have "no just ground (juste sujet) for making war" upon neutral States.[109] Therefore, neutral States that have acquired the neutral status independently of neutrality treaties can enjoy the same legal right as neutral States that have concluded neutrality treaties can, that is, the right not to be involved in a war.

B CONDITIONS FOR THE LEGAL STATUS OF NEUTRALITY

According to eighteenth-century writers, although it is not necessary for States to conclude neutrality treaties with belligerents in order to become neutrals, certain conditions should be fulfilled: the abstention from giving assistance to any belligerents and the impartialiality towards all belligerents. For example, Vattel states:

> In order to have a clear understanding of this question, we must avoid confusing the policy a Nation may pursue when it is free from any obligation, with the conduct it must observe during a war *if it desires to be treated as perfectly neutral*. So long as a neutral Nation desires to be *secure in the enjoyment of its neutrality* (veut jouïr sûrement de cet état), it must show itself in all respects *strictly impartial* (*une exacte impartialité*) towards the belligerents; for if it favours one to the prejudice of the other, it can not complain if the latter treats it as an adherent and ally of the enemy.[110]

According to Vattel, the strict impartiality that a State desiring to be treated as perfectly neutral must show towards belligerents includes: (1) to give no help, when States are not under obligation to do so, nor voluntarily to furnish either troops, arms, or munitions, or anything that can be directly made use of in the

34 Origins of the concept of neutrality

war (non-assistance); (2) in all that does not bear upon the war, a neutral State must not refuse to one of the parties, what it grants to the other (impartiality).[111] Wolff also states that States can be neutrals "in so far as it furnishes to neither of the belligerent parties the things which can be useful to it in war, which are usually furnished by allies, or furnishes to each party those things which nation owes to nation by nature independently of war.[112]

Bynkershoek, who states that "[i]f I am a neutral I may not lend aid to one to an extent that brings injury to the other", also considers the non-assistance to belligerents as a condition for the status of neutrality.[113]

According to eighteenth-century writers, the conditions for a State to be a neutral are to maintain an impartial attitude by abstaining from giving assistance to belligerent States. As stated by Vattel, a State fulfils those conditions because it "desires to be treated as perfectly neutral" and "desires to secure in the enjoyment of its neutrality". "[T]he enjoyment of its neutrality" refers to enjoying the legal effects of neutrality as clarified in section A, that is, not to be viewed as an enemy by belligerents and not to be involved in the war.

Then, why did they formulate the conditions for becoming a neutral as the non-assistance to and impartiality towards belligerents? One reason is that eighteenth-century writers referred to the conditions of neutrality that were provided for in typical neutrality treaties. As observed in section 1.2 of this chapter, in typical neutrality treaties, a contracting State (a belligerent) accorded neutrality to the other contracting State on the conditions that the latter would observe neutrality. Although the details of those conditions varied in each treaty, their minimum content was to abstain from involving in the war and to abstain from providing assistance to belligerents, which was referred to by writers. For example, Wolff has delimited the scope of what "[t]hose who are adherents of neither party [neutrals] ought to do for each of the belligerent parties" on the basis that "in a treaty of neutrality it is merely agreed that the nation which wishes to be neutral should not give aid to either of the belligerent parties".[114]

However, those writers, when formulating the conditions for the status of neutrality as non-assistance and impartiality, not only referred to the pattern of typical neutrality treaties, but also offered more substantial explanations. For example, Bynkershoek states: "We must rather consider the enemies of our friends from two different points of view, not only as our friends, but also as enemies of our friends. If we consider them only as friends we may properly help them with advice, with troops, arms, and whatever else they need in war. But in so far as they are enemies of our friends we may not do this, because we would then show preference to one side in the war".[115] According to Bynkershoek, States should not show preference to one of the belligerents because "by aiding the one against the other in any manner we intervene in the war", "we *would ourselves appear in a manner to be making war on our friends*".[116] In order to avoid such a consequence, "[i]t is better to preserve friendship with both than to show preference to one in war, and thus tacitly to renounce the friendship of the other".[117] In other words, to provide assistance to one belligerent is to show hostile intention to the other belligerent, and by doing so "we *would ourselves appear in a manner to be making war on our friends*"; thus, States that do not wish to be viewed in this way, that is, States that wish to remain neutral, should not assist either belligerent State.

C THE THEORETICAL BASIS OF NEUTRALITY

As shown above, according to eighteenth-century scholars, belligerents are prohibited from making war against a neutral State, as long as the neutral State abstains from providing assistance to any belligerents and take an impartial attitude towards belligerents. The next question we should ask is: why were belligerents prohibited from waging war on a neutral State? In State practice prior to the eighteenth century, only States that had concluded neutrality treaties with belligerents were regarded as neutrals, and the belligerents that had concluded such treaties were prohibited from making war on the neutral States. The grounds for this prohibition were agreements, namely, a neutrality treaty, concluded between a belligerent and a neutral. On the other hand, since eighteenth-century scholars recognised that States could become neutrals even if they had not concluded neutrality treaties with belligerents, it became necessary to find a basis other than the agreement between belligerents and neutrals for the prohibition of war against neutral States.

A careful consideration of eighteenth-century legal literature reveals that the basis for such prohibition is found in the just war doctrine. For example, according to Wolff, "[a]gainst those who are neutrals in war the belligerents have no right of war (jus belli), *since they are doing them no injury* (injuriam), *which alone gives a right of war* (jus ad bellum)".[118] Vattel, discussing the status of States providing limited assistance to belligerents on the basis of defensive alliance treaties concluded before the war, which are also regarded as neutrals in Vattel's opinion,[119] observes that

> [t]he assistance which they give to my enemy is a debt which they are paying; and in discharging it *they do me no wrong* (*injure*), and consequently give me *no just ground* (*juste sujet*) *for making war* upon them (§ 26).[120]

In sum, according to those writers, neutral States which abstain from giving assistance to belligerents do not carry out *injuries* (*injuria*; *injure*) against any belligerent: and the only just cause of war is injury inflicted upon the State; therefore, belligerents have no grounds to make war against neutral States.

On the other hand, what is the legal consequence of providing assistance to a belligerent? According to Vattel, for example, providing assistance to a belligerent is an act "certainly inconsistent with neutrality (contraire sans doute à la Neutralité)",[121] and the other belligerent is justified in regarding such assistance as an "act of hostility (un acte d'hostilité)"[122] and the State providing assistance as an enemy.[123] To be justified in regarding that State as an enemy (regarder comme mon ennemie) means, according to Vattel, to "have a right to make war against him [that State] (en droit de lui faire la guere)".[124] Also, according to

36 Origins of the concept of neutrality

Wolff, "[h]e who allies himself with my enemy, as by sending him troops or subsidies, or by assisting him in war in any manner, *is my enemy*", and "it is allowable to enter his territory with an armed force, and to conduct hostile operations there, or *bring war upon him*".[125]

However, a question now arises: Is a belligerent justified in regarding a State providing assistance to the other belligerent as an enemy, even when the former belligerent is carrying on an unjust war? According to the just war doctrine, which is supported by eighteenth-century writers: (1) It is permissible to assist a State that is carrying out a just war;[126] (2) to assist a State waging an unjust war is an "injury (*injuria*; injure)"[127] against the State carrying out a just war; and (3) in order for a State to wage war, a just cause is needed, and the only just cause of war is an "injury" inflicted.[128] This being so, it seems that the provision of assistance to a belligerent amounts to an injury against the other belligerent, namely, a just cause of a war for the latter belligerent, *only when the former belligerent carries out an unjust war*. Actually, Wolff states that the right of war against other States is based on "the right of defence against an aggressor (jure defensionis adversus aggressorem)" and that, "*it is allowable to give aid to one carrying on a just war*, but he who does anything for the sake of one who is carrying on an unjust war does a wrong to him on whose side the war is just, and in this respect he is then on an equality with an aggressor".[129]

Then, it seems possible to think that it is sufficient for a State to abstain from assisting a State engaging in an *unjust war*, in order to avoid being regarded as an enemy and involved in war. It seems unnecessary to abstain from assisting a State carrying out a *just* war, which is perfectly lawful according to the just war doctrine. Nevertheless, eighteenth-century scholars formulated the conditions for the status of neutrality as non-assistance to and impartiality towards *all* belligerents. Why did they do so?

They do not directly answer this question. The key to answering this question is: according to those writers, as States are mutually independent and equal, each State may decide for themselves as to whether war is just.[130] In a war between State X and State Y, it is permissible for State A, which is not participating in the war, to judge that State X has a just cause and to give assistance to State X. As discussed below, a third State is not prohibited from making a judgement on the justice or injustice of a war between other States. However, as each belligerent may also make their own judgement on the justice or injustice of the war, State A's judgement will not necessarily be accepted by State Y, and State Y may view the assistance given by State A to State X as a support for an unjust war, that is, as an injury against State Y. In such circumstances, if State A wishes to remain outside the war, the safest option is to abstain from assisting either State X or State Y. As long as assistance is not given to either belligerent, no injury is carried out on either belligerent.

In sum, the conception of neutrality as presented by eighteenth-century scholars – the idea according to which belligerents are prohibited from waging war on neutral States that abstain from assisting either belligerent and take impartial attitudes towards all belligerents – was based on the just war doctrine.

According to the just war doctrine, since the only just cause for war is an injury inflicted upon a State, and neutral States which do not assist either belligerent do not inflict an injury on either belligerent, neither belligerent may wage war against such neutral States.

The statement that the conception of neutrality was based on the just war doctrine may appear to be paradoxical at first glance. This statement appears to be paradoxical because most contemporary scholars have assumed and regarded as self-evident that the conception of neutrality is incompatible with the just war doctrine: Under the just war doctrine, belligerents are divided into just and unjust, and they are not equal with each other; therefore, third States are obliged to assist a just belligerent, rather than treating them impartially. However, according to the thesis of this book, neutral States were required to abstain from assisting either belligerent and to take impartial attitudes towards both belligerents, not because belligerents were equal, but because assistance to a belligerent could be regarded as an injury against the other belligerent and could be invoked as a just cause of war by that belligerent, which should be avoided if the third State wished to remain outside the war. Moreover, as discussed below, in the just war doctrine, assistance to a just belligerent was not always seen as the obligations of States but States were permitted to abstain from assisting a just belligerent in consideration of their own interests, namely, the interests of remaining outside the war and thereby securing their peace. In this sense, the conception of neutrality is by no means incompatible with the just war doctrine, and rather, the latter was the theoretical basis of the former.

D RELATIONSHIP BETWEEN NEUTRALITY AND THE OBLIGATION TO
ASSIST A BELLIGERENT WAGING A JUST WAR

Eighteenth-century writers, as earlier writers did, affirm that under the law of nature it is the obligation of States to render assistance to States that wage a just war. For example, Wolff states that "[t]o a nation carrying on a just war it is allowable to send auxiliaries and subsidies and to aid it in war in any manner, nay more, by nature (naturaliter) nation is bound to nation as to those things, if that is possible".[131] Vattel also states that "*[i]t is lawful and praiseworthy (louable) to assist in every way a Nation which is carrying on a just war; and such assistance even becomes a duty (un devoir) for every Nation which can give it without injury to itself (sans se manquer à elle-même)*". He calls this principle as the "incontestable principle".[132]

However, according to those writers, the obligation to assist a just belligerent and the conception of neutrality are compatible and by no means contradict each other. That is because States are obliged to assist a just belligerent only in so far as it does not present a risk to themselves, and it is allowable for States to give priority to their own interests, the interest of remaining out of war and securing their own peace. It is therefore permissible to take an attitude of neutrality by abstaining from assisting either belligerent.

38 *Origins of the concept of neutrality*

For example, Wolff, in considering the issue of "whether neutrality is allowable by nature", raises two cases in which it is allowable.[133] The first is a case where it is to be the interest of the State to remain neutral. According to Wolff, "by nature it is certainly illegal to give aid to one carrying on an unjust war". However, this does not mean that it is an obligation to provide assistance to States carrying out a just war: "[S]ince every right of a people (populi) by nature should be determined by the purpose of the state, if it shall be to the interest of the state (si e re civitatis fuerit) rather to abstain from war than to involve itself in it,… it is not bound by nature to give assistance". Therefore, "[i]t is allowable by nature for any nation to be neutral in war". The second is a case where the justice or injustice of the war is unclear. If a State provides assistance to either belligerent in such a case, and if that State does not have an ability to make a correct judgement on the justice of the war, it might commit a sin (peccet). It might give assistance to an unjust belligerent, which is contrary to the law of nature, based on an incorrect judgement on the justice of the war. Therefore, according to Wolff, "it is evident that it is allowable to be a neutral in a doubtful case".

The argument of Vattel is similar to that of Wolff. Vattel, considering "[t]he right to remain neutral (Du droit de demeurer neutre)", states that "[w]hen a war breaks out between two Nations, all the others who are not bound by treaties are free to remain neutral". According to Vattel, there are two factors to be taken into consideration when making a judgement as to whether States are free to remain neutral:

1   The justice of the cause. If that is clear, they cannot aid the unjust party; on the contrary, it is honourable to give their aid to oppressed innocence when they can do so. If the cause be of doubtful justice, the other Nations may suspend their judgement, and not enter into a quarrel which does not concern them.
2   When they are convinced which party is in the right, it still remains for them to determine whether it be for the good of the State (est du bien de l'État) to intervene in the affair and take up the war.[134]

In sum, Wolff and Vattel discuss cases where States are not obliged to give assistance to a State carrying on a just war and therefore may remain neutral on two levels. The first is the level of the just causes of war. When a State cannot make a correct judgement on the justice or injustice of a war between other States, it is permissible to abstain from giving assistance to either belligerent, in order to avoid committing acts that are not permissible in the law of nature, that is, to assist a State carrying on an unjust war. The second is the level of the interests of a State. Even if the justice or injustice of the war is clear, a State may take an attitude of neutrality if it is to the interest of the State. The interest of the State in this case refers to the interest of remaining neutral and enjoying the right not to be involved in war.

This means that a State may remain neutral even when the justice or injustice of the war is clear.[135] However, even in that case, the judgement itself, made by a neutral State as to the justice or injustice of the war is not contrary to neutrality. As Wolff says, "there is no need that neutral nations should suspend their judgement concerning the justice of the war, although *it may be wiser (consultum)* that they should not express it openly".[136] In other words, even if a judgement is made regarding the justice or injustice of the war, as long as no assistance is given to a belligerent based on that judgement, a neutral is not regarded as inflicting an injury on the other belligerent, and it may remain neutral.

It is to be noted here that to abstain from assisting either belligerent is what should be done by a State that wishes to be a neutral and to remain outside the war, and the provision of assistance to a belligerent waging a just war is by no means prohibited; on the contrary, it is rather "honourable". As stated above, according to eighteenth-century scholars, as States are independent and equal each other, in a war between State X and State Y, these States may make their own judgement regarding the justice of the war. However, State A, which does not participate in the war, may also make its own judgement regarding the justice or injustice of the war. According to Vattel, as States are equal and independent, States "can not set themselves up as judge (s'ériger en juges) over one another", but "[t]hat does *not prevent other Nations from passing judgment* on the question *for themselves* in order to decide what their attitude must be and to assist the Nation which appears to them to be in the right".[137] The provision of assistance by State A to the belligerent that is deemed to be just is assistance to a just belligerent, and assistance to a just belligerent, as stated earlier, is "honourable" according to the just war doctrine. Certainly, the provision of assistance to a belligerent may be regarded as an injury and invoked as a just cause of war by the other belligerent even if the State providing such assistance believes that it is assistance for a just war. Although the judgement as to which belligerent has a just cause may be made by third States, it may also be made by belligerents; therefore, there is no guarantee that the judgement made by third States will be accepted by belligerents. Considering such possibilities, States that attempt to ensure their own security by avoiding being regarded as inflicting an injury on either belligerent should abstain from giving assistance to either belligerent and remain neutral. However, for those States that pay no heed to the risk of being regarded as inflicting injury on either belligerent and being involved in war, assistance to the State that is considered to have a just cause is not prohibited, or even regarded as "honourable".[138]

3 The place of the so-called "neutral commerce" in the historical development of the law of neutrality

Existing studies have described the historical development of the law of neutrality largely as the history of maritime commerce of third States with belligerents during wartime (the so-called freedom of "neutral commerce"), and, from the perspective of belligerents, the history of the right of capture at sea exercised against third States' commerce in times of war, more specifically, the

40   *Origins of the concept of neutrality*

history of the law of capture of enemy property, the law of contraband of war, the law of blockade, and the law of visit and search.[139]

Certainly, maritime commerce with belligerents in times of war brought about greater economic gains for third States than commerce in times of peace, and it was a matter of great interest for States. This is because when war breaks out, the number of vessels belonging to the belligerents decreases and maritime freight increases. This brings profits for third States and also opens up the kinds of trade that the belligerent States had monopolised in times of peace (such as colonial trade).[140]

However, it is by no means self-evident that the issue of third States' maritime commerce with belligerents in times of war was always discussed within the framework of "neutrality" prior to the eighteenth century. Rather, in view of what we have seen in this book so far, the essence of the conception of neutrality was the idea that neutral States are legally entitled to remain outside war on certain conditions. Of course, many neutral States also have interest in the economic profits gained by maritime commerce with belligerents. However, there might be neutral States that have no interest in such economic profits, but only pursue their security interests by remaining outside war.

Thus we shall consider the relationship of the so-called "neutral commerce" with the conception of neutrality (section 3.2), the essential meaning of which has been identified so far in this book. But before that, we will briefly outline the history of the so-called "neutral commerce" (section 3.1).

3.1 Overview of the history of so-called "neutral commerce"

The so-called freedom of "neutral commerce" refers to the principle that subjects of third States can freely carry on maritime commerce with belligerents during wartime. Belligerents may seize all things belonging to the enemy at sea, namely enemy vessels and enemy cargoes, and confiscate them in accordance with certain procedure. Historically, several doctrines have been advocated as to whether and to what extent vessels and cargoes that do not belong to the enemy may be seized and confiscated.

The practice of distinguishing between the enemy and non-enemy and limiting the target of capture to vessels and cargoes belonging to the enemy emerged in the middle of the fourteenth century.[141] For example, the treaty concluded in 1351 between England and the Kingdom of Castile and the treaty concluded between England and Portugal in 1353 provided that, if the subjects of one contracting State seized an enemy vessel, and cargo belonging to the subjects of the other contracting State were discovered on the same vessel, such cargo was to be returned to its owner.[142] Also, the King of England issued ordinances in 1346, 1375 and 1378, to the effect that in cases where enemy goods were being transported on vessels belonging to States other than the enemy, only enemy goods were to be confiscated, and the vessel itself was not to be confiscated, and the freight that would have been gained from transporting the enemy goods to the destination were to be paid to the captain.[143]

Furthermore, the *Consolato del mare*, which is generally considered as being compiled in Barcelona between the end of the thirteenth century and the middle of the fourteenth century, provides that vessels and cargoes belonging to the enemies (enemichs) may be seized, but vesels and cargoes belonging to the friends (amichs) were not to be seized and confiscated.[144]

However, between the middle of the sixteenth century and the middle of the seventeenth century, the practice of seizing and confiscating non-enemy goods transported by enemy vessels and non-enemy vessels transporting enemy goods spread in Europe. One of the doctrines for justifying such practice is the so-called doctrine of "hostile infection", according to which non-enemy vessels transporting enemy goods are infected with hostile character and regarded as enemy vessels, and the non-enemy goods transported by enemy vessels are also infected with hostile character and being regarded as enemy goods. This doctrine, which was first adopted by an edict of France in 1543, was adopted in 1557 by England and in 1584 by France, among others.[145] When the doctrine of hostile infection is applied, exemption from seizure and confiscation is limited to the case where non-enemy vessels transport non-enemy cargoes only. This is almost identical with the total prohibition of maritime commerce between third States and the enemy. The practice of total prohibition of the maritime commerce between the enemy and third States during this period also includes cases such as the British Order in Council in 1601, which, while not relying on the doctrine of hostile infection, totally prohibited the trade with the enemy, on the ground that the enemy (Spain) "hath sought to disturb the general peace of Christendome", and Spain could not continue the war "without the helpe and assistance of those who be her Highnes' confederates, frendes, or allies" and that "stopping hinderance and impeaching all commerce and traffick with him in his territories of Spaine and Prtingall will qucickly, in likelyhood, give an ende to these bloudie and unnnaturall warres, which disturbe the generall peace and quiet of all theise partes of Christendom".[146]

The practice of total (or nearly total) prohibition of maritime commerce with the enemy mostly disappeared by the latter half of the seventeenth century.[147] Between the latter half of the seventeenth century and the eighteenth century, many treaties were concluded between States that provided for the principle of the freedom of maritime commerce of third States with belligerents, except the transportation of contraband of war and blockade-running. Therefore, in this period and thereafter, the issue was not whether belligerents were able to totally prohibit maritime commerce between third States and the enemy but rather the extent of the right of capture.[148] There were mainly two doctrines concerning the right of capture that were provided for in those treaties. The first is the doctrine of *Consolato del mare*, according to which while enemy goods are seized and confiscated regardless of whether they are transported by enemy vessels or by non-enemy vessels, non-enemy goods are not confiscated even when transported by enemy vessels. This doctrine uses the enemy or non-enemy character of *cargo* as a criteria of capture. The second is the doctrine of *free ships free goods* (or the "free ships make free goods" doctrine), according to which while all

42 Origins of the concept of neutrality

goods are seized and confiscated when transported by enemy vessels, regardless of whether they are enemy goods or non-enemy goods, even enemy goods are not confiscated when transported by non-enemy vessels. This doctrine uses the enemy or non-enemy character of the *vessels* as a criteria of capture. According to the second doctrine, the vessels belonging to third States were not to be seized and confiscated even when they were transporting enemy cargo, which was advantageous for maritime States such as the Netherlands; thus, this doctrine was chiefly supported by the Netherlands.

Initially, the doctrine of *free ships free goods* was considered as a privilege specially accorded by treaties concluded between two or several States, and the doctrine of the *Consolato del mare* was regarded as a principle of general international law. Since the eighteenth century, there were movements to establish this doctrine as a principle of general international law. One of these movements was the so-called First Armed Neutrality between 1780 and 1783, in which several European States such as Russia, Denmark, Sweden, and the Netherlands asserted the principle: enemy goods on neutral vessels, contraband excepted, should not be seized by belligerents.[149] However, this doctrine was not immediately established as a principle of general international law. It was by the 1856 Paris Declaration that this principle was recognised as a principle of general international law.[150]

3.2 The relationship of the so-called "neutral commerce" with the conception of neutrality

As briefly outlined above, while the extent to which belligerents could capture vessels and cargoes changed with the period, it was generally recognised, with the exception of the period between middle of the sixteenth century and the first half of the seventeenth century, that belligerents could not capture all the vessels and cargoes belonging to third States; on the contrary, maritime commerce of third States with belligerents was in principle free (the so-called "freedom of neutral commerce"). In particular, since the latter half of the seventeenth century, no States denied such freedom itself, and the issue shifted to the extent of the right of capture; for example, conflict between the doctrine of the *Consolato del mare* and the doctrine of *free ships free goods*.

What we must consider here is whether the status of third States that could enjoy the freedom of maritime commerce with belligerents was considered to be neutral during this period. Regarding this point, it is necessary to recall that, as discussed in section 1.3 of this chapter, in State practice prior to the eighteenth century, neutrality was not a status automatically created by the outbreak of war, but the legal status contractually constituted by neutrality treaties concluded between a belligerent and a third State, and there were also categories of third States other than neutrals, namely allies and other States.

Then, in order to be guaranteed the freedom of maritime commerce with belligerents, was it necessary for a third State to be a neutral, or was it sufficient to be an ally or other State?

Origins of the concept of neutrality 43

One clue to this question is found in municipal laws of several States during this period. These laws provided that while all vessels and cargoes "belonging to our enemies (appartenans à nos ennemis)" were seized and confiscated,[151] any other vessels and cargoes, that is, vessels and cargoes not belonging to the enemies, were in principle exempt from seizure and confiscation. As the term meaning States not belonging to the enemies, various terms were used, such as "our allies, confederates and friend States (our allies, confederattes, and frendes)" (the 1557 Order in Council of England), "our allies, confederates or friend States (nos alliez, confederez ou amis)" (the 1584 edict of France) and "our allies, friend and neutrals (Onse Geallieerden, Vrunden ende Neutralen)" (the 1652 ordinance of the Netherlands).[152] In short, all States not belonging to the enemy – not only neutrals, but also allies, friends or other States – were guaranteed the freedom of maritime commerce with belligerents.

This becomes clearer from a number of bilateral treaties concluded during this period that contained provisions concerning maritime commerce in times of war. For example, seventeen treaties cited by Ishimoto as treaties that recognised "the freedom of neutral commerce" include peace treaties, alliance treaties, commercial treaties and maritime treaties; but no neutrality treaties are included.[153] These treaties provide that, when contracting State X is at war with State A, which is not party to the treaties, and when the other contracting State Y does not participate in the war, the subjects of State Y are in principle free to engage in maritime commerce with State A. Many of these treaties do not clearly define the legal nature of the relationship between State X and State Y, but at the very least do not characterise it as the relation of "neutrality". For example, in alliance treaties which provided that subjects of State Y were free to carry on maritime commerce with State A, the legal relation between State X and State Y was not defined as the relation of "neutrality", but as the relation of "amity (amité)", "peace (paix)" or "alliance (alliance; confédération)".[154] Moreover, some of those treaties provided for the obligation of State Y, as an ally of State X, to provide assistance to State X.[155] Treaties that are often cited as treaties recognising the freedom of "neutral commerce" even include alliance treaties by which a contracting State agreed to provide assistance to the other contracting State, and at the same time guaranteed the freedom of commerce with the other belligerent.

In sum, not only neutral States but also other third States (namely, allies or other States) were guaranteed the freedom of commerce with belligerents in the practice of States during this period. Therefore, we cannot consider that in State practice from the sixteenth to the eighteenth centuries, the issue of maritime commerce of third States with belligerents was essentially an issue of "neutrality".[156] Of course, this does not mean that neutral States were not guaranteed the freedom of maritime commerce. On the contrary, since the vessels and cargoes of a neutral State do not belong to the enemy, they are in principle exempt from being seized and confiscated, except for cases of contraband of war or blockade running. In fact, some neutrality treaties provided for the freedom of commerce of a contracting State, the neutral status of which is recognised by the neutrality treaty.[157]

44 *Origins of the concept of neutrality*

Lastly, according to the just war doctrine, which was supported by pre-seventeenth century scholars, it is self-evident that the vessels and cargoes not belonging to the enemy may not be seized and confiscated. The just war doctrine regarded war as a means of remedy for violations caused by injuries inflicted, or, in other words, as a means of recovering one's rights by force. Therefore, according to the just war doctrine, it is permissible to "to acquire things as recovery of debts that can only be recovered by force, or as an appropriate punishment for illegal acts".[158] However, that is all that is permissible in accordance with the just war doctrine, and there is no basis for the seizure or confiscation of things that do not belong to the enemy, that is, States that have not inflicted an injury on the State waging a just war. For example, based on this reasoning, Grotius observes that "things ... of which the owners are neither subjects of the enemy nor hoslilely inclined, cannot be acquired by war" because "[i]n order that something may become ours by the law of war, it must belong to the enemy".[159]

Notes

1 Very few scholars have correctly understood that in State practice before the eighteenth century the legal relation of neutrality was set up contractually, that is, only through a treaty of neutrality. Other than Miele, Grewe and Oeter, see Schopfer, *Le principe juridique de la neutralité*, 74–118; Nys, "Notes sur la neutralité", 477–490.

2 Regarding Miele's and Grewe's views on the legal character of neutrality treaties, see notes 35 and 36 of this chapter.

3 Oeter, "Ursprünge der Neutralität", 481. Miele, Grewe and Oeter refer to neutrality in State practice from the sixteenth to eighteenth centuries as "contractual neutrality (vertragliche Neutralität)" in the sense that neutrality during this period was contractually set up by an agreement concluded between a belligerent and a third State, and they refer to neutrality in the theory of eighteenth century scholars as "institutional neutrality (institutionelle Neutralität)", which is set up independently of an agreement between States. See literature cited in note 57 of the Introduction.

4 See Taoka, "Meaning of the Term Neutrality", 46–48 [in Japanese].

5 Wolff, *Jus gentium*, § 672 [italics in the original].

6 See Steiger und Schweitzer, "Neutralität", 315.

7 Although I have been unable to confirm the fact by primary historical resources, Knight has reported a case in which Liège formally declared that she would preserve "a full and entire neutrality (bonne et vraie Neutralité)" during the war between Louis XI and Maximilian of Burgundy in 1477–8. See Knight, "Neutrality and Neutralisation in the Sixteenth Century", 99–100. Apart from official documents such as treaties, Niccolò Machiavelli (1492–1550) used the term "neutralità" in his *Il principe* (1532) and Jean Bodin (*c.*1529–96) argued about "neutralité" in chapter 6, book 5 of his *Les six livres de la république* (1576). See Machiavelli, *Il principe*, 111 (Cap. XXI); Bodin, *Les six livres de la république*, 5:178–184 (Liv. V, Chap. VI). However, Machiavelli and Bodin, who argued solely about the political utility or danger of neutral attitudes, did not use the term "neutrality" as a legal concept. They neither considered neutrality as having a legally protected status nor a status accompanying rights and duties under international law. On Machiavelli's and Bodin's discussion about neutrality, see also, Truyol y Serra, "Zur Entstehungsgeschichte der Neutralitätslehre", 449–460.

Origins of the concept of neutrality   45

8 Traité de Neutralité entre les DUCHE' & COMTE' DE BOURGOGNE, passe en consideration des Suisses entre FRANÇOIS I. Roi de France, & MARGUERITE Archiduchesse d'Autriche, à S. Jean de Laone, le 8 de Juillet 1522, Du Mont, *Corps universel*, 4(1): 378–381.

9 Traité entre les Députez de HENRI IV. Roi de France, de PHILIPPE II. Roi d'Espagne, & des CANTONS SUISSES, pour le rétablissement de la Neutralité entre le Duché & Comté de Bourgogne, à Lion, le 22 Septembre 1595, Du Mont, *Corps universel*, 5(1): 517–518.

10 Lettres de Neutralité octroyées par HENRI IV. Roi de France, à CHARLES Duc de Lorraine, pour les Païs, Durant la Guerre dudit Roi contre l'Espagne, à Abbeville, le 19. Juin 1596, Du Mont, *Corps universel*, 5(1): 527–528; Autres Lettres de Neutralité acordées par HENRI IV. Roi de France à CHARLES. Duc de Lorraine, pour son Fils le Cardinal, pour les Evêchez de Metz, Toul, & Verdun, & l'Abbaïe de Gorze, pendant la Guerre contre le Roi d'Espagne, à Abbeville, le 19. Juin 1596, Du Mont, *Corps universel*, 5(1): 528.

11 Traité de Neutralité entre GUSTAVE ADOLPHE, Roi de Suède, et les Etats de Catoliques d'Allemagne, fait à Maience le 29. Janvier 1632, Du Mont, *Corps universel*, 6(1): 29–30.

12 Captitulatio Electoris Trevirensis PHILIPPI CHRISTOPHORI, cum AXELIO OXENSTIRN Regiæ Majestatis Suecica Legato, super acceptata Neutralitate Suecica per Legatos Christianissimi Regis Gallia Ludovici XIII, negotiata Moguntiæ die 12. Aprilis 1632, Du Mont, *Corps universel*, 6(1): 36–38.

13 Traité de Neutralité entre LOUIS XIV. Roi de France, & FERDINAND II. Grand Duc de Toscane, à Florence le 11. Mai 1646, Du Mont, *Corps universel*, 6(1): 343.

14 Traité de neutralité, Fait entre ANSELME CASIMIR WAMBOLT DE UMSTAT, Electeur de Mayence; & le Maréchal de Turenne, General de l'Armée de Louis XIV. Roi de France en Allemagne, à Frankfort sur le Mein, le 9. Mai 1647, Du Mont, *Corps universel*, 6(1): 394–395.

15 Pacta Neutralitatis perpetuæ à Regia Majestate Sueciæ CHRISTINA Illustrissiomo Duci Curlandiæ JACOBO indultæ, dat. Holmiæ die 4. Junii 1647, Du Mont, *Corps universel*, 6(1): 395.

16 Articles, par lesquels Monsieur le Duc de MODENE, au nom de S.M.T.C. et en vertu des Pouvoir qu'il en a receu, accorde la Neutralité à Monsieur le Duc de Mantoue, fait à Modene, 9. Juillet 1658, Du Mont, *Corps universel*, 6(2): 225.

17 Traité de Neutralité entre CHRISTIAN V. Roi de Dannemarc, FRIDERIC GUILLAUME Electeur de Brandenbourg & CHRISTOPHLE BERNARD Evêque & Prince de Münster d'une part, & JEAN FREDERIC Duc de Brunswic-Lünebourg-Hanover d'autre part, portant que ledit Duc ne s'opposera point aux Armes des trois Princes confederés contre la Suede de quelque costé qu'elles se tournent, & qu'en échange ils auront soin que leurs Expeditions, Passages, & Campements ne causent aucun dommage à ses Terres, Païs & Sujets, mais qu'au contraire ils le maintiendront & defendront en cette Neutralité, à Hanover, le 11/21. Septembre 1675, Du Mont, *Corps universel*, 7(1): 305–306.

18 Traité de Neutralité entre LOUÏS XIV. Roi de France, et JEAN FREDERIC Duc de Brunswic et Lunebourg, fait à Linsbourg, le 18. Ottobre 1675, Du Mont, *Corps universel*, 7(1): 312–313.

19 Traité de Neutralité entre LOUIS XIV. Roi très-Chréstien de France d'une part, & le Louable Corps HELVETIQUE d'autre part, contenant, que de la part de la France il ne sera pris aucun Passage par la Suisse, & que les Louables Cantons ne l'accorderont aussi à nulle autre Puissance étrangere, fait à Bade en Argouw, le 7. Mai 1689, Du Mont, *Corps universel*, 7(2): 228–229.

20 Convention or Act of Neutrality between France and the Netherlands, signed at The Hague, 24 November 1733, *CTS* 34:139–142. This treaty, named the "convention

46 Origins of the concept of neutrality

of neutrality" by Parry, compiler of the *Consolidated Treaty Series*, is also referred to as "[c]ette convention ou acte de neutralité" in the treaty text itself. Ibid., 142.

21 Neutrality Convention between Austria–Hungary and France, signed at Versailles, 1 May 1756, *CTS* 40:331–334. This treaty, named the "Neutrality Convention" by Parry, is also referred to as "une Convention ou Acte de Neutralité" in another treaty signed on the same day between the same parties. See Treaty of Union and Defensive Amity between Austria–Hungary and France", signed at Versailles, 1 May 1756, *CTS* 40:337, 340, 349, 350.

22 Among the fourteen treaties listed in section 1 (p. 19), (1) was concluded during the Italian Wars (1494–1559), (2) and (3) were concluded during the Religious Wars (Guerres de Religion) (1562–98), (4), (5), (6), (7), (8) and (9) were concluded during the Thirty Year's War (1618–48), (10) and (11) were concluded during the Dutch War (1672–78) (12) was concluded during the Nine Years' War (the War of the League of Augsburg) (1688–97), (13) was concluded immediately after the outbreak of the War of Polish Succession (1733–38) and (14) was concluded immediately before the outbreak of the Seven Years' War (1756–63).

23 Du Mont, *Corps universel*, 6(1): 29.

24 Ibid., 29 [italics added].

25 Ibid., 37 [italics added].

26 *CTS* 40:333 [italics added].

27 Du Mont, *Corps universel*, 7(1): 312.

28 Neutrality treaties, which provide that a contracting State shall "accord (accorder; indulgeo)" neutrality, also provide that it shall "grant (octroyer)" neutrality to the other contracting State, or that a contracting party shall "respect (colo; observo; observer)" the other contracting party's neutrality.

29 Du Mont, *Corps universel*, 5(1): 527. A letter of neutrality (lettre de neutralité), which is a unilateral act by a belligerent State, is distinguished from a treaty of neutrality, an agreement between a belligerent State and a third State. They, however, share something in common as they create an obligation for a contracting State (a belligerent in a war) not to resort to war against the other contracting State (a third State in the war). See Miele, *L'estraneità ai conflitti armati*, 1:105.

30 Du Mont, *Corps universel*, 6(1): 343.

31 *CTS* 34:141. As stated in the text of the treaty, the Austrian Netherlands was not a territory of the Netherlands but "at present under the possession of His Imperial Majesty [the Emperor of the Holy Roman Empire]". However, since the 1715 treaty provided that the Austrian Netherlands "shall serve as barrier for the Republic [of the Netherlands]", a promise of not involving the Austrian Netherlands in the war had the same significance as a promise of not involving the Netherlands itself in the war.

32 *CTS* 40:333–334.

33 Du Mont, *Corps universel*, 6(1): 37 [italics added].

34 Wolff, *Jus gentium*, § 680 [italics in the original]. The words translated as "neutral(s)" in the main text are, in the original text, "ei, qui neutrarum partium est" and "eos, qui in bello medii sunt". As Wolff used these phrases synonymously with neutral(s) (see note 83 of this chapter), we will translate them as "neutral" in this book and enclose the term neutral(s) within brackets ([neutral(s)]), indicating that it is not a faithful translation from the original.

35 Grewe, *Epochen der Völkerrechtsgeschichte*, 443–444.

36 Miele, *L'estraneità ai conflitti armati*, 1:104.

37 Du Mont, *Corps universel*, 5(1): 527 [italics added].

38 Oeter, "Ursprünge der Neutralität", 457.

39 Miele, *L'estraneità ai conflitti armati*, 1:107–109.

40 Textor, *Synopsis juris gentium*, 101. Textor affirms that the status of neutrality may be created by a tacit agreement. According to him, "it was tacitly understood that

Origins of the concept of neutrality   47

neutrality was agreed on through the practice of an equal friendship, the enemies of each side knowing about it and not making any opposition to it". Ibid., 105.

41 See Oeter, "Ursprünge der Neutralität", 459–462.

42 See Carter, "Dutch as Neutrals", 828; Nys, "Notes sur la neutralité", 489–490. For the treaty of neutrality concluded between the Netherlands and France in the Polish Succession War, see note 20 of this chapter.

43 Wolff, *Jus gentium*, § 681.

44 See e.g. Tabata, *New Lecture on International Law*, 2:173–205 [in Japanese].

45 With regard to the prevailing view today, according to which there has been a transition in the legal status of war in international law from (1) the period in which the just war doctrine was supported, to (2) the period in which the unlimited freedom of States to resort to war was recognised, and to (3) the period in which war and the use of force by States have been in principle prohibited, Taira Nishi points out that the prevailing view focuses on literature in relation to (1), on the realities of State practice in relation to (2), and on the rules of positive international law in relation to (3), and therefore that the emphasis of the arguments in the prevailing view diverges in each period. He also doubts whether "the scholastic doctrine of just cause succeeded in regulating the actual conduct of war by monarchs of the time by its transcendent authority". See Nishi, "Turn of the Concept of War", 64 [in Japanese].

46 See Neff, *War and the Law of Nations*, 69, 91.

47 Textor, *Synopsis juris gentium*, 101. "[T]he recent Germano-Gallic War" referred to in the cited text seems to indicate the Franco–Dutch War (1672–78).

48 When State X and State Y are at war with each other, and State A, which does not participate in the war, has concluded a neutrality treaty with State X but has not concluded such a treaty with State Y, State X is prohibited to go to war against State A by virtue of the neutrality treaty. In contrast, State Y, non-party to the neutrality treaty, is not prohibited to resort to war against State A. In other words, State A is considered to be a neutral State in relation to State X but is not considered so in relation to State Y. We may call this the "relativity of the status of neutrality". A neutrality treaty between State X and State A usually provided that State A should not assist State Y but did not expressly provide that State A would not assist State X. However, considering that a neutrality treaty did not oblige State A to assist State X and that it often provided that State A would not "involve itself in the war", we can consider that it was assumed that State A would assist neither State X nor State Y.

49 Order in Council as to Enemy Goods in Friends' Ships, and Friends' Goods in Enemy Ships, in Marsden, *Documents*, 1:165–166.

50 Edit sur l'admirauté, du mois de mars 1584, in Pardessus, *Collection*, 4:316.

51 Ordonnance des Etats Généraux des PROVINCES-UNIES, qui défend tout commerce avec l'Angleterre. Faite à la Haye, le 5. Decembre, 1652, Du Mont, *Corps universel*, 6(2): 36, 37.

52 Traités de Confédération & Alliance, entre LOUIS XIII. Roi de France & les Etats Evangeliques des Cercles & Provinces Electorales de FRANCONIE, SUAVE & du RHIN, fait à Francfort, le 20. Septembre 1634, Du Mont, *Corps universel*, 6(1): 78 [italics added].

53 See Nys, "Traité de subside et troupes auxiliaires", 173–196.

54 See Oeter, "Ursprünge der Neutralität", 454–455.

55 See Naruse, Yamada, and Kimura, *Outline of German History I*, 499 [in Japanese].

56 See Grewe, *Epochen der Völkerrechtsgeschichte*, 323–331.

57 See Horn, *Die geschichtliche Entwicklung*, 6.

58 See Miele, *L'estraneità ai conflitti armati*, 1:104.

59 Du Mont, *Corps universel*, 6(1): 29 [italics added].

60 Ibid., 5(1): 527 [italics added].

61 See Schopfer, *Principe juridique de la neutralité*, 100.

62 See above, pp. 17–18.

48 Origins of the concept of neutrality

63 On the just war doctrine, see generally, Haggenmacher, *Grotius et la doctrine de la guerre juste*; Johnson, *Ideology, Reason, and the Limitation of War*; Nussbaum, "Just War"; Russell, *Just War in the Middle Ages*; Vanderpol, *La doctrine scolastique du droit de guerre*.

64 Thomae Aquinatis, *Summa Theologiae*, II-II, q. 40, a. 1.

65 Victoria, *De indis*, 279 (*De jure belli*, 13).

66 Suárez, *Selections from Three Works*, 804 (Disp. XIII, *De bello*, sec. 4, n. 1).

67 Grotius, *De jure belli ac pacis*, Lib. II, Cap. I, § I.

68 See Onuma, "War", 57–121; Ota, *Political Thought of Hugo Grotius*, 133–163 [in Japanese].

69 Suárez, *Selections from Three Works*, 804–807 (Disp. XIII, *De bello*, sec. 4). See in this regard, Ito, *Suárez' Theory of International Law*, 69–78 [in Japanese]. According to the traditional scholastic doctrine of just war, one of the conditions for a war to be just is that it is based on the authority of a prince (*auctoritas principis*) or that a legitimate authority declares the war. This is because war is considered to be based on a State's *potestas jurisdictionis*. Thus, private individuals, who do not possess the *potestas jurisdictionis*, cannot wage war. Private individuals should resort to the State's judicial system when their own rights are injured. However, "war" in this context means offensive war. It was considered self-evident that even private individuals were entitled to wage defensive war, since anyone has the right to defend oneself in accordance with natural law. See Ito, "Idea of *Bellum Vindicativum*", 1–20 [in Japanese].

70 Grotius, *De jure belli ac pacis*, Lib. II, Cap. I, § II.

71 On the obligation to assist a belligerent carrying out a just war, see for example, Ito, "Legal History of the Right of Self-Defence", 35–38 [in Japanese].

72 Gentili, *De jure belli*, Lib. I, Cap. XV.

73 Grotius, *De jure belli ac pacis*, Lib. I, Cap. V, § I, § II.

74 Ibid., Lib. II, Cap. XXV, § VI.

75 Gentili, *De jure belli*, Lib. I, Cap. XV.

76 Grotius, *De jure belli ac pacis*, Lib. II, Cap. XXV, § VII.

77 Ito, "Legal History of the Right of Self-Defence", 38 [in Japanese].

78 See above, p. 19.

79 Gentili, *Hispanicae advocationis*, Lib. I, Cap. I.

80 Grotius, *De jure belli ac pacis*, Lib. III, Cap. XVII.

81 Ibid., Lib. III, Cap. XVII, § I.

82 Ibid., Lib. III, Cap. XVII, § III.

83 Although few writers used the terms "neutrality" or "neutral" before the seventeenth century, as an exception, Johann Wolfgang Textor used these terms in his book published in 1680. He called "[those States that] were called medii in Roman history" *neutrales* and the status of such States as *neutralitas*. Textor, *Synopsis juris gentium*, 101. In the eighteenth century, these terms were used more commonly. For instance, in his book of 1764, Christian Wolff, while using such terms as "ei, qui neutrarum partium est" and "eos, qui in bello medii sunt", used by writers in the preceding periods, also used the terms *neutrales* and *neutralitas*. Wolff, *Jus gentium*, § 672–683. In his book of 1758, Vattel consistently used the terms "neutralité", "États neutres", "Nations neutres" and "Peuples neutres", without using such terms as "middle in the war". Vattel, *Le droit des gens*, Liv. III, Chap. VII, § 103–135. Hübner also used the terms "neutralité" and "États neutres". Hübner, *De la saisie des batimens neutres*, 1:30–49. However, some scholars still avoided using the terms "neutrality" even in the eighteenth century. For example, Bynkershoek, in his *Quaestionum juris publici* (1737), used terms such as *non-hostes*, *amici* and *communem amicum* instead of *neutralitas* and *neutrales*. Bynkershoek, *Quaestionum juris publici*, 67–69.

84 See Taoka, "Meaning of the Term Neutrality", 48 [in Japanese].

Origins of the concept of neutrality 49

85 Victoria, *De indis*, 288, 290 (*De jure belli*, 36, 40); Suárez, *Selections from Three Works*, 816 (Disp. XIII, *De bello*, sec. 7, n. 10).
86 Grotius, *De jure belli ac pacis*, Lib. III, Cap. XVII, § I.
87 Ibid., Lib. III, Cap. XVII, § III.
88 Regarding this question, see Onuma, "War", 179–181; Kasai, "Grotian Conception of *jus gentium*", 45–50 [in Japanese].
89 Hübner, *De la saisie des batimens neutres*, 1:16–17 [italics in the original].
90 Wolff, *Jus gentium*, § 617, 618; Vattel, *Le droit des gens*, Liv. III, Chap. III, § 26.
91 Vattel, *Le droit des gens*, Liv. III, Chap. III, § 26. On the concept of "perfect rights" in Wolff's and Vattel's theories, see Yanagihara, *Theory of International Law of Christian Wolff*, 241–249 [in Japanese].
92 Wolff, *Jus gentium*, § 777–958; Vattel, *Le droit des gens*, Liv. III, Chap. XII, § 188–192.
93 As discussed in detail by Masaharu Yanagihara, while Wolff and Vattel use the same term ("voluntary law of nations"), their theoretical foundations for the concept of voluntary law of nations are different. According to Wolff, the voluntary law of nations is the positive general international law that the "supreme state (*civitas maxima*)", as a fiction, enacts by exercising its legislative power (*jus ferendi leges*). In contrast, Vattel, who denies the existence of the "supreme state", has to seek other foundations and bases the voluntary law of nations on the principle of States' sovereign equality. Therefore, in Vattel's theory, the content of the voluntary law of nations is largely determined by the intent of States actually expressed in State practice. According to Yanagihara's analysis, the practical consequences of the difference in the theoretical foundations for the voluntary law of nations between Wolff and Vattel clearly appear in the field of the law of war, and Vattel uncritically tends to bring actual State practice into the content of the voluntary law of nations. See Yanagihara, *Theory of International Law of Christian Wolff*, 131–166, 238–263 [in Japanese].
94 E.g. Ishimoto, *Changing Structure of International Law*, 65 [in Japanese].
95 Bynkershoek, *Quaestionum juris publici*, 2, 3.
96 Ibid., 71–72 [italics added].
97 Kinji Akashi has pointed out that, in Bynkershoek's *Quaestionum juris publici*, passages that appear to negate the just war doctrine coexist with passages that appear to support it. Akashi, as an example of the former, refers to the passages in which Bynkershoek argues about neutrality (*commumem amicum*). See Akashi, *Cornelius van Bynkersyhoek*, 94–95. Akashi seems to assume that the status of neutrality is incompatible with the just war doctrine. However, as we will discuss in section 2.2.2 of this chapter, the just war doctrine is compatible with the status of neutrality; rather, the eighteenth century theory of neutrality was based on the just war doctrine. In this regard, Bynkershoek's statement that "[i]n my judgement, the question of justice and injustice does not concern the neutral, and it is not his duty to sit in judgement between his friends who may be fighting each other ... ([s]i recte judico, belli justitia vel injustitia nihil quicquam pertinet ad communem amicum, ejus non est, inter utrumque amicum, sibi invicem hostem, federe judicem...)" (Bynkershoek, *Quaestionum juris publici*, 69) has often been cited as a passage that indicates Bynkershoek's negation of the just war doctrine. See e.g. Ishimoto, *Changing Structure of International Law*, 65, 69 [in Japanese]. However, Bynkershoek argues in this passage that it is better for a State that wishes to remain a common friend (*communem amicum*) of both belligerents not to assist one of the belligerents based on the judgment of justice and injustice of the war. He does not contend that the justice and injustice of a war are incapable to be judged or should not be judged by any third State. According to Bynkershoek, as a State that assists a belligerent "would ourselves appear in a manner to be making war on our friends" (ibid., 70), a State that wishes to avoid being regarded as making war on one of the belligerents,

50 *Origins of the concept of neutrality*

as a "common friend", should refrain from any assistance to either belligerent. However, Bynkershoek does not contend that all third States are obliged to become "common friends"; a State may become an ally. Bynkershoek, immediately after arguing about "common friends (*commumem amicum*)" (ibid., 67–71), states that "[t]he theory is quite different regarding allies and confederates (Foederatis & Sociis)" (ibid., 71), thus clearly distinguishing between "common friends (*commumem amicum*)" and "allies (*foederatis*)". Furthermore, Bynkershoek, considering the situation in which a third State has concluded alliance treaties with two belligerents at war with each other, argues that such a State should judge "whether they have a just cause for war" and aid an ally "which has the juster cause (qui justiorem causam habet)". Ibid., 71–72. In short, according to Bynkershoek, "the question of justice and injustice does not concern the neutral" only when a State remains a "common friend" of both belligerents. It is not a general statement regarding States not participating in a war. A state which is an "ally" of the belligerents needs to judge the justice and injustice of war to decide which belligerent it should aid.

98 Wolff, *Jus gentium*, § 673.

99 Vattel, *Le droit des gens*, Liv. III, Chap. VII, § 107.

100 Wolff, *Jus gentium*, § 682.

101 Ibid., § 681.

102 Vattel, *Le droit des gens*, Liv. III, Chap. VII, § 108.

103 Wolff, *Jus gentium*, § 673 [italics added].

104 Hübner, *De la saisie des batimens neutres*, 1:32–33.

105 Vattel, *Le droit des gens*, Liv. III, Chap. VII, § 106 [italics added].

106 Wolff, *Jus gentium*, § 680 [italics added].

107 Ibid.

108 Vattel, in chapters 6 and 7 of book III of *Le droit des gens*, distinguishes between situations in which a belligerent may regard a third State as an enemy (regarder comme Ennemi) and situations in which it may not. According to Vattel, examples of the former situations are as follows: a third State assists an enemy in accordance with an offensive alliance (Vattel, *Le droit des gens*, Liv. III, Chap. VI, § 98); a third State assists an enemy in accordance with a defensive alliance that has either been concluded specifically against the belligerent or been concluded during the war or when it is observed that war is about to be declared (ibid., Liv. III, Chap. VI, § 99); a third State assists an enemy without being under treaty obligation to do so (ibid., Liv. III, Chap. VI, § 97). An example of the latter situations is a situation where a third State takes a position of neutrality, including the situation in which a State assists a belligerent, in accordance with a defensive alliance treaty concluded before the outbreak of a war (ibid., Liv. III, Chap. VI, § 101, Chap. VII, § 103–134).

109 Ibid., Liv. III, Chap. VI, § 101. According to Vattel, "when a sovereign furnishes moderate help (sécours modéré) which he owes in virtue of an earlier defensive alliance he does not thereby become a party to the war (il ne s'associe point à la Guerre) (§ 101). Hence he may fulfil his obligation, and at the same time maintain a strict neutrality". Ibid., Liv. III, Chap. VII, § 105. This argument of Vattel is the origin of the theory of so-called "qualified neutrality". On the theory of qualified neutrality, see below, Chapter 2, section 1.4.2.

110 Vattel, *Le droit des gens*, Liv. III, Chap. VII, § 104 [italics added].

111 Ibid.

112 Wolff, *Jus gentium*, § 673.

113 Bynkershoek, *Quaestionum juris publici*, 69. The words in the quoted sentence translated as "[neutral]" are, in the original text, *medius*. Bynkershoek, in his *Quaestionum juris publici*, never did use the terms *neutralitas* or *neutralis*, instead used the terms such as *medius, non-hostes, amici, communem amicum*. The reason for this might be that, Bynkershoek, like writers before the seventeenth century, avoided using the terms *neutralitas* and *neutralis*, words of Vulgar Latin that appeared in the Middle

Origins of the concept of neutrality 51

Ages. See above, pp. 28–29. What Bynkershoek argues by using such terms as *medius, non-hostes, amici* and *communem amicum* is the conception that a third State avoids to be involved in a war by abstaining from giving assistance to either belligerent, and it is substantially the same conception as Wolff's and Vattel's theories of neutrality.

114 Wolff, *Jus gentium*, § 683.
115 Bynkershoek, *Quaestionum juris publici*, 69.
116 Ibid., 70 [italics added].
117 Ibid., 69.
118 Wolff, *Jus gentium*, § 680 [italics added].
119 See note 109 of this chapter.
120 Vattel, *Le droit des gens*, Liv. III, Chap. VI, § 101 [italics added].
121 Ibid., Liv. III, Chap. VII, § 113.
122 Ibid., Liv. III, Chap. VI, § 97.
123 Ibid., Liv. III, Chap. VI, § 98, 99, Chap. VII, § 113.
124 Ibid., Liv. III, Chap. VI, § 95.
125 Wolff, *Jus gentium*, § 730, 733 [italics added].
126 Ibid., § 656; Vattel, *Le droit des gens*, Liv. III, Chap. VI, § 83.
127 Wolff, *Jus gentium*, § 656–657; Vattel, *Le droit des gens*, Liv. III, Chap. VI, § 83.
128 See above, section 2.1.1 and 2.2.2 of this chapter.
129 Wolff, *Jus gentium*, § 733 [italics added].
130 Ibid., § 888; Vattel, *Le droit des gens*, Liv. III, Chap. III, § 40.
131 Wolff, *Jus gentium*, § 656.
132 Vattel, *Le droit des gens*, Liv. III, Chap. VI, § 83 [italics in the original].
133 Wolff, *Jus gentium*, § 674.
134 Vattel, *Le droit des gens*, Liv. III, Chap. VII, § 106.
135 According to Bynkershoek, "[i]t is not our duty to avenge (vindicare) all the wrongs of every sovereign; it is sufficient if we avenge our own and our allies". Bynkershoek, *Quaestionum juris publici*, 71. In other words, according to Bynkershoek, a State is obliged to assist a belligerent State only when they have concluded an alliance treaty. A State that has not concluded alliance treaties with any belligerents may remain neutral by abstaining from assisting any belligerents.
136 Wolff, *Jus gentium*, § 674 [italics added].
137 Vattel, *Le droit des gens*, Liv. III, Chap. III, § 40 [italics added].
138 Eighteenth-century writers clearly distinguish between "neutrals", which do not assist any belligerents, and "allies", which assist one of the belligerents. For instance, in Book III of Vattel's *Le droit des gens*, allies (associés de l'ennemi; sociétés de guerre; alliés) and neutrals (neutralité; neutre) are dealt with in separate chapters; Chapters 6 and 7. Vattel, *Le droit des gens*, Liv. III, Chaps. VI, VII. The subjects of neutrals (*neutralitas*) and allies (*fœderatio*) are also dealt with in separate sections in Wolff's *Jus gentium methodo scientifica pertractatum*. Wolff, *Jus gentium*, § 653–671, 672–685. Furthermore, Bynkershoek clearly distinguishes States that assist belligerents from States that do not, referring to the former as *foederatis & sociis* and the latter as *non-hostes, amici* or *communem amicum*. Bynkershoek, *Quaestionum juris publici*, 67, 69, 71. It is noteworthy that eighteenth-century writers assume not only situations in which a State assists a belligerent by entering the war and itself becoming a belligerent but also situations in which a State assists a belligerent without entering the war. This is clear from the fact that they define "auxiliaries (*auxiliares*)" as "troops ... which one nation, *not engaged in the war*, sends to another nation carrying on war" and "subsidies (*subsidia*)" as "moneys, which are paid to a nation carrying on war by another nation, *not engaged in the war*" [italics added]. See Wolff, *Jus gentium*, § 653, 654.
139 See e.g. Ishimoto, *Historical Study on the Law of Neutrality* [in Japanese]; Jessup and Deák, *Neutrality, Its History, Economics and Law*, Vol. 1, *The Origins*; Kulsrud, *Maritime Neutrality*; Neff, *Rights and Duties of Neutrals*; Pares, *Colonial Blockade*.

52 *Origins of the concept of neutrality*

140 See Kulsrud, *Maritime Neutrality*, 322–323.

141 See Gardiner, "History of Belligerent Rights", 521–546; Marsden, *Documents*, 1:vi–xxx; Sanborn, *Origins of the Early English Maritime and Commercial Law*, 122–123, 319–323.

142 Traité conclu pour vingt ans, entre EDOUARD III. Roi d'Angleterre & les Députés des Villes maritimes du Royaume de CASTILLE & du Comté de BISCAYE, pour le bien du Commerce réciproque, donné à Londres, le 1. Août 1351, Du Mont, *Corps universel*, 1(2): 265–267; Traité de Commerce conclu pour cinquante ans entre EDOUARD III. Roi d'Angleterre & les Députés des Villes maritimes du Royaume de PORTUGAL, donné à Londres le 20. Octobre 1353, ibid., 1(2): 286–287.

143 Marsden, *Documents*, 1:x, 75–77, 102–104, 106–107.

144 Droit maritime connu sous le nom de Consulat de la Mer, in Pardessus, *Collection*, 2:303–307. *Consolato del mare* is a code of maritime law that codified customary law arising from the practice of merchants engaged in the Mediterranean trade. It is considered to be compiled in Barcelona at the end of the thirteenth or the middle of the fourteenth century. See Matsukuma, "Consolato del mare", 401 [in Japanese].

145 Order of Council as to Enemy Goods in Friends' Ships and Friends' Goods in Enemy Ships, in Marsden, *Documents*, 1:165–166; Edit sur l'amiraute, du mois de mars 1584, Art. LXIX, in Pardessus, *Collection*, 4:316.

146 Proclamation Prohibiting the Trade with Spain or Portugal, in Marsden, *Documents*, 1:313–317.

147 The practice of general interdiction of maritime commerce between third States and enemy States did not completely disappear. For example, in 1689, England and the Netherlands, in a war against France, instituted a general interdiction against third States' trade with France. See Neff, *Rights and Duties of Neutrals*, 39.

148 Ishimoto, *Historical Study on the Law of Neutrality*, 75–87 [in Japanese].

149 On the Armed Neutralities, see e.g. Bergbohm, *Die bewaffnete Neutralität*; Madariaga, *Britain, Russia, and the Armed Neutrality*; Yokota, *Freedom of the Sea*, 53–139 [in Japanese].

150 The Declaration of Paris resolved a long-standing conflict between the principle of *free ships free goods* and the principle of *Consolato del mare* by combining these principles in the most favourable manner for neutrals. In other words, it adopted the former principle for goods on neutral vessels (the second principle of the Declaration of Paris states: "The neutral flag covers enemy's goods, with the exception of contraband of war") and the latter principle for goods on enemy vessels (the third principle of the Declaration of Paris states: "Neutral goods, with the exception of contraband of war, are not liable to be captured under the enemy's flag"). On the Declaration of Paris, see Fujita, "1856 Paris Declaration respecting Maritime Law", 61–75.

151 For example, article 4, title 9 of the 1681 Maritime Ordinance of France provided that "all vessels belonging to our enemies will be good prizes". Ordonnance touchant la marine du mois d'aout 1681, Titre IX, Art. VII, in Pardessus, *Collection*, 4:384.

152 For the sources of these municipal laws, see notes 49–51 of this chapter.

153 Ishimoto, *Historical Study on the Law of Neutrality*, 75–77 [in Japanese].

154 E.g. Articles d'Alliance & de Commerce entre le Serenissime & tres-puissant Prince CHARLES SECOND, par la grace de Dieu, Roi d'Angleterre. d'Ecosse, France, & Irlande, Deffenseur de la Foy, etc. Et le Serenissime & tre-puissant Prince, CHRISTIAN CINQUIEME, par la grace de Dieu Roy de Danemarc, Norwege, etc., conclu à Copenhague, le 11. jour de Juillet, 1670, Du Mont, *Corps universel*, 7(1): 132–137; Renouvellement, Prorogation, & Explication de l'Alliance entre LOUIS XIV. Roi de France & CHARLES XI. Roi de Sued", à Stockholm le 14. Avril 1672, Du Mont, *Corps universel*, 7(2): 166–171.

155 E.g. Traité d'Alliance entre LOUIS XIV. Roi de France & FREDERIC III. Roi de Danemarc, signé par M. Hannibal Seftel, Ambassadeur de Dannemarc, à Paris le 3.

Origins of the concept of neutrality   53

Aoust 1663, Du Mont, *Corps universel*, 6(2): 470–473; Renouvellement, Prorogation, & Explication de l'Alliance entre LOUIS XIV. Roi de France & CHARLES
XI. Roi de Sued, à Stockholm le 14. Avril 1672, Du Mont, *Corps universel*, 7(2):
166–171. Some alliance treaties, which provided freedom of maritime commerce for
subjects of State A towards State Y, did not insist on State A's obligation to aid State
X, providing only State A's duty of non-assistance to State Y. See e.g. Traité de Paix
& d'Alliance entre ALFONSE Roi de Portugal & les PROVINCES-UNIES des
Pays-Bas, fait à la Haye, le 6. Août 1661, Du Mont, *Corps universel*, 6(2): 366–371;
Articles d'Alliance & de Commerce entre le Serenissime & tres-puissant Prince
CHARLES SECOND, par la grace de Dieu, Roi d'Angleterre. d'Ecosse, France, &
Irlande, Deffenseur de la Foy, etc. Et le Serenissime & tre-puissant Prince, CHRIS-
TIAN CINQUIEME, par la grace de Dieu Roy de Danemarc, Norwege, etc.,
conclu à Copenhague, le 11. jour de Juillet, 1670, Du Mont, *Corps universel*, 7(1):
132–137.

156 By the nineteenth century, the maritime commerce of States remaining outside the
war had fallen under "neutral commerce", which was due to the fact that, in State
practice in the nineteenth century, all States remaining outside the war could
become neutrals, even if the State had not concluded a neutrality treaty with belligerent States, and it was *presumed* that a State that remained outside the war intended
to remain neutral, providing the State did not explicitly declare intent to participate
in the war. See below, pp. 107–108.

157 Among the fourteen neutrality treaties listed in section 1.1 of this chapter, while
Article 2 of (1), Paragraph 9 of (3), Article 13 of (4), Article 11 of (5), Article 7 of
(7), Article 5 of (8) and Article 2 of (9) provided that commerce between neutral
States and belligerent States was free, the other treaties did not contain provisions to
that effect.

158 Yamauchi, *History of Legal Conception of Looting*, 214 [in Japanese]. For example,
Vitoria stated:

> There is no doubt that everything captured in a just war vests in the seizor
> (*occupantium*) up to the amount which provided satisfaction for the things that
> have been wrongfully seized and which covers expenses also. This needs no
> proof, for that is the end and aim of war.
>
> Victoria, *De indis*, 293 (*De jure belli*, 50)

Grotius also observed:

> According to the law of nature, by a lawful war we acquire things which either
> equal to that which, although it was owed to us, we could not otherwise obtain,
> or we inflict upon the guilty a loss that does not exceed an equitable measure of
> punishment…
>
> Grotius, *De jure belli ac pacis*, Lib. III, Cap. VI, § I

159 Grotius, *De jure belli ac pacis*, Lib. III, Cap. VI, § V. This is a passage in which
Grotius discusses the principles under *jus gentium*. According to Grotius, while
there is no ground for a belligerent to acquire things from the enemy in excess of
the debt or disproportional to the punishment that the enemy deserves,

> [b]y the law of nations (jure gentium) not merely he who wages war for a just
> cause, but in a public war (bello solenni) also any one at all becomes owner
> (dominus), without limit or restriction (sine fine modoque), of what he has
> taken from the enemy.
>
> Ibid., Lib. III, Cap. VI, § II

However, as quoted above, Grotius does not admit, even as a principle under *jus
gentium*, that a belligerent acquires things not belonging to the enemy. The reason

54 *Origins of the concept of neutrality*

why Grotius admits that a belligerent may acquire things belonging to the enemy "without limit or restriction" under *jus gentium* is, as Naoya Kasai has pointed out:

> While the question of the right to kill or wounded persons ceases to be a major question between enemies when actual combat ends, the question of booty and prisoners of war may very well be carried over to the post-war period, thus occasionally providing a reason for starting another war.... As long as there is no realistic hope of taking back booty and prisoners seized by the victor, it would be more practical to confer legal effects on the actual results at the level of the law of nations, divorced from the effect of natural law.
>
> Kasai, "Laws of War", 263–264

2 The law of neutrality as an institution of general international law
1793–1918

This chapter considers the process by which the law of neutrality was established as an institution of positive general international law. According to the theory of neutrality as presented by eighteenth-century writers, third States, even if they had not concluded neutrality treaties with belligerents, could become neutral States and enjoyed the right not to be involved in war on the condition that they abstained from assisting either belligerent. This theory was accepted in the practice of States from the end of the eighteenth century to the nineteenth century, and the law of neutrality was established as an institution of positive general international law. Since the end of the eighteenth century, it became common for third States to remain neutral without concluding neutrality treaties with belligerents, by unilaterally issuing a declaration or proclamation of neutrality, and enacting municipal laws called "neutrality laws".[1] As Miele observes as a result of examining the practice of States at the end of the eighteenth century, "in this way, the constitutive fact of the relation of neutrality ceased to be the mutual intention of belligerents and neutrals, but the establishment of it now depends the unilateral intention of the State outside the conflict".[2]

The theory that a third State had the right to remain neutral, without concluding neutrality treaties with belligerents, by unilaterally expressing such an intention, that is, the theory of neutrality as presented by eighteenth-century writers, was first put into actual practice by the United States in the French Revolutionary Wars (1792–1802).[3] As observed by Amos S. Hershey, "[t]he theory of neutral rights and obligations was formulated by Bynkershoek, Hübner, De Martens, and Vattel in the eighteenth century, but it was the first put into actual practice by the United States during the Washington administration".[4] Thus, section 1 of this chapter shall consider the process in which the law of neutrality was established as an institution of general international law, with the starting-point being the practice of the United States in the French Revolutionary Wars, and section 2 shall consider the concept of the "right to remain neutral", which is the key concept in the traditional law of neutrality.

56 *The law of neutrality 1793–1918*

1 The emergence of the law of neutrality as an institution of general international law

1.1 The practice of the United States in the French Revolutionary Wars[5]

1.1.1 Proclamation of neutrality of 22 April 1793

On 22 April 1793, the year in which Great Britain, the Netherlands and Spain entered the French Revolutionary Wars, which had initially been fought between France on the one hand, and Austria and Prussia on the other, George Washington, President of the United States, issued a proclamation.[6] In this proclamation, President Washington declared that it was "the disposition of the United States" to "with sincerity and good faith adopt and pursue a conduct friendly and impartial toward the belligerent Powers", and warned "the citizens of the United States carefully to avoid all acts and proceedings whatsoever, which may in any manner tend to contravene such disposition". He also announced that "whosoever of the citizens of the United States shall render himself liable to punishment or forfeiture under the law of nations, by committing, aiding, or abetting hostilities against any of the said Powers", and gave instructions to officers throughout the United States "to cause prosecutions to be instituted against all persons, who shall, within the cognizance of the courts of the United States, violate the law of nations, with respect to the Powers at war, or any of them". Although the words "neutral" or "neutrality did not appear in this proclamation, as it declared the intention of the United States to adopt and pursue a conduct *friendly* and *impartial* towards the belligerent Powers, it was later referred to as the "Proclamation of Neutrality".[7]

Despite this proclamation, there were frequent cases in which citizens of the United States "commit[ed], aid[ed], or abett[ed] hostilities" against the belligerent Powers. The biggest issue was the privateering carried out at the order of French Minister Charles Edmond Genet.[8] French plenipotentiary minister Genet, who was appointed to the United States in April 1793, enlisted persons to engage in privateering at the ports of the United States and gave these persons commissions to carry out privateering and to fit out and arm privateers. Those privateers captured merchant ships of the enemies of France.

The United States government took measures to prosecute and punish private individuals – mainly citizens of the United States but including foreigners – who engaged in privateering based in the territory of the United States or the fitting out and arming of privateers within the territory of the United States. The legal basis for such measures was identified in the *Henfield* case, which is considered below.

The law of neutrality 1793–1918   57

1.1.2 The Henfield *case (1793)*

The *Citizen Genet*, a privateer commissioned by the French government, was fitted out in Charlestown, South Carolina. Gideon Henfield, a citizen of the United States, was an officer of the *Citizen Genet*. The *Citizen Genet* seized and took as a prize, a British merchant ship called the *William* on the high seas, and Henfield returned to the United States on board the *William* as a prize master. Henfield was arrested and prosecuted for carrying out a breach of neutrality, and a trial was held at the Circuit Court for the District of Pennsylvania.[9]

The judges delivered charges to the grand jury to the effect that the defendant Henfield should be found guilty. But the grand jury delivered a verdict of "Not Guilty". While we cannot know the reasoning behind this verdict, what is important here is the legal opinions presented by the judges and the prosecutor (District Attorney Rawle, Chief Justice Jay and Judge Wilson) to the grand jury. As stated below, regardless of the conclusion of the verdict in this case, the legal opinions presented by the judges and prosecutor, or, in other words, the view that private individuals should be punished for carrying out privateering based in the territory of a neutral State, was adopted in the Neutrality Act of 1794 and was later accepted in the municipal laws of other States in the nineteenth century.

The charges and legal opinions presented to the grand jury by the judges and prosecutor in this case are summarised as follows.

First, according to the judges and prosecutor, the acts carried out by Henfield were "breaches of the neutrality".[10] As identified in the indictment by District Attorney Rawle, Henfield was engaged in privateering as a member of the crew of the *Citizen Genet*, and therefore, he was obstructing the neutrality of the United States by taking and destroying the ships, goods and moneys of British subjects and waging war against them on the high seas.[11]

According to the judges and the prosecutor, the United States had to punish those who carried out acts that breached neutrality within the territory of the United States or based in the territory of the United States. As "the United States are in a state of neutrality relative to all the powers at war, and that it is their duty, their interest, and their disposition to maintain it: that, therefore, they who commit, aid, or abet hostilities against these powers or either of them, offend against the laws of the United States, and ought to be punished".[12] "When the offending citizen escapes into his own country, his nation should oblige him to repair the damage, if reparation can be made, or should punish him according to the measure of his office.... If the nation refuse to do either, it renders itself in some measure an accomplice in the guilt, and becomes responsible for the injury",[13] and "an infraction of this kind, unless punished, becomes a good cause of war on the part of the offended nation".[14]

"Breaches of the neutrality" by private individuals based in the territory of a neutral State, such as privateering against belligerents, if left unpunished by the government of a neutral State, became a "good cause for war" on the part of the offended belligerent. Conversely, a neutral State punishes persons who

58 *The law of neutrality 1793–1918*

committed "breaches of neutrality" based in its territory, in order to avoid giving a good cause for war to a belligerent. In other words, the punishment of those who have committed "breaches of neutrality" is justified by "the common welfare" of a State to avoid a situation in which "a few individuals, for avaricious purposes, might involve the nation in a war".[15]

The judges and prosecutor also justified the above conclusion from the perspective of the power to declare war within a State.[16] According to them, nature has given man the right to use force for their defence and the preservation of their rights; however, since the establishment of a political society, namely a State, that right no longer belongs to private individuals but to the State itself or its sovereigns. For example, Article 1 Section 8 Clause 11 of the United States Constitution confers the power to declare war not on private individuals but on Congress. As stated above, "breaches of neutrality" carried out by private individuals, if left unpunished, becomes a good cause for war for the offended belligerent, and in this sense may be considered as "war" on the part of private individuals. In other words, such acts of private individuals should be punished because they infringe the power to declare war that belongs solely to the State.

1.1.3 The Neutrality Act of 1794

As stated in section 1.1.1, the United States government issued the Proclamation of Neutrality in 1793, which prohibited private individuals from committing, aiding or abetting hostilities against the belligerents, and, in particular, carrying out privateering against the belligerents based in the territory of the United States, and the fitting out and arming of privateers within the territory of the United States.

However, as there was no statute that could be the legal basis for such prohibition in the United States at that time, the courts and the government invoked the "law of nations" as the legal basis for the prohibition.[17] The domestic courts of the United States at that time regarded the "law of nations" as the law of nature applied between States[18] and in the *Henfield's* case, the concept of the "law of nations" was understood as such.[19]

According to the case law of the United States domestic courts, the "law of nations" is part of the law of the United States and can be applied by the courts.[20] Then, one may consider that the "law of nations" provides a sufficient legal basis for the punishment of private individuals who have carried out privateering and the fitting out and arming of privateers. However, since, according to Article 1 Section 8 Clause 10 of the United States Constitution, the power "[t]o define and punish ... offenses against the law of nations" belongs to Congress,[21] there was an argument that the courts could not punish "offenses against the law of nations" by directly applying "the law of nations", and that statutes enacted by Congress was indispensable to punish such offences.[22] In view of the existence of such an argument, it was unclear if privateering and the fitting out and arming of privateers would be punished by directly applying the

The law of neutrality 1793–1918 59

"law of nations", and, in order to ensure that such acts were definitely punished, it was preferred that a statute be established.

Against such background, "An Act in addition to the Act for Punishment of Certain Crimes against the United States", commonly known as "the Neutrality Act", was enacted in 1794.[23] This Act prohibited any person from committing the following acts within the territory or jurisdiction of the United States, and defines the penalties for violations: (1) to accept and exercise a commission to serve a foreign prince or state in war by land and sea (section 1); (2) to enlist or enter himself in the service of any foreign prince or state (section 2); (3) to fit out or arm any ship or vessel with intent that such ship or vessel shall be employed in the service of any foreign prince or state to cruse or to commit hostilities upon the subjects, citizens or property of another foreign prince or state with whom the United States are at peace (section 3); (4) to increase or augment the force of any ship of war, cruiser or other armed vessel in the service of a foreign prince or state being at war with another foreign prince or state with whom the United States are at peace (section 4); (5) to begin or set on foot any military expedition or enterprise to be carried on against the territory or dominions of any foreign prince or state with whom the United States are at peace (section 5).

The Neutrality Act was revised in 1817 and 1818. The background to these revisions was as follows.[24] The Wars of Independence had been waging among the Spanish colonies in South America since around 1810. Two defects seemed to exist in the Neutrality Act of 1794 in relation to those wars. The first defect is that the penalties for violations of the Act are not sufficiently effective. For example, President James Madison, in his message to Congress on 26 December 1816, stated that "the existing laws have not the efficacy necessary to prevent violations of the obligations of the United States as a nation at peace toward belligerent parties", and recommended to the consideration of Congress the expediency of further legislative provisions as may be requisite for detaining vessels that were equipped in the ports of the United States in violation of the Neutrality Act.[25] The second defect is that the Neutrality Act of 1794 does not apply to civil wars. The Act forbids acts of hostility by private individuals against a "foreign prince or state", but it does not apply to acts of hostility against parties in a civil war, who are not a "foreign prince or state". Actually, in the *Gelston* v. *Hoyt* case (1818), the Supreme Court of the United States held that the Neutrality Act of 1794 did not apply to civil wars.[26] In view of these defects, the "Act to More Effectively Preserve the Neutral Relations of the United States" of 3 March 1817 (the Neutrality Act of 1817), authorised and required the collectors of customs of the United States to "detain any vessel manifestly built for warlike purposes, and about to depart from the United States".[27] "An Act in addition to the 'Act for the Punishment of Certain Crimes against the United States,' and to Repeal the Acts Therein Mentioned" of 20 April 1818 (the Neutrality Act of 1818) replaced the term "a foreign prince or State", which was used in the Neutrality Act of 1794, with the term "a foreign prince, state, colony, district, or people", making the Neutrality Act applicable to civil wars as well.[28]

60 *The law of neutrality 1793–1918*

1.2 The practice of enacting neutrality laws in the early nineteenth century

The practice of enacting municipal laws in order to maintain neutrality (commonly called "neutrality laws") spread to States other than the United States in the nineteenth century. We will consider the law of Great Britain, which enacted a detailed special law as the United States did, and the laws of other States, including France, which incorporated general and abstract provisions concerning neutrality in the penal codes.

1.2.1 The law of Great Britain

Great Britain enacted the so-called "Foreign Enlistment Act" in 1819.[29] This Act prohibited any person from committing "without the leave or licence of His Majesty, His Heirs or Successors",[30] the following acts within any part of the United Kingdom, or in any part of British Dominions beyond the seas: (1) to accept any military commission to serve as soldier, or serve in any warlike or military operation in the service of any foreign State, or of any persons exercising or assuming to exercise any powers of government in any colony or province (Article 2); (2) to enlist or enter himself to enlist in the service of any foreign State, or of any persons exercising or assuming to exercise any powers of government in any colony or province (Article 2); (3) to equip, furnish, fit out or arm a ship or vessel with the intent or in order that such ship or vessel shall be employed in the service of any foreign State, or of any persons exercising or assuming to exercise any powers of government in any colony or province (Article 7); and (4) to increase or augment the warlike force of any ship or vessel of war, or cruiser, or other armed vessel in the service of any foreign State, or of any persons exercising or assuming to exercise any powers of government in any colony or province (Article 8). This Act applies not only to wars between sovereign States but also to civil wars, because this Act prohibits acts such as the fitting out and arming of vessels employed in the service of "any Person or Persons exercising or assuming to exercise any powers of Government in or over any Foreign State, Colony, Province, or part of Province or People" as well as vessels employed in the service of "any Foreign Prince, State, or Potentate".

The background to the enactment of the Foreign Enlistment Act was as follows.[31]

In the 1810s, Spanish colonies in South America carried out wars of independence in order to become independent from Spain. In these wars, the British government, in order to maintain friendly relations both with Spain and with the South American colonies, declared the determination to preserve strict neutrality and abstain from assisting either party.[32] Great Britain needed to maintain good relations with Spain, as a vital ally against Napoleon during the period of the Napoleonic wars, and after the wars, as an important element in the European collective security system constructed to prevent the re-emergence of French dominance. At the same time, in order to maintain the commercial

The law of neutrality 1793–1918   61

links that Great Britain was developing with the emergent States in Spanish America, it was necessary to maintain good relations with the Spanish–American colonies as well.

In April 1817, however, the systematic recruitment of British military personnel for service with the rebel forces in Spanish America began to be carried out within the territory of Great Britain. The circumstances were favourable for such recruitment, as there were large numbers of veterans of the Napoleonic wars who had been discharged from the British forces and were unemployed. The Spanish government made a protest to the British government regarding such recruitment, which forced the British government to take measures.

As a statute that seemed to be applicable to this situation, there existed the statute of 1735–6 (9 Geo. 2(1735–6) c.30), which provides that a British subject who enlists or enters himself to serve "any foreign prince, state, or potentate" shall be adjudged to be guilty of a felony, and shall suffer death in cases of felony without benefit of clergy.[33] However, clearly, Spanish colonies in South America were not "foreign princes, states or potentates". In order to overcome this difficulty, it would have been necessary for the British government to recognise Spanish colonies as sovereign States. However, the British government could not take this option, as doing so would damage the friendly relation with Spain. On 27 November 1817, the British government issued a proclamation that strictly charges and commands all and every British natural-born subjects not to serve in the military forces or ships of war raised or set forth by "the Persons exercising or assuming to exercise the Powers of Government" in "divers Provinces or Parts of Provinces in Spanish America".[34] But this proclamation was not very effective in preventing the acts of private individuals.

Against this background, the British government considered a new statute to be necessary, and presented a bill for the Foreign Enlistment Act to Parliament on 13 May 1819. In Parliament, the opinion was divided over the need for this bill.

The ground for those who supported this bill was the need for a State to prevent and punish certain acts of private individuals in order to maintain peaceful relations with other States. For example, according to Sir W. Scott, "it was the right of states, and states only, to determine whether they would continue neutral, or assume a belligerent attitude – that they had the power of preventing their subjects from becoming belligerent, if they pleased to exert it".[35] Robert Grant also stated:

> Every government, in its foreign relations, was the representative of the nation to which it belonged; and it was of the highest importance to the peace of nations, that government should be so considered. Nation announced their intentions to each other through the medium of their rulers.... But all this system was inverted and thrown into confusion, if the government might act in one way and the nation in another. – All this system was at an end if, while we were professedly at peace with Spain, she was to be attacked by a large army of military adventurers from our own shores...[36]

62 The law of neutrality 1793–1918

Furthermore, according to Earl Bathurst, "[a State] that its subjects made war at pleasure upon states with whom their government was at peace, and without any interruption from that government to their pursuits" is "a state incapable of maintaining the relations of peace and amity with other powers".[37] In short, the opinion of those who supported this bill was that, as stated by Lord Castlereagh, "[t]his law was necessary to prevent us from giving cause of war to Spain against us".[38]

On the other hand, those who opposed this bill also recognised the need for preventing and punishing certain acts of private individuals that could harm peaceful relations with other States. For example, Sir James Mackintosh stated, "[i]t was impossible to deny that the sovereign power of every state could interfere to prevent its subjects from engaging in the wars of other states, by which its own peace might be endangered or its own interests effected".[39]

The issue is whether, in order to prevent and punish acts of private individuals that might endanger peaceful relations with other States, a statute is necessary, or whether the common law or the royal prerogative is sufficient for that purpose.[40]

As regards this issue, those who opposed this bill maintained that the acts under consideration in the bill could be punished based on the existing statue (i.e. 9 Geo. 2 (1735–6) c.30), the common law or the royal prerogative in Great Britain; the circumstances differed from those of the United States where a new statute was required.[41] For example, Sir Mackintosh stated: "[T]hough the common law in England was sufficient for the required purpose, in America it was not. The power of making war and peace was vested in the president of America, as it was in the king of England. In America, therefore, a legislative act was necessary. But, as his majesty's proclamation of 1817 was still in force, how could any legislative measure be necessary in this country?"[42]

On the other hand, those who favoured this bill maintained that the existing statute was insufficient for the following two reasons. The first was that the existing statute only applied to "foreign princes, states or potentates", that is, recognised sovereign States: it did not apply to civil wars between Spain and the insurgents in Spanish America.[43] The second is that the existing statute did not prohibit private individuals from fitting out vessels employed in war; however, "[i]t was extremely important, for the preservation of neutrality, that the subjects of this country should be prevented from fitting out any equipments, not only in the ports of Great Britain and Ireland, but also in the other ports of the British dominions, to be employed in the foreign service".[44] In addition, they rebutted the argument of those who opposed the bill according to which acts under consideration could be punished based on the common law or the royal prerogative, by pointing out that the King, who certainly could punish such acts based on the royal prerogative *after* the acts were committed, had no authority under the common law to *prevent* such acts *in advance*,[45] and maintained that "[t]o empower the crown to preserve that neutrality, the legislature must afford it the necessary means".[46]

In the end, the Foreign Enlistment Bill was supported by the majority and passed by Parliament, and the Foreign Enlistment Act came into effect on

The law of neutrality 1793–1918   63

1 August 1819. The purpose of this Act was, as clarified in the discussion of the bill in Parliament, "the preservation of neutrality" of Great Britain: If Great Britain did not prevent or punish hostile acts by private individuals against belligerents (including rebels in civil war) based in the territory of Great Britain, it would be regarded as "virtually departing from its neutral character, and assuming that of an enemy".[47] In order to avoid such a result and to preserve neutrality of the State, hostile acts by private individuals had to be punished.[48] There were conflicting opinions regarding the means of preventing and punishing such hostile acts – whether the royal prerogative was sufficient or whether a new statute was needed. However, everyone in Parliament agreed that there were certain acts of private individuals that should be punished for the preservation of neutrality.

1.2.2 The penal codes of France and other states

In contrast to the detailed special neutrality laws enacted by the United States and Great Britain, various other States incorporated general and abstract provisions for the maintenance of neutrality in their penal codes. The model for such provisions was Article 84 of the French Penal Code (1810), which provides that "[w]hoever shall have exposed the state to a declaration of war by hostile acts (actions hostiles) not approved by the government shall be punished by banishment, and, if war should follow, by deportation".[49] Examples of the provisions of penal codes which forbids hostile acts by private individuals that expose the State to the risk of war, in the same way as Article 84 of the French Penal Code, include Article 84 of the Penal Code of the Netherlands,[50] Article 123 of the Penal Code of Belgium,[51] Article 148 of the Penal Code of Spain,[52] Article 148 of the Penal Code of Portugal,[53] Article 174 of the Penal Code of Sardinia,[54] Article 174 of the Penal Code of Italy,[55] Article 90 of the Penal Code of Brazil,[56] Article 160 of the Penal Code of Bolivia[57] and Article 84 of the Penal Code of the Dominican Republic.[58]

These provisions of penal codes were later cited in the proclamations of neutrality issued by those States, as the legal basis for the punishment of hostile acts by private individuals that would compromise the neutrality of the State. For example, the declaration of neutrality issued by France during the American Civil War (1861–65) provides that "it is prohibited for all French nationals to take commission from either of the two parties to arm vessels of war, or to accept letters of marques to make privateering at sea, or to participate in a manner whatsoever in equipment or armament of a vessel of war or privateer of either of the two parties", and provides that those who violate the provisions of this declaration shall be prosecuted in accordance with Articles 84 and 85 of the Penal Code.[59] Also, the Decree concerning neutrality issued by Spain during the Franco–Prussian War (1870–71) provides that "[a]ccording to the same Article [Article 151] of the Penal Code, the arming, furnishing, or equipping of any ship against either of the belligerent Powers is prohibited in all the ports of Spain and her colonies, no matter with what flag it may be covered".[60] In short,

64   *The law of neutrality 1793–1918*

in these declarations of neutrality, the aforementioned provisions of the penal codes were invoked as the legal basis for prosecuting private individuals who commit acts such as the fitting out and arming vessels of war that may endanger the neutrality of the State. Therefore, as stated by the United States government in the *Alabama* claims arbitration in 1872, "these laws, although not bearing the title of 'Neutrality Laws', are quite as clearly neutrality laws in fact as the foreign-enlistment acts of the United States and of Great Britain".[61]

The ground for the punishment of private individuals in accordance with those provisions of the penal codes is that "hostile acts" of private individuals towards belligerent States, if left unpunished, expose the State to the risk of being involved in the war. For example, a commentary to Article 151 of the Penal Code of Spain states that "[w]ar is in itself a fact of too serious a character, and such armaments may too greatly endanger the safety of the country, that we should think it fit or justifiable for any person whatsoever to embark in such an enterprise without being duly authorized to do so".[62] Also, according to a commentary to Article 148 of the Penal Code of Portugal, for an act to constitute a crime under that article, it is necessary that "it be in itself of an hostile character" and that it in itself is such as to "give just reason for war according to international right (segundo o direito internacional … podesse justo motivo de guerra)".[63] Hostile acts of private individuals against a belligerent, if left unpunished by a neutral State, "give just reason for war according to international right", and "may too greatly endanger the safety of the country", and, in order for States to avoid giving a belligerent a just cause for war, the hostile actions of private individuals should be punished.

1.3 The practice of applying neutrality laws

The neutrality laws enacted by various States in the early nineteenth century were frequently applied throughout the nineteenth century, and as a result of the accumulation of the practice of States, the law of neutrality was established as an institution of general international law. In this section, we will consider (1) cases related to military expeditions (section 1.3.2) and (2) cases related to the fitting out and arming of ships intended for warlike purposes (section 1.3.3), and will identify the grounds for the need for preventing such conducts. As shown by the cases considered in sections 1.3.2 and 1.3.3, the practice of applying the neutrality laws includes many cases of civil wars; thus, we will first consider the applicability of the law of neutrality in civil wars to the extent necessary to proceed with the argument set forth in this book.

1.3.1 Neutrality in civil wars

According to the general understanding today, in the case of civil wars, unless insurgents were recognised as a belligerent, other States did not become neutrals.[64] Regarding the time when the recognition of belligerency came into existence as an institution of international law, the prevailing opinion is that the institution of the recognition of belligerency were already in existence in the wars of independence of Spanish America in the 1810s and in the Greek War of Independence in the 1820s.[65] However, as pointed out by Lord McNair and Syndham Legh Walker, probably, the concept of the recognition of belligerency was first used in the eighth edition of Wheaton's *Elements of International Law* published with annotations by Dana in 1866.[66] Legal literature, diplomatic documents and judgements of domestic courts prior to that had never used the concept of the recognition of belligerency.[67] The ground for the prevailing opinion today is that declarations of neutrality were issued by foreign States or, in other words, the implied recognition of belligerency was made, in the Spanish–American wars of independence and in the Greek War of Independence. However, the idea that a declaration of neutrality amounts to implied recognition of belligerency is an idea that did not exist in the first half of the nineteenth century but emerged in the later half of the century, and it is not appropriate to apply this idea when evaluating State practice in the first half of the nineteenth century. The idea that foreign States may – or are obliged to – assume the status of neutrality in civil wars even if they do not recognise insurgents as a belligerent can be valid, and as shown below, such an idea was in fact supported by State practice in the first half of the nineteenth century.

This book, therefore, following the view of McNair and Walker according to which the institution of the recognition of belligerency did not exist in the first half of the nineteenth century, divides the phase into the period when the recognition of belligerency did not exist as an institution of international law (the first half of the nineteenth century) and the period when it had emerged as an institution of international law (the latter half of the nineteenth century).

A THE FIRST HALF OF THE NINETEENTH CENTURY

In the first half of the nineteenth century, when the concept of the recognition of belligerency did not yet exist, State practice supported the view that foreign States were free to choose either to remain neutral or to take part in a civil war. The basis for such practice was the view presented by Vattel in his *Le droit des gens* of 1758. According to Vattel, "[i]t clearly follows from the liberty and independence of Nations that each has the right to govern itself (se gouverner) as it thinks proper, and that no one of them has the least right to interfere (se mêler) in the government (Gouvernement) of another" (the principle of non-intervention).[68] However, the situation changes when a civil war occurs: "When a party (un parti) is formed within the State which ceases to obey the sovereign and is strong enough to make a stand against him, or when a Republic is divided into two opposite factions (factions), and both sides take up arms, there exists a *civil war* (une *Guerre Civile*)."[69] "[W]henever such dissension reaches the state of civil war, foreign Nations may assist that one of the two parties which seems to have justice on its side." This is because "[w]hen ... the political bonds (les liens de la Société Politique) between a sovereign and his people are broken, or at least suspended, they may be considered as two distinct parties (deux

66   The law of neutrality 1793–1918

Puissances distinctes), and since both are independent of all foreign authority, no one has the right to judge them."[70] In sum, according to Vattel, a civil war is considered as a war between two distinct parties, between whom there are no "political bonds"; therefore, in a civil war, as in an international war between States, the parties must abide by the laws of war,[71] and foreign States may either assist the party that is deemed to be just, or they may abstain from assisting either party and remain neutral.

Vattel's view was supported by writers in the first half of the nineteenth century. For example, Henry Wheaton, in the first edition of *Elements of International Law* (1836), wrote:

> Until the revolution is consummated, whilst the civil war involving a contest for the government continues, other states may remain indifferent spectators of the controversy, still continuing to treat the ancient government as sovereign, and the government *de facto* as a society entitled to the rights of war against its enemy; or may espouse the cause of the party which they believe to have justice on its side. In the first case, the foreign state fulfils all its obligations under the law of nations; and neither party has any right to complain, provided it maintains an impartial neutrality. In the latter, it becomes, of course, the enemy of the party against whom it declares itself, and the ally of the other; and as the positive law of nations makes no distinction, in this respect, between a just and an unjust war, the intervening state becomes entitled to all the rights of war against the opposite party.[72]

According to Wheaton, this principle is applicable not only in cases of revolution with the aim of a change of government within a State, but also in cases of civil wars with the aim of independence from an existing State: "[W]hilst the contest for the sovereignty continues, and the civil war rages", "other nations may either remain passive,... or may join in alliance with one party against the other". In the case of the former, "neither party has any right to complain so long as other nations maintain an impartial neutrality".[73]

In sum, according to Vattel and Wheaton, in cases where civil war breaks out within a State, foreign States may choose either to remain neutral or to participate in the civil war on the side of the party deemed to be just. Vattel and Wheaton did not use the term "recognition of belligerency". According to them, in a civil war, the existing government (the sovereign) and the insurgent are viewed as two distinct parties in the war. The status of the insurgent as a party in the war are not conferred by acts of recognition of belligerency, but is based on the fact that "the political bonds" between the existing government and the insurgent have been broken as the insurgent "ceases to obey the sovereign and is strong enough to make a stand against him".

Such a view advanced by Vattel and Wheaton was supported by the practice of States in the first half of the nineteenth century. For example, in the insurrection that broke out in Russian Poland in 1831, the British government, citing

Vattel's *Le droit des gens*, stated: "as if the war was carried on between Two Belligerent Nations", in this civil war, "Austria, having determined not to interfere in the contest between Russia and Poland, must be considered as neutral in that contest".[74] The Austrian government, also citing Book 3, Chapter 18, Section 296 of Vattel's *Le droit des gens*, according to which foreign States may decide which party in a civil war is just or unjust and provide assistance to the party deemed to be just, explained: While "she [Austria] could have pursued a system of neutrality in the strict sense of the word (un système de neutralité proprement dite); she could also have chosen an intermediate line between a belligerent State and a neutral State (une ligne intermédiaire entre celle de puissance belligérante et celle de puissance neutre)". Austria as an ally of Russia took a "middle line", not the attitude of strict neutrality, in this civil war.[75] Also, in the revolt that took place in British Canada in 1837, the United States government, without referring to the concept of recognition of belligerency, characterised this revolt as a "civil war", expressed the view that "civil wars are not distinguishable from other wars as to belligerent and neutral rights",[76] and took measures to "arrest and punish under the laws of the United States" "any persons who shall compromise the neutrality of the government".[77]

B THE LATTER HALF OF THE NINETEENTH CENTURY

The concept of the recognition of belligerency emerged in State practice and legal literature in the latter half of the nineteenth century, particularly after the 1880s.[78] According to State practice and writers, the conditions that justify the recognition of belligerency are as follows: (1) the existence of an armed conflict of a general character; (2) that the insurgents must occupy and administer a substantial portion of territory; (3) that the insurgents must conduct the hostilities in accordance with the laws of war and through organised armed forces acting under a responsible authority; and (4) the existence of circumstances that make it necessary for third States to define their attitude by means of the recognition of belligerency.[79] There are two modes of recognition of belligerency: express recognition, which takes place by a declaration clearly announcing the intention of recognition, and implied recognition, which takes place through acts implying the intention of recognition, such as the issuance of a declaration of neutrality or recognising the validity of the blockade made by the insurgents. The legal effects of recognition of belligerency include that the insurgents recognised as belligerents are entitled to exercise belligerent rights, and that the soldiers of the insurgents recognised as belligerents are treated as prisoners of war.

While there are many other issues with regard to the conditions, modes and legal effects of recognition of belligerency,[80] what is crucial for the present study is that, in State practice and legal literature in the latter half of the nineteenth century, there was a general support for the view that the legal status of neutrality was created only when recognition of belligerency was accorded to the insurgents. For example, Rougier, in his book of 1903, states: In cases of an

68   The law of neutrality 1793–1918

international war between States, "[neutrality] exists by the operation of law (en plein droit), and is presumed in case of silence of the State", but "[i]n a civil war, on the contrary, neutrality does not exist by the operation of law and is not presumed; neutrality is created by the act of recognition of belligerency by third States".[81]

There were few writers who clearly answered the question as to whether a third State that had accorded recognition of belligerency may take part in the civil war. But as observed by Oppenheim, it seems reasonable to conclude that "[a]s a civil war becomes real war through recognition of the insurgents as a belligerent power", "[f]oreign States may either become party to the war or remain neutral".[82]

1.3.2 Military expeditions

A "military expedition" is defined as the organisation of a number of men into a body, within the territory of a neutral State, with a common intent or purpose to engage in carrying out armed hostilities against the territory of any belligerent with which the neutral State is at peace.[83] In other words, a military expedition exists when the two conditions are fulfilled: (1) the hostile intentions and (2) the organisation of the expedition.[84]

As we have seen in sections 1.1.3 and 1.2.1 of this chapter, the Neutrality Act of the United States and the British Foreign Enlistment Act prohibited private individuals, within the territories of those States, from preparing and commencing military expeditions against belligerents.[85] The provisions of the penal code of other States, which were incorporated for the maintenance of neutrality, only prohibited private individuals from carrying out hostile actions that may expose the State to the risk of war, without any specific reference to the concept of "military expeditions". But military expeditions were considered to be included in the concept of "hostile actions" that were prohibited by these provisions.[86]

Why should a neutral State prohibit and prevent the organisation and commencement of military expeditions within its own territory? We shall answer this question by examining the Terceira Affair, which is known as one of *causes célèbres* concerning military expeditions,[87] and the practice of the United States, where there were frequent cases of military expeditions in the nineteenth century.

A THE TERCEIRA AFFAIR[88]

With the death of King João VI in March 1826, the inheritance of the throne became an issue, as Don Pedro, the eldest son of João VI, had already become the Brazilian emperor. Pedro handed over the Portuguese throne to his minor daughter, Donna Maria, and made his younger brother (namely, Maria's uncle) Don Miguel, regent. However, in 1828, as Don Miguel usurped the throne from Donna Maria and declared himself king, the supporters of Don Miguel

The law of neutrality 1793–1918 69

and the supporters of Donna Maria fought, putting Portugal into a state of civil war. The supporters of Donna Maria requested aid from Great Britain on the basis of the alliance treaties between Great Britain and Portugal (the alliance treaties of 1373, 1571, 1642, 1654 and 1810), but the British government maintained that the purpose of these alliance treaties was "the protection of Portugal from Foreign Invasion", which did not apply to "internal revolt or dissention", thereby declaring its intention to remain neutral in this civil war.[89] In the meantime, a large number of Portuguese supporters of Donna Maria found refuge in the southwest of Great Britain, where they organised military expeditions to assist Donna Maria. The British government demanded that the expeditionary force of Portuguese refugees be dissolved and that the individuals be repatriated to Portugal, but the Portuguese refugees did not comply with. In January 1829 the expeditionary force left Great Britain, falsely stating that it was heading to Brazil, but actually went to Terceira, one of the group of islands known as the Azores in Portugal. Meanwhile, the British government gave instructions to the British Navy to prevent the expeditionary force from landing on Terceira, and to use force after giving a warning if the expeditionary force resisted. Based on these instructions, the British Navy forcibly intercepted the expeditionary force's landing on Terceira.

A debate arose in British Parliament over the legality of the forcible measures taken in this case. Those who maintained that the measures taken by the British Navy were illegal under international law submitted to the House of Commons, a resolution which read that such measures were "violation[s] of the sovereignty of the state to which the Island of Terceira belonged".[90]

Those who opposed this resolution, that is, those who maintained that the measures taken by the British Navy were legal under international law argued that "the Portuguese refugees were an armed body of men" and fulfilled the organisation requirement of the concept of military expeditions.[91] They argued that if an expedition for the purpose of carrying out hostilities was not a breach of neutrality, they were "incapable of understanding wherein that breach could consist".[92] Therefore, they concluded that Great Britain, which declared its intention to maintain neutrality in this civil war, had to prevent such expeditions.[93]

They argued that the measures taken by the British government to forcibly obstruct the expedition by dispatching the Navy to the seas off Terceira were justified under international law. The grounds for this argument are as follows.[94] Despite the demand made by the British government to dissolve the expeditionary troops, the Portuguese refugees requested the continuation of the expeditionary force on the condition that they would go to Brazil and not to Portugal. The British government accepted this request, but only on the condition that the expeditionary force was to go to Brazil and that the Navy would prevent the expeditionary force from going to Portugal. Therefore, although the measures enforced by the British Navy on the high seas led to bloodshed, it was the responsibility of the Portuguese refugees and not the responsibility of the British government. According to them, the measures are justified even if it is assumed

70 The law of neutrality 1793–1918

that the forcible measure of the British Navy were carried out not on the high seas but in the territorial sea of Portugal: If it is assumed that Terceira belonged to the party of Don Miguel, the measures had the objective of preventing actions that would harm the party of Don Miguel, which would not cause any problem. On the contrary, if it is assumed that Terceira belonged to the party of Donna Maria, the British Navy did nothing more than to enter the territory of a party that was attempting an illegal expedition, which would not cause any problem either.

On the other hand, those who favoured the resolution and criticised the measures taken by the British Navy argued as follows. First, they criticised the fact that the place where the measures taken by the British navy in order to prevent the expeditionary force was on the high seas or in the territorial sea of Portugal. It was certainly necessary for a neutral State to take measures to prevent military expeditions organised within its territory from heading to belligerent States, but such measures are only to be taken within its territory or jurisdiction. This is because it is not permissible to stop, visit and search foreign vessels on the high seas or in the territorial seas of foreign States, except the measures taken as an exercise of belligerent rights permitted by the international law of war.[95] Those who favoured the resolution also argued that no military expeditions were organised or carried out in this case. The first ground for this argument was that Terceira was under the authority of the party of Donna Maria, and the fact that the supporters of Donna Maria had gone to Terceira did not amount to an attack against the party of Don Miguel.[96] "The Portuguese refugees went unarmed to a place in possession of their own sovereign."[97] The second ground is that the Portuguese refugees went unarmed to Terceira and "they did not go to make an hostile attack".[98]

In the end, the majority in the House of Commons rejected the resolution.[99]

The issue in this case was whether the forcible measures taken by the British Navy in the seas off Terceira – either on the high seas or in the territorial sea of Portugal – were permissible under international law. However, putting aside the legality of dispatching the Navy and taking forcible measures in the area outside the territory of Great Britain, even those who favoured the aforementioned resolution acknowledged that, as a neutral State in the civil war in Portugal, Great Britain had to prevent the organisation of military expeditions to be carried out against Portugal, and that the measures of prevention were lawful if taken within the territory of Great Britain. Furthermore, there was no conflict of opinion in Parliament regarding the ground for the necessity of preventing the organisation of military expeditions within the neutral territory. That ground is that military expeditions are "acts of private warfare",[100] and if a neutral State does not prevent such acts being prepared within its territory, it may become involved in the war by the belligerent. Regarding this point, Horace Twice in the House of Commons explained:

> If the neutral willingly connived at the damage, the belligerent so injured has no remedy but a war against such injurious neutral. But it is precisely to

The law of neutrality 1793–1918   71

prevent neutral States from being absorbed into the vortex of an existing war, that the rule of their conduct has been prescribed by the law of nations, and if they mean to take the benefits and immunities of that rule, they must also be strict in their fulfilment of its obligations.[101]

In other words, if a neutral State "willingly connive[s]" military expeditions organised within its territory, the belligerent State thereby injured are permitted to resort to war against the neutral State; thus, a State that does not wish to be involved in the war should prevent the organisation of military expeditions within its territory.

B THE PRACTICE OF THE UNITED STATES

Besides the Terceira Affair, which is frequently referred to as one of the *causes célèbres* concerning the law of military expeditions, most cases of military expeditions in the nineteenth century were expeditions organised within the territory of the United States and dispatched to neighbouring States, particularly States in Central America, where civil wars frequently occurred due to the unstable political situations and governments lacking sufficient ability to prevent military expeditions.[102] Among the numerous cases of military expeditions dispatched from the United States to neighbouring States,[103] we will select and examine cases in which the legal basis for preventing the organisation of military expeditions was clearly presented.

i Canadian Rebellion (1837–38)   In 1837, a rebellion took place in Canada, then a British colony, with the objective of separating from the rule of Great Britain. Having been defeated in Canada, the rebels took temporary refuge in Buffalo, New York State in the United States, where they enlisted a number of American citizens as soldiers, took weaponry and ammunition from weapons storehouses of the United States government and organised troops, after which they occupied Navy Island, located in British Canada, which they then used as a base to attack Canada.[104] The United States government acknowledged that the rebellion occurring in Canada was a "civil war", and took measures to arrest and punish under the law of the United States "any persons who shall compromit the neutrality of this government by interfering in an unlawful manner with the affairs of the neighboring British Provinces".[105]

Daniel Webster, Secretary of State of the United States, explained the basis for such measures as follows.[106] The acts of the rebels in enlisting personnel, and acquiring weaponry and ammunition in Buffalo were "military expeditions against the British Government in Canada". The United States government, which was strictly neutral in this civil war, should take measures to arrest and punish American citizens taking part in the military expeditions. That is because: "[I]t is a manifest and gross impropriety for individuals to engage in the civil conflicts of other states, and thus to be at war, while their Government is at peace. War and peace are high national relations, which can properly be

72 *The law of neutrality 1793–1918*

established or changed only by nations themselves." According to Webster, "the United States have been the first among civilized nations to enforce the observance of this just rule of neutrality and peace, by special and adequate legal enactments". And "[t]he rule is founded in the impropriety and danger of allowing individuals to make war on their own authority, or by mingling themselves in the belligerent operations of other nations to run the hazard of counteracting the policy, or embroiling the relations of their own Government". In short, private individuals conducting military expeditions against a belligerent State are tantamount to "individuals making war on their own authority", and if such acts by private individuals conducted within the territory of a neutral State are left unpunished, the neutral State itself will be viewed as participating in the war, which damages the external relations of the government and compromises the neutrality of the government; therefore, a neutral State, in order to avoid such a consequence, should prevent the organisation of military expeditions within its territory, by means of neutrality laws.

ii The military expeditions of William Walker (1853–60) William Walker, an American citizen, organised and carried out military expeditions several times against States of Central America such as Nicaragua, Mexico and Costa Rica between 1853 and 1860. The United States government took measures to arrest Walker and his associates by dispatching the Navy to the shores of those States of Central America.[107]

James Buchanan, President of the United States, explained the basis of taking such measure in his message to Congress in 1858:[108] "The crime of setting on foot, or providing the means for, a military expedition within the United States" is tantamount to "mak[ing] war against a foreign state with which were are at peace" and is "a usurpation of the war-making power, which belongs alone to Congress". The United States prohibited such acts by the Neutrality Act of 1794 because "the Government itself, at least in the estimation of the world, becomes an accomplice in the commission of this crime, unless it adopts all the means necessary to prevent and to punish it". In sum, a neutral State prevents and punishes the organisation of military expeditions within its territory, in order to avoid the consequences of being regarded as an "accomplice" in the "war" made by private persons against a foreign State.

iii The Second Cuban War of Independence (1895–98) In the Spanish colony of Cuba, a rebellion took place with the aim of independence from Spain between 1895 and 1898 (the so-called Second Cuban War of Independence). During this rebellion, at least seventy-one military expeditions were dispatched from the territory of the United States to Cuba, and the United States government invoked the Neutrality Act and took measures to prevent and punish the organisation of such military expeditions within its territory.[109]

In contrast to the cases considered in sections (i) and (ii), which occurred during the period when the institution of recognition of belligerency were not yet established and the legal status of neutrality could be created without recognition of belligerency, in this rebellion, which took place in the period when the institution of recognition of belligerency had already been established, the United States, which had not recognised the insurgents in Cuba as a belligerent, was not a neutral State.[110] Actually, even in the Proclamation of 1895, wherein the Neutrality Act of the United States was invoked, the United States government avoided using the term "neutrality".[111]

Nevertheless, the United States government invoked the Neutrality Act in this rebellion since that Act was applicable not only to situations in which the United States was a neutral but also to situations in which the United States was not a neutral. As the Supreme Court of the United States held in *Wiborg v. United States* (1895), "[t]he statute was undoubtedly designed in general to secure neutrality in wars between two other nations, or between contending parties recognized as belligerents, but its operation is not necessarily dependent on the existence of such state of belligerency".[112] In other words, while the main purpose of the Neutrality Act is "to secure neutrality in wars between two other nations, or between contending parties recognized as belligerents", there are some secondary purposes.[113]

The meaning of the term "to secure neutrality", namely the main purpose of the Neutrality Act, was clarified by the District Court of Delaware in the *Laurada* case (1898), the issue of which was whether a vessel named the *Laurada*, which had transported personnel to engage in military expeditions in Cuba, may be forfeited. The Court, after stating that it is not the purpose of the Neutrality Act to prohibit commercial activities of private persons such as transportation of arms and munitions of war to belligerents, which "involve no breach of a real neutrality" of the United States, held: "The purpose of the neutrality laws is, however, to prohibit acts and preparations on the soil or waters of the United States, not originating from a due regard for commercial interests, but of a nature distinctively hostile in a material sense to a friendly power, engaged in hostilities, and calculated or tending to involve this country in war".[114]

In sum, the main purpose of the Neutrality Act prohibiting the organisation of military expeditions within the territory of the United States is to "ensures neutrality", and to prevent and punish acts "calculated or tending to involve this country in war". Of course, the United States was not a neutral in this rebellion since it did not recognise the insurgents as a belligerent. In this sense, the above-quoted passages of the judgments in *Wiborg v. United States* and the *Laurada* were only *obiter dicta*. Nevertheless, these judgments are important in identifying the main purpose of the Neutrality Acts of the United States.

C ESTABLISHMENT OF THE PRINCIPLES RELATING TO MILITARY EXPEDITIONS

As seen above, while most of the cases relating to military expeditions are those of the United States, excluding the Terceira Affair, there was no objection in State practice and literature to the principle according to which a neutral State

74   *The law of neutrality 1793–1918*

should prevent the organisation of military expeditions within its territory.[115] This is illustrated by the provisions of the 1907 Hague Convention (V) respecting the Rights and Duties of Neutral Powers and Persons in Case of War on Land and their *travaux preparatoires*. Articles 4 and 5 of the Convention provide that a neutral Power must not allow the formation of corps of combatant to assist the belligerents on its territory. According to the minutes of the drafting history, the corps of combatant includes not only those formed by the belligerent States but also those formed and carried out by "private individuals (particuliers)";[116] thus the Hague Convention (V) confirms the principle that a neutral State should prevent the organisation of military expeditions within its territory. The report of Colonel Borel to the second commission states: "It goes without saying that the neutral State must prevent its frontier being crossed by corps or bands which have already been organized on its territory without its knowledge."[117] There was no objection to this statement at the Conference.

The basis for preventing the organisation of military expeditions within the neutral territory, which we have identified so far, will now be summarised once more: Military expeditions carried out by private persons against belligerent States are regarded as "war" or "acts of private warfare". If a neutral State does not take measures to prevent the organisation of military expeditions within its territory, it would be regarded as an "accomplice" in "war" or "acts of private warfare" and might be involved in the war by the belligerent. In order to avoid such a consequence, a neutral State takes measures to prevent the organisation of military expeditions within its territory.

1.3.3 Fitting out and arming of vessels employed for warlike purposes

In addition to military expeditions, the Neutrality Act of the United States and the British Foreign Enlistment Act prohibit the fitting out and arming, within their territory, of vessels employed for hostilities by belligerents. Other States, which did not have detailed and special neutrality laws, also prohibited the fitting out and arming of such vessels within their territories in their proclamations or declarations of neutrality.[118]

We shall identify the basis for the prohibition of fitting out and arming of such vessels by examining the case law of the United States domestic courts and the *Alabama* claims arbitration, which played an important role in the formation of the legal principles related to this issue.

A CASE LAW OF THE UNITED STATES

As we have seen in section 1.1.3 of this chapter, Article 3 of the Neutrality Act of the United States prohibits the fitting out and arming vessels within the ports and other territory of the United States with intent that such vessels shall be employed in the service of belligerents to commit hostilities upon the subjects, citizens or property of another foreign prince, state, colony, district or people. We shall examine three leading cases relating to this provision: The

The law of neutrality 1793–1918 75

Santassima Trinidad (1822); The *Gran Para* (1822); and *United States* v. *Quincy* (1832).

i The Santissima Trinidad (1822) The *Independencia del Sud*, after being fitted out and armed in Baltimore in the United States, sailed to Buenos Aires to go on sale, where it became a privateer commissioned by the government of Buenos Aires.[119] The *Santissima Trinidad*, a Spanish merchant vessel, was one of the vessels captured by the *Independencia del Sud*. The original owner of the *Santissima Trinidad* made a claim to the United States court, contending that the fitting out and arming of the *Independencia del Sud* in Baltimore was a violation of the Neutrality Act, and therefore, the original owner is entitled to restitution as the capture made by the *Independencia del Sud* was infected by the character of tort.[120]

The Supreme Court of the United States considered whether there had been a violation of the Neutrality Act and delivered the following opinion:

> It is apparent, that though equipped as a vessel of war, she [the *Independencia del Sud*] was sent to Buenos Ayres on a commercial adventure, contraband, indeed, but in no shape violating our laws on our national neutrality. If captured by a Spanish ship of war during the voyage she would have been justly condemned as good prize, and for being engaged in a traffick prohibited by the law of nations. But there is nothing in our laws, or in the law of nations, that forbids our citizens from sending armed vessels, as well as munitions of war, to foreign ports for sale. It is a commercial adventure which no nation is bound to prohibit; and which only exposes the persons engaged in it to the penalty of confiscation. Supposing, therefore, the voyage to have been for commercial purposes, and the sale at Buenos Ayres to have been a *bona fide* sale, (and there is nothing in the evidence before us to contradict it,) there is no pretence to say, that the original outfit on the voyage was illegal, or that a capture made after the sale was, for that cause alone, invalid.[121]

The *Independencia del Sud* was already a vessel of war when it left the port of Baltimore for Buenos Aires. A vessel of war, being contraband of war, would receive the "penalty of confiscation" if captured by a Spanish warship. According to the Court, however, if one is prepared for such a penalty, it is free to engage in "a commercial adventure" of manufacturing contraband articles and exporting them to belligerent States, and the neutral governments do not have to prevent such manufacture or export.[122]

ii The Gran Para (1822) In the *Santissima Trinidad* case, the Court has held that the building, fitting out and arming of vessels of war within the United States for export to belligerent States is nothing more than a "commercial adventure", which does not violate the Neutrality Act of the United States. On the other hand, in the judgment in the *Gran Para* case, which was delivered the

76 *The law of neutrality 1793–1918*

day after the judgment of the *Santassima Trinidad* (13 March 1822), and where the circumstances of the case were similar to those of the *Santassima Trinidad*, the Court found that the fitting out and arming of a vessel of war within the United States violated the Neutrality Act of the United States.

The *Irresistible*, after being built, fitted out and armed in Baltimore in the United States, sailed to Buenos Aires, where it was commissioned as a privateer by the Banda Oriental, which was engaged in a civil war with the objective of independence from Spain and a related war with Portugal. The *Irresistible* seized a large sum of money in silver and gold coins on board the Portuguese merchant ship the *Gran Para* on the high seas, after which it returned to Baltimore where the monies were deposited in the Marine Bank of Baltimore. The original owner of the seized monies brought a claim to the court for the restitution of the monies taken from the *Gran Para* as the fitting out and arming of the *Irresistible* in Baltimore was in violation of the Neutrality Act of the United States.

The Supreme Court of the United States, considering whether there was a violation of the Neutrality Act, delivered the following opinion:

> That the Irresistible was purchased, and that she sailed out of the port of Baltimore, armed and manned as a vessel of war, for the purpose of being employed as a cruizer against a nation with whom the United States were at peace, is too clear for controversy.... There is nothing resembling a commercial adventure in any part of the transaction. The vessel was constructed for war, and not for commerce. There was no cargo on board but what was adapted to the purposes of war. The crew was too numerous for a merchantman, and was sufficient for a privateer. These circumstances demonstrate the *intent* with which the Irresistible sailed out of the port of Baltimore.[123]

This judgment, following the doctrine of "commercial adventure" as presented in the *Santassima Trinidad* case, established the criteria of distinguishing between the lawful fitting out and arming of vessels forming part of "commercial adventure" on the one hand, and the unlawful fitting out and arming of vessels that violate the Neutrality Act on the other. According to the Court, the criteria of distinguishing them is the "intent" of the parties concerned: whether the parties concerned (such as the owners of the vessels) had intent to employ such vessels in war, or whether they had only intent to sell such vessels in a market as merchandise. In this case, the Court inferred the intent of the owner of the *Irresistible* from the content and volume of its cargo and crews, and held that the intent of the owner was not of commercial character but of warlike character, and that the fitting out and arming of the *Irresistible* with the knowledge of such intent was in violation of the Neutrality Act of the United States. The doctrine presented by this judgment is more clearly developed in the *United States* v. *Quincy* in 1832.

iii United States v. Quincy (1832) The *Bolivar*, after being fitted out in the port of Baltimore in the United States, sailed out from Baltimore to St. Thomas in the West Indies on 27 September 1827, where it was commissioned as a privateer by the United Provinces of Rio de la Plata, which was at war with Brazil. The *Bolivar* captured several merchant vessels belonging to Portugal, Brazil and Spain. The defendant in this case, John D. Quincy, was prosecuted on the basis of Article 3 of the Neutrality Act of the United States for participating in the fitting out of the *Bolivar* in the port of Baltimore. As stated in the judgment, the war between Brazil and the United Provinces Rio de la Plata was not a civil war but an international war between States, as "the United Provinces of Rio de la Plata had been regularly acknowledged as an independent nation by the executive department of the government of the United States, before the year 1827".[124]

The Supreme Court of the United States, after stating that, in order to find the defendant as guilty, the existence of the intention to employ the vessel in hostilities such as privateering must be established, and that whether such intention has existed is a question belonging exclusively to the jury to decide, explains the reason why there must be such intention:

> It [Intention] is the material point on which the legality or criminality of the act must turn; and decides whether the adventure is of a commercial or warlike character.
>
> The law does not prohibit armed vessels belonging to citizens of the United States from sailing out of our ports; it only requires the owners to give security (as was done in the present case) that such vessels shall not be employed by them to commit hostilities against foreign powers at peace with the United States...
>
> All the latitude, therefore, necessary for commercial purposes, is given to our citizens; and they are *restrained only from such acts as are calculated to involve the country in war*.[125]

This judgment has more clearly than the judgment of the *Gran Para* made clear that "intent" or "intention" is the criteria of distinguishing the lawful fitting out and arming of vessels and the illegal fitting out and arming: whether the parties concerned had the intent to employ a vessel for the warlike purposes (such as privateering), or whether they had only intent to sell the vessel as merchandise.

iv The legal doctrine of intent The results of a consideration of the leading cases regarding Article 3 of the Neutrality Act of the United States are summarised as follows.

Private persons are free to manufacture contraband goods – in cases of vessels war, building, fitting out and arming vessels – within the territory of a neutral State and to export those goods to belligerent States as "commercial adventures". These persons must accept the risk of such goods being captured by the belligerents as contraband of war, but are not prohibited from engaging in such "adventures". And the neutral government is not required to prohibit such "adventures". However, as held by the court in the *United States* v. *Quincy*,

78 *The law of neutrality 1793–1918*

private persons are restrained from such acts as are calculated to involve the State in war. These acts thus restrained are the acts prohibited by the Neutrality Act of the United States.

According to the jurisprudence of the Supreme Court of the United State, the acts not prohibited by the Neutrality Act of the United States – "commercial adventures" of private persons – and the acts prohibited by that Act are distinguished by the "intent": The fitting out and arming of vessels within the territory of the United States are illegal when (1) the parties concerned (such as the owners of the vessels) have the intention, before the vessels leave a port of the United States, to employ such vessels for the warlike purposes (such as privateering); and (2) those who engage in fitting out or arming the vessels know such intent. This doctrine developed by the jurisprudence of the Supreme Court of the United States is known as "the legal doctrine of intent".[126]

John Westlake elaborates this doctrine:[127]

> When a ship or a cargo of arms is despatched by a neutral owner in search of a market, his motive is the expectation that it will find a belligerent purchaser who will use it in war, but the intent so to use it can only be formed by the purchaser, and remains contingent as long as the expectation exists, so that *the expectation is not an assistance knowingly given to it*. But when a ship is despatched from a neutral port by a belligerent owner, his intent to employ her in war has been formed while she was still in neutral territory, so that her despatch is *an act of war* and a usurpation of the neutral state's authority, and any one who has contracted with the belligerent owner or worked for him about the ship *with knowledge of his intent* has *identified himself with it*.

A neutral government prevents and punishes the fitting out and arming of vessels with intent that such vessels shall be employed in war because otherwise it would be regarded as committing itself an act of war against the belligerent.

Therefore, military expeditions, which we have considered in section 1.3.2 of this chapter, and the fitting out and arming of vessels are placed under the same legal principle. Privateering, which is a hostile act by private persons against merchant vessels of a belligerent, is a naval military expedition.[128] As noted in section 1.3.2, a military expedition is regarded as a "war" carried out by private persons against a belligerent State, and if a neutral State does not take necessary measures to prevent the organisation of the military expedition within its territory, it would be regarded as an "accomplice" in the war. On the other hand, according to the "legal doctrine of intent", persons who fit out or arm vessels with knowledge of the intent of other persons to employ such vessels in war are also regarded as being engaged in or assisting the naval military expedition. Therefore, if the neutral government does not take necessary measures to prevent not only a military expedition itself but also the fitting out and arming of vessels used for a naval military expedition, it would be regarded as an "accomplice" in the "war" carried out by private persons. In other words, as

The law of neutrality 1793–1918 79

stated by the Supreme Court of the United States in the *United States* v. *Quincy*, the purpose of Article 3 of the Neutrality Act is to prevent and punish such acts as are calculated to involve the State in war.

B THE *ALABAMA* CASE

i The facts of the case On 14 May 1861, after the outbreak of the American Civil War, the British government issued a proclamation of neutrality, and demanded that British subjects observe the Foreign Enlistment Act.[129] Nevertheless, many vessels were built and fitted out within the territory of Great Britain and were used for hostilities by the Confederate States.

One of those vessels, the *Alabama*, which was initially called "No. 290" but later renamed the "*Alabama*", was built by a ship-building firm in Birkenhead in Great Britain at the order of government of the Confederate States, and after being transported to Liverpool and delivered to the ordering party, it was launched on 15 May 1862 and fitted out at the port of Liverpool.[130]

On 23 June 1862, Earl Russell, British Foreign Minister, received from Adams, United States Minister at London, a note stating that there was the strongest reason to believe that the *Alabama*, which was then being fitted out and was nearly ready for departure from the port of Liverpool and expected to proceed directly to Nassau, had been there engaged in completing her armament, provisioning, and crew for making war upon the United States.[131] In response to this note, the British government promised to immediately refer the matter to the proper department of the British government (25 June 1862), and requested the Law Officers of the Crown to give an opinion on this matter.[132] According to the report submitted by the Law Officers of the Crown on 30 June, assuming that the representation made to the British government by Adams is in accordance with the facts, the building and equipment of the *Alabama* is a "manifest violation of the foreign-enlistment act, and steps ought to be taken to put that act in force and to prevent the vessel from going to sea", but whether these measures are actually taken depends upon the nature and sufficiency of any evidence of a breach of the law.[133]

The issue, then, was whether there was sufficient evidence to support Adams' assertion, and, in this regard, the United States government presented evidence to the British government on 21 July. However, for the British government, this evidence was "very scanty, consisting in reality of the testimony of one witness, who states facts within his own knowledge, that of the other deponents being wholly or chiefly hearsay",[134] and thus the United States government presented additional evidence on 23 and 25 July. The British government requested the opinion of Law Officers on 23 July, who reported their opinion on 29 July. Their opinion was that the proper authorities should seize the *Alabama*.[135] On 31 July, following up on this opinion, the British government ordered the collectors of customs at Liverpool to seize the *Alabama*,[136] but it had already left the port of Liverpool on the morning of 29 July, before the report of the Law Officers of the Crown had reached the government.

80 *The law of neutrality 1793–1918*

Thereafter, the *Alabama* arrived at Terceira of Portugal, where it was supplied with weapons, ammunition, military equipment, coal and personnel by the *Agrippina* and the *Bahamas* coming from Great Britain. After that, the *Alabama* was commissioned as a ship of war by the government of the Confederate States, and captured merchant ships belonging to the Union.

The United States government claimed compensation to the British government for the damages caused by the acts of ships of war that were built or fitted out within the territory of the Great British States, including the *Alabama*. The negotiations between the United States government and the British government over the issue of compensation continued during the Civil War until after the war had ended. In the end, both governments concluded the Washington Treaty in 1871 and thereby agreed to submit the dispute to arbitration.[137]

Article 6 of the Washington Treaty provides for the rules, which are agreed upon by the contracting States, as rules applicable to the case (the so-called "three rules of Washington"). The first rule is that a neutral government is bound to

> use due diligence to prevent the fitting out, arming, or equipping, within its jurisdiction, of any vessel which it has reasonable ground to believe is intended to cruise or to carry on war against a Power with which it is at peace; and also to use like diligence to prevent the departure from its jurisdiction of any vessel intended to cruise or carry on war as above, such vessel having been specially adapted, in whole or in part, within such jurisdiction, to warlike use.[138]

The main issue in this arbitration was whether the British government had used due diligence to prevent the building, fitting out and departure of the *Alabama*. More specifically, the issue was whether, as the United States government argued, there was "gross negligence" on the part of the British government with regard to "the delay of eight days" between 21 July 1861, when the United States government presented evidence regarding the *Alabama*, for which the British government requested additional evidence, and 29 July, when the *Alabama* had departed the port of Liverpool.[139]

On this issue, the British government maintained that the government had employed all the means at its disposal to prevent the fitting out and departure of the *Alabama*. The powers possessed by the British government to prevent the fitting out and departure of the *Alabama* were powers defined by the Foreign Enlistment Act of 1819. One of the modes of prevention provided by the Act was the seizure of the ships. According to the Act, after a seizure was made, it was necessary that proceedings for the condemnation of the vessel seized should be instituted in the court of exchequer and brought to trial before a jury. In order to obtain a condemnation, it was necessary to prove, based on evidence sufficient to create in the mind of the judges or jury a reasonable and deliberate belief, that the fitting out or arming of vessels was done with intent that the vessels should be employed in belligerent operations. According to the British

The law of neutrality 1793–1918   81

government, the *Alabama* had departed Liverpool while the government was waiting for the opinion of the Law Officers, but this was due to the sudden illness of a Law Officer whose written opinion was delayed; thus, the British government had sufficiently exercised the powers available to it, even if it was unable to prevent the departure.[140] On the other hand, the United States government maintained that a neutral government was bound to use all the means in its power to prevent the fitting out and arming, within its territory, of vessels intended to cruise against a State with which it was at peace, if there was reasonable suspicion, even if the grounds for suspicion fell short of legal proof. If the means provided by the domestic laws were inadequate, the British government should have amended the laws, as to put new and more effective means in the hands of its Executive.[141]

The rules of Washington contained a proviso, which provided that "Her Majesty's Government cannot assent to the foregoing Rules as a statement of principles of International Law which were in force at the time when the claims mentioned in Article I arose...". Although the British government accepted the Washington rules as rules applicable to the present case, it denied their status as existing rules of positive international law.

ii Award   The Arbitral Tribunal, largely supporting the argument of the United States, held that "...the government of Her Britannic Majesty cannot justify itself for a failure in due diligence on the plea of insufficiency of the legal means of action which it possessed", and that "it omitted, notwithstanding the warnings and official representations made by the diplomatic agents of the United States during the construction of the said number '290,' to take in due time any effective measures of prevention, and that those orders which it did give at last, for the detention of the vessel, were issued so late that their execution was not practicable". The Tribunal concluded that the British government had lacked due diligence and ordered the sum of $15,500,000 in gold to be paid by Great Britain to the United States.[142]

iii Basis of the Washington rules   In this arbitration, the parties agreed to the three rules of Washington as rules applicable to the case. Therefore, the Arbitral Tribunal could simply apply the rules to the case, without considering the rationale of the rules. On the other hand, the British and the United States governments, in the documents submitted to the Tribunal, discussed in detail the basis and rationale of the three rules of Washington, referring to a large amount of literature and State practice.[143]

There was no difference of opinions between the British and the United States governments as to the principles concerning military expeditions and contraband of war: A neutral government is bound to use due diligence to prevent its territory from being used "as a base or point of departure for a military or navy expeditions, or for hostilities on land or sea", but is not bound to prevent or restrain the export of articles of contraband of war from its territory to a belligerent.[144]

82 The law of neutrality 1793–1918

The opinions of the two governments differ as to which principle – the principle concerning military expeditions or the principle concerning contraband of war – applies to the fitting out and arming, within the territory of a neutral State, of vessels intended for the warlike use.

According to the British government, "[t]he case of a vessel which is dispatched from a neutral port to or for the use of a belligerent, after having been prepared within the neutral territory for warlike use, is one which may be regarded from different points of view, and may fall within the operation of different principles": It may be regarded as "falling within the scope of the principles applicable to the sale, manufacture, shipment, and transportation of articles contraband of war". Or on the other hand, it may be regarded as "being really and in effect the preparation and commencement of a hostile expedition". "But the difficulty of drawing a clear, precise, and intelligible line between these two classes of transactions has always been considerable in theory, and still greater in practice." According to the British government, as there were no States other than the United States and Great Britain that had regarded the fitting out and arming of vessels as "the preparation and commencement of a hostile expedition", the rules of Washington cannot be considered as reflecting existing rules of positive international law.[145]

On the other hand, the government of the United States maintained that the rules of Washington reflected the existing rules of positive international law. The basis for this argument is that the general practice of States has regarded the fitting out and arming of vessels intended for warlike purposes as the preparation and commencement of hostile naval expeditions, which should be prevented by neutral States. According to the United States government, the fitting out and arming of vessels intended for warlike purposes "has been and is regarded as organized war".[146]

In sum, the difference in opinion between the two governments was the difference as to whether, in the practice of States, the fitting out and arming of vessels intended for warlike use was viewed as the preparation of military expeditions (the view of the United States government), or whether it was viewed as the manufacture and exportation of contraband articles (the view of the British government).

From the viewpoint of the United States government, the reason why a neutral government should prevent the fitting out and arming, within its territory, of vessels intended for warlike purposes is explained as follows.[147] According to the United States government, both "the right to maintain peace and to stand neutral whilst other sovereigns are belligerent" and "the right to give cause of war to another sovereign" are "inherent in the quality of sovereignty". "Such cause of war may consist in acts of professed warfare." "Acts of professed warfare" include the capture of merchant vessels and affording aid to one belligerent, as well as the invasion of a foreign State in arms, the reduction of its cities and the military devastation of its territory. Therefore, if *a State* captures merchant ships of another State, the former has committed "acts of professed warfare" against the latter, and the latter has a "cause of war" to the former.

According to the United States government, the capture of merchant ships *by private persons* also entails the same consequences as the case of capture by a State. This is because "in questions of international peace or war, and in all which regards foreign States, the will of the subjects (or of commorant aliens) is merged in that of the local sovereign; that sovereign is responsible if he permits or knowingly suffers his subjects (or commorant aliens) to perpetrate injury to a foreign State". If a State "permits or knowingly suffers his subjects" to capture foreign merchant ships, the State itself is regarded as carrying out "acts of professed warfare" against the foreign State and produces "causes of public war on the part of such foreign State". Therefore, according to the United States government, a neutral State prevents the fitting out and arming, within its territory, of vessels intended for warlike purposes, in order to avoid giving "causes of public war" to a belligerent State and converting itself into a belligerent.

C THE DEVELOPMENT AFTER THE *ALABAMA* CASE

In the *Alabama* case, there was debate as to whether the fitting out and arming of vessels intended for warlike purposes was nothing more than the manufacture, transportation and sale of contraband articles, or whether it was as a part of an organised military expedition against belligerent States. After the *Alabama* arbitration, there were still some writers, in particular British writers, who were of the opinion that a neutral State does not need to prevent the fitting out and arming of vessels, which is nothing more than the manufacture of contraband articles.[148]

However, the prevailing opinion in the period after the *Alabama* arbitration was that a neutral State should, within its territory, prevent the fitting out and arming of vessels with intent to carry out hostilities on belligerents or, in other words, that the rules of Washington reflected the existing rules of general international law. For example, Charles Calvo, in his report presented in the 1874–75 session of the *Institut de Droit International*, surveyed national legislations of various States, diplomatic correspondence between States and opinions of publicists, and concluded that the Treaty of Washington did not create new rules but confirmed the pre-existing rules of international law.[149] In the same session, many other members of the *Institut* were in favour of Calvo's opinion,[150] and the *Institut* adopted a resolution declaring that the rules contained in the Treaty of Washington reflected the existing rules of the current international law.[151]

In the end, the rules of Washington were adopted in Article 8 of the 1907 Hague Convention (XIII) concerning the Rights and Duties of Neutral Powers in Naval War. In other words, States supported the same view adopted by the United States in the *Alabama* arbitration, namely, the view that the rules of Washington were not merely rules applicable to the case but rules of general application.

84 *The law of neutrality 1793–1918*

1.4 Other categories of acts that should be performed or abstained from by a neutral state

As we have seen in the previous sections, in the nineteenth century, States which wished to remain neutral in wars between other States or civil wars prevented private persons form organising military expeditions and fitting out and arming vessels intended for warlike use, by applying their neutrality laws. However, the acts that should be performed or abstained from by neutral States were not limited to the matters regulated by the neutrality laws of States. For example, there was general agreement in State practice and among writers that a neutral State should abstain from providing military assistance to a belligerent, although the neutrality laws of no States provided so.

We will consider main categories of acts that a neutral State should perform or abstain from, and categories of acts that a neutral State may carry out.

1.4.1 Military assistance to a belligerent

It was generally and consistently recognised in State practice and literature in the nineteenth century that a State should abstain from providing belligerent States with any military assistance.[152] Materials and services with which neutral States should not provide a belligerent include arms, ammunition, vessels of war, military provisions, loans and military information, etc. The reason why neutral States should abstain from such assistance was that

> to give assistance to either of the belligerents would be *indirectly to take part in the war*, and would afford a sufficient reason to the one those enemy was thus assisted, for having recourse to force to prevent such assistance from being given.[153]

In other words, as stated by the United States government in the *Alabama* claims arbitration, "affording aid to one belligerent against another" is "acts equivalent to professed warfare" on the other belligerent, which gives that belligerent a cause of war; thus, a State that wishes to avoid such consequences and to remain outside the war should abstain from providing military assistance to a belligerent State.[154]

However, there were not so many actual instances where neutral States provided military assistance to belligerent States during the nineteenth century. Neutral States generally abstained from providing such assistance if they wished to remain outside the war, as providing a belligerent with military assistance would be an "act equivalent to professed warfare" on the other belligerent, which would become a cause of war for the belligerent.[155] Rather, instances that actually and frequently arose were the situations in which despite the determination of a neutral government to observe neutrality and remain outside the war, private persons carried out acts that might compromise such determination of the government, such as military expeditions against the belligerent.[156]

The law of neutrality 1793–1918 85

On the other hand, it was generally recognised in State practice and legal literature that a neutral State was not bound to abstain from expressing sympathy towards a belligerent, although the expression of sympathy was a kind of moral support for a belligerent and discrimination against the other belligerent.[157] The reason for this, according to Bluntschli, is that the expression of sympathy "is not an act of war, nor is it the participation in the war (Blosse Meinungen und Meinungsäusserungen über Recht und Unrecht und über die Gegensätze der Politik sind *keine kriegerischen Acte* und *keine Theilnahme am Krieg*)".[158] This clearly shows that the extent of the acts which neutral States should abstain from is delimited not on the basis of the principle that a neutral State should not discriminate between belligerents, but on the basis of the principle that a neutral State should abstain from acts equivalent to the "participation in the war". Neutral States need to abstain from the provision of military assistance to a belligerent because it is regarded as "indirectly taking part in the war" or "an act equivalent to professed warfare". In contrast, neutral States need not abstain from expressing sympathy towards a belligerent because it is not regarded as the participation in the war.

1.4.2 Limited assistance based on a defensive alliance treaty concluded prior to the war: the so-called "qualified neutrality"

While, in principle, the provision of military assistance to a belligerent is an act contrary to the status of neutrality, there was controversy as to whether *limited assistance* provided on the basis of a *general and defensive* alliance treaty *concluded prior to the war* was compatible with the status of neutrality. In the first half of the nineteenth century, many writers affirmed the compatibility of the provision of such assistance with the status of neutrality, and they refer to the status of States providing such assistance as "qualified neutrality (neutralité limité; beschränkte Neutralität)" or "imperfect neutrality (neutralité imparfaite; unvollständige Neutralität)", as opposed to "perfect neutrality (neutralité parfaite; vollständige Neutralität)", the status of States providing no military assistance to either belligerent.[159] In the latter half of the nineteenth century, writers who supported the conception of "qualified neutrality" decreased, and many writers opposed the conception of "qualified neutrality" and took the view that the provision of military assistance was incompatible with the status of neutrality, even if it was based on a defensive alliance treaty.[160]

Those writers who supported the conception of qualified neutrality argued that an alliance treaty concluded *before the outbreak of war* and *of a general character* – that is, not specifying the State against which the treaty is aimed – did not have a hostile character against any State, and thus implementing it did not violate neutrality. For example, George Fréderic de Martens, in his *Precis du droit des gens moderne de l'europe* of 1801, observes that a State providing limited assistance to a belligerent on the basis of a general and defensive alliance treaty concluded prior to the war "does not thereby announce the intention to harm the actual enemy (l'intention de nuire à l'ennemi actuel), but rather simply

86 The law of neutrality 1793–1918

announces the will to satisfy its obligation [under the alliance treaty]"; therefore such a State is "not treated as enemy" by the other belligerent.[161] Also, J. C. Bluntschli, in his *Das moderne Völkerrecht der civilisierten Staten* of 1872, states that a State providing limited assistance based on "an earlier treaty that has been concluded without anticipating the outbreak of war" is not treated as violating neutrality because "the peaceful attitude (die friedliche Gesinnung)" of such a State is doubtless and it is not regarded as participating in the war.[162]

In contrast, those writers who opposed the conception of qualified neutrality argued that the provision of assistance to a belligerent, irrespective of the nature of the alliance treaty in accordance with which such assistance is provided, is undoubtedly of hostile character towards the other belligerent. For example, in his *Commentaries upon International Law* of 1857, Robert Phillimore writes: "it is idle to contend that either this previous stipulation, or the limited character of the succour can take away the *hostile* and *partial* character of such an action".[163] Pasquale Fiore, in his *Nouveau droit international public* of 1886, also states that the existence of an alliance treaty concluded before the war and the limited nature of assistance "cannot change the essence of the thing for the belligerent against which assistance is provided, because it cannot change the partial and hostile character of the act".[164]

Those writers who supported and opposed the conception of qualified neutrality differ as to whether the hostile character of military assistance is removed by the existence of a general defence alliance treaty concluded prior to the outbreak of war. According to those who support this conception, general and defensive alliance treaties concluded prior to the war do not target any specified States, nor do they have the objective of opposing those States; therefore, assistance provided on the basis of such treaties does not have hostile character. On the other hand, according to those who oppose the conception of qualified neutrality, whether or not assistance is provided on the basis of a general and defensive alliance treaty concluded prior to the outbreak of war does not change the fact that assistance is provided, and the *hostile* character of such assistance is not removed by the existence of such a treaty. If the provision of assistance is of a *hostile* character, as observed by Kleen, "the opposite party, against which the assistance is furnished, has a right on its side to consider such neutrality, which is no longer perfect, as abandoned and void (comme abandonnée et nulle), and the assistance as an actual act of hostility (un véritable acte d'hostilité). And consequently, it may, if it wishes, refuse the immunity of neutrality to the State acting in this manner, and treat such a State as enemy (le traiter en ennemi)".[165] On the contrary, if the assistance is not of a hostile character, the belligerent may not treat a State providing the assistance as enemy. That is why the *hostile* character of the assistance was debated among writers.

It is to be noted here that those who opposed the conception of qualified neutrality did not insist on the *illegality* of assistance to a belligerent, but rather they insisted on the *incompatibility* of any assistance *with the status of neutrality*. For example, according to Kleen, who states that neutrality "is either perfect or void (parfaite ou nulle)" and therefore clearly opposes the conception of

The law of neutrality 1793–1918 87

qualified neutrality, it is "the *moral duty* (le *devoir moral*)" of a State to assist another State that has been unjustly attacked; however, such a State "can no longer be considered as neutral nor claim the advantages of neutrality (préten-dre aux avantages de la neutralité)".[166] In other words, the debate regarding the conception of qualified neutrality was not a debate regarding the legality or ille-gality of providing assistance to a belligerent on the basis of a general and defen-sive alliance treaty concluded prior to the outbreak of war, but rather the debate as to whether States providing such assistance can claim the status and advant-ages of neutrality.

1.4.3 Export and transport of contraband articles by private persons

As noted in section 1.4.1, a neutral State should abstain, *as a State*, from pro-viding a belligerent with goods such as arms, ammunition, vessels of war and military provisions. In contrast, when such goods are exported and transported *by private individuals* to a belligerent, the other belligerent may capture those goods at sea as contraband of war;[167] however, a neutral State is not bound to prevent private persons from exporting and transporting contraband articles to belligerent States. This principle was widely recognised in State practice and legal literature in the nineteenth century, and was codified in Article 7 of the 1907 Hague Convention (V) respecting the Rights and Duties of Neutral Powers and Persons in Case of War on Land and Article 7 of the Hague Convention (XIII) concerning the Rights and Duties of Neutral Powers in Naval War.

What is the rationale of this principle? In other words, why is it not necessary for a neutral State to prevent private individuals from exporting contraband articles, which the neutral State itself should not supply to belligerents?

In answering this question, what is crucial is how to understand the character of the acts of private individuals in exporting and transporting contraband articles to belligerents. Certainly, there were some writers and decisions of the domestic courts that took the view that the export and transportation of contra-band articles by private individuals was an "unneutral act" or "hostility".[168] However, the view generally supported by the practice of States and writers in the nineteenth century was that the export and transportation of contraband articles to belligerents by private persons was neither "unneutral" nor "hostile" in character, but it was simply a commercial act. For example, the Supreme Court of the United States held in the *Santassima Trinidad* case (1822): "[T] here is nothing in our laws, or in the law of nations, that forbids our citizens from sending armed vessels, as well as munitions of war, to foreign ports for sale. It is a commercial adventure which no nation is bound to prohibit."[169] In the *Chavasse* case (1865), the Lord Chancellor Lord Westbury held: "In fact, the act of the neutral trader in transporting munitions of war to the belligerent country is quite lawful, and the act of the other belligerent in seizing and appro-priating the contraband articles is equally lawful. These conflicting rights are co-existent, and the right of the one party does not render the act of the other

88   *The law of neutrality 1793–1918*

party wrongful or illegal."[170] This view, according to which the export and transportation of contraband articles by private individuals are prohibited neither by international law nor by municipal laws but only exposed to the risk of being captured at sea by the belligerents, was widely supported by the practice of States and writers in the nineteenth century.[171]

Then, why is the export and transportation of contraband articles by private individuals regarded as a commercial activity? With regard to this question, Hall explains:

> An act of the state which is prejudicial to the belligerent is necessarily done with the intent to injure; but the commercial act of the individual only affects the belligerent accidentally. It is not directed against him; it is done in the way of business, with the object of getting a business profit, and however injurious in its consequences, it is not instigated by that wish to do harm to a particular person which is the essence of hostility. It is prevented because it is inconvenient, not because it is a wrong[.][172]

According to Hall, the essence of hostility lies in the "wish to do harm to a particular person": Private persons exporting and transporting contraband articles to belligerent States only have the object of getting a "business profit". They do not have "the intention to injure" a belligerent State, and thus do not commit hostilities against the belligerent. In contrast, when a neutral State itself provides a belligerent with military supplies, as "trade is not one of the common functions of a government", it is regarded as being based on an "extraordinary motive", or, in other words, it is considered as an act of "hostility" inspired by the "intention is to injure" the other belligerent.[173]

If the acts of private individuals in exporting and transporting contraband articles to belligerents are not acts of hostility in themselves, a neutral State is by no means regarded as committing acts of hostility, even if it leaves such export and transport unpunished. On the other hand, as we have seen in section 1.3.2 of this chapter, military expeditions, which are also carried out by private individuals, are not commercial acts but private acts of war against belligerent States. If a neutral State does not take necessary measures to prevent the organisation of military expeditions within its territory, the neutral State itself is regarded as being complicit in the military expeditions, namely, acts of war against the belligerents. A neutral State takes the measures to prevent the organisation of military expeditions within its territory in order to avoid being regarded as an accomplice in acts of war against a belligerent, and providing the belligerent with a legal ground for a war. In contrast, as the export of contraband articles by private persons is nothing more than a commercial activity, a neutral State which does not prevent such export is only regarded as supporting the commercial activity, not acts of hostility.

While a neutral State is not bound to prohibit the export and transportation of contraband articles by private individuals, contraband articles are subject to the capture at sea by a belligerent. Today, the legal relations between belligerent and neutral States concerning the capture of contraband articles are often referred to as the "duties of acquiescence" or "duties of toleration" on the part of neutral States. However, writers in the nineteenth century did not use the concept of the "duty of acquiescence".[174] Of course, those writers affirmed that belligerents had the right to capture and confiscate certain neutral ships and goods at sea (including contraband of war). However, in treatises of international law published in the nineteenth century, the issue of the capture of neutral ships and goods were discussed in a chapter entitled "rights of neutrals (droits des neutres; Rechte der Neutralen)", rather than a chapter discussing the "duties of neutrals": The right of neutrals to engage in maritime commerce with belligerents are restricted by the right of capture exercised by belligerents.

The concept of the "duty of acquiescence" has come into use in the twentieth century. But the precise meaning of this concept has not been made entirely clear. When it is stated that a neutral State is obliged to *acuiese* or *torelate* damages caused to its nationals by the exercise of belligerent rights at sea, the meaning of this statement is: While a State would be entitled to demand reparation for damages caused to its nationals in times of peace, "during wartime, a neutral State must tolerate damages caused to its nationals in so far as they are caused in accordance with the law of war".[175] Does this mean that a neutral State can demand reparation for damages caused by the lawful exercise of belligerent rights, but such a demand is merely a *legally invalid* demand (the belligerent is not obliged to make reparation)? Or, does this mean that a neutral State is *prohibited* from demanding reparation to the belligerent, and the demand for reparation in such a case is regarded as a violation of the neutral duty? Many writers seem to use the concept of duty of acquiescence in the former sense. The duty of acquiescence in this sense, as correctly pointed out by Julius Stone, is "no-right" on the part of a neutral State, rather than "duties": According to Stone, the so-called "belligerent rights" are not rights in the strict sense of the term, but rather the "privileges" of belligerent States; and a neutral State has *no right* to demand reparation for damages caused by the lawful exercise of such privileges by belligerents.[176]

There were a few writers and decisions of domestic courts that took the view according to which the demand for reparation for damages caused by the lawful exercise of belligerent rights were acts contrary to the status of neutrality.[177] For example, Vattel, after stating that articles such as arms and ammunitions transported by neutral subjects to a belligerent are captured by the other belligerent but the neutral State itself does not bear any responsibility, states: "If their sovereign should undertake to protect (protéger) them, the act would be equivalent to a desire on his part to furnish such help – an attitude certainly inconsistent with neutrality."[178] Also, in the case of *Seton, Maitland & Co.* v. *Low* (1799), Judge Lewis of the New York State Supreme Court held that in cases where contraband articles and blockade-running vessels have been seized and confiscated by a belligerent State, "the neutral power, by demanding compensation, would avow itself a party to the war".[179] Furthermore, in the case of *Richardson v. Maine Fire and Marine Insurance Company* (1809), the Massachusetts

90 The law of neutrality 1793–1918

Supreme Court held: In cases where contraband articles transported by neutral subjects had been seized and confiscated by a belligerent States, "[s]hould their sovereign offer to protect them, his conduct would be incompatible with his neutrality".[180]

Such a view, however, was not supported by most other writers and decisions of the domestic courts, and the practice of States in the nineteenth century. The prevailing view in the nineteenth century was that demanding reparation for damages caused by the exercise of belligerent rights was not in itself an act contrary to neutrality. According to this view, belligerent States have privileges or rights to seize and confiscate contraband articles in times of war, and thereby the rights of neutral States are restricted in comparison to the rights they have in times of peace.[181]

1.4.4 Passage of troops and the sick and wounded belonging to belligerents through the land territory of a neutral State

Pre-eighteenth century scholars affirmed that troops of belligerents had the right to pass through the land territory of neutral States (the right of innocent passage; *transitus innoxius*, passage innocent).[182] In contrast, scholars in the first half of the nineteenth century denied the existence of such a right and took a view that a neutral State *may refuse* the passage of troops of belligerents through its land territory. But they still affirmed that a neutral State *may allow* troops of belligerents to pass through its land territory if such approval was impartially given to all belligerents.[183]

The view that a neutral State should not allow troops of any belligerent to pass through its territory was generalised among writers in the latter half of the nineteenth century.[184] According to this view, a neutral State should not allow troops of any belligerent State to pass through its land territory because to do so would be to promote the war being carried out by a belligerent State and "to intervene in the war by its very nature".[185]

There was a difference of opinions among writers even in the latter half of the nineteenth century as to whether a neutral State may allow the passage of the sick and wounded belonging to the armed forces of belligerents through its land territory. Opinions of writers differed because, if approval was given for the passage of the sick and wounded through the territory of a neutral State, the troops of belligerent States would be exempted from the burden of transporting the sick and wounded, while on the other hand, the humanitarian consideration requires that the sick and wounded should be promptly taken back to their own State for medical treatment, and passage through the neutral territory is needed in order to take the shortest distance to their own State.[186] In view of such differences of opinions, the Brussels Conference, which was held in 1874 with the objective of drawing up a draft treaty regarding the laws of war, giving priority to the humanitarian consideration, adopted an article providing: "A neutral State may authorize the passage through its territory of the wounded or sick belonging to the belligerent armies, on condition that the trains bringing them

The law of neutrality 1793–1918   91

shall carry neither personnel nor material of war" (Article 55 of the Brussels Declaration).[187] Provisions with almost identical wording were adopted in Article 59 of Annex to the 1899 Convention of the Laws and Customs of War on Land (the 1899 Hague Regulations)[188] and in Article 14 of the 1907 Hague Convention (V) respecting the Rights and Duties of Neutral Powers and Persons in Case of War on Land.

1.4.5 Treatment of troops and soldiers of belligerents within the land territory of a neutral State

Troops of a belligerent, having been pressed back to the border of a neutral State by the enemy troops, might seek refuge in the territory of the neutral State. In such a case, if the neutral State approved of the troops taking refuge in the territory and their subsequent departure, the troops could use the neutral territory as a location for a temporary refuge and could return to their own State at the most convenient time; thus, such approval would amount to the provision of a military convenience to the belligerent State. However, there would be no problem if it were ensured that the troops could not leave the neutral territory and not once again engage in military activities during the wartime. The "neutral asylum" is an institution based on such an idea: A neutral State may receive troops of a belligerent State into its territory for asylum, on the conditions that the neutral State disarms and interns the troops until the end of war. In the nineteenth century, the legality of neutral asylum was consistently supported by State practice and writers. Article 53 of the 1874 Brussels Declaration and Article 57 of the 1899 Hague Regulations provided: "A neutral State which receives in its territory troops belonging to the belligerent armies shall intern them, as far as possible, at a distance from the theatre of war." These provisions confirmed the principle supported by the consistent practice of States that a neutral State might grant asylum to the troops of belligerents on the conditions that it interns the troops.

On the contrary, a general and consistent practice of States did not exist, and opinions of writers were divided as to the following issues: (1) the treatment of individual soldiers escaping into the territory of a neutral State; (2) the treatment of soldiers belonging to a belligerent who were interned as prisoners of war by the other belligerent being granted asylum in the neutral territory; (3) the treatment of goods and materials which the troops being granted asylum in the neutral territory had taken from enemy troops; and (4) the treatment of escaped prisoners of war in the territory of a neutral State.[189] There were no provisions concerning these four issues in the 1874 Brussels Declaration or the 1899 Hague Regulations. As we will see below, these issues were resolved by the 1907 Hague Peace Conference.

92 The law of neutrality 1793–1918

1.4.6 Belligerent warships in the territorial waters or ports of a neutral State

As seen in sections 1.4.4 and 1.4.5, a neutral State may not allow the passage of troops of belligerents – excluding the sick and wounded – through its land territory, and in cases where a neutral State grants asylum for troops of belligerents in its territory, it must disarm and intern the troops until the end of the war. In contrast, different principles apply at sea: A neutral State may allow the passage of belligerent warships through its territorial waters, and may allow belligerent warships entering and staying at its ports without disarming and interning these warships.

While there were various explanations as to the reason for such a difference of principles between land and sea,[190] there was a general agreement in State practice and among writers that a neutral State may allow the passage of belligerent warships through its territorial waters and the entry and stay in its ports, and at the same time, that certain conditions had to be fulfilled when a neutral State allowed such passage, entry and stay.

In the nineteenth century, however, a general and consistent practice of States did not exist as to what those conditions were. More specifically, the practice of States was inconsistent regarding: (1) whether any restrictions should be imposed on the reasons for which belligerent warships entered a neutral port (for example, whether the entry and stay at a neutral port for the purpose of escaping the pursuit of enemy warships should be refused); (2) whether a neutral State may allow a belligerent to bring prizes into its port; (3) the period for which a neutral State may allow belligerent warships to stay at its port; (4) the number of belligerent warships that may be allowed to stay in a single neutral port; (5) whether a neutral State may allow belligerent warships to replenish their supply of war material or their armament at its ports, and if so, the extent to which supply could be approved; (6) whether a neutral State may allow the repair of belligerent warships in its ports, and if so, whether the provision of such repair was differentiated according to the reason the repair was needed (for example, whether a neutral State should refuse repairs if the damage was caused in battle with enemy warships). Taking the issue of (2) as an example, while States such as Austria (1854), Brazil (1861, 1866, 1898), France (1877, 1898), Spain (1861), Haiti (1898) and Honduras (1866) allowed the belligerents to bring prizes into their ports, other States such as Great Britain (1861, 1864, 1866), Chile (1870), Italy (1864, 1877, 1895), Japan (1898) and the Netherlands (1866, 1898) forbade the entrance of prizes into their ports.[191] With regard to the issue of (3), since the British regulation enacted in 1862 during the American Civil war to limit the period of stay of belligerent warships in its ports to twenty-four hours, many other States such as France (1864), Italy (1864 and 1877), the United States (1870 and 1904) Denmark (1898), the Netherlands (1898), Russia (1898) and Japan (1898) enacted similar regulations; whereas other States such as the Netherlands (1866), France (1898) and Haiti (1898) set no time limit for the stay, and Portugal in 1866 admitted stays of "short period of time".[192] In short, the practice of States concerning these issues was divergent.

1.5 The 1907 Hague Conventions

As we have seen in the previous section, during the nineteenth century, a general and consistent practice of States did not exist with regard to many issues such as the treatment of belligerent troops and soldiers in the land territory of a neutral State (see section 1.4.5) and the treatment of warships in the territorial waters of a neutral State (see section 1.4.6).

Under these circumstances, two conventions concerning the law of neutrality were adopted at the Second Hague Peace Conference held in 1907: Convention (V) respecting the Rights and Duties of Neutral Powers and Persons in Case of War on Land, and Convention (XIII) concerning the Rights and Duties of Neutral Powers in Naval War. As discussed below, the purpose of these conventions was twofold: first, to confirm the established rules of international law, which had been formed by a general and consistent practice of States during the nineteenth century; second, to make new rules based on the compromise among States participating in the Conference, with regard to the issues for which there had been no consistence practice of States and no rules of customary international law.

1.5.1 Background to the Hague Peace Conferences in 1899 and 1907[193]

On 24 August 1898, the Russian government addressed a circular letter to the representatives of several States accredited to St. Petersburg, proposing to hold an international conference regarding disarmament and arms control. Russia intended to improve the difficult economic circumstances of the State by curtailing military expenditure through disarmament. However, States other than Russia, despite being in favour of holding a conference, implied their negative intentions towards disarmament. To avoid the conference becoming unproductive, the Russian government addressed another circular letter (12 August 1898) to governments of the States, indicating that issues other than disarmament such as the pacific settlement of disputes and the law of war would be discussed at the conference.

At the First Hague Peace Conference held in 1899, not even one convention regarding disarmament was adopted, although that was the original purpose of the conference, whereas one convention regarding the pacific settlement of international disputes and two conventions and three declarations regarding the laws of war were adopted. However, the issue of the law of neutrality was not discussed at this conference, and no conventions or declarations were adopted. The proposal to use this opportunity to make a comprehensive treaty regarding the law of neutrality came from the Second Subcommittee of the Second Committee, but as the mandate of the subcommittee was limited to making and considering draft conventions regarding the laws of war between belligerents, a

94 *The law of neutrality 1793–1918*

convention regarding the law of neutrality was not produced.[194] In the end, the First Hague Peace Conference only declared its "hope (*væu*)" for the intention to discuss the issue of neutrality at a conference in the future.

Proposals to hold another conference to reconsider the conventions and declarations adopted at the First Hague Peace Conference and to draw up conventions for the issues not covered by the 1899 Conventions and Declarations were made since 1904. At the Second Hague Peace Conference thus held in 1907, one convention regarding the pacific settlement of international disputes, two conventions regarding restrictions on the commencement of wars, eight conventions and one declaration regarding the law of war between belligerents, and two conventions regarding the law of neutrality were adopted. The issue of neutrality was on the agenda for this conference from the beginning on the basis of the aforementioned "*væu*" declared at the 1899 conference. After discussions in the committees and the plenary meeting of the conference, two conventions concerning the law of neutrality were adopted.

We will summarise the content of the Hague Convention (V) respecting the Rights and Duties of Neutral Powers and Persons in Case of War on Land and the Hague Convention (XIII) concerning the Rights and Duties of Neutral Powers in Naval War, and will identify the significance of these conventions in the historical development of the law of neutrality.

1.5.2 Content of the two conventions

A CONVENTION (V) RESPECTING THE RIGHTS AND DUTIES OF
NEUTRAL POWERS AND PERSONS IN CASE OF WAR ON LAND

Convention (V) respecting the Rights and Duties of Neutral Powers and Persons in Case of War on Land consists of five chapters with twenty-five articles. The content of Chapters 1 through 4 is outlined below, excluding the final provisions provided in Chapter 5.

i Chapter 1 (Articles 1 to 10) Chapter 1 of the Convention (V) provides for the acts that a belligerent State is forbidden to perform against a neutral State. According to this chapter, "[t]he territory of neutral Powers is inviolable" (Article 1). Belligerent States are forbidden: (1) "to move troops or convoys of either munitions of war or supplies across the territory of a neutral Power" (Article 2); (2) to "[e]rect on the territory of a neutral Power a wireless telegraphy station or other apparatus for the purpose of communicating with belligerent forces on land or sea" (Article 3); and (3) to form "[c]orps of combatants" to assist the belligerents (Article 4).

Chapter 1 of the Hague Convention (V) next provides for the acts that a neutral State is bound to perform and the acts that it is not bound to perform. The latter category of acts are: (1) A neutral State is not called upon to prevent persons from "crossing the frontier separately to offer their services to one of the belligerents" (Article 6); (2) A neutral State is not bound to "prevent the

The law of neutrality 1793–1918 95

export or transport, on behalf of one or other of the belligerents, of arms, munitions of war, or, in general, of anything which can be of use to an army or a fleet" (Article 7); (3) A neutral State is not called upon to "forbid or restrict the use on behalf of the belligerents of telegraph or telephone cables or of wireless telegraphy apparatus belonging to it or to companies or private individuals" (Article 8). A neutral State may voluntarily prohibit or restrict those acts provided in Articles 7 and 8, but in that case, the prohibitions and restrictions must be "impartially applied by it to both belligerents" (Article 9). On the other hand, "[a] neutral Power must not allow (ne doit tolérer) any of the acts referred to in Articles 2 to 4 to occur on its territory" (Article 5). The acts that a neutral State must not allow include: (1) the passage of troops or convoys of munitions of war or supplies across its territory (Article 2); (2) the erection of a wireless telegraphy station (Article 3); and (3) the formation of corps of combatants to assist the belligerents (Article 4).

Regarding those provisions, there were no major differences of opinions among States participating in the Conference, and no difficulties arose when drafting and adopting the provisions.[195] This was because these provisions reflected the existing rules of customary international law, which had been formed by a general and consistent practice of State practice in the nineteenth century. For example, as stated in section 1.4.4 of this chapter, there were absolutely no objections in State practice and among writers since the latter half of the nineteenth century as to the rule that a neutral State should not allow the passage of belligerent troops through its land territory, which was codified by Articles 2 and 5 of the Convention. Also, Article 7 codified the established principle that a neutral State was not bound to prevent private individuals from exporting and transporting contraband articles to belligerents, which was supported by a general and consistent practice of States in the nineteenth century (see section 1.4.3 of this chapter).

ii Chapter 2 (Articles 11 to 15)   As noted in section 1.4.5 of this chapter, a neutral State may receive in its territory and grant asylum to belligerent troops on the condition that it disarms and interns the troops until the end of the war. This principle was codified by Article 53 of the 1874 Brussels Declaration and Article 54 of the 1899 Hague Regulations on land warfare. The Brussels Declaration and the 1899 Hague Regulations also contains provisions regarding the provision of food, clothing and relief required by humanity to the interned armed forces. Furthermore, the Brussels Declaration and the 1899 Hague Regulations provide that a neutral State may authorise the passage through its territory of the sick and wounded belonging to a belligerent and that the 1864 Geneva Convention applies to the sick and wounded interned in the neutral territory.

Articles 11, 12, 14 and 15 of the 1907 Hague Convention (V), which were substantially the same as the corresponding articles of the Brussels Declaration and the 1899 Hague Regulations,[196] were adopted without any substantial objection at the 1907 Hague Conference.[197]

96 *The law of neutrality 1793–1918*

On the other hand, with regard to the treatment of soldiers belonging to a belligerent who were interned as prisoners of war by the other belligerent being granted asylum in the neutral territory or the treatment of escaped prisoners of war in the territory of a neutral State, a general and consistent practice of States did not exist in the nineteenth century, and there were no provisions in either the Brussels Declaration or the 1899 Hague Regulations. As the preamble to the Hague Convention (V) illustrates ("[w]ith a view to ... regulating the position of the belligerents who have taken refuge in neutral territory"), one of the major objectives of the 1907 Conference was to provide a solution to these issues.

Article 13 of the Hague Convention (V) provides that a neutral State which receives escaped prisoners of war (paragraph 1) and prisoners of war brought by troops taking refuge in the neutral territory (paragraph 2) shall leave them at liberty ("les laissera en liberté"). In other words, a neutral State should not intern those prisoners of war, but it should permit the repatriation of those prisoners of war to their own State if they wish so.

The drafter of the Convention explained the rationale of this article as follows. As regards escaped prisoners of war (paragraph 1), since "[t]he only obstacle to the freedom of the prisoners here referred to lies in the actual power that the belligerent forces which captured them are exercising over them" and such actual power vanishes when such soldiers successfully escape to the territory of neutral States; thus, such prisoners of war should become free, rather than interned.[198] As regards prisoners of war brought by troops taking refuge in the neutral territory (paragraph 2), if the troops of a belligerent were not to be granted asylum by the neutral State, their only option is to surrender to the enemy, in which case, the prisoners of war would return to their own State; therefore, when granting asylum to the troops of a belligerent, the neutral State should liberate the prisoners of war. If the neutral State were to intern those prisoners of war in this case, it would injure the belligerent State to which the prisoners of war belonged: It would then be disadvantaged by being unable to recover the soldiers captured as prisoners of war by the enemy.[199]

iii Chapter 3 (Articles 16 to 18) The German government submitted draft provisions to the Conference, which distinguished between nationals of belligerent States and "neutral persons (personne neutre)" (nationals of neutral States) in the territory of belligerent State and provided for more favourable treatment of the latter over the former. According to this draft, a belligerent State shall not ask neutral persons to render them war services (services de guere) – excluding sanitary services or sanitary police services – even though voluntary; no war tax (contribution de guerre) shall be levied on neutral persons; neutral vessels and their cargoes can be expropriated or used by a belligerent party only if these vessels are used for river navigation within its territory or within the enemy territory.[200] However, a general and consistent practice of States in the nineteenth century was according equal treatment to private individuals within the territories of belligerent States, regardless of their nationality.[201] Therefore, the draft provisions proposed by the German government were opposed by other States[202] and not adopted, except for the provisions defining the term "neutral persons" (Articles 16–18) and Article 19 concerning railway material coming from the territory of neutral States. As stated in the preamble to the Convention, the possibility of settling, in its entirety, the position of neutral individuals in their relations with the belligerents was expected to take place in the future. However, as no treaty that distinguishes between the treatment of neutral persons and the treatment of nationals of belligerents has been made, Articles 16 to 18 of the Hague Convention (V) defining the term "neutral persons" has remained meaningless.[203]

iv Chapter 4 (Article 19) Article 70 of the German draft provisions regarding neutral persons provided: "Belligerent parties are authorized to expropriate or use (à exproprier ou à utiliser) for any military purpose, through immediate payment therefore in specie, all neutral movable property found in their country." Regarding this article, the delegate of Luxembourg insisted that public transportation owned by neutral persons should be excluded from the scope of Article 70 of the German draft, on the ground that public transportation was, unlike other movable property, essential to the economic activities of nationals.[204] As this issue was also related to Article 54 of the 1899 Hague Regulations on land warfare, which provided that "[t]he plant of railways coming from neutral States, whether the property of those States, or of companies, or of private persons, shall be sent back to them as soon as possible", States participating in the Conference, reconciling the German draft and the Luxembourger proposal of amendment, adopted Article 19, which provides: "Railway material coming from the territory of neutral Powers, whether it be the property of the said Powers or of companies or private persons, and recognizable as such, shall not be requisitioned or utilized by a belligerent except where and to the extent that it is absolutely necessary."

B CONVENTION (XIII) CONCERNING THE RIGHTS AND DUTIES OF NEUTRAL POWERS IN NAVAL WAR

In contrast to the Hague Convention (V) respecting the Rights and Duties of Neutral Powers and Persons in Case of War on Land, the Hague Convention (XIII) concerning the Rights and Duties of Neutral Powers in Naval War is not divided into chapters, but it can largely be divided into (1) general provisions (Articles 1 to 8), (2) provisions related to the status of belligerent warships in the territorial waters and ports of neutral States (Articles 9 to 27),[205] and (3) final clauses (Articles 28 to 33). We will summarise the content of those provisions, excluding the final clauses.

i General Provisions (Articles 1 to 8) The Hague Convention (XIII) provides for the acts that a belligerent State is forbidden to perform against a neutral State. Article 1 provides: "Belligerents are bound to respect the sovereign rights

98   *The law of neutrality 1793–1918*

of neutral Powers and to abstain, in neutral territory or neutral waters, from any act which would, if knowingly permitted by any Power, constitute a violation of neutrality." More specifically, belligerents are forbidden: (1) to conduct "[a]ny act of hostility, including capture and the exercise of the right of search, committed by belligerent war-ships in the territorial waters of a neutral Power" (Article 2); (2) to set up a prize court on neutral territory or on a vessel in neutral waters (Article 4); (3) "to use neutral ports and waters as a base of naval operations against their adversaries, and in particular to erect wireless telegraphy stations or any apparatus for the purpose of communicating with the belligerent forces on land or sea" (Article 5).

Next, the Convention provides for the measures to be taken by a neutral State in its territorial waters. According to these provisions: (1) "When a ship has been captured in the territorial waters of a neutral Power, this Power must employ, if the prize is still within its jurisdiction, the means at its disposal to release the prize with its officers and crew, and to intern the prize crew" (Article 3). (2) "A neutral Government is bound to employ the means at its disposal to prevent the fitting out or arming of any vessel within its jurisdiction which it has reason to believe is intended to cruise, or engage in hostile operations, against a Power with which that Government is at peace. It is also bound to display the same vigilance to prevent the departure from its jurisdiction of any vessel intended to cruise, or engage in hostile operations, which had been adapted entirely or partly within the said jurisdiction for use in war" (Article 8). While it is not a matter limited to territorial waters, Article 6 provides that neutral States shall not supply "in any manner, directly or indirectly,... to a belligerent Power,... war-ships, ammunition, or war material of any kind whatever".

Regarding these provisions, there were no major differences in opinions among the States participating in the Conference, and there were no difficulties when drawing up and adopting the provisions.[206] This was because these provisions reflected the existing rules of customary international law, which had been formed by a general and consistent practice of States in the nineteenth century. For example, the rule codified in Article 8 of the Convention, which requires neutral States to prevent the fitting out and arming of vessels intended for hostile use, originated in Article 3 of the 1794 Neutrality Act of the United States and Article 7 of the 1819 British Foreign Enlistment Act, and was applied in the 1872 *Alabama* claims arbitration. Although there was an objection as to whether this rule was a rule of general international law immediately after the *Alabama* arbitration, the rule had become recognised as a rule of general international law by the early twentieth century. Therefore, it was not difficult to codify this rule in the 1907 Hague Peace Conference.[207]

ii Status of belligerent warships in neutral ports (Articles 9 to 27)   Contrary to the general provisions (Articles 1 to 8) of the Convention, there were conflicting opinions among the States participating in the 1907 Hague Conference regarding the issue of the status of belligerent warships in "neutral ports, roadsteads, or territorial waters" (referred to simply as "neutral ports" hereafter),

The law of neutrality 1793–1918 99

and various draft articles with varying contents were presented by different States.[208] For example, "one of the most difficult issues" regarding maritime neutrality was the issue of the length of stay for belligerent warships in neutral ports. As regards this issue, while some States such as Russia presented draft articles according to which neutral States were free to establish the length of stay, other States such as Great Britain, Japan and Spain presented draft articles which provided that, except for exceptional circumstances, the length of stay was limited to twenty-hour hours. And even among the latter group of States, there was a difference of opinion as to what constituted "exceptional circumstances". Such differences of opinion among States were due to the absence of a consistent practice of States regarding this issue during the nineteenth century (see section 1.4.6. of this chapter).

The States participating in the Hague Conference overcame such differences of opinion by "the spirit of conciliation (l'espirit de conciliation)",[209] and the following provisions were adopted: (1) "The neutrality of a Power is not affected by the mere passage through its territorial waters of war-ships or prizes belonging to belligerents"(Article 10). (2) As regards the length of stay in neutral ports, Article 12 provides that "[i]n the absence of special provisions to the contrary in the legislation of a neutral Power, belligerent war-ships are not permitted to remain in the ports, roadsteads, or territorial waters of the said Power for more than twenty-four hours, except in the cases covered by the present Convention" (Article 12). However, in cases of "damage or stress of weather", neutral States may permit the stays of belligerent warships beyond the length of time provided for in Article 12 (Article 14). (3) As regards the maximum number of belligerent warships that a neutral State may permit the stay in a single port, Article 15 provides that "[i]n the absence of special provisions to the contrary in the legislation of a neutral Power, the maximum number of warships belonging to a belligerent which may be in one of the ports or roadsteads of that Power simultaneously shall be three" (Article 15). (4) "When warships belonging to both belligerents are present simultaneously in a neutral port or roadstead, a period of not less than twenty-four hours must elapse between the departure of the ship belonging to one belligerent and the departure of the ship belonging to the other. The order of departure is determined by the order of arrival, unless the ship which arrived first is so circumstanced that an extension of its stay is permissible" (Article 16). (5) "In neutral ports and roadsteads belligerent war-ships may only carry out such repairs as are absolutely necessary to render them seaworthy, and may not add in any manner whatsoever to their fighting force" (Article 17). (6) As regards the supply of material in neutral ports, Article 18 provides that "[b]elligerent war-ships may not make use of neutral ports, roadsteads, or territorial waters for replenishing or increasing their supplies of war material or their armament, or for completing their crews", and Article 19 provides that belligerent warships in neutral ports "may only ship sufficient fuel to enable them to reach the nearest port in their own country". Article 19 also provides that "[t]hey may, on the other hand, fill up their bunkers built to carry fuel, when in neutral countries which have adopted this

100 *The law of neutrality 1793–1918*

method of determining the amount of fuel to be supplied". (7) As regards the bringing of prizes into neutral ports, Article 21 provides that "[a] prize may only be brought into a neutral port on account of unseaworthiness, stress of weather, or want of fuel or provisions", and Article 23 provides that "[a] neutral Power may allow prizes to enter its ports and roadsteads, whether under convoy or not, when they are brought there to be sequestrated pending the decision of a Prize Court".

1.5.3 *Significance of the Hague Conventions*

As outlined in section 1.5.2, the two Hague Conventions defined the measures that neutral States should take and those acts that neutral States should abstain from. The provisions of the two Hague Conventions can be categorised into (1) provisions that were adopted without objection because they reflected the existing rules of customary international law (for example, Chapter 1 of the Hague Convention (V) and Articles 1–8 of the Hague Convention (XIII), and (2) provisions concerning those issues that no consistent practice of States existed during the nineteenth century, and were adopted by overcoming differences of opinions by "the spirit of conciliation" at the Conference (for example, provisions regarding the status of belligerent warships in neutral ports (Articles 9–27 of the Hague Convention (XIII))).

However, there was no objection among the States participating in the Hague Conference as to the underlying principle behind those provisions, that is, the principle that "one of the duties of neutral States is absolute abstention from any aid, direct or indirect, in the operations of the belligerents", which was considered by those States as "a universally recognized and accepted principle of international law".[210] In other words, while there was no difference of opinion among States at the level of legal principles, opinions of States differed when articulating those principles into the form of legal rules, depending on whether the acts at issue amounted to "[direct or indirect] aid ... in the operations of the belligerents". As stated by the president of the Second Committee of the Conference, at the time when the Hague Conference were held, there were "a certain number of generally admitted principles" but "the application of these principles may differ in certain respects in the different States".[211]

Why, then, was it necessary for a neutral State to absolutely abstain from "any aid, direct or indirect, in the operations of the belligerents"? Regarding this point, it is to be noted that, at the Hague Conference, the principle of "absolute abstention from any aid, direct or indirect, in the operations of the belligerents" was often regarded as a synonym with the principle of "abstaining from all participation in hostilities (de s'abstenir de toute participation aux hostilité)".[212] In other words, a neutral State should abstain from providing military assistance to belligerent States because the provision of military assistance to belligerents is equivalent to the "participation in hostilities". The principle that a neutral State should abstain from those acts that would be regarded as "participation in hostilities" closely related to the right of a neutral State not to be

The law of neutrality 1793–1918   101

involved in war by belligerents, the existence of which was generally recognised among the States participating in the Hague Conference.

That the States participating in the Conference recognised the existence of the right of neutral States not to be involved in war by belligerents is confirmed by the following facts recorded in the official minutes of the Hague Conference. For instance, the Committee of Examination, which drafted the Convention (XIII) concerning the Rights and Duties of Neutral Powers in Naval War, as an idea which should be the starting-point for drafting articles, refers to the principle that "[the] sovereignty of [a neutral State] should be respected by belligerents, who *cannot implicate it in the war (ne peuvent l'impliquer dans la guerre)* or molest it with acts of hostility".[213] Also, in the Second Subcommission of the Second Commission, which drafted the Hague Convention (V) respecting the Rights and Duties of Neutral Powers and Persons in Case of War on Land, the Belgian delegate states that "[b]eing themselves strangers to the hostilities they [neutral States] have the primordial right (le droit primordial) to demand that they be not implicated in them directly or indirectly",[214] and there were no objections to this statement from the other States.

The existence of the principle that neutral States have the right not to be involved in war by belligerents is also supported by Article 10 of the Hague Convention (V) respecting the Rights and Duties of Neutral Powers and Persons in Case of War on Land and its drafting history. Article 10 provides: "The fact of a neutral Power resisting, even by force, attempts to violate its neutrality cannot be regarded as a hostile act ([n]e peut être considéré comme un acte hostile le fait, par une Puissance neutre, de repousser même par la force les atteintes à sa neutralité)." The purpose of this provision, according to its drafter, is to clarify that "the use of force by the neutral State with the sole object of resisting an attempt to violate its neutrality cannot be invoked as a *casus belli* by the State responsible for this necessity of a recourse to this extreme measure".[215] The concept of "an hostile act (un acte hostile)" used in this provision, as explained by Bassompiere, means "acts by which a State shows itself to be the enemy of another State; therefore, all acts that permit the latter State to treat the former as enemy, and to declarer war against it". Therefore, if a belligerent State declares war on a neutral State resisting attempts to violate its neutrality, the former would declare war "without the right to declare war (sans droit pour déclarer la guerre)" and thereby would commit a "wrongful act (tort)".[216] Article 10 of the Convention (V) presupposes that there must exist a "*casus belli*" or "hostile act" on the part of a neutral State in order for a belligerent to lawfully resort to war against the neutral State. This is an idea that presupposes the existence of the right of a neutral State not to be involved in war. Article 10, which distinguishes cases where it is permissible for a belligerent to wage war against a neutral State and cases where it is not permissible to do so, would lose its practical value, if a neutral State did not have the right not to be involved in war, and therefore a belligerent were free at any time to wage war against a neutral State.

Neutral States should abstain from any act that would be considered as "participation in hostilities", because they are States claiming to remain outside

102 *The law of neutrality 1793–1918*

the war. The obvious prerequisite for claiming to remain *outside* the war is that a neutral State must refrain from acts that would be regarded as entering by itself *inside* the war. If a neutral State commits conduct that is regarded as "participation in hostilities", the belligerent State against which such conduct is committed may regard the neutral State as abandoning the right to remain outside the war and may declare war against it. If a neutral State wishes to avoid such a result, it is required to observe the provisions of the Hague Conventions (V) and (XIII).

The Hague Conventions (V) and (XIII) were based on the same basic idea as that adopted by the practice of States in the nineteenth century: the idea that a neutral State had the right not to be involved in war, and, in order to enjoy the right, it was required to abstain from acts that were regarded as participation in hostilities. As we have seen so far, and as discussed in detail below, a neutral State is a State abstaining from acts that would be regarded as "acts of war" or "participation in war", and remains outside the war by avoiding giving any belligerent State a legal basis for making war against it.

The Hague Conventions (V) and (XIII), being based on the same idea as that adopted by the practice of States in the nineteenth century, established more detailed rules identifying those acts that are regarded as participation in war, namely those acts that a neutral State should abstain from in order not to be involved in war. For example, it was generally recognised in State practice in the nineteenth century that a neutral State should prevent the organisation of military expeditions within its territory and that a neutral State as a State should not provide any military assistance to either belligerent. Regarding those issues, the Hague Peace Conference could simply confirm and restate the existing principles and rules in the Conventions, and there were no particular difficulties in the drafting process. On the other hand, since there had been no consistent practice regarding issues such as the stay of belligerent warships in neutral ports, the Hague Conference had to establish provisions that resolved the inconsistency of practice. As pointed out by John Westlake, although it is generally recognised that neutral States "ought to avoid acts of war as long as they decline to enter on a state of war", but "the hopelessness of a complete agreement on theoretical grounds between belligerents and neutrals as to what are acts of war, makes positive rules imperatively necessary".[217] It was the 1907 Hague Peace Conference that established and completed such "positive rules" regarding the law of neutrality.[218]

2 The right to remain neutral and its conditions

In the previous section, we have considered the historical development of the law of neutrality leading to the 1907 Hague Peace Conference. As we have seen, it was generally recognised in State practice and legal literature in the nineteenth century that States wishing to remain neutral were required to abstain from certain acts (such as the provisions of military assistance to either belligerent) and to take certain measures (such as the prevention of the organisation of military

The law of neutrality 1793–1918   103

expeditions within their territory), and that they were required to do so in order not to give belligerent States causes of war and not to be involved in war.

If neutral States are required to abstain from certain acts and to take certain measures in order not to be involved in war, then they should be *legally entitled* not to be involved in war as long as they abstain from these acts and take these measures. Otherwise, belligerents would be free at any time to make war against neutral States regardless of the conduct of the neutral States, and the law of neutrality would lose its practical value as an institution defining those acts that neutral States should abstain from and those measures that they should take in order not to be involved in war. As we will discuss in this section, it was generally recognised in State practice and by writers that neutral States had the right not to be involved in war.

2.1 The concept of the right to remain neutral

In State practice and legal literature from the nineteenth century to the early twentieth century it was often stated that a belligerent State was permitted to "treat as an enemy (traiter en ennemi; als Feind behandeln)" any State violating its neutrality (for example, a State providing military assistance to the other belligerent).[219] Such statement presupposes, on the contrary, that a belligerent may not treat as an enemy any neutral State that strictly observes it neutrality, or in other words, that such a neutral State has the right not to be treated as an enemy and not to be involved in war by the belligerent States. If a belligerent State were free to declare war on a neutral State at any time regardless of the cause, it would not be necessary to state that belligerent States are permitted to treat a neutral State as an enemy under certain circumstances.

In fact, it was recognised in State practice and by writers during this period that neutral States had the right not to be involved in war, which was generally referred to as "the right to remain neutral (le droit de rester neutre; das Recht, neutral zu bleiben)". For example, in the *Alabama* claims arbitration, the United States government observes that "the right to maintain peace and to stand neutral whilst other sovereigns are belligerents, is inherent in the quality of sovereignty".[220] Many treatises of international law published before the First World War contained the statement to the effect that States had the right to remain neutral.[221] As seen below, writers who denied the existence of the right to remain neutral first appeared in the early twentieth century. As far as the present author is aware, there were no writers during the nineteenth century who denied the existence of this right.

"The right to remain neutral" means the "right to be treated as a neutral".[222] In other words, as observed by Martens and Vergé, "[a]s long as a neutral State perfectly observes the obligations of neutrality, it has the right to demand that the belligerents States treat it as such (il est en droit d'exiger que la puissance belligérante le traite comme tel)".[223] Corresponding to this right, belligerents are obliged "not to involve the pacific State in the hostilities, either by carrying out hostile acts (actes hostiles) against them or by trying to transform them into

104 *The law of neutrality 1793–1918*

co-operators (coopérateurs) or auxiliaries of war (auxiliaires de la guerre)".[224] In short, a neutral State has the right not to be involved in the war and not to be regarded as a belligerent and, conversely, a belligerent State is obliged not to force a neutral State into participating in the war as an ally or to involve the neutral State in the war as an enemy.[225] As remaining neutral is the *right* of a neutral State, the act of a belligerent involving a neutral State in the war is a violation of the right protected by international law and constitutes a "violation of the rules of positive international law".[226]

The right to remain neutral is the right of a State to *choose* and *maintain* the status as a neutral State. In contrast to this right, there are various rights known as the "rights of neutrals (droits des neutres; Rechte der Neutralen)", which neutral States have *as long as they are neutral States*. The rights of neutrals are distinguished from the right to remain neutral, in that the latter is the right to choose and maintain *the neutral status itself.*

The main examples of the rights of neutrals are the inviolability of the neutral territory and the freedom of commerce.[227] But these rights are nothing more than the rights that States have under peacetime international law. These rights are even subject to special restrictions during wartime. For example, while neutral States have the freedom for maritime commerce during wartime, it is restricted by the belligerent rights of capture, which does not exist in peacetime. Therefore, as observed by Hautefeuille, "the state of war arising between two States does not increase the rights of States that remain neutral", but "these rights are, in reality, diminished".[228]

Nevertheless, it is of benefit for a State to remain neutral. That is because, if a State is forced to become a belligerent, it cannot enjoy even the rights accorded by peacetime international law such as the inviolability of territory and the freedom of maritime commerce. While the territory of a neutral State is inviolable and may not be attacked, invaded or occupied by belligerents, the territory of a belligerent is the region of war, which may be lawfully attacked, invaded or occupied by the other belligerent.[229] As regards the freedom of maritime commerce, neutral vessels and cargoes are not to be seized and confiscated except in certain cases (such as cases when cargo is contraband of war or cases of a breach of blockade), whereas all the belligerent vessels and belligerent cargoes on board, regardless of whether such vessels and cargoes are useful in carrying out war, are subject to seizure and confiscation in accordance with prize law. The right to remain neutral is the right of a State not to be forced to become a belligerent, and not to be placed in the situation where a State loses even the rights accorded under international law of peace. If a State did not have the right to remain neutral, belligerent States would be free at any time to wage war on a neutral State and change it to a belligerent, and to deprive that State of the rights accorded by international law of peace. From the viewpoint of a neutral State, the right to remain neutral means that a neutral State is not arbitrarily deprived of the rights accorded by international law of peace.

In State practice and legal literature from the nineteenth to the early twentieth centuries, the right to remain neutral was considered as a corollary of the

The law of neutrality 1793–1918 105

sovereignty, liberty and independence of States. For example, Geffcken states that "the right of every independent State to remain neutral during a war between other States … is derived from sovereignty".[230] Rivier also states: "The voluntary neutrality (La neutralité volontaire) is the rule, and it arises from independence. All States, being independent, have the right to remain neutral when other States are at war".[231] Furthermore, the United States government, in the *Alabama* claims arbitration in 1872, observes that "the right to maintain peace and to stand neutral whilst other sovereigns are belligerent is inherent in the quality of sovereignty".[232]

2.2 Conditions for the right to remain neutral

Neutral States are required to abstain from certain acts or take certain measures in order to enjoy the right to remain neutral. What we have examined in section 1 of this chapter is the extent and kind of acts to be abstained from and measures to be taken by neutral States in order to enjoy the right to remain neutral.[233] Examples of those measures to be taken by a neutral State include the prevention of the organisation of military expeditions within its territory, and examples of those acts to be abstained from by a neutral State include the provision of military assistance to belligerents.

Why is a neutral State required to abstain from such acts and to take such measures in order to enjoy the right to remain neutral? This was explained as follows in State practice and by writers from the nineteenth to the early twentieth centuries.[234] The right to remain neutral is the right of a neutral State not to be involved in war and to remain outside the war. But if such States carried out acts that were regarded as the "participation in the war", it would either be regarded as participating by itself in the war, or, at least, would be regarded as having abandoned the right to remain outside the war. For example, a neutral State should abstain from providing a belligerent with military assistance because the provision of military assistance was considered as being equivalent to "indirectly taking part in the war".[235] Also, a neutral State should prevent the organisation of military expeditions within its territory because military expeditions are considered as "war" carried out by private individuals against a belligerent State, and a neutral State would be an "accomplice" in "war" against the belligerent if it left such acts unpunished.[236] On the other hand, a neutral State is free to express sympathy for a belligerent State, because the expression of sympathy is "not an act of war, nor is it participation in the war".[237] In sum, if a neutral State claims the right to remain *outside* the war, it is quite natural that it is required to abstain from acts that are regarded as entering itself *inside* the war.

As seen above, the criteria for distinguishing between those acts that a neutral State is required to abstain from and those that it is not required to abstain from was whether these acts were regarded as "participation in the war". Therefore, for many writers in the nineteenth century, the essence of neutrality was not impartiality. For example, Funck-Brentano and Sorel state that "neutrality is not impartiality" but "neutrality consists in the abstention from any act of war".[238]

106 *The law of neutrality 1793–1918*

Bluntschli also states that "neutrality does not mean indifference or impartiality towards the belligerent parties and the progress of the war", and that "the natural prerequisite of neutrality (die natürliche Voraussetzung der Neutralität) is the actual non-participation in the war (die thatsächliche Nichtbetheiligung am Kriege)".[239] Certainly, there were writers who considered the impartiality as an essential element of neutrality, but the basis for this view was that a partial attitude towards a belligerent State constituted the participation in the war. For example, Kleen, who maintains that the impartiality is "a condition *sine quá non* of neutrality", stated that "all inequality in the treatment [of belligerents], in some manner, implicates assistance of war (un secours de guerre) in favour of one of the parties, and, by such assistance a neutral State would *indirectly take part in the hostilities* (aurait *pris une part indirecte aux hostiltités*)".[240] In other words, a neutral State was required to take an impartial attitude towards all belligerents because a partial attitude towards a belligerent was considered as participation in the war or in hostilities, not because an impartial attitude itself was required.

Acts that a neutral State is required to abstain from or carry out, as conditions to claim the right to remain neutral, tended to be referred to as "the duties of neutrality" or "the duties of neutral States" in State practice and legal literature in the nineteenth century.[241] However, Gareis criticised such tendency by stating: "These conditions of neutrality (diese Bedingungen der Neutralität) are *wrongly* (*mit Unrecht*) called duties of a neutral. This is wrong in so far as the neutral, when abandoning the attitude of inactivity (die Inakitivität aufgibt) and taking part in the war (Kampfe), does not violate any duties (keine Pflicht verletzt), but merely change its policy (nur seine Politik ändert)." Therefore, according to Gareis, "the so-called duties of neutrality (Die sog. Neutralitätspflichten)" should be referred to as "the conditions under which a State may demand the respect for its neutrality on its part (die Bedingungen, unter welchen en Staat seinerseits die Respektierung seiner Neutralität fordern darf)".[242] Ullmann also calls what is "commonly referred to as the duties of a neutral" as the "conditions (Bedingungen)" for demanding that belligerent States respect its neutrality.[243]

How should we consider this issue raised by Gareis and Ullmann? It depends on whether it was prohibited by international law prior to the First World War for a State to carry out acts that were regarded as "acts of war" or "participation in the war". As discussed above, a neutral State should abstain from providing a belligerent with military assistance because the provision of military assistance to a belligerent was regarded as "indirectly taking part in the war"; on the contrary, a neutral State was free to express sympathy for a belligerent because the expression of sympathy was not regarded as an "act of war, nor is it participation in the war". In other words, those acts violating the so-called "duties of neutrals" were acts equivalent to the "participation in the war" or "acts of war".[244]

Then, were "the participation in the war" or "acts of war" prohibited by international law? Since a State was not prohibited from entering a war between other States in international law prior to the First World War,[245] acts equivalent to "the participation in the war", namely, acts violating the so-called "duties of neutrals", were not acts prohibited by international law.[246]

Of course, as stated previously, a neutral State providing military assistance to a belligerent would be regarded as "indirectly participating in the war", and the other belligerent may treat such a State as an enemy and may make war against it. As observed by Sir Alexander Cockburn in the *Alabama* claims arbitration, "the consequence of a violation of neutrality is the right of the offended belligerent to treat the offending neutral as an enemy, and declare war against him".[247] In order to avoid such a consequence, a neutral State abstains from acts such as the provision of military assistance to a belligerent.

A neutral State was required to abstain from certain acts that are regarded as "participation in the war" or "acts of war" because it wished to remain outside the war, not because those acts were *prohibited* by international law. On the contrary, assisting a belligerent was a legal duty for a State that had concluded an alliance treaty with the belligerent, and assisting a belligerent unjustly attacked was sometimes considered as a moral duty of States.[248] That being so, it is more appropriate to refer to the so-called "duties of neutrals" not as the *duties*, but, as maintained by Gareis and Ullmann, as the *conditions* for claiming and enjoying the right to remain neutral.

However, there is no great substantial difference of understanding regarding the legal nature of the so-called "duties of neutral States" between those writers who use the term "duties of neutral States" and those writers who criticise the term and used the term "conditions" of neutrality. For both groups of writers, the legal consequence of a violation of the "duties of neutral States" is the right of the offended belligerent to treat the offending neutral as an enemy and to declare war against it, and States are required to observe the "duties of neutral States" only if they wish not to be treated as enemies. Therefore, those writers who use the term "duties of neutrality" often emphasise that States should observe such duties only if they wish to remain neutral. For example, Piédelièvre observes: "Neutrality entails certain duties that the States are required to perform, *if they wish to enjoy the advantages which neutrality gives them (s'ils veulent jouir des avantages qu'elle leur offre)*."[249] Ottolenghi also states that "the duties of neutrality" are the duties States are required to observe, "*as long as they want to remain neutrals (in tanto e fino a quando essi vogliano essere neutrali)*".[250] In this way, the term "duties of neutral States" often had a meaning that is close to the term "conditions" of neutrality, and, in fact, there were many cases in which the term "duties of neutrality" was used interchangeably with the term "conditions" of neutrality.[251]

According to the practice of States and writers from the nineteenth to the early twentieth centuries, in order for States to become neutrals and to enjoy the right to remain neutral, it is sufficient if the conditions of neutrality were fulfilled. It was not necessary for States to issue declarations of neutrality. It is presumed that a State has an intention to remain neutral, unless it clearly expresses a contrary intention, that is, an intention to participate in a war.[252] As regards the basis for such presumption, Fiore explains: "The ordinary relations

108 *The law of neutrality 1793–1918*

between States are those of amity and peaceful commerce. Therefore, it must be admitted that such relations are continued, until the time when they are ruptured by a declaration of war or by an alliance treaty with a State that has made the declaration of war."[253] As identified in section 2.1 of this chapter, the essence of the traditional conception of neutrality consisted in the right of a neutral State to maintain peaceful relations with belligerents, that is, the right not to be involved in a war. As stated by Fiore, as the normal relations between States are peaceful relations, the intention of a third State during a war between other States is presumed to be that of maintaining the peaceful relations with the belligerents, that is, the intention to remain neutral unless the third State explicitly expresses the intention to the contrary.

2.3 The legal status of third States not fulfilling the conditions of neutrality

2.3.1 The possibility of military assistance without entering the war

As stated above, a belligerent is permitted to "treat as an enemy" any State violating its neutrality (for example, a State providing military assistance to the other belligerent). In other words, "the consequence of a violation of neutrality is the right of the offended belligerent to treat the offending neutral as an enemy, and declare war against him".[254] However, to treat such a State as an enemy is the right or faculty – not the duty – of a belligerent, and it is possible that a belligerent State does not treat that State as an enemy. For example, Hautefeuille, referring to the principle that a belligerent has the faculty (faculté) to treat a third State providing the other belligerent with military assistance as an enemy, observes: "This principle, however, cannot damage the right of the offended belligerent not to exercise this faculty, and to consent to regard as neutral the nation that is not in reality neutral, in order to have less enemies to combat."[255]

On the other hand, third States fulfil the conditions of the right to remain neutral in order to remain outside the war by abstaining from acts equivalent to participation in the war, which were not prohibited by international law prior to the First World War. Thus, States not wishing to remain outside the war are not bound to fulfil those conditions. In traditional international law, it was completely lawful for a hitherto neutral State to enter the war on the side of one of the belligerents and assist it.

However, this does not mean that States could not assist a belligerent unless entering the war. It was not prohibited to provide such assistance without entering the war. As pointed out by Pradier-Fodéré, in cases where a third State take "a vague attitude (une attitude équivoque)", belligerent States "do not have the right to demand the other States to declare whether they intend to remain neutral or to participate in the hostilities".[256]

As a result, there may be situations in which a State provides one of the belligerents with military assistance without entering the war, while the other belligerent does not declare war on such a State. The most typical example of such situations is the case of Portugal in the First World War.

2.3.2 Portugal in the First World War

On 4 August 1914, immediately after the outbreak of the First World War, the foreign minister of Portugal told Carnegie, British Minister at Lisbon: "...Portugal had no wishes in the matter, as she would throw her lot in with Great Britain, and would direct her policy in accordance with the advice of His Majesty's Government".[257] The "advice" of the British government was that "[i]n the meantime,... [the Portuguese government would] defer issuing any declaration of neutrality".[258] In response to this advice, the Portuguese government stated that "although Portugal would in the meantime remain neutral, she would not in any circumstances make a formal declaration of neutrality",[259] but at the same time, the Portuguese government were ready to assist Great Britain at any moment if it were necessary.[260] According to the Portuguese government, the reason why Portugal would aid Great Britain was that it did not want a victory of Germany in this war.[261]

Later, Portugal did provide military assistance to Great Britain.[262] Then, both the Portuguese government and the British government regarded the legal status of Portugal as being neither a belligerent State nor a neutral State. For example, the British Foreign Office, in a document drawn up on 13 August 1914, wrote:

> ...Portugal is not a neutral power. She is an ally of Great Britain, she has not issued a Proclamation of neutrality and does not intend to do so. She cannot be considered as a neutral power merely because she is not taking any active part in belligerent operations.[263]

In February 1916, the Portuguese Foreign Minister told Carnegie, British Minister at Lisbon: "Portugal is an ally of Great Britain, is not neutral."[264] Furthermore, the British Foreign Office, in a document drawn up in July 1915, described the status of Portugal as an "embarrassing situation as neither neutral nor belligerent".[265] While the German government made a protest against the provision of assistance by Portugal to Great Britain as constituting "a grave violation of neutrality",[266] the Portuguese government, in consultation with the British government, did not respond to this protest.[267]

Why, then, did Portugal take such a vague attitude as being neither a neutral nor a belligerent? The background to this was the different expectations between the Portuguese government and the British government. On the one hand, the Portuguese government wished to enter the war. It hoped that, by entering the war and contributing to the victory, Portugal would be able to "have the right to make her voice heard when the final settlement was made" (in particular, the treatment of African colonies).[268] On the other hand, the British government, after comparatively weighing the advantages and

110   *The law of neutrality 1793–1918*

disadvantages for Great Britain of Portuguese participation in the war, reached a conclusion that the participation of Portugal in the war would not be of benefit to Great Britain politically.[269] In particular, regarding the expectations of the Portuguese government in terms of exercising the right to have her voice in the final settlement, the British government thought that, if Portugal was allowed to participate in war,

> [w]e should lose our freedom in the settlement of Africa after the war, and might find ourselves faced with the alternative of ingratitude or the surrender to Portugal of some part of Northern German South-West Africa and Southern German East Africa.[270]

The demand made by the British government to the Portuguese government to refrain from entering the war was based on this kind of political decision.[271] However, the British government expected to benefit from the military assistance supplied by Portugal, and it actually received such assistance.[272] Although the Portuguese government repeatedly conveyed its hope to enter the war to the British government,[273] it maintained the aforementioned basic stance of forming its policies in this war on the "advice" of the British government. Portugal merely provided aid without entering the war.

The Portuguese government realised the possibility that the provision of assistance by Portugal to Great Britain, which was considered as "a violation of neutrality", might invite the declaration of war by Germany against Portugal. For example, on 15 July 1915, Soares, Portuguese Minister for Foreign Affairs said to Carnegie, British Minister at Lisbon: "By numerous breaches of neutrality Portugal had given Germany just cause for declaring war, but so far she had done nothing beyond making protests."[274]

Why, then, did Germany not declare war against Portugal? It was because Germany did not want to lose its merchant ships staying in the ports of Portugal. According to the prevailing view of international lawyers at that time, while a third State may not requisition merchant ships staying in its ports, a belligerent State may, under certain conditions, requisition the merchant ships staying in its ports. Germany wished to avoid a situation in which Portugal would become a belligerent and would requisition the German merchant ships staying at Portuguese ports.[275] In March 1916, Germany ultimately declared war against Portugal. That was because the Portuguese government, contrary to the prevailing view, had requisitioned the German merchant ships in the ports of Portugal on 27 February 1916. In other words, while the original reason why Germany had not declared war against Portugal was to avoid a situation in which Portugal would become a belligerent and would requisition the German merchant ships, this reason had disappeared as a result of the requisition measures taken by Portugal on 27 February. Therefore, Germany declared war against Portugal on the basis of the fact that "[t]he Portuguese Government has assisted the enemies of the German Empire since the beginning of the war by unneutral acts".[276]

2.3.3 Settlement of disputes by payment of compensation

As we have seen in the preceding sections, the legal consequence arising from not fulfilling the conditions of the right to remain neutral was that the offended belligerent was permitted to treat the offending State as an enemy and to wage war on that State. A State that was prepared for such legal consequences was free to provide a belligerent with military and other assistance. However, if both the belligerent and the third State wished to avoid such legal consequences, the controversy between them could be resolved by the payment of compensation, not by war.[277] For example, in the *Alabama* claims arbitration, the United States government, which took the view that a violation of neutrality on the part of a third State produced "causes of public war" on the part of the offended belligerent, did not declare war against Great Britain, but submitted the dispute to arbitration based on the agreement with Great Britain and settled the dispute by the acceptance of compensation paid by Great Britain. However, it must be noted that, in order to settle the dispute by paying compensation, it was necessary that both a belligerent and a third State wished to avoid the outbreak of war. Regarding this point, in the *Alabama* claims arbitration, Judge Cockburn, after stating that the responsibility of States for violations of neutrality is not "absolute and unlimited", explained the reason for that: "[I]t must be remembered that the consequence of a violation of neutrality is the right of the offended belligerent to treat the offending neutral as an enemy, and declare war against him. He is not bound to accept pecuniary amends as an alternative."[278] In other words, in cases where a third State violating neutrality refused to pay compensation, the only option for the offended belligerent was to declare war against the third State.[279]

2.4 Theoretical basis for the right to remain neutral

As we have seen in section 2 of Chapter 1, the origin of the concept of the right to remain neutral, or, in other words, the conception that belligerents should not make war on neutral States is found in the doctrine presented by writers in the eighteenth century such as Wolff and Vattel. The theoretical basis for such conception was found in the just war doctrine: According to the just war doctrine, a just cause of war is necessary for a State to make war against other States, and a just cause of war is an injury (injure; *injuira*) inflicted by another State; however, a neutral State that does not provide any assistance to belligerents does not inflict injury against any belligerent; therefore, the belligerent States have no just cause of war and may not wage war against the neutral State.

However, it is generally understood that the just war doctrine was not supported by writers and State practice in the nineteenth century. That being so, what was the theoretical foundation for the concept of the right to remain neutral in the doctrine and State practice of the nineteenth century? We shall consider this question below.

112 *The law of neutrality 1793–1918*

2.4.1 *The just war doctrine and its decline*

Clarifying the legal status of war in international law between the nineteenth and the early twentieth centuries vastly exceeds the scope of this book. However, according to recent studies, there were some writers who adopted the just war doctrine or similar doctrine even in the nineteenth century.[280] For instance, Jean Louis Klüber, in his book published in 1819, writes that "war must be just (juste)", and for a war to be just, it must be based on "the necessity to conserve the external rights (droits externes) threatened to be or already being injured".[281] Halleck, in his book of 1866, distinguishes between *justifiable* and *unjustifiable* causes of war, and states that "justifiable causes of war" are "injuries received or threatened".[282]

As long as the just war doctrine was maintained, the theoretical basis of the right to remain neutral would not be challenged. As stated below, early twentieth-century writers who denied the existence of the right to remain neutral relied on the assumption that international law allowed the unrestricted freedom of States to resort to war. If one did not share such an assumption, there was no reason to deny the existence of the right to remain neutral, which had been recognised by writers since the eighteenth century. Actually, Klüber and Halleck affirmed that States had the right to remain neutral.[283]

However, between the latter half of the nineteenth century and the early twentieth century, the just war doctrine declined, and the prevailing view among writers was that the distinction between just and unjust causes of war was not a matter of positive international law.[284] Oppenheim, for example, in his book published in 1906, states that the alleged rules which determine and define just causes of war "are rules of writers, but not rules of International Law based on international custom or international treaties". According to Oppenheim, although writers sometimes assert "that whereas all wars waged for political causes are unjust, all wars waged for international delinquencies are just, if there be no other way of getting reparation and satisfaction", in actuality, "wars have often been waged by both parties for political reasons only".[285] Also, Hershey, in his book published in 1912, describes war as a "political fact" carried out with a "purely political motive, or as a means of self-help", and states that the justice or injustice of war "belong to the domain of International Ethics or Morality rather than to that of International Law".[286]

As we shall see below, with the decline of the just war doctrine, writers who denied the existence of the right to remain neutral appeared in the early twentieth century.

2.4.2 *Writers who denied the existence of the right to remain neutral*

It was in the early twentieth century that there appeared writers who denied the existence of the right to remain neutral. For example, Oppenheim, in the first edition of his *International Law* published in 1906, while acknowledging that many writers such as Vattel, Wheaton and Kleen assert the existence of the right

The law of neutrality 1793–1918   113

to remain neutral, maintains that "[j]ust as third States have not duty to remain neutral in a war, so they have no right to demand to remain neutral", and therefore there is "no duty for a belligerent to abstain from declaring war against a hitherto neutral State".[287] Cavaglieri also states that "as a neutral State does not have any legal right to demand that its neutrality be indefinitely respected by belligerents", "it is legal for belligerents to violently involve neutral States in the conflict".[288]

The ground for those writers who deny the existence of the right to remain neutral is that "international law in its present development apparently allows nations to go to war whenever they please":[289] Since States are free to declare war against any other State at any time, regardless of the reason, it is impossible to think that only wars against neutral States are illegal.

The appearance of the view denying the existence of the right to remain neutral in the twentieth century was due to the decline of the just war doctrine, which had been the theoretical basis of the right to remain neutral in the earlier doctrine. However, even in this period when the just war doctrine was almost entirely unsupported, there were still many writers such as Rivier, Hershey and de Visscher, while denying the just war doctrine, at the same time affirmed the existence of the right to remain neutral.[290] That seems to be because the view denying the existence of the right to remain neutral had some serious defects, which will be considered below.

2.4.3 Defects of the view denying the existence of the right to remain neutral

The view that denied the existence of the right to remain neutral had the following three defects: (1) It was not compatible with the views expressed by States; (2) There was no State practice supporting the view; and (3) It could not explain the basis of the so-called "duties of neutral States".

A INCOMPATIBILITY WITH THE VIEWS EXPRESSED BY STATES

According to those who negate the existence of the right to remain neutral, whether a belligerent will respect the neutrality of a neutral State, or whether it will make war on a neutral State and thereby depriving its neutral status, is dependent on the political decisions of the belligerent; thus, neutrality is not a legally protected status, but is "a purely de facto situation (rein tatsächlicher Zustand)".[291] The legal issue concerning neutrality is the rights and duties that neutral States have *as long as they remain neutral States*, or, in other words, "the content of neutrality (der Inhalt der Neutralität)".[292] Moreover, the "content of neutrality" is the duties of neutral States, rather than their rights. As stated by Max Huber, "the so-called rights of neutrals" (such as the inviolability of their territory) are not "new rights that neutral States did not have in times of peace". Moreover, neutral States would lose even such rights if the State becomes involved in the war and becomes a belligerent. Therefore, from the viewpoint of

114 *The law of neutrality 1793–1918*

those who deny the existence of the right to remain neutral, the essence of neutrality is "all the duties of neutral States", and neutral States are considered to bear "only burden (nur Lasten)" under the law of neutrality.[293]

However, the view advanced by those who denied the existence of the right to remain neutral was not consistent with the views expressed by States, such as the views expressed by States at the Second Hague Peace Conference held in 1907. For example, as quoted above, the Committee of Examination that drafted the Convention (XIII) concerning the Rights and Duties of Neutral Powers in Naval War, as an idea which should be the starting-point for drafting articles concerning the law of neutrality, referred to the principle that "[the] sovereignty of [a neutral State] should be respected by belligerents, who *cannot implicate it in the war (ne peuvent l'impliquer dans la guerre)* or molest it with acts of hostility".[294] Also, the delegates of States at the Conference expressed the view that "[n]eutrality [is] the *absolute right* of all States", and the view that "[b]eing themselves strangers to the hostilities they [neutral States] have the primordial right (le droit primordial) to demand that they be not implicated in them directly or indirectly".[295] In sum, the States participating in the Hague Conference recognised that neutral States had the right not to be involved in war, and therefore, neutrality was beneficial to States that chose to be neutral. If neutrality was only a "burden" to neutral States, it would not have been considered as "the absolute right" of States that chose to be neutral.[296]

B NON-EXISTENCE OF STATE PRACTICE SUPPORTING THE VIEW

Oppenheim, in the first edition of his *International Law*, states: "[h]istory reports many cases in which States, although they intended neutrality, were obliged by one or both belligerents to make up their minds and choose the belligerent with whom they must throw in their lot".[297] However, Oppenheim does not identify what "many cases" were and when these cases happened. As discussed in section 1 of Chapter 1, in State practice prior to the eighteenth century, neutrality was the legal status created by neutrality treaties concluded between belligerents and third States, and belligerents were free to wage war against third States with which they had not concluded neutrality treaties. It was after the end of the eighteenth century that it was recognised in State practice that third States were entitled to remain neutral even if they had not concluded neutrality treaties. Then, the issue to be considered is whether there were any cases in which it was recognised as lawful for belligerents to declare war against neutral States in State practice since the end of the eighteenth century.

Before considering this question, it must be noted that even those who negated the existence of the right to remain neutral considered as illegal for belligerents to carry out hostilities against *neutral States*, as provided for in Articles 1–4 of the 1907 Hague Convention (V) respecting the Rights and Duties of Neutral Powers and Persons in Case of War on Land and Articles 1 and 2 of the Hague Convention (XIII) concerning the Rights and Duties of Neutral Powers

The law of neutrality 1793–1918   115

in Naval War. The opinions of writers were divided as to whether belligerent States were free to wage war on neutral States and to convert hitherto neutral States to *belligerent States*, and, by so doing, hostilities against such States that were no longer neutrals became legal. In other words, the issue was whether "the declaration of war supersedes the violation of neutrality (La décralation de guerre couvre la violation de la neutralité)".[298]

Cases that prove the non-existence of the right to remain neutral must be cases in which *wars* were waged against neutral States and such wars were considered as lawful in accordance with international law. Cases in which belligerents *did not make war* against neutral States but carried out *hostilities short of war* against *neutral* States neither prove nor deny the existence of the right to remain neutral. Such hostilities against *neutral* States were considered as illegal even by those who denied the existence of the right to remain neutral, unless justified by some grounds such as self-defence.[299]

In the period under consideration in this chapter (1793–1918), there were several cases in which belligerent States carried out some kind of hostilities against neutral States or within the territory of neutral States.[300] Such cases include: (1) Great Britain (a belligerent) bombarded Copenhagen, the capital of Denmark (a neutral), and expropriated the Danish fleet in 1807 (the Danish Fleet incident). (2) In 1813, during the Napoleonic Wars, the troops of the Allied Powers against France passed through the territory of Switzerland (a neutral). (3) During the Canadian Insurrection of 1837, the armed forces of Great Britain (a belligerent) invaded the territory of United States (a neutral in the civil war) and attacked the steamship the *Caroline* staying at the Fort Schlosser, within the territory of the United States (the *Caroline* incident).[301] (4) In February 1904, at the outbreak of the Russo-Japanese War, the Japanese troops (a belligerent) landed in the territory of Korea (a neutral). (5) During the Russo-Japanese War, Japanese warships pursued the Russian warship *Reshitelni* (the enemy of Japan) into the Chefoo port in China (a neutral) and seized it there (August 1904). (6) At the outbreak of the First World War, the German troops (a belligerent) passed through the territory of Belgium (a neutral) in order to attack France (the German violation of Belgian neutrality). (7) In September 1914, during the First World War, the Japanese troops (a belligerent) landed in Lungkow in China (a neutral) in order to capture Tsingtao, which had been leased to Germany (the enemy of Japan), and the seized the Shantung railways. (8) During the First World War, the troops of the Allied Powers landed in and occupied Salonika of Greece (a neutral) (from October 1915 to February 1916).

It is not necessarily clear whether those hostilities by the belligerents against the neutral States were carried out as *wars*;[302] rather, many of the hostilities can be interpreted as being carried out not as wars. For example, with regard to the cases (7) and (8), China entered the First World War on 14 August 1917 and Greece on 2 July 1917.[303] This means that, when the hostilities were carried out and immediately thereafter (in September 1914 in the case of China, and from October 1915 to February 1916 in the case of Greece), China and Greece were

116 *The law of neutrality 1793–1918*

not yet belligerents, and that the hostilities against these States were not conducted as wars.

In contrast, there are some cases in which the hostilities against neutral States are considered as being carried out as wars. For example, as regards the case (1) (the Danish Fleet Incident), Taoka states: "As a result of the battles [that was fought between Denmark and the United Kingdom from August to October 1807], Denmark and England *entered a state of war*."[304] Also, as regards the case (6) (the German Violation of Belgian Neutrality), some writers maintain that the notification by the German government to the Belgian government made on 2 August 1914, demanding permission for the German troops to pass through the Belgian territory was an *ultimatum*, and as a result of its refusal by the Belgian government (3 August 1914), a state of war was created between Germany and Belgium.[305]

However, even if some of the hostilities against neutral States were conducted as wars, what is crucial is that there was no single case in which a war by a belligerent against a neutral was considered as lawful at any time; rather, belligerents always attempted to justify their acts by invoking some grounds. For example, regarding case (1), the British government, facing criticism in Parliament for having committed "a violation of neutrality" and a "violation of international law", attempted to justify the acts of the British navy as a measure of "necessity" or "self-protection" in response to the imminent threat of the capture of the Danish fleet by France.[306] In the case (6) (the German violation of Belgian neutrality), the German government attempted to justify its acts by asserting that, as the French army intended to attack the west side of Germany by passing through the territory of Belgium, and, as Belgium was unable to resist this, it was necessary for Germany to invade Belgian territory before France would do so for "self-preservation (Selbsterhaltung)" and the "legitimate defence (Notwehr)" of Germany.[307]

Also, in the cases wherein the hostilities by belligerents against neutral States were conducted not as wars and in those wherein this was not clear, belligerent States always made some kind of justification, and there was no single case in which belligerents took a view that the hostilities against neutral States were always lawful if carried out as wars. When carrying out hostilities against neutral States, belligerents have always attempted to justify their actions by invoking such grounds as self-preservation, necessity, self-defence,[308] consent given by a neutral State,[309] or a violation of neutrality on the part of a neutral State.[310]

In sum, in the period from the end of the eighteenth to the early twentieth centuries, there are no cases that prove the non-existence of the right to remain neutral. To the best of the author's knowledge, there have been no cases in which it was asserted that war against neutral States is always free, and no such cases have been shown by any writer who denies the existence of the right to remain neutral.[311]

The law of neutrality 1793–1918 117

C INABILITY TO EXPLAIN THE BASIS FOR THE DUTIES OF NEUTRAL STATES

The third and most crucial defect of the view negating the existence of the right to remain neutral is that it was unable to explain the basis of the so-called "duties of neutral States". As we have seen so far, according to the traditional doctrine of neutrality, which originated in eighteenth-century writers and was accepted by the practice of States and writers in the nineteenth century, the basis of the so-called "duties of neutral States" are explained as follows: A neutral State should abstain from certain acts such as the provisions of military assistance to a belligerent, because such acts were regarded as acts equivalent to "the participation in the war" or "acts of war" against the other belligerent, which gives that belligerent "a cause of war"; therefore, if a neutral State wished to avoid giving the belligerent a cause of war and to enjoy the right to remain neutral, it was required to observe the so-called "duties of neutral State". Such explanation, however, cannot be maintained if one negates the existence of the right to remain neutral. According to those who denied the existence of the "right to remain neutral", belligerent States were free at any time to make war against neutral States *regardless of the acts taken by neutral States*. They could not explain that States should observe "the duties of neutral States" in order not to be involved in war. That being so, they should have presented some kind of new explanation as to the reason why neutral States should observe "the duties of neutral States", but no such explanation was presented by most writers who negated the existence of the right to remain neutral. For example, Oppenheim and Cavaglieri did not offer any explanation on this point.[312]

However, there were a few writers who tried to explain this point. For example, in his article published in 1918, Alex Lifschütz, who denied the existence of the right to remain neutral,[313] observes that the principle underlying the law of neutrality is that "no neutral States must aid belligerent States either directly or indirectly", and that this principle is based on "the idea of bringing to an end as quickly as possible any war that breaks out", that is, the "shortening of the war (Die Abkürzung der Kriege)".[314] In other words, according to him, the duties of neutrality are based on the idea of ending the war as quickly as possible by not providing goods to either belligerent that would be useful in the execution of war.

This explanation by Lifschütz, however, contained a fatal flaw. If the purpose of the duties of neutrality were to shorten the war, as explained by Lifschütz, the supply of contraband articles by private individuals to belligerent States should also be inconsistent with this purpose, and neutral States should prevent it (Lifschütz did actually assert so[315]). However, according to the existing rules of positive international law at that time, private individuals were free to export and transport contraband articles to belligerents as long as they were prepared for the risk of capture by belligerents, and neutral States were not obliged to prevent such export and transport.[316] Lifschütz, who

118 *The law of neutrality 1793–1918*

criticized such rules as a proposal of *lex ferenda*,[317] was unable to explain the basis of the existing rules of positive international law. Therefore, Lifschütz's argument about the basis of the duties of neutral States was completely unsupported by other writers.

2.4.4 Limitations on war by the concept of the causes of war

In view of the aforementioned defects of the view negating the existence of the right to remain neutral, it was natural that many writers in the early twentieth century still affirmed its existence.[318] The issue was how to explain the theoretical basis of the right to remain neutral, which had once been based on the just war doctrine, in the early twentieth century, a time when the just war doctrine was almost entirely unsupported. As regards this issue, Charles de Visscher presented remarkable arguments in his articles in 1916 and 1917.[319]

A ARGUMENTS OF DE VISSCHER

In his articles published in 1916 and 1917, de Visscher argues that cases in which a State resorts to war against another State should be divided into two categories. The first is cases in which State A, for example, declares war on State B in order to acquire part of the territory of State B, which is a case of "*direct* aggression that arises from completely individual disputes between the two States (l'aggression *directe*, née d'un différend absolument personnel aux deux Puissances)". The second is cases in which State A, which is already at war with State B (the war in the first case), declares war on State C in order to use the territory of State C as a base for military operations to attack State B, in which "the attack is not an *immediate* and *direct* consequence of the individual disputes between the two States involved (aggression n'est pas la suite *immédiate* et *directe* d'un différend *personnel* aux deux parties)".[320]

According to de Visscher, in the first category of cases, "[i]t is perfectly – and unfortunately – true that in the actual state of international relations, *in a conflict limited to the two principal parties (un conflit limité aux deux parties principales), the cause of war does not matter*". "The ancient discussion on the distinction between just and unjust wars is a matter outside modern positive international law."[321]

On the other hand, according to de Visscher, in the second category of cases, the war of State A against the neutral State C is "an *illegitimate extension (extention illégitime) of military operations to her territory*",[322] which is "a violation of the rules of positive international law".[323] Such a war is an extension of the war against "*the States that intend to remain outside the dispute (les Etats qui entendent rester étranger à leur différend)*", and the protection of third States unrelated to the dispute from an extension of the war is the purpose of the law of neutrality. In other words, the law of neutrality "protects the right of *third States* not to be involved in war (de protegér le droit d'une *troisième Puissance* de n'être pas impliquée dans la guerre)".[324]

The law of neutrality 1793–1918 119

De Visscher maintains that war is restricted by the "dispute (différend)", which is the origin and source of the war (cause of war), and the right of neutral States not to be involved in war is based on the concept of the causes of war. According to de Visscher, in view of the reality of international relations, international law has to tolerate the resort to war by a State against another State in order to resolve disputes or issues between these States. That is why the rules of positive international law that distinguishes between just and unjust causes of war has not yet been established. However, since war is an ultimate means of resolving disputes or issues with other States, war must be limited to the relationship between the those States involved in the dispute. For example, when State A demands the cession of some of the territory of State B, which State B refuses, State A may declare war in order to enforce its demand on State B. However, in the war that breaks out due to the dispute over the cession of the territory of State B, State A does not have reasons to wage war on State C, which is unrelated to this dispute. Based solely on the need for military operations – for example, the need to pass through the territory of State C in order to attack State B – it is not permissible to extend the war to State C, which is unrelated to the dispute. In other words, according to de Visscher, even if just and unjust causes of war cannot be distinguished, it is still possible to identify the causes of war, which limit the war to the States involved in the dispute.

B CONCEPT OF THE CAUSES OF WAR

As discussed above, de Visscher clearly denies the just war doctrine, which distinguishes between just and unjust causes of war. However, he affirms that the causes of war themselves can be identified, which form the basis of the right to remain neutral (the right of neutral States not to be involved in war). Thus, the concept of the causes of war is a crucial and essential concept in the traditional law of neutrality. We shall further elaborate this concept, with reference to writers other than de Visscher in this period.

There were writers other than de Visscher who clearly denied the just war doctrine while at the same time assuming the concept of the causes of war. For example, Hershey, for whom the justice or injustice of war "belong to the domain of International Ethics or Morality rather than to that of International Law", stated that the major causes of modern wars were: (1) the desire for commercial or colonial expansion; (2) the desire to secure or maintain political or racial supremacy in certain quarters of the globe; (3) the motives of humanity mixed with considerations of political and commercial interest; (4) the desire for the realisation of a more perfect nationality; (5) wars of conquest or aggression; (6) the suppression of revolutionary or democratic movements; (7) wars of self-preservation and (8) wars for political independence.[325] Also, Oppenheim, who maintained that there existed no rule of positive international law that distinguished just and unjust causes of war, wrote that there were innumerable causes of war, including "the necessity upon a State of acquiring more territory" and "the desire for national unity", as discussed in the section entitled "Causes of War".[326]

120 *The law of neutrality 1793–1918*

De Visscher's theory of neutrality is an idea that the causes of war thus identified limit the personal scope of a war. For example, when State A demands the cession of some of the territory of State B, which State B refuses, State A may declare war on State B in order to enforce its demand, which is a sufficient cause for war to be waged against State B. However, war cannot be declared on State C (a neutral State), which is unrelated to this cause of war. By identifying the causes of war in this way, the personal scope of war is restricted to State A and State B.

The causes of war restrict not only the personal scope of war but also, *theoretically*, the "ends of war", which thereby restricts the temporal scope of the war. As stated by Oppenheim, "[t]he cause or causes of war determine at its inception the ends of such war". "Ends of war" refers to "those objects for the realisation of which a war is made". Theoretically, "a belligerent [must] stop the war when his opponent is ready to concede the object for which war was made". However, according to Oppenheim, there was no rule of positive international law that prohibited the alteration or modification of the ends of war, and a belligerent was allowed to continue the war even in cases where the ends of war at the start of the war had been achieved.[327]

To put the above in other words, those writers who affirmed the existence of the right to remain neutral and those writers who negated it in the early twentieth century, although having different conclusions about the law of neutrality, shared the same basic idea about the concept of war. Of de Visscher, Hershey and Oppenheim, although the former two affirmed the right to remain neutral, and Oppenheim denied it, all three writers shared the same opinions with regard to the concept of war: (1) Rules of positive international law that distinguished between just and unjust causes of war had not been established, and the distinction of this point was an issue of "International Ethics or Morality" rather than that of international law and was "outside law" (denial of the just war doctrine). (2) However, the causes of war itself could be identified. For example, when State A demands the cession of some of the territory of State B, which State B refuses, State A may declare war on State B in order to enforce its demand. In this case, the cause of war is the controversy over the cession of territory between State A and State B. (3) The concept of the causes of war, at least in theory, restricts the personal and temporal scope the war. In the example above, in a war that starts over the controversy of the cession of a territory, State A must end the war as soon as it has acquired the territory demanded from State B (restriction on the temporal scope of war), and State A must not involve State C (neutral State), which is unrelated to the controversy.[328] As noted earlier, Oppenheim also recognised that the cause of war restricts the temporal scope of a war in theory. However, while recognising that the cause of war theoretically restricts the temporal and personal scope of a war, Oppenheim denied the existence of positive rules that limited the temporal and personal scope of war, in view of the fact that such limitation was not observed in the actual practice of States.[329] On the contrary, de Visscher and Hershey were of view that the restrictions on the personal scope of war by the causes of war were reflected in rules of positive international law.[330]

The law of neutrality 1793–1918 121

The idea that the personal scope of war was restricted by the causes of war was a suitable idea for the reality of international relations in the nineteenth century. In the nineteenth century, States did actually resort to war in order to resolve disputes or controversies in their relationships with other States. However, belligerent States refrained from extending the war to States that were unrelated to the original dispute or controversy that caused the war. During this period, wars between States were restrained as far as possible, and in cases where war did break out, the territorial scope of war was limited as much as possible in order not to extend the States involved. Even if it was inevitable that States would resort to war in order to resolve controversies in their relationships with other States, war for the sake of resolving controversies should be limited to States involved in the controversy, and it was not to be extended to unrelated States. The main cause of such restrictions on war was the sense of fear that was shared among the European Great Powers regarding war as a cause of revolution, which was based on the experience of the French Revolutionary and Napoleonic Wars, so war was prevented from being unreasonably extended. Even after the fear of revolution dissipated in the latter half of the nineteenth century, the extension and prolongation of wars were considered as causing interventions by other Great Powers, by which the result of a victory might be deprived, and therefore should be avoided as far as possible.[331]

Notes

1 The "General Chronological List" of the *Consolidated Treaty Series* compiled by Parry confirms that although neutrality treaties were concluded until 1805, the conclusion of such treaties ceased after 1805. The neutrality treaties included in this list during the period from 1790 to 1918 are as follows: (1) Treaty of Peace and Neutrality between France and Solms, signed at Offenbach, 19 October 1800, *CTS* 55:395–398, (2) Treaty of Peace and Neutrality between France and Wied, signed at Offenbach, 22 October 1800, ibid., 399–402, (3) Treaty of Peace and Neutrality between France and Hesse-Homburg, signed at Offenbach, 23 October 1800, ibid., 403–406, (4) Convention of Peace and Neutrality between Erbach and France, signed at Offenbach, 20 November 1800, ibid., 407–410, (5) Convention of Neutrality and Subsidy between France and Spain, signed at Paris, 19 October 1803, *CTS* 57:201–205, (6) Convention respecting Neutrality and Subsidies between France and Portugal, signed at Lisbon, 19 March 1804, ibid., 327–370, (7) Treaty of Neutrality between France and the Two Sicilies, signed at Paris, 21 September 1805, *CTS* 58:211–214. The "General Chronological List" was compiled not only from the *Consolidated Treaty Series* but also from other treaty compilations, and it is considered that this list includes almost all treaties concluded during this period.
2 Miele, *L'estraneità ai conflitti armati*, 2:178.
3 Even prior to 1793, the practice of maintaining neutrality by enacting municipal laws without concluding neutrality treaties with belligerents existed. For example, in the American War of Independence (1775–83), Italian states such as Tuscany, the Papal States, the Republic of Genoa and the Republic of Venice, in order to maintain neutrality in the war, enacted municipal laws that forbade the arming of warships or privateers in their ports. See Regolamento fatto per il Gran Duca di Toscana toccante la navigazione e il commercio in tempo di guerra del 1. Agosto 1778, in Martens, *Recueil de traités*, 3:24–35; Edito del Papa toccante la navigazione e il

122 *The law of neutrality 1793–1918*

commercio in tempo di guerra d. 4. Mars 1779, in ibid., 52–59; Edito della Repubblica di Gênova toccante la navigazione e il commercio in tempo di guerra del 1. Juill. 1779, in ibid., 64–73; Edito della republica di Venezia toccante la navigazione e il commercio in tempo di guerra del 9. Sept. 1779, in ibid., 74–87. As discussed in section 1.1 and 1.2 of this chapter, neutrality laws enacted by several States in the nineteenth century also forbade the arming of vessels in their ports. In this sense, municipal laws enacted by Italian States in the American War of Independence are certainly the origins of the law of neutrality. However, initially, other States were unaware of these laws of the Italian States. See Hyneman, *First American Neutrality*, 16. Rather, the model for nineteenth-century State practice was the practice of the United States in the French Revolutionary Wars. For instance, among a large number of State practice cited by the governments of Great Britain and the United States in the *Alabama* claims arbitration (1872), the oldest practice was that of the United States in 1793. See Case of the United States, *PRTW* 1:47–88; Case of Great Britain, *PRTW* 1:236–269; Counter Case of the United States, *PRTW* 1:417–856, *PRTW* 2:1–196; Counter Case of Great Britain, *PRTW* 2:197–410; Argument of the United States, *PRTW* 3:5–51. Thus, in terms of the strength of influence on later practice, it seems to be justified to start the examination of State practice from that of the United States in 1793 while not considering the practice of Italian States in the American War of Independence in further detail. In addition, with regard to the practice of Italian States in the American War of Independence, no materials are available other than the texts of the municipal laws; therefore, no further consideration can be provided beyond what is contained in this footnote.

4 Hershey, *Essentials of International Public Law*, 453. Indeed, the theory of neutrality presented by eighteenth-century writers, especially that of Vattel, was frequently cited in judgments of domestic courts, diplomatic documents and parliamentary debates of many States from the end of the eighteenth century to the first half of the nineteenth century. See e.g. Henfield's Case, 11 F. Cas. 1099, 1107–1108, 1117–1118 (C.C.D. Pa. 1793) (No. 6,360); Jefferson to Morris, 16 August 1793, *American State Papers*, 1, *Foreign Relations* 1:168; *Hansard Parliamentary Debates*, 1st ser., vol. 40 (1819), cols. 1096–1097, 1246, 1407, 1413.

5 For further details regarding the practice of the United States concerning neutrality in the French Revolutionary Wars, see Hyneman, "Neutrality during the European Wars", 279–309; Hyneman, *First American Neutrality*; Thomas, *American Neutrality in 1793*.

6 By the President of the United States of America; A Proclamation, *American State Papers*, 1, *Foreign Relations* 1:140.

7 See Walker, *Science of International Law*, 431.

8 Privateering is the practice in which States authorise private individuals to conduct maritime capture, by issuing a commission (letters of marque), and permit them to appropriate captured vessels and cargoes after prize procedure. Privateering was abolished by the 1856 Declaration of Paris, to which States such as the United States and Spain did not accede. For further details regarding privateering, see Stark, *Abolition of Privateering*, 1–160.

9 Henfield's Case, 11 F. Cas. 1099, 1099–1122 (C.C.D. Pa. 1793) (No. 6,360).

10 Id., at 1101, 1116.

11 Id., at 1111.

12 Id., at 1104.

13 Id., at 1108.

14 Id., at 1117.

15 Id.

16 Id., at 1103–1104, 1108–1109, 1116–1117.

17 Id., at 1102, 1107, 1120; Jefferson to Morris, 16 August 1793, *American State Papers*, 1, *Foreign Relations* 1:167–172.

The law of neutrality 1793–1918 123

18 Unemura, *Relationship between International Law and Municipal Law*, 210–219 [in Japanese].

19 *Henfield's Case*, at 1119.

20 Unemura, *Relationship between International Law and Municipal Law*, 204–240 [in Japanese].

21 U.S. Const. Art. 1, § 8, cl. 10.

22 *Henfield's Case*, at 1120–1122.

23 An Act in addition to the Act for the Punishment of Certain Crimes against the United States, 5 June 1794, in Deák and Jessup, *Collection*, 2:1079–1083.

24 See Dumbauld, "Neutrality Laws of the United States", 262–263.

25 Message of the President, 26 December 1816, *PRTW* 1:465.

26 Gelston v. Hoyt, 16 U.S. (3 Wheat.) 246, 323–324 (1818).

27 An Act More Effectually to Preserve the Neutral Relations of the United States, 3 March 1817, in Deák and Jessup, *Collection*, 2:1084.

28 An Act in addition to the "Act for the Punishment of Certain Crimes against the United States" and to Repeal the Acts Therein Mentioned, 20 April 1818, in Deák and Jessup, *Collection*, 2:1085–1086.

29 An Act "to Prevent the Enlistment or Engagement of His Majesty's Subjects to Serve in Foreign Service, and the Fitting Out or Equipping, in His Majesty's Dominions, Vessels for Warlike Purposes, without His Majesty's License", 3 July 1819, in Deák and Jessup, *Collection*, 1:125–133.

30 Acts that are prohibited by the Foreign Enlistment Act are those performed "without the leave or licence of His Majesty, His Heirs or Successors". This indicates, on the contrary, that a King or Queen can permit private individuals to perform acts that are prohibited by the Foreign Enlistment Act. Such permission was actually given in the Spanish Civil War in 1835. Order in Council Permitting British Subjects to Engage in the Military and Naval Service of Spain, 10 June 1835, in Deák and Jessup, *Collection*, 1:170–171.

31 On the background to the enactment of the Foreign Enlistment Act, see Waddell, "British Neutrality and Spanish-American Independence", 1–18.

32 *Hansard Parliamentary Debates*, 1st ser., vol. 40 (1819), col. 1379.

33 Wheeler, *Foreign Enlistment Act*, 17.

34 Proclamation of the Prince Regent Prohibiting British Subjects from Taking Part in the Contest between Spain and the Spanish-American Provinces, 27 November 1817, in Deák and Jessup, *Collection*, 1:168.

35 *Hansard Parliamentary Debates*, 1st ser., vol. 40 (1819), col. 1233.

36 Ibid., col. 1244.

37 Ibid., col. 1380.

38 Ibid., col. 368.

39 Ibid., col. 366.

40 The "prerogative" or "royal prerogative" in England refers to various inherent common law powers and privileges that the Crown possesses. The prerogative includes powers such as making treaties, declaring war and peace, sending troops into armed conflict, and appointing ministers. A small number of prerogative powers may be exercised only by the monarch personally or at her express personal command, such as the dissolution and summoning of Parliaments. Most others are exercised indirectly by minsters in the name of the Crown. See Greenberg, *Jowitt's Dictionary of English Law*, 2:1774.

41 *Hansard Parliamentary Debates*, 1st ser., vol. 40 (1819), cols. 1263–1265.

42 Ibid., col. 1094.

43 Ibid., cols. 363–364.

44 Ibid., col. 364.

45 Ibid., col. 874.

46 Ibid., col. 374.

124 *The law of neutrality 1793–1918*

47 Ibid., col. 1247.
48 Ibid., col. 368.
49 Code Pénal, 1810, in Deák and Jessup, *Collection*, 1:583.
50 Extract from the Penal Code, *PRTW* 2:135.
51 Code Pénal, 1867, in Deák and Jessup, *Collection*, 1:50.
52 Penal Code, *PRTW* 2:87.
53 Code and Commentary, *PRTW* 2:55.
54 Penal Code, 20 November 1859, in Deák and Jessup, *Collection*, 1:712.
55 Codice penale del regno d'Italia, *PRTW* 2:52–53.
56 Penal Code, 11 October 1890, in Deák and Jessup, *Collection*, 1:80.
57 Penal Code, 3 November 1834, in Deák and Jessup, *Collection*, 1:75.
58 Penal Code, 20 August 1884, in Deák and Jessup, *Collection*, 1:538.
59 Declaration of Neutrality in the American Civil War, 10 June 1861, in Deák and Jessup, *Collection*, 1:590–591.
60 Decree concerning Neutrality in the Franco–Prussian War, 26 June 1870, in Deák and Jessup, *Collection*, 2:934–935.
61 Argument of the United States, *PRTW* 3:36.
62 *El codigo penal, concordado y comentado por Don Joaquin Francisco Pacheco*, tomo 11, pp. 91, 92, 96, 97 (Madrid, 1870), quoted in *PRTW* 2:88.
63 *Theoria do direito penal, applicada as codigo penal portuguez, comparado com o codigo do Brazil, leis patrias, codigos e leis criminaes dos povos antigos e modernos. Offerecida a S. M. I. O. SR. D. Pedro II. – Imperador no Brazil per F. A. F. Da Silva Ferrao.* Vol. IV (Lisboa, 1857), pp. 181, 231, quoted in *PRTW* 2:55, 56.
64 See e.g. Dinstein, *Non-International Armed Conflicts*, 109–113, 221–222.
65 See e.g. Eustathiadès, "La première application", 22–43; Lauterpacht, *Recognition*, 175–269.
66 Wheaton (Dana ed.), *Elements of International Law*, 8th ed., 29–32.
67 McNair, *International Law Opinions*, 2:337; Walker, "Recognition of Belligerency", 177–210.
68 Vattel, *Le droit des gens*, Liv. II, Chap. IV, § 54.
69 Ibid., Liv. III, Chap. XVIII, § 292 [italics in the original].
70 Ibid., Liv. II, Chap. IV, § 56.
71 Ibid., Liv. III, Chap. XVIII, § 293–294.
72 Wheaton, *Elements of International Law*, 71.
73 Ibid., 73.
74 Palmerston to Cowley, 19 June 1831, TNA: PRO, O 7/226, fos. 50–59.
75 Mémorandum, 6 juillet 1831, in Schiemann, *Kaisser Nikolaus im Kampf mit Polen*, 466–469.
76 Stevenson to Palmerston, 22 May 1838, *BDFA*, pt. 1, ser. C, vol. 1, p. 33.
77 See below, p. 71.
78 See e.g. Hall, *Treatise on International Law*, 29–39; Lawrence, *Principles of International Law*, 302–306; Rivier, *Principes du droit des gens*, 213; Rougier, *Les guerres civiles*, 192–231; Wheaton (Dana ed.), *Elements of International Law*, 8th ed., 29–32; The Carondelet, 37 F. 799 (S.D.N.Y. 1889); The Conserva, 38 F. 431, 436 (E.D.N.Y. 1889); The Itata, 56 F. 505, 512 (9th Cir. 1893); The Three Friends, 166 U.S. 1, 57, 62–63 (1896).
79 See e.g. Lauterpacht, *Recognition*, 176.
80 See e.g. Castrén, *Civil War*, 135–206; Chen, *International Law of Recognition*, 301–407; Lauterpacht, *Recognition*, 175–328.
81 Rougier, *Les guerres civiles*, 416.
82 Oppenheim, *International Law*, 1st ed., 2:321. However, it is generally assumed today that in traditional international law, third States that recognised insurgents as a belligerent were obliged to remain neutral and abstain from assisting either the lawful government or the belligerent. See e.g. Doswald-Beck, "Legal Validity of

The law of neutrality 1793–1918 125

Military Intervention", 196–197; Roth, *Governmental Illegitimacy*, 177–179. On this issue, see also, Lieblich, *International Law and Civil Wars*, 71–106.

83 See United States v. Murphy, 84 F. 609, 614 (D.Del. 1898). On military expeditions, see generally Curtis, "Hostile Military Expeditions", 1–37, 224–255; García-Mora, *Hostile Acts of Private Persons*, 49–66.

84 See Curtis, "Hostile Military Expeditions", 10–18.

85 While the 1819 British Foreign Enlistment Act did not contain any provision for military expeditions, Article 11 of the same Act amended in 1870 forbade preparing or fitting out any naval or military expedition. An Act to Regulate the Conduct of Her Majesty's Subjects during the Existence of Hostilities between Foreign States with Which Her Majesty is at Peace, 9 August 1870, in Deák and Jessup, *Collection*, 1:137.

86 See García-Mora, *Hostile Acts of Private Persons*, 60.

87 McNair and Watts, *Legal Effects of War*, 451.

88 On the factual circumstances of the Terceira Affair, see McNair, *International Law Opinions*, 2:340; Wheaton (Dana ed.), *Elements of International Law*, 8th ed., 472–473; Kinshichi, *Portuguese History*, 175–178 [in Japanese]. As the 1819 Foreign Enlistment Act contained no provisions prohibiting military expeditions (see above, note 85 of this chapter), the measures employed to prevent military expeditions in this case were not based on the Foreign Enlistment Act but on royal prerogative. See Argument of the United States, *PRTW* 3:27. Nevertheless, this case is worthy of consideration because it was considered that the United Kingdom, as a neutral State, needed to prevent the organisation and beginning of military expeditions and it clarified the grounds for this.

89 Aberdeen to Barbacena, 13 January 1829, *BFSP* 16:424–433; Wellington to Palmella, 30 December 1828, ibid., 454–455; Aberdeen to Barbacena, 11 March 1829, ibid., 518–520.

90 *Hansard Parliamentary Debates*, 2d ser., vol. 24 (1830), col. 127.

91 Ibid., col. 176.

92 Ibid., col. 153.

93 Ibid., cols. 177–178.

94 Ibid., cols. 154–175.

95 Ibid., cols. 143–146, 151.

96 Ibid., cols. 131–132.

97 Ibid., col. 205.

98 Ibid., col. 204.

99 Ibid., col. 213.

100 Wellington to Palmella, 23 December 1828, *BFSP* 16:446.

101 *Hansard Parliamentary Debates*, 2d ser., vol. 24 (1830), col. 169.

102 See Curtis, "Hostile Military Expeditions", 2–3, 252.

103 Moore, *Digest of International Law*, 7:909–934.

104 See, Taoka, *Right of Self-Defence*, 15–16.

105 Proclamation Enjoining Neutrality as to Canada, 5 January 1838, in Deák and Jessup, *Collection*, 2:1177–1178.

106 Webster to Fox, 24 April 1841, *BDFA*, pt. 1, ser. C, vol. 1, pp. 153–160. This note, sent by Webster, Secretary of State of the United States, to Fox, British Minister at Washington, concerns the famous *Caroline* incident. The *Caroline*, a small steamer used by the insurgents in the Canadian revolt for the transportation of persons and goods from the American mainland to the Navy island, was attacked by the British force while stationed at Fort Schlosser, within United States territory, at midnight on 29 December 1837. This incident became a subject of dispute between the United States and the United Kingdom. In the *Caroline* incident, which is famous as a precedent for the concepts of self-defence and self-preservation, these concepts were invoked as an exception to the principle of inviolability of neutral territory. For

126   *The law of neutrality 1793–1918*

instance, Stevenson, Minister of the United States at London, in a note on 22 March 1838, stated "[o]f all the principles of public law there are none more sacred than those which secure the immunity of neutral territory from the exercise of acts of hostility or war by a foreign Power". According to him, while "it will be said there are exceptions to this rule, and cases arising out of necessity and self-preservation, which suspend in favour of a belligerent *sub-modo* the rights of a neutral nation, and justify the invasion of its territory", "the necessity which justifies invasion of neutral territory must be imminent and extreme" [italics in the original]. Stevenson to Palmerston, 22 May 1838, *BDFA*, pt. 1, ser. C, vol. 1, pp. 30–35. In the abovementioned note of 4 April 1841, Webster, after pointing out that the United States government "[holds] itself above reproach in everything respecting the preservation of neutrality", stated that, under these circumstances, the British government had to show "a necessity of self-defence, instant, overwhelming, leaving no choice of means, and no moment for deliberation" if it wanted to justify its entry into United States territories and the destruction of the *Caroline*. For further details regarding the concept of "self-defence" in the *Caroline* incident, see Jennings, "The Caroline and McLeod Case", 82–99; Mori, *The Right of Self-Defence*, 62–68 [in Japanese].

107 On the military expeditions of William Walker, see Curtis, "Hostile Military Expeditions", 243–244.

108 Message of the President of the United States, Communicating, in Compliance with the Resolution of the Senate of 4 January 1858, the Correspondence, Instructions, and Orders to the United States Naval Forces on the Coast of Central America, Connected with the Arrest of Wm. Walker and His Associates, at or near the Port of San Juan de Nicaragua, 7 January 1858, *PRTW* 1:668–671.

109 See Benton, *Spanish-American War*, 42–46.

110 See Moore, *Digest of International Law*, 1:198–200. On the problem as to when recognition of belligerency came into existence as an institution of international law, see section 1.3.1 of this chapter.

111 By the President of the United States, A Proclamation, *FRUS 1895 II*, 1195.

112 Wiborg v. United States, 163 U.S. 632, 647 (1895).

113 However, it is unclear from the judgment itself what the secondary objectives are and on what they are grounded.

114 The Laurada, 85 F. 760, 769–770 (D.Del. 1898).

115 See e.g. Bluntschli, *Das moderne Völkerrecht*, 420–421; Hall, *Rights and Duties of Neutrals*, 59–60; Lawrence, *Principles of International Law*, 503–508, 530–535; Walker, *Science of International Law*, 457.

116 Ministère des Affaires Étrangères, *Deuxième conférence*, 3:54. The English translation of this material is printed in Scott, *Proceedings of the Hague Peace Conferences*.

117 Ministère des Affaires Étrangères, *Deuxième conférence*, 3:55.

118 E.g. Decree concerning Argentine Neutrality in the Crimean War, 16 June 1854, in Deák and Jessup, *Collection*, 1:5–6; Declaration of Neutrality in the American Civil War, 10 June 1861 [France], in ibid., 1:590–591; Declaration of Neutrality in the Russo-Turkish War, 6 May 1877 [France], in ibid., 1:592; Proclamation of Neutrality in the Franco–Prussian War, 24 October 1870 [Peru], in ibid., 2:872–873; Decree of the King-Regent of Portugal, Declaring the Neutrality of Portugal in the Crimean War, 5 May 1854, in ibid., 2:902; Royal Decree regarding Neutrality in the American Civil War, 29 July 1861 [Portugal], in ibid., 2:903; Royal Decree regarding Portuguese Neutrality in the War between Austria, etc., and Prussia and Italy, 2 July 1866, in ibid., 2:904; Royal Decree concerning Neutrality in the Crimean War, 12 April 1854 [Spain], in ibid., 2:933; Royal Decree concerning Neutrality in the American Civil War, 17 June 1861 [Spain], in ibid., 2:933–934; Decree concerning Neutrality in the Franco–Prussian War, 26 June 1870 [Spain], in ibid., 2:934–935.

The law of neutrality 1793–1918   127

119 As stated in the judgment, since Buenos Aires had not been recognised as a sovereign State, the war between Spain and Buenos Aires was a civil war. Nevertheless, the Court examined the issues of neutrality without referring to the recognition of belligerency. The Santissima Trinidad, 20 U.S. (7 Wheat.) 283, 337 (1822). This fact seems to prove that the concept of recognition of belligerency did not exist at that time. See, section 1.3.1 of this chapter.

120 According to the case law of the United States municipal courts, captures made by vessels that have been fitted out and armed in violation of the Neutrality Law of the United States are unjust enrichment arising out of illegal acts and were subject to restitution, that is, restoration to the original owners. See e.g. Talbot v. Janson, 3 U.S. (3 Dall.) 133 (1795); The Brig Alerta, 13 U.S. (9 Cranch) 359 (1815); L'Invincible, 14 U.S. (1 Wheat.) 238 (1816); The Estrella, 17 U.S. (4 Wheat.) 298 (1819).

121 The Santissima Trinidad, 20 U.S. (7 Wheat.) 283, 340–341 (1822).

122 Nevertheless, the Court concluded that there was a violation of the Neutrality Act in this case: The *Independencia*, after sailing to Buenos Aires and receiving commission from the government of Buenos Aires, returned to Baltimore and augmented its force by undergoing considerable repairs and enlisting more persons. The Court found that the augmentation of force of the *Independencia* at the Baltimore violated Article 4 of the 1819 Neutrality Act, and ordered restitution of vessels that had been captured by the *Independencia*. Id. at 341–355.

123 The Gran Para, 20 U.S. (7 Wheat.) 471, 486 (1822) [italics added].

124 United States v. Quincy, 31 U.S. (6 Pet.) 445, 467(1832).

125 Id. at 466 [italics added].

126 Westlake, *International Law*, pt. 2, 213.

127 Ibid., 213–214 [italics added].

128 Curtis, "Hostile Military Expeditions", 9.

129 Russell to Lyons, 15 May 1861, Enclosure, By the Queen, A Proclamation, *BDFA*, pt. 1, ser. C, vol. 5, pp. 202–205.

130 While the *Alabama* was armed at the island of Terceira, outside the territory of Great Britain, the United States and Great Britain agreed on the fact that the *Alabama* had been built and fitted out within the territory of Great Britain before it went to Terceira. See Case of the United States, *PRTW* 1:146–155; Case of Great Britain, *PRTW* 1:308–353.

131 Adams to Russell, 23 June 1862, *PRTW* 1:308.

132 Russell to Adams, 25 June 1862, *PRTW* 1:310. Law Officers of the Crown are those who have advised the King or Queen on questions concerning international law in England since the sixteenth century. According to McNair's *International Law Opinion*,

> in the sixteenth century the Crown developed the practice of consulting groups of civilians, members of Doctors' Commons, upon questions of international law which arose in the conduct of foreign affairs [...] From about 1600 until the retirement of the last holder of the office, Sir Travers Twiss, Q.C., in 1872, the Crown's standing adviser on these questions was the Queen's (or King's) Advocate, who was always (or with rare exceptions) a civilian and a member of Doctors' Commons. He was consulted alone or with other civilians, and from the seventeenth century onwards the Attorney- and Solicitor-General were associated with him when the question was one of great importance or, frequently, upon his own request; these three officers are comprised in the term "the Law Officers".
>
> McNair, *International Law Opinions*, 1:xvii–xviii

133 The Law-Officer of the Crown to Russell, 30 June 1862, *PRTW* 1:310.

134 Case of Great Britain, *PRTW* 1:352.

135 The Law-Officers of the Crown to Russell, 29 July 1862, *PRTW* 1:325–326.

128   *The law of neutrality 1793–1918*

136 Case of Great Britain, *PRTW* 1:326.

137 Treaty between Great Britain and the United States for the Amicable Settlement of All Causes of Difference between the Two Countries, signed at Washington, 8 May 1871, *CTS* 143:145–162.

138 *PRTW* 1:14. The second rule of Washington provides that a neutral government is bound "not to permit or suffer either belligerent to make use of its port or waters as the base of naval operations against the other, or for the purpose of the renewal or augmentation of military supplies or arms, or the recruitment of men". The third rule provides that a neutral government is bound "to exercise due diligence in its own ports and waters, and, as to all persons within its jurisdiction, to prevent any violation of the foregoing obligations and duties".

139 Case of the United States, *PRTW* 1:149.

140 Case of Great Britain, *PRTW* 1:272–273, 351–353.

141 Case of the United States, *PRTW* 1:63.

142 Decision and Award, Made by the Tribunal of Arbitration Constituted by Virtue of the First Article of the Treaty Concluded at Washington the 8th of May, 1871, between the United States of America and Her Majesty the Queen of the United Kingdom of Great Britain and Ireland, *PRTW* 4:49–54.

143 It is not very clear why the two governments, which had agreed that the rules of Washington were applicable to the case, had to discuss the basis of the rules in detail. A possible explanation for this is as follows. First, the purpose of the British government was probably to emphasise the difficulty in legally establishing the ship owner's or ship operator's intent, which was the criteria distinguishing between the fitting out of ships that should be prevented by a neutral government and those that did not need to be prevented, and thereby to contend that the careful consideration of proof concerning the intent of the *Alabama* in this case did not constitute a lack of "due diligence" on the part of the British government. See Case of Great Britain, *PRTW* 1:239–244. On the other hand, the United States government probably attempted to insist that the prevention of fitting out and arming of vessels intended for warlike use concerned the matter of peace or war between States, which could have been regulated by the royal prerogative in Great Britain without relying on statues, and therefore that the deficiency of the statute (the Foreign Enlistment Act) could not be invoked as a reason for the failure of preventing the departure of the Alabama. See Argument of the United States, *PRTW* 3:17–27.

144 Case of Great Britain, *PRTW* 1:236–237; Case of the United States, *PRTW* 1:80–81; Argument of the United States, *PRTW* 3:22–23.

145 Case of Great Britain, *PRTW* 1:239.

146 Case of the United States, *PRTW* 1:63–88.

147 Argument of the United States, *PRTW* 3:22–25.

148 E.g. Hall, *Rights and Duties of Neutrals*, 61–73; Oppenheim, *International Law*, 1st ed., 2:360.

149 Calvo, "Examen des trois règles", 453–532.

150 Woolsey, "Les trois règles de Washington", 559–560; Rolin-Jaequemyns, "Les trois règles de Washington", 561–569; Bluntschli, "Résolutions proposées à l'Institut", 581.

151 Institut de Droit International, *Annuaire de l'Institut de Droit International* 1:139–140.

152 E.g. Kleen, *Lois et usages de la neutralité*, 1:233–255; Oppenheim, *International Law*, 1st ed., 2:376–386.

153 Opinions of Sir Alexander Cockburn, *PRTW* 4:234 [italics added].

154 Argument of the United States, *PRTW* 3:22.

155 Ibid.

156 For instance, the bulk of State practice that appears in Chapter 28 (Neutrality) of Moore's *Digest of International Law* concerns acts by private individuals, such as

The law of neutrality 1793–1918   129

military expeditions and fitting out and arming of vessels. See Moore, *Digest of International Law*, 7:859–1109.

157 See e.g. Kleen, *Lois et usages de la neutralité*, 1:113; Piédelièvre, *Précis de droit international public*, 2:486; Rivier, *Principes du droit des gens*, 2:384–385; Verraes, *Les lois de la guerre*, 2:45. While there have not been many instances where neutral States actually express sympathy for one of the belligerents, we can find one such instance, in which the Foreign Minister of El Salvador, upon the United States' entrance into the First World War, stated that "El Salvador would remain neutral, but reserving all its sympathies in the conflict for the people and Government of the United States". Deák and Jessup, *Collection*, 1:564. This statement shows that it was believed that a State could remain neutral while at the same time expressing sympathy for one of the belligerents.

158 Bluntschli, *Das moderne Völkerrecht*, 418 (§753) [italics added].

159 See e.g. Martens, *Précis du droit des gens*, 2e éd., 452; Klüber, *Droit des gens*, 436–437; Kent, *Commentaries on American Law*, 2:108; Wheaton, *Elements of International Law*, 281–283; Manning, *Commentaries on the Law of Nations*, 167–168; Heffter, *Das europäische Völkerrecht*, 243–244; Halleck, *Elements of International Law*, 230–231; Bluntschli, *Das moderne Völkerrecht*, 415; Woolsey, *Introduction to the Study of International Law*, 277–278; Calvo, *Le droit international*, 4:486–487.

160 In addition to the sources cited at notes 163 to 165 of this chapter, see e.g. Rivier, *Principes du droit des gens*, 2:377–379; Lawrence, *Principles of International Law*, 484–485; Liszt, *Das Völkerrecht*, 240–241.

161 Martens, *Précis du droit des gens*, 2e éd., 447–448.

162 Bluntschli, *Das moderne Völkerrecht*, 415, 421 (§746, 759).

163 Phillimore, *Commentaries upon International Law*, 3:202 [italics in the original].

164 Fiore, *Nouveau droit international public*, 3:423.

165 Kleen, *Lois et usages de la neutralité*, 1:112–113.

166 Ibid., 76, 111.

167 Cargoes may be captured and confiscated as contraband of war when: (1) they are susceptible of a belligerent use and (2) they have an enemy destination. State practice was inconsistent with respect to whether and under what conditions neutral vessels carrying contraband articles and non-contraband articles on those vessels may be confiscated. See Colombos, *Treatise on the Law of Prize*, 186–230.

168 See e.g. The Commercen, 14 U.S. (1 Wheat.) 382, 387 (1816); Baker, *Halleck's International Law*, 2:245; Moore, *Digest of International Law*, 7:749. If one characterises the export and transportation of contraband articles by private individuals as an "unneutral act" or "hostility", a question arises as to why a neutral government does not need to prevent such conduct. In this regard, Woolsey points out that since "it is difficult for a government to watch narrowly the operations of trade, and it is annoying for the innocent trader", State practice leave the punishment of contraband trade "in the hands of those who are most interested", namely, belligerent States. Woolsey, *Introduction to the Study of International Law*, 297.

169 The Santissima Trinidad, 20 U.S. (7 Wheat.) 283, 340 (1822).

170 *Ex parte* Chavasse, (1865) 4 De G.J. & S. 655, 659.

171 E.g. Seton, Maitland & Co. v. Low, 1 Johns. Cas. 1, 14 (N.Y. 1799); Richardson v. Maine Fire and Marine Insurance Company, 6 Mass. 102, 113 (1809); The Laurada, 85 F. 760, 769 (D.Del. 1898); Case of Great Britain, *PRTW* 1:236–237; Argument of the United States, *PRTW* 3:23; Lawrence, *Principles of International Law*, 599–603; Westlake, *International Law*, pt. 2, 194–197.

172 Hall, *Treatise on International Law*, 76.

173 Ibid., 76, 555.

174 According to most writers in the nineteenth century, the "duties of neutrals" are the abstention and impartiality. See e.g. Calvo, *Le droit international*, 4:523–566.

130 *The law of neutrality 1793–1918*

It was only after the twentieth century, especially after the interwar period, that the duty to acquiesce the lawful exercise of the right of capture at sea by belligerents has been mentioned as one of the "duties of neutrals". See e.g. Oppenheim, *International Law*, 1st ed., 2:333; Holland, *Lectures on International Law*, 490; Kunz, *Kriegsrecht und Neutralitätsrecht*, 228; Verdross, *Völkerrecht*, 320; Taoka, *Outline of International Law*, 2:404–405 [in Japanese]; Tachi, *International Law in Times of War*, 430–431[in Japanese]. It should be considered whether it is appropriate to regard the abstention and impartiality as the "duties". We shall discuss this point in section 2.2 of this chapter.

175 Tabata, *New Lecture on International Law*, 2:287 [in Japanese].
176 Stone, relying on Hohfeld's classification of "rights", argues that the so-called "duties of acquiescence" of neutral States are "no-rights" correlative to privileges of belligerent States in the sense that the neutral States have no legal redress against the lawful exercise of belligerent rights. Stone, *Legal Controls of International Conflict*, 383, 478. According to Hohfeld, "rights" in a broad sense are categorised into (1) right (in a narrow sense), (2) privilege, (3) power, and (4) immunity, and they are correlative to another person's (1) duty, (2) no-right, (3) liability, and (4) disability. Hohfeld, *Fundamental Legal Conceptions*, 36–64.
177 Note that the term the "duty of acquiescence" was not used even in such a case.
178 Vattel, *Le droit des gens*, Liv. III, Chap. VII, § 113.
179 Seton, Maitland & Co. v. Low, 1 Johns. Cas. 1, 14 (N.Y. 1799).
180 Richardson v. Maine Fire and Marine Insurance Company, 6 Mass. 102, 113 (1809).
181 On the legal foundations or rationale of the rights of belligerents to capture neutral vessels and cargoes, see Wani, "Legal Foundations of Prize Law", 45–70 [in Japanese].
182 See Grotius, *De jure belli ac pacis*, Lib. II, Cap. II, § XIII; Wolff, *Jus gentium*, § 686–704; Vattel, *Le droit des gens*, Liv. III, Chap. VII, § 119–135.
183 See e.g. Martens, *Précis du droit des gens*, 2e éd., 455–456; Wheaton, *Elements of International Law*, 284.
184 See e.g. Hautefeuille, *Des droits et des devoirs des nations neutres*, 1:211–215; Bluntschli, *Das moderne Völkerrecht*, 429; Fiore, *Nouveau droit international public*, 3:432–434; Kleen, *Lois et usages de la neutralité*, 1:503–504.
185 Hall, *Treatise on International Law*, 558.
186 The following case illustrates such a difference of opinion: In the Franco–Prussian War (1870–71), Prussia, a belligerent in the war, asked permission for the passage of the sick and wounded belonging to its army through the territories of Belgium and Luxembourg. France, the enemy of Prussia, requested Belgium and Luxembourg to refuse Prussia's request. Belgium refused passage, while Luxembourg granted permission. See Oppenheim (Lauterpacht ed.), *International Law*, 7th ed., 2:691–692; Ochsner, *Transit von Personen und Gütern*, 73. In this case, Prussia and Luxemburg were of opinion that the sick and wounded belonging to a belligerent had the right to pass through neutral territory, whereas France and Belgium took a contrary view.
187 Projet d'une déclaration internationale concernant les lois et coutumes de la guerre, in Samwer et Hopf, *Nouveau recueil général*, 2e sér., 4:212–228. The English translation of the Brussels Declaration is printed in Schindler and Toman, *Laws of Armed Conflicts*, 21–28. The Brussels Declaration did not enter into force as a treaty.
188 Convention (II) with Respect to the Laws and Customs of War on Land, signed at The Hague, 29 July 1899, Annex: Regulations respecting the Laws and Customs of War on Land, CTS 187:429–443. The authentic text of the Convention is French. The English translation is printed in Schindler and Toman, *Laws of Armed Conflicts*, 55–87.
189 For example, as regards the issue (2), in theory, if a neutral State refuses asylum to belligerent troops, the troops have no other choices other than capitulating to the

The law of neutrality 1793–1918 131

enemy troops at the border of the neutral State; therefore, soldiers captured as prisoners of war by the capitulating troops would be returned to their own State. That being so, a neutral State that grants asylum to a belligerent troops must repatriate those who have been captured as prisoners of war by the troops. If that were not the case, the neutral State would be putting the other belligerent at a disadvantage by providing asylum to the belligerent troops (the disadvantage of being unable to recover one's own soldiers captured as prisoners of war). However, in State practice, Germany, France and others detained those who have captured as prisoners of war by the troops being granted asylum until the end of the war. In contrast, Switzerland in the Franco–Prussian war repatriated an equal number of previously detained French soldiers when releasing Prussian soldiers captured as prisoners of war by the French troops that had been granted asylum in the Swiss territory. See Shinobu, *International Law in Times of War*, 4:326 [in Japanese]. For further details about the issues of (1) – (4) listed in the main text, see e.g. Heilborn, *Rechte und Pflichten der neutralen Staaten*, 12–65; Sauser-Hall, *Des belligérants internés*, 57–247; Wilson, "Escaped Prisoners of War", 519–523.

190 For example, Hall points out that "[p]artly as a consequence of the habit of freely admitting foreign public ships of war belonging to friendly powers to the ports of a state as a matter of courtesy, partly because of the inevitable conditions of navigation, it is not the custom to apply the same rigour of precaution to naval as to military forces". Hall, *Treatise on International Law*, 585. Other writers, such as Calvo, explain the reason for the difference of treatment between land forces and warships by the so-called "floating territory" theory, according to which a ship (especially a warship) is a "part of the territory of the State whose flag the ship flies". Calvo, *Le droit international*, 4:541.

191 See [Harvard Law School] "Rights and Duties of Neutral States in Naval and Aerial War", 455.

192 See ibid., 468–469.

193 For further details regarding the Hague Peace Conferences, see Higgins, *The Hague Peace Conferences*, 39–59.

194 Annex to the 1899 Hague Convention (II) with respect to the Laws and Customs of War on Land (see note 188 of this chapter) contains some provisions regarding neutrality. (1) Article 54 provides: "The plant of railways coming from neutral States, whether the property of those States, or of companies, or of private persons, shall be sent back to them as soon as possible." (2) Article 57, paragraph 1 provides: "A neutral State which receives in its territory troops belonging to the belligerent armies shall intern them, as far as possible, at a distance from the theatre of war." (3) Article 58, paragraph 1 provides: "Failing a special convention, the neutral State shall supply the interned with the food, clothing, and relief required by humanity." (4) Article 59, paragraph 1 provides: "A neutral State may authorize the passage over its territory of wounded or sick belonging to the belligerent armies, on condition that the trains bringing them shall carry neither combatants nor war material." (5) Article 60 provides: "The Geneva Convention applies to sick and wounded interned in neutral territory." Among these provisions, (5) became Article 15 of the 1907 Convention (V) respecting the Rights and Duties of Neutral Powers and Persons in Case of War on Land without any modification. (2), (3) and (4) became Articles 11, 12 and 14 of the 1907 Hague Convention (V) without any major revisions except for a change in wording from "a neutral State (l'État neutre)" to "a neutral Power (la Puissance neutre)". (1) was introduced into article 19 of the 1907 Hague Convention (V) with substantial revisions.

195 Ministère des Affaires Étrangères, *Deuxième conférence*, 3:32–37, 51–57, 179–182.

196 See note 194 of this chapter.

197 Ministère des Affaires Étrangères, *Deuxième conférence*, 3:59–60.

198 Ibid., 59.

132 *The law of neutrality 1793–1918*

199 Ibid., 38–39.
200 Propositions de la délégation d'Allemagne: Projet d'une nouvelle section à ajouter au Règlement de 1899 concernant les lois et coutumes de la guerre sur terre, in ibid., 268–270.
201 See Huber, "Die Fortbildung des Völkerrechts", 587. On the treatment of neutral persons and property in the territories of belligerents and the occupied territories, see e.g. Albrecht, *Über Requisitionen von neutralen Privateigentum*, 1–66; Frankenbach, *Die Rechtsstellung von neutralem Staatsangehörigen*, 1–132; Giebler, *Die rechtliche Stellung der Angehörigen neutraler Staaten*, 1–34.
202 Ministère des Affaires Étrangères, *Deuxième conférence*, 3:63–73.
203 See Boidin, *Les deux conférences de La Haye*, 131.
204 Ministère des Affaires Étrangères, *Deuxième conférence*, 3:214–217.
205 Although the Hague Convention (XII) does not define the term "territorial waters (eux territoriales)", it is considered as including both territorial sea and internal waters.
206 Ministère des Affaires Étrangères, *Deuxième conférence*, 3:489–496.
207 With regard to the issue of the fitting out and arming, within the territory of a neutral State, of vessels intended for warlike purposes, see section 1.3.3 of this chapter. There are some differences in wording between the Washington rules, which were agreed as applicable rules in the *Alabama* claims arbitration, and Article 8 of the Hague Convention XIII on Neutral Powers in case of Naval War. The term "due diligence" as used in the former was replaced by the term "the means at its disposal (moyens dont il dispose)" in the latter. That was because the term "due diligence" had been criticised as being vague. Ibid., 493.
208 Ibid., 460–514, 569–652.
209 Ibid., 460, 462, 464, 479, 499.
210 Ibid., 461.
211 Ibid., 180.
212 Ibid., 467, 487, etc.
213 Ibid., 488 [italics added].
214 Ibid., 180.
215 Ibid., 60. "*Casus belli*" means "a legitimate cause of initiating war". See Kotzsch, *Concept of War*, 165.
216 Bassompierre, "L'article 10 de la cinquième convention", 237–238.
217 Westlake, *International Law*, pt. 2, 197.
218 However, the Hague Conference left some issues unresolved. For example, while the Dutch delegate proposed to make an article concerning the treatment of war material captured by troops and brought with them into the territory of a neutral State, no provisions was made on this issue. See Ministère des Affaires Étrangères, *Deuxième conférence*, 3:59–60, 258. Also, some articles, while inserted in the Hague Conventions, left room for possible conflicting interpretations in the future. For example, in the *Altmark* case of 1940, Norway and Great Britain disputed over the issue of the meaning of the term "the mere passage (le simple passage)" in Article 10 of the Hague Convention XIII. See below, section 1.3.1 of Chapter 3.
219 See e.g. Geffcken, "Die Neutralität", 607; Hautefeuille, *Des droits et des devoirs des nations neutres*, 1:168, 169; Kleen, *Lois et usages de la neutralité*, 1:113; Opinions of Sir Alexander Cockburn, *PRTW* 4:235.
220 Argument of the United States, *PRTW* 3:22. In the *United States* v. *O'Sullivan* (1851), the District Court for the Southern District of New York, although it did not use the very term the "right to remain neutral", stated that the law of neutrality "springs out of and rests upon that code of natural law which recognizes and declares *the right of every nation to remain at peace*, and *not to be unjustly or wrongfully driven into war by the aggressions of another*" [italics added]. United States v. O'Sullivan, 27 F. Cas. 367, 374 (S.D.N.Y. 1851) (No. 15,974).

The law of neutrality 1793–1918 133

221 See e.g. Martens, *Summary of the Law of Nations*, 310; Martens, *Précis du droit des gens*, 2e éd., 450; Schmalz, *Das europäische Völkerrecht*, 278; Klüber, *Droit des gens*, 434; Wheaton, *Elements of International Law*, 281; Heffter, *Das europäische Völkerrecht*, 244; Martens (Vergé éd.), *Précis du droit des gens*, nouvelle éd., 2:291–294; Ortolan, *Règles internationales et diplomatie de la mer*, 77; Hautefeuille, *Des droits et des devoirs des nations neutres*, 1:174–175; Halleck, *Elements of International Law*, 231; Wheaton (Dana ed.), *Elements of International Law*, 8th ed., 426; Bluntschli, *Das moderne Völkerrecht*, 417; Baker, *Halleck's International Law*, 2:173; Geffcken, "Die Neutralität", 606; Fiore, *Nouveau droit international public*, 3:418–419, 431; Calvo, *Le droit international*, 4:501; Rivier, *Principes du droit des gens*, 2:377; Kleen, *Lois et usages de la neutralité*, 1:75. See also literature cited in note 290 of this chapter. While some of the literature cited above uses the phrase "the right to remain peace" instead of the phrase "the right to remain neutral", intended meanings of those phrases are the same.
222 Fiore, *Nouveau droit international public*, 3:431.
223 Martens (Vergé éd.), *Précis du droit des gens*, nouvelle éd., 2:294.
224 Pradier-Fodéré, *Traité de droit international public*, 8:873–874.
225 The institution of permanent neutrality and the institution of neutrality under general international law, share something in common in that a belligerent is prohibited from involving a neutral State in the war. The institution of permanent neutrality that was established by treaties in the nineteenth century for Switzerland, Krakow, Belgium and Luxembourg imposed the following obligations upon Contracting States: (1) the obligation of permanently neutral States (Switzerland, Krakow, Belgium and Luxembourg) to remain neutral in wars between other States; (2) the obligation of Contracting States other than permanently neutral States to respect the neutrality of permanently neutral States (the obligation to respect); and (3) the obligation of guarantor States to guarantee the neutrality of permanently neutral States (the obligation to guarantee). In addition to the permanently neutral States, the Great Powers such as Austria, France, Great Britain, Prussia and Russia participated in such treaties as guarantor States, namely, States which assumed both the obligation to respect and the obligation to guarantee. The obligation of Contracting States other than permanently neutral States to respect the neutrality of the permanently neutral States includes both "the prohibition of transforming a permanently neutral State into a belligerent State by forcing the permanently neutral State participate in a war as an ally or by declaring war on the permanently neutral State" and "the prohibition of the use of a permanently neutral State's territory for military passage to attack an enemy, the establishment of a military base in the territory of a permanently neutral State or the demand for the supply of armed forces or munitions from a permanently neutral State". See Taoka, *Permanent Neutrality and Japan's Security*, 212 [in Japanese]. The obligation to guarantee the neutrality of a permanently neutral State is the obligation to eliminate, even by resorting to war when necessary, the violation of the neutrality of a permanently neutral State by other States. In the law of neutrality under general international law, which is the object of study of this book, a belligerent State is obliged to respect the neutrality of a neutral State as long as the neutral State maintains strict neutrality. But no State is obliged to guarantee the neutrality of a neutral State in the law of neutrality under general international law. In other words, the law of permanent neutrality and the law of neutrality under general international law differ in terms of the existence of the obligation to guarantee and the obligation to remain neutral, but they share something in common in that a belligerent State is obliged to respect the neutrality of a neutral State.
226 De Visscher, "La théorie de la nécessité", 79.
227 See e.g. Calvo, *Le droit international*, 4:523; Hautefeuille, *Des droits et des devoirs des nations neutres*, 1:247–250.

134 The law of neutrality 1793–1918

228 Hautefeuille, *Des droits et des devoirs des nations neutres*, 1:249.

229 "Region of war" is an area in which belligerents are *entitled* to conduct hostilities and it is distinguished from "theatre of war", which means an area where hostilities *are actually conducted*. See Oppenheim, *International Law*, 1st ed., 2:80.

230 Geffcken, "Die Neutralität", 606.

231 Rivier, *Principes du droit des gens*, 2:377. According to Rivier, the concept of "voluntary neutrality" is opposite to the concept of "obligatory or conventional neutrality (Neutralité obligatoire, ou conventionnelle)". The latter concept refers to the status of States that are obliged by treaties to remain neutral in every war between other States, that is, the status of permanently neutral States such as Switzerland and Belgium.

232 Argument of the United States, *PRTW* 3:22.

233 According to what this book has argued so far, the law of neutrality is an institution that regulates the acts that should be performed by neutral States in order to enjoy the right to remain neutral. From the perspective of belligerent States, it is an institution that regulates the circumstances in which they may or may not wage war on neutral States. In this sense, the law of neutrality is an institution that belongs to the area of the *jus ad bellum* rather than the *jus in bello*. However, it is to be noted, as pointed out by Kolb, that the terms *jus ad bellum* and *jus in bello*, and the idea clearly distinguishing between them as distinct branches of international law, which first appeared in the 1930s, did not exist in the literature or State practice before the nineteenth century. See Kolb, "Origin of the Twin Terms", 553–562. Therefore, in the literature and State practice before the nineteenth century, it was not discussed whether the law of neutrality was an issue of *jus ad bellum* or *jus in bello*.

234 See e.g. Fiore, *Nouveau droit international public*, 3:431; Bluntschli, *Das moderne Völkerrecht*, 419.

235 See note 153 of this chapter and text accompanying it.

236 See Chapter 2, Section 1.3.2.

237 See note 158 of this chapter and text accompanying it.

238 Funck-Brentano et Sorel, *Précis du droit des gens*, 346, 347.

239 Bluntschli, *Das moderne Völkerrecht*, 418, 419.

240 Kleen, *Lois et usages de la neutralité*, 1:209–210 [italics added].

241 E.g. Fiore, *Nouveau droit international public*, 3:430; Hershey, *Essentials of International Public Law*, 458; Geffcken, "Die Neutralität", 656; The Gran Para, 20 U.S. (7 Wheat.) 471, 489 (1822).

242 Gareis, *Institutionen des Völkerrechts*, 215 [italics added].

243 Ullmann, *Völkerrecht*, 519–520.

244 "Act of war" means either (1) an act that itself creates a state of war, or (2) an act of a State against another State that legally permits the latter State to resort to war against the former. See Kotzsch, *Concept of War*, 163–175. "Act of war" in the latter sense is synonymous with *un acte hostile* and *casus belli*. On the concept of *un acte hostile* and *casus belli*, see above, p. 101. and note 215. When it is said that the military assistance provided by a neutral State to a belligerent amounts to an "act of war" against the other belligerent State, the term "act of war" is used in the latter sense.

245 See e.g. Martens, *Précis du droit des gens*, 2e éd., 439; Bluntschli, *Das moderne Völkerrecht*, 416; Gareis, *Institutionen des Völkerrechts*, 215; Lawrence, *Principles of International Law*, 485. However, from the viewpoint of the just war doctrine, participating in a war in support of an unjust belligerent is not permitted. See e.g. Vattel, *Le droit des gens*, Liv. III, Chap. III, §40.

246 However, there were some instances in which "acts of war" against another State were prohibited by international law. For example, Gareis, who states that "a neutral which takes part in the war by giving up a passive attitude does not violate any duty … but only changes its policy", raises cases where there is a special treaty obligation

The law of neutrality 1793–1918 135

and "the case of surprise attack contrary to international law" (völkerrechtswidrigen Überrumpelung) as cases in which acts of war against another State violate international law. See Gareis, *Institutionen des Völkerrechts*, 215. Although Gareis assumes that a "surprise attack" is prohibited by international law, it is very doubtful whether there was, before the adoption of the 1907 Hague Convention (III) relative to the Opening of Hostilities, any rule of positive international law prohibiting a "surprise attack", namely, resorting to war without making any previous declaration of war. On this issue, see Taoka, *International Law III*, 358–389 [in Japanese].

247 Opinions of Sir Alexander Cockburn, *PRTW* 4:235.

248 Kleen, *Lois et usages de la neutralité*, 1:76. The law of neutrality emerged as an institution of international law in the nineteenth century not because neutrality was regarded as morally legitimate. Rather, neutrality was often criticised from a moral perspective. It was often argued that a State should intervene in a war between other States to terminate it as soon as possible or support the just belligerent. According to this argument, neutrality is a State's attitude, which only considers its own security, to avoid intervening in a war, and it is not morally justified. See e.g. Lorimer, *Institutes of the Law of Nations*, 121–130; Westlake, *International Law*, pt. 2, 190–191. However, as is clear from Westlake's statement that "neutrality is not *morally* justifiable" [italics added], a criticism against neutrality was an argument from a moral viewpoint. In positive international law, a State was permitted to remain neutral by prioritising its national interests, that is, its own security, over the interests of international society as a whole. See above, pp. 104–105.

249 Piédelièvre, *Précis de droit international public*, 2:489 [italics added].

250 Ottolenghi, *Il rapporto di neutralità*, 18 [italics added].

251 E.g. Fiore, *Nouveau droit international public*, 3:431.

252 E.g. Ibid., 419; Hautefeuille, *Des droits et des devoirs des nations neutres*, 1:177–178, 184; Lawrence, *Principles of International Law*, 474; Phillimore, *Commentaries upon International Law*, 3:202; Piédelièvre, *Précis de droit international public*, 2:486–487.

253 Fiore, *Nouveau droit international public*, 3:419.

254 Opinions of Sir Alexander Cockburn, *PRTW* 4:235.

255 Hautefeuille, *Des droits et des devoirs des nations neutres*, 1:181.

256 Pradier-Fodéré, *Traité de droit international public*, 8:927–928.

257 Carnegie to Grey, 4 August 1914, TNA: PRO, FO 371/2164, file 30342, paper 37964.

258 Grey to Carnegie, 4 August 1914, TNA: PRO, FO 371/2161, file 30342, paper 35645.

259 Carnegie to Grey, 19 August 1914, TNA: PRO, FO 371/2105, file 36169, paper 40850.

260 Hardinge to Grey, 20 August 1914, TNA: PRO, FO 371/2105, file 39169, paper 43227.

261 For example, the Minister of Portugal, while in conversation with the British Ambassador in San Sebastian, Spain, in August 1914, stated, as a reason that Portugal intended to support Great Britain, "[t]he victory of Germany ... would be the end of their independence and would mean the loss of all their colonies...". Hardinge to Grey, 20 August 1914, TNA: PRO, FO 371/2105, file 39169, paper 43227.

262 The specific details of the aid provided to Great Britain by Portugal included giving the British army the right of passage through Mozambique (Portuguese territory), supplying coal to British warships (German warships were denied the supply of coal), approving the harbouring of British warships at Portuguese ports beyond the period allowed in the law of neutrality and providing Great Britain with munitions and anti-torpedo boat destroyers. Carnegie to Grey, 11 March 1916, Enclosure in No. 1, Declaration Read by Portuguese Minister for Foreign Affairs in Congress, 10 March 1916, TNA: PRO, FO 371/2759, file 110, paper 52095.

263 Minute, 13 August 1914, TNA: PRO, FO 371/1883, file 38309, paper 38669.

136 *The law of neutrality 1793–1918*

264 Carnegie [to Grey], 14 February 1916, TNA: PRO, FO 371/2759, file 110, paper 29240.

265 Minute: "Portugal and the War", 20 July 1915, TNA: PRO, FO 371/2472, file 91547, paper 106315.

266 German Legation, 9 June 1915, TNA: PRO, FO 372/706, file 59380, paper 110322.

267 Grey to Carnegie, 30 July 1915, TNA: PRO, FO 372/706, file 59330, paper 88894; Carnegie to Grey, 22 September 1915, TNA: PRO, FO 372/706, file 59330, paper 136486.

268 Carnegie to Grey, 15 July 1915, TNA: PRO, FO 371/2472, file 100366, paper 100366; Carnegie to Grey, 9 December 1915, TNA: PRO, FO 371/2472, file 91547, paper 193272.

269 Minute: "Portuguese co-operation", 21 July 1915, TNA: PRO, FO 371/2472, file 100366, paper 100366.

270 Ibid.

271 Carnegie to Grey, 17 November 1914, TNA: PRO, FO 371/2105, file 51771, paper 72191; The Secretary of State for the Colonies to the Governor-General of the Union of South Africa, 4 January 1915, TNA: PRO, FO 371/2231, file 1058, paper 1058; Grey to Carnegie, 7 July 1915, TNA: PRO, FO 371/2472, file 91547, paper 91547.

272 Edmond W. Slade, Admiralty, 3 August 1914, TNA: PRO, FO 371/2188, file 35792, paper 35792.

273 Carnegie to Grey, 17 November 1914, TNA: PRO, FO 371/2105, file 51771, paper 72191.

274 Carnegie to Grey, 15 July 1915, TNA: PRO, FO 371/2472, file 100366, paper 100366.

275 Ibid. On the problem concerning a third State's power to requisition belligerent merchant vessels, see e.g. Garner, *International Law and the World War*, 1:176–180; Stone, *Legal Controls of International Conflict*, 440; Woolsey, "Taking of Foreign Ships", 497–506.

276 Carnegie to Grey, 11 March 1916, Enclosure in No. 1: Declaration Read by Portuguese Minister for Foreign Affairs in Congress, 10 March 1916, TNA: PRO, FO 371/2759, file 110, paper 52095.

277 See e.g. Despagnet, *Cours de droit international public*, 1246; Ullmann, *Völkerrecht*, 520.

278 Opinions of Sir·Alexander Cockburn, *PRTW* 4:235.

279 In this regard, the resolution adopted by the Institut de Droit International at the Hague session in 1875 can be understood as a proposal of *lex ferenda*. The resolution, while admitting that the primary legal consequence arising from a violation of neutrality is a war by an offended belligerent against a violating neutral, recommends nonetheless that States resolve disputes concerning the violations of neutrality by the payment of compensation as far as possible and thereby attempts to reduce the chance of war. Article 6 of the resolution stipulates:

> The State injured by a violation of the duties of neutrality has the right to *consider the neutrality as extinct*, and to resort to armes to defend itself from the violating State, *only in the grave and urgent case*, and only during the war. In the less grave and not urgent cases, or when the war has been terminated, a dispute of this sort belongs exclusively to arbitral procedure [italics added].

This resolution, while admitting that if a neutral State has committed acts contrary to neutrality, an injured belligerent may consider that neutrality as extinct and resort to war against that State, recommends the settling of disputes by arbitral procedure and avoiding resorting to war "[i]n the less grave and not urgent cases". See Institut de Droit International, *Annuaire de l'Institut de Droit International*, 1:139–140.

The law of neutrality 1793–1918 137

280 Takane Sugihara refers to Halleck, Woolsey, Bluntschli and Klüber as writers who took the "just-war-like theory" in the nineteenth century, according to which war was a means of redress for the violations of rights. See Sugihara, "Legal Character of Modern International Law", 96–98 [in Japanese]. On the concept of war in the legal literature in the nineteenth century, see also Yanagihara "War as a Means of Settlement of International Disputes", 2–22 [in Japanese].

281 Klüber, *Droit des gens*, 375–376.

282 Halleck, *Elements of International Law*, 145–147.

283 Klüber, *Droit des gens*, 434; Halleck, *Elements of International Law*, 231.

284 For instance, Lammasch stated in an article of 1916, "[t]oday, however, the question, When is war justified? has almost ceased to be discussed". Lammasch, "Unjustifiable War", 689.

285 Oppenheim, *International Law*, 1st ed., 2:56, 69, 71.

286 Hershey, *Essentials of International Public Law*, 349, 352.

287 Oppenheim, *International Law*, 1st ed., 2:322, 336. Oppenheim, who had denied the existence of the right to remain neutral in the first edition (1906) and second edition (1912) of his *International Law*, affirmed this right in the third edition of the same book (1921). See below, Chapter 3, section 2.1.

288 Cavaglieri, "Belligeranza, neutralità e posizioni giuridiche intermedie", 335.

289 "The Hague Conventions and the Neutrality of Belgium and Luxemburg", 959.

290 Rivier stated in his book published in 1896 that "all States, being independent, have the right to remain neutral (a le droit de rester neutre) when other States make war with each other", while affirming that "[t]he distinction between just war and unjust war is juridically of no value". Rivier, *Principes du droit des gens*, 2:202–203, 377. Moreover, Hershey, who admitted that the justice and injustice of war "belong[s] to the domain of International Ethics or Morality rather than to that of International Law", stated in a book published in 1912 that "[a]n independent State has an inalienable right to remain neutral in a war, and a belligerent is bound to respect this neutrality". Hershey, *Essentials of International Public Law*, 352, 455. On De Visscher's view regarding the "right to remain neutral", see below, section 2.4.4.A. As other writers who affirmed the existence of the "right to remain neutral" in the early twentieth century, see, for example, Thonier, *De la contrebande de guerre*, 54; Verraes, *Les lois de la guerre*, 2:6; Pradier-Fodéré, *Traité de droit international public*, 8:873–879, 913–914; Hershey, *Russo-Japanese War*, 71; Phillimore, "The Future Law of Neutrality", 47.

291 Lifschütz, "Neutralität", 42.

292 Ibid., 45, 60.

293 Huber, "Die Fortbildung des Völkerrechts", 586.

294 Ministère des Affaires Étrangères, *Deuxième conférence*, 3:488 [italics added].

295 Ibid., 180, 578 [italics added].

296 The so-called "rights of neutral States" such as the territorial inviolability and the freedom of commerce are nothing but rights that States have even in times of peace. However, from the perspective of those writers who affirm the existence of the right to remain neutral, a neutral State is legally guaranteed to remain a neutral State, and therefore legally guaranteed to continue to enjoy the rights that it has in times of peace, namely, the rights of a neutral State. This is the benefit of the status of neutrality. In contrast, according to those who deny the existence of the right to remain neutral, a belligerent State is at any time free to convert a hitherto neutral State into a belligerent State by declaring war against it; in other words, a neutral State is in a position to be taken away at any time the rights which it has in times of peace. From this perspective, neutrality is not the benefit for a neutral State.

297 Oppenheim, *International Law*, 1st ed., 2:322.

298 De Visscher, "De la belligérance", 98.

138 *The law of neutrality 1793–1918*

299 Lawrence states that "all authorities admit that the exigencies of self-defence will justify a temporary violation of neutral territory". Lawrence, *Principles of International Law*, 501. On the concept of self-defence or self-preservation as an exception to the principle of the inviolability of neutral territories, see also, Calvo, *Le droit international*, 4:536–537; Hall, *Treatise on International Law*, 247–248; Hershey, *Essentials of International Public Law*, 458; Woolsey, *Introduction to the Study of International Law*, 271.

300 On the question of hostilities or the use of force by a belligerent State against a neutral State, see Brownlie, *Use of Force*, 309–316; Miele, *L'estraneità ai conflitti armati*, 2:529–560; Schindler, "L'emploi de la force", 847–864; Morita, "Legitimate Use of Force against Non-Belligerent States", 137–156 [in Japanese].

301 See above, pp. 71–72.

302 In traditional international law the terms "war" and "use of force" were not synonymous, and there existed circumstances in which armed force was used without creating a state of war and, conversely, circumstances in which a state of war came into existence without any use of armed force. Traditional international law admitted that the use of force short of war, such as reprisals, intervention, self-defence and pacific blockade, existed. According to the majority view, the decisive criterion for the existence of war was the intentions of the concerned State, namely *animus belligerendi*: A state of war was considered to exist either (1) when the concerned States expressly manifested *animus belligerendi* by a declaration of war or some other formal pronouncement, or (2) when *animus belligerendi* was inferred from the States' conducts. However, there were cases in which it was difficult to judge whether there existed *animus belligerendi*. On the concept of war in traditional international law, see e.g. Greenwood, "Concept of War", 284–287; McNair and Watts, *Legal Effects of War*, 1–34; Wolff, *Kriegserklärung und Kriegszustand*, 21–134.

303 Garner, *International Law and the World War*, 1:38.

304 Taoka, *Right of Self-Defence*, 36 [italics added].

305 See e.g. "The Hague Conventions and the Neutrality of Belgium", 961.

306 *Hansard Parliamentary Debates*, 1st ser., vol. 10 (1808), cols. 156–162, 190–194, 642–661, 736–752, 920–921, 1179–1182, 1185–1235, 1247–1250, 1284–1290.

307 Deutsche Note an Belgien, 2 August 2014, in Grewe, *Fontes historiae iuris gentium*, Bd. 3/1, 653; Belgian Minister at Berlin to Belgian Minister for Foreign Affairs, 4 August 1914, in *AJIL Supplement* 9 (1915): 70.

308 For instance, in the case (3), the British government and the United States government disputed about whether a violation of the principle of "immunity of neutral territory from the exercise of acts of hostility or war by a foreign Power" would be justified by "necessity and self-preservation" or "self-defence". See *supra*, note 106 of this chapter. Similarly in the case (5), the Japanese government maintained that

> since the neutral character of the [Cheffo] port has already been destroyed when the Russian vessel of war [*Reshitelni*] escaped from Port Arthur and entered into the port, it is a matter of course that Japan is entitled to take necessary measures of self-defence there.
>
> Komura to the Chinese Minister in Japan, 20 August 1904, *Documents on Japanese Foreign Policy*, Supplement II to Vols. 37 and 38, Doc. No. 1302

309 For instance, in the case (4), the Japanese government attempted to justify the landing of its troops in the Korean territory by referring to "the distinct consent of the Corean [*sic.*] Government". Komura to Hayashi, 4 March 1904, *Documents on Japanese Foreign Policy*, Supplement I to Vols. 37 and 38, p. 78 (Doc. No. 81). Furthermore, in the case (8), the Entente Powers attempted to justify their action on the basis of the Greek government's consent to the entry to and occupation of the Greek territory. Memorandum by Lord E. Percy Respecting Negotiations with Greece, 22 October 1915, TNA: PRO, FO 371/2278, file 164598, paper 174823.

The law of neutrality 1793–1918 139

310 For instance, in the case (7), the Japanese government attempted to justify the entry of its troops into the Chinese territory (namely, a neutral territory) by referring to the alleged facts that "[China], having tolerated Germany, a belligerent State, to arm Jiaozhou Bay and remain there, has clearly violated the duties of neutrality", and that "as a result of China's allowing Germany the free use of the Shantung railway, China has completely failed to abide by the duties of neutrality". Kato to Chinda, 2 September 1914, *Documents on Japanese Foreign Policy* 1914, vol. 3, Doc. No. 395; Kato to Okida, 30 September 1914, ibid., Doc. No. 448. Moreover, in the case (2), the Allied Powers against France, in a declaration of 21 December 1813 in which those powers attempted to justify the invasion of the Swiss territory, maintained that Switzerland was "a subordinate State (un Etat subordonné)" of France and that Switzerland's "alleged neutrality (La prétendu Neutralité)" was in name only, and therefore belligerent States were not obliged to respect it. See Déclaration des Puissances Alliées, en entrant sur le Territoire Suisse, le 21 Décembre, 1813, *BFSP* 1:1165–1169.

311 What I intend to argue here is that there are no cases which prove the non-existence of the right to remain neutral and it is not my intention to positively prove the existence of the right to remain neutral, relying on the cases listed in the main text. The fact that belligerents resorting to war against neutral States have attempted to justify their acts neither proves nor denies the existence of the right to remain neutral. While such justification might be legal justification, we cannot deny the possibility that it was merely political or moral justification. As we shall argue, a more positive basis for the existence of the right to remain neutral is that the denial of this right makes it impossible to explain the reason why neutral States are required to perform the so-called "duties of neutral States".

312 Oppenheim states:

> But for the interest of belligerents to remain during the war on good terms with neutrals, and but for the *interest of the neutrals not to be dragged into the war*, the institution of neutrality would never have developed so favourably as it actually has done during the nineteenth century.
>
> Oppenheim, *International Law*, 1st ed., 2:313–314 [italics added]

However, according to Oppenheim, who denies the existence of the right to remain neutral, the status of a neutral State "not to be dragged into the war" is not legally guaranteed, even if it observes the "duties of neutral States". In other words, Oppenheim fails to prove that the "duties of a neutral" are legally grounded by "the interest of the neutrals not to be dragged into the war".

313 Lifschütz, "Neutralität", 44, 46.

314 Ibid., 66, 73.

315 Ibid., 71.

316 Regarding the principle that neutral States were not required to prohibit private individuals from exporting and transporting contraband articles, see to section 1.4.3 of this chapter.

317 Lifschütz, "Neutralität", 68–73.

318 See above, p. 112.

319 Regarding this point, Heilborn presents another solution. According to Heilborn, neutrality is a "contract (Vertrag)" that comes into existence by an "offer (Offerte)" on the part of a third State and its "acceptance (Annahme)" on the part of a belligerent State, and in such a contract, the third State (neutral State) have "the right (Anspruch) to demand not to be involved in the war". See Heilborn, *Das System des Völkerrechts*, 336–351. For Heilborn, the basis of the right of a neutral State not to be involved in the war is a contract (agreement) with a belligerent State. However, many writers criticised the existence of contracts between a belligerent State and a neutral State as being nothing more than a fiction (see e.g. Ullmann, *Völkerrecht*,

140 *The law of neutrality 1793–1918*

519), and no writers supported Heilborn's theory. Furthermore, according to Heilborn's theory, a belligerent State which has not accepted the offer by a third State may wage war on the third State only because it has not accepted the offer of the third State, but as discussed in the section 2.4.3.B, there is no State practice which supports this view.

320 De Visscher, "De la belligérance", 98 [italics in the original].

321 Ibid., 98–99 [italics in the original].

322 Ibid., 98 [italics in the original].

323 De Visscher, "La théorie de la nécessité", 79.

324 De Visscher, "De la belligérance", 99 [italics in the original].

325 Hershey, *Essentials of International Public Law*, 350–351.

326 Oppenheim, *International Law*, 1st ed., 2:69–70.

327 Ibid., 72–73.

328 According to this view, a State directly related to the cause of war cannot demand respect for its neutrality from belligerent States. For example, Lawrence described the Russo-Japanese War as "war for Korea and in Korea, if not with Korea": Japan and Russia began the war over the issue of Korea. In other words, the issue of Korea was the cause of war itself, and thus Korea was not in a position to claim the neutral status in this war. See Lawrence, *War and Neutrality in the Far East*, 216.

329 De Visscher and Hershey, who take the view that the causes of war limit the personal scope of war, have not expressed their view as to whether the causes of war also limit the temporal scope of war.

330 According to writers such as de Visscher, Hershey and Oppenheim, war is considered as a means of resolving a dispute or a conflict of interest between States or as a means of forcing a demand on another State. In sharp contrast to this conception of war, Quincy Wight, in his article of 1924 observed that "[w]ar is not a lawful institution but an event, an unfortunate event". See Wright, "Changes in the Conception of War", 761. According to Wright, war, like natural disasters in municipal law, is an incident that is neither legal nor illegal, and special rules as suitable to the emergency of war (namely, the laws of war) apply when such "an unfortunate event" occur. In Wright's conception of war, the causes of war, or in other words, the objects for which States resort to war do not matter, and there is no idea of limiting the personal scope of war based on the causes of war. In contrast, the conception of war shared by de Visscher, Hershey and Oppenheim, which assumes and identifies the causes of war, deviates from the just war doctrine in that it abandons the idea that causes of war are divided into just and unjust ones, but still rooted in the just war doctrine as it assumes and identifies the causes of war.

331 See Bridge and Bullen, *Great Powers and the European States System*, 10–11, 97.

3 The development of the law of neutrality in the period 1919–45

To summarise and restate what we have discussed in Chapter 2, the traditional law of neutrality was a means for a neutral State to guarantee its peace and security. In the traditional law of neutrality, a neutral State was legally entitled not to be involved in war as long as it fulfilled the conditions for the right to remain neutral.[1] However, as the duty of a State to remain neutral did not exist in international law, a State did not need to guarantee its peace and security by means of the law of neutrality. A State could guarantee its peace and security by other means, such as alliances with other States.[2] The choice between neutrality or an alliance as the means of guaranteeing the peace and security of a State was a political decision to be made by each State.[3]

After the First World War, collective security appeared as a new means of guaranteeing the peace and security of States.[4] Collective security is a system in which "many different States, including opposing States, promise to refrain from the use of force amongst themselves, and in the case in which any State breaks peace by going against this promise, the related States shall combine the forces of the group in an attempt to maintain peace".[5] The system of collective security was adopted in the interwar period, for example, by the Covenant of the League of Nations (1919)[6] and the Locarno Treaty (1925).[7] States participating in the collective security system bear the burden of applying sanctions when another member State is attacked (for example, the measures provided for in Article 16 of the Covenant of the League of Nations). However, States would also benefit if they were attacked, as the other member States would then take measures to eliminate such an attack. While the specific details of the sanctions that were to be taken if a member State was attacked differed in individual treaties, Article 16 of the Covenant of the League of Nations included measures incompatible with the status of neutrality (see section 1.1 of this chapter). After the First World War, many States participated in the League of Nations and agreed to take sanction measures that would be incompatible with neutrality. In fact, the member States did not invoke the status of neutrality when they took the measures provided for in Article 16 of the Covenant. That is why, the law of neutrality, at a glance, seemed to temporarily disappear as an institution of international law between the 1920s and the first half of the 1930s.

142 *The development of the law of neutrality*

However, as each State is free to decide by itself whether to participate in the League of Nations, it was a matter of political decision for each State to select, as a means of guaranteeing its peace and security, either the collective security system of the League of Nations or the traditional law of neutrality. Prior to the First World War, a State had the option of guaranteeing its peace and security by means of either the law of neutrality or alliances, and in the interwar period, the option of collective security was added to this selection. Therefore, the decisions of States which had relied on the law of neutrality as a means of guaranteeing its peace and security before the First World War to participate in the League of Nations and to attempt to guarantee its peace and security by means of the collective security system were nothing more than a change of security policy. Although many States made such changes of policies, the law of neutrality remained valid as an institution of international law, which could be used again at any time.

This chapter considers the development of the law of neutrality from 1919 to 1945: Between the 1920s and the first half of the 1930s, many States changed their security policies from a policy based on the law of neutrality to a policy based on the collective security system. But, as the ineffectiveness of the collective security system of the League of Nations became clear in the latter half of the 1930s, many States returned to the policies of guaranteeing their peace and security by relying on the law of neutrality. In the Second World War, where many States actually attempted to guarantee their security by adopting the status of neutrality, the law of neutrality functioned just as it had been prior to the First World War (section 1). This chapter also argues that some writers presented a conception of neutrality that was fundamentally different to the traditional conception of neutrality, and this causes much confusion in the debates about the law of neutrality today (section 2).

1 Reliance and non-reliance on the law of neutrality during the interwar period and the Second World War

1.1 Reliance on the collective security system

1.1.1 Collective security system of the League of Nations and neutrality[8]

Articles 12, 13 and 15 of the Covenant of the League of Nations restricted the freedom of States to resort to war. Article 12 provides: "if there should arise between them any dispute likely to lead to a rupture", the members of the League shall "submit the matter either to arbitration or judicial settlement or to enquiry by the Council", and they shall "in no case to resort to war until three months after the award by the arbitrators or the judicial decision or the report by the Council". Articles 13 and 15 apply after three months have passed from the award by the arbitrators or the judicial decision, or the report by the Council. Paragraph 4 of Article 13 prohibits the members of the League from resorting to war against a member of the League that complies with the award or the judicial decision. Paragraph 6 of Article 15 prohibits the members of the League from going to war with any party to the dispute which complies with the recommendations of the report of the Council that had been unanimously agreed to by the members thereof other than the representatives of one or more of the parties to the dispute. In sum, the League Covenant prohibits (1) wars carried out without exhausting peaceful means such as arbitration, judicial settlement or enquiry of the League Council; (2) wars carried out before three months have passed from the award by the arbitrators or the judicial decision, or the report by the Council; and (3) wars against States that comply with the award by the arbitrators or the judicial decision, or the report by the Council that has been unanimously agreed to by the members thereof other than the Representatives of one or more of the parties to the dispute.

Article 16 provides for two types of sanctions against a member of the League that resorts to war in violation of Articles 12, 13 or 15 (referred to as a "covenant-breaking State" hereafter). The first is economic measures. Paragraph 1 of Article 16 of the Covenant provides that all other members of the League "undertake immediately to subject it to the severance of all trade or financial relations, the prohibition of all intercourse between their nationals and the nationals of the covenant-breaking State, and the prevention of all financial, commercial or personal intercourse between the nationals of the covenant-breaking State and the nationals of any other State, whether a Member of the League or not". The second type of sanction is military measures. Paragraph 2 of Article 16, which provides that the League Council shall "recommend to the several Governments concerned what military, naval or air force the members of the League shall severally contribute to the armed forces to be used to protect the Covenants of the League", assumes the possibility of military measures being taken against a covenant-breaking State. While the members of the League are not legally bound to participate in these military measures, paragraph 3 of Article 16 provides that the members of the League "will take the necessary steps to afford passage through their territory to the forces of any of the Members of the League which are co-operating to protect the Covenants of the League".

These measure provided for in Article 16 of the Covenant include measures incompatible with neutrality.[9]

First, in cases where members of the League take economic measures *within their territories*, the discriminatory nature of such measures would become an issue. In the traditional law of neutrality, neutral States were free to discontinue their trade and financial relations with belligerent States or to prohibit intercourse between their nationals and the nationals of belligerents. But neutral States had to apply such measures impartially to all belligerent States.[10] Therefore, discontinuing the trade and financial relations only with the covenant-breaking State or prohibiting intercourse of their nationals only with the nationals of the covenant-breaking States would be measures that are incompatible with neutrality.[11]

Second, another issue arises in cases where members of the League enforce economic measures against vessels of non-member States *outside their territory*

144   *The development of the law of neutrality*

(on the high seas or in the territorial seas of the covenant-breaking States). Based on paragraph 1 of Article 16 of the Covenant, members of the League are bound to prevent "all financial, commercial and personal intercourse between the nationals of the covenant-breaking State and the nationals of *any other State, whether a Member of the League or not*" [italics added]. There would be cases in which members of the League should prevent maritime intercourse between the nationals of the covenant-breaking State and the nationals of non-members of the League. However, such maritime intercourse cannot be prevented by means of a pacific blockade. According to the prevailing opinion at that time, while a State enforcing a pacific blockade may seize the vessels of the blockaded State, it may not seize the vessels of third States.[12] Therefore, in order to carry out such measures lawfully according to international law, members of the League have no other option than establishing belligerent blockades. In cases of belligerent blockades, all the vessels and their cargoes that have breached the blockade may be seized and confiscated, regardless of whether they are enemy vessels or neutral vessels. However, by establishing and enforcing a belligerent blockade, a blockading State becomes a belligerent; thus, this measure is incompatible with the status of neutrality.

Finally, as regards military measures, while members of the League are not bound to take the measures provided for in paragraph 2 of Article 16 (use of military, naval and air force), they are bound to take the measures provided for in paragraph 3 of the same Article (the necessary measure of allowing the armed forces of League member States to pass through their territory). According to the traditional law of neutrality, a neutral State should not allow the armed forces of belligerents to pass through its territory.[13] Therefore, measures provided for in paragraph 3 are incompatible with neutrality.

In sum, in cases where war breaks out in violation of Articles 12, 13 and 15 of the Covenant, members of the League are obliged by Article 16 to take a number of measures that are not compatible with neutrality.[14] Nevertheless, forty-two States participated in the League of Nations as original members, including States that had guaranteed their peace and security relying on the law of neutrality. What was the background behind the participation of these States in the League of Nations? We shall consider this point below.

1.1.2 Participation of small European States in the League: change of their security policies

Small European States such as Belgium, Denmark, the Netherlands, Norway, Sweden, and Switzerland had adopted security policies based on neutrality before the First World War.[15] As discussed in Chapter 2, in the traditional law of neutrality, neutral States had the right not to be involved in war as long as they observed neutrality. Small European States, by relying on the law of neutrality, had adopted policies to avoid being involved in war.

However, these States participated in the League of Nations after the First World War, although their participation meant bearing the duty to take measures incompatible with neutrality. This fact signified a change of security policies for these States from one based on the law of neutrality to a security policy based on collective security. Why did these States change their security policies? The controversy over the Switzerland's participation in the League of Nations provides a clue to this question.

The participation of Switzerland in the League was decided following a resolution adopted at the second Council of the League of Nations (February 1920), the approval of the Swiss government (3 and 4 March 1920) and a national referendum (16 May 1920).[16] However, there was much controversy in Switzerland about the pros and cons of participation in the League, and there were various debates before the participation in the League was finally decided. When the Swiss government decided to participate in the League, it declared that it would participate in "no military action of the League of Nations" based on Article 16 of the Covenant,[17] which was approved by the League Council. But it was acknowledged that Switzerland had the "duty to participate in commercial and financial measures".[18] Therefore, the issue for Switzerland was whether to favour or oppose undertaking the duty to enforce the economic measures by participating in the League of Nations.

For example, the report of the minority of the National Defence Committee (Landesverteidigungskommission), which was a committee established within the Swiss Military Department (das schweizerische Militärdepartment), opposed the participation of Switzerland in the League. This was one of the reports drafted and presented by the National Defence Committee, which had been requested by the government to study the issue of participation in the League. As there were conflicting opinions within the committee and the committee has failed to draft a single report, the committee presented a report of the majority and a report of minority to the government (July 1919).[19]

The minority report contended: "[T]here is only *absolute* neutrality (*absolute* Neutraltät) for Switzerland in the future as well as in the World War that is strictly enforced not only in military relations but also in economic relations, *if we will estimate the recognition of it by both belligerents*." The ground of this contention is the importance of economic warfare in contemporary wars. According to the report, "in the World War, it was made clear that economic warfare (der wirtschaftliche Krieg), that is, starvation blockade (Hungerblockade), has been proven obviously as the most fruitful and *the most effective means of warfare*". Therefore, "it would be perfectly absurd to demand that the advantages of neutrality, particularly that of territorial inviolability, from both belligerent States, while exercising such means of [economic] warfare as a member of the League to benefit one belligerent and to disadvantage the other belligerent". The belligerent disadvantaged by such measures would surely "declare this conduct as being not *neutral* but as being *hostile (feindselig)*". For these reasons, the minority report of the National Defence Committee concluded that Switzerland should not participate in the League because "Switzerland would run the risk of being involved in all wars and enforcement [measures] carried out by the League of Nations" if it did.[20]

146 *The development of the law of neutrality*

On the other hand, the report of the majority of the National Defence Committee contended that Switzerland should participate in the League of Nations. This report acknowledges that the measures provided for in paragraph 1 of Article 16 of the Covenant amount to the "unequal treatment" of belligerents, and that such unequal treatment might provide the belligerent thus disadvantaged with "a ground that justifies the intended attack against the territorial integrity of Switzerland". It also acknowledges that "[n]aturally Switzerland must avoid giving [belligerents] a justifiable cause (berechtigten Anlass) to violate its neutrality". However, according to the report, the unequal treatment of belligerents provided for in paragraph 1 of Article 16 of the Covenant is a "secondary issue", and "a secondary issue should not be given too much importance". That is because "the participation [of Switzerland in economic measures] ... can only inflict a small amount of damage on the blockaded State". On the other hand, there are major benefits for Switzerland of participating in the League; for example, the aid that would be received from League members if it were attacked by another State. In the end, while recognising that the measures provided for in paragraph 1 of Article 16 of the Covenant would bring about certain disadvantages for Switzerland, this report supported the participation of Switzerland in the League for the reason that such disadvantages were regarded as being minor and that the advantages of participation in the League were greater than the disadvantages.[21]

The argument in favour of the participation in the League was also developed in the message of the Swiss Federal Council addressed to the Swiss Federal Assembly (4 August 1919).[22] In this message, the Federal Council acknowledges that the participation in the League and undertaking the duty to take the economic measures provided for in paragraph 1 of Article 16 of the League Covenant would entail a certain level of "disadvantage and risk (Nachteile und Gefahren)". The "disadvantage and risk" is the possibility that the taking of such economic measures would be seen as unequal treatment of belligerents, which would be invoked as an "excuse (Vorwand)" by covenant-breaking States to violate the neutrality of Switzerland. According to the Federal Council, however, in actuality, "the unequal treatment itself would not be an actual cause of war". That is because "what is important for belligerents ... is only the military operations (militärischen Unternehmungen) of neutral States, or, in other words, that neutral States do not participate in the military operations of the enemy State and that the direct use of the territory of neutral States for the military operations of [the enemy State] ... is prevented". The economic measures taken by Switzerland against the covenant-breaking State would be only of "relatively small significance" to the covenant-breaking State. Moreover, in the situation in which many members of the League take economic measures, it would be almost meaningless for the covenant-breaking State to attack only Switzerland in order to prevent the economic measures taken by Switzerland, which would rather carry the risk of a counterattack from the other members. Hence, the actual risk of Switzerland being attacked by the covenant-breaking State would be minor. On the other hand, by participating in the League,

Switzerland would receive the benefits of the "peacekeeping systems established by Articles 12 to 17 of the Covenant of the League of Nations". In the end, the Federal Council, emphasising the benefits of participation over the smaller disadvantages and risks, concluded that Switzerland should participate in the League.

The conflicting views over the participation of Switzerland in the League of Nations can be summarised as follows. Both the arguments in favour of and against the participation in the League shared the view that the economic measures provided for in paragraph 1 of Article 16 of the Covenant were the "unequal treatment" of the covenant-breaking State, which could be invoked as a "ground" or "excuse" by the covenant-breaking State to violate the neutrality of Switzerland and to make war on Switzerland. The opinions were divided as to the actual risk for the covenant-breaking State to invoke such basis or excuse so as to make war on Switzerland. The argument in favour of the participation in the League argued that the economic measures were of no more than minor significance to the covenant-breaking State, and that the benefits of the protection of the collective security system of the League outweighed the minor possibility that the covenant-breaking State would wage war on Switzerland. On the other hand, the arguments against the participation in the League was that as economic warfare had an important role in contemporary war, "Switzerland would face the risk of being involved in all wars carried out by the League of Nations" if it participated in the League. Ultimately, the argument in favour of the participation in the League, according to which Switzerland could guarantee the relatively greater security by participating in the League, attracted general support, and Switzerland decided to participate in the League.

The circumstances behind and the reasons for Switzerland's decision to participate in the League seems to be the same as those in cases of many other small States. For example, Hiroshi Momose, discussing the participation of the Scandinavian States in the League of Nations, states:

> The thing that made an impression on *small* Scandinavian States from the experience of the First World War was the decreasing potential of ensuring one's security and independence on the basis of *neutrality* during wars between Great Powers, and thus the Scandinavian States, putting aside their traditional diplomatic policy of wartime neutrality, found a means of guaranteeing their security in the organised international relations, and decided to participate in the League of Nations.[23]

As shown by the case of the German violation of Belgian neutrality in the First World War, the effectiveness of the law of neutrality as a means of guaranteeing the security of the State was in doubt. In such circumstances, many small States, having considered that relying on the collective security system of the League of Nations offered greater security than relying on the law of neutrality, decided to participate in the League.

Many States that participated in the League of Nations in the 1920s entrusted their security not to the law of neutrality but to the collective security

148 *The development of the law of neutrality*

system of the League of Nations. Therefore, there were only a few cases in which the status of neutrality was invoked in State practice between the 1920s and the first half of the 1930s. For example, in the Chaco War between Bolivia and Paraguay (1933–35), in which an embargo on weapons and military goods was enforced against Paraguay on the basis of recommendations by the General Assembly and the Council of the League, only five States (Argentina, Brazil, Chile, Peru and Uruguay) issued declarations of neutrality.[24] Also, in the Italo–Ethiopian War (1935–36), while some non-member States such as Germany and the United States issued declarations of neutrality,[25] member States of the League, based on Article 16 of the Covenant, enforced economic sanctions against Italy, and did not invoke the status of neutrality.[26]

It must be noted here that the prerequisite for the decision of States, and small States in particular, to participate in the League in the 1920s was the expectation that their peace and security would be effectively guaranteed by the collective security system of the League. Due to such expectations, many States decided to bear the burden of taking the measures provided for in Article 16 of the Covenant despite the risk of being invoked as the "ground" for the covenant-breaking State to declare war on States taking such measures. But there would be no reason to bear this burden if such expectations were not met. Actually, as seen below, in the mid-1930s and thereafter when it became clear that the collective security system of the League of Nations was not functioning effectively, various small States advocated an exemption from the burden of Article 16 of the Covenant and returned to the traditional security policies based on the law of neutrality.

1.2 Collapse of the Versailles system and returns to traditional neutrality[27]

The League of Nations constituted an important part of the Versailles system, which was the international order based on the peace treaties after the First World War. Although the Versailles system ensured stability for a while in the 1920s, it had collapsed by the 1930s due to the several incidents brought about by Germany, Italy and Japan, which criticised the Versailles system as being an international order only for the "haves" States.[28] These incidents included the Manchurian Conflict (1931), the Nazi takeover of the German government (1933), the withdrawal of Japan and Germany from the League of Nations (1933), the German declaration of rearmament (1935), the Italo–Ethiopian war (1935–36) and the German occupation of Rhineland (1936).

Of these incidents, the one that had the largest impact on the security policies of small States was the Italo–Ethiopian war. In this war, although the Council of the League of Nations determined that "the Italian government has resorted to war in disregard of its covenants under Article 12 of the Covenant of the League of Nations" (7 October 1935),[29] which was supported by fifty member States at the Assembly, and economic measures based on paragraph 1 of Article 16 were taken, Italian aggression against Ethiopia did not come to an

The development of the law of neutrality 149

end. The reason was that oil, which was all-important in the execution of the war, was excluded from the list of items for economic sanction. The background to this was that Great Britain, which was promoting economic sanctions against Italy, did not have "the determination to risk of waging war in order to prevent the aggressive behaviour of Italy", but "the sanctions were limited to those that did not risk the outbreak of war".[30]

As a result, small European States that had ensured their security by means of the collective security system of the League of Nations, having realised that "the League of Nations and the Anglo-French power was unreliable", took up a policy of "being released, if possible, from the duty in Anglo-French centric League of Nations to sanction aggressors".[31] This policy was put into practice by denying the obligatory nature of Article 16 of the Covenant, and returning to the traditional neutrality.

First, small European States, referring to the inconsistent application of Article 16 of the Covenant in practice (such as the non-application in the Manchurian Conflict in 1931), asserted that the implementation of the measures provided for in Article 16 was a matter left to the discretion of each member State and that these measures were not necessarily to be enforced in all wars that were in violation of Articles 12, 13 and 15. For example, on 1 July 1936, Belgium, Denmark, Finland, the Netherlands, Norway, Spain, Sweden and Switzerland made a joint declaration stating that "so long as the Covenant as a whole is applied only incompletely and inconsistently, we are obliged to bear that fact in mind in connection with the application of Article 16".[32] Also, the Swiss Ministry of Foreign Affairs in February 1938 stated: "Article 16 [of the Covenant] has no longer functioned. It is the general opinion that Article 16 has been proven to be inapplicable in certain cases. It has therefore become actually optional (tatsächlich fakultative)."[33]

After denying the obligatory nature of Article 16 of the Covenant, small European States declared their intention to return to the policies of ensuring their security based on the law of neutrality. For example, in 1938, based on the "need to protect the security of [Switzerland]", the Swiss government declared its intention to return to "perfect neutrality (netralité intégrale ou compléte)" or "traditional neutrality (neutralité traditionnelle)".[34] On 27 May 1938, Denmark, Finland, Iceland, Norway and Sweden declared that those States would enact neutrality laws with common contents, "[c]onsidering that it is highly desirable that the rules of neutrality applied by them in case of war between foreign Powers should be similar".[35] The details of these neutrality laws generally followed the rules that were established at the 1907 Hague Conventions.[36] These States therefore declared their intention to rely on the traditional law of neutrality in future wars.

The reason why small European States returned to the policies of ensuring their security based on the traditional law of neutrality was that it was necessary to "protect the security" of the States, as stated by the Swiss government.[37] States undertook the duties of Article 16 of the Covenant, even though they carried the risks of being invoked by the covenant-breaking State as the basis to

150 *The development of the law of neutrality*

declare war on States that took such measures, because the States deemed that the risks would be outweighed by the benefits of the collective security system of the League of Nations. However, as it had become clear that the security of small States could not be effectively ensured by the League of Nations, the reason to dare to risk applying Article 16 of the Covenant disappeared. And thus, such States returned to the traditional policies of ensuring their security based on the law of neutrality. In fact, as shown below, these States attempted to ensure their peace and security in the Second World War by relying on the law of neutrality.

1.3 Reliance on the law of neutrality in the Second World War

The Second World War broke out with the invasion of Poland by the German army (1 September 1939) and the declaration of war against Germany made by Great Britain and France (3 September 1939). Following that, forty States issued declarations of Neutrality.[38] However, it was difficult for these neutral States to maintain their neutrality. During the Second World War, there were frequent cases of wars or hostilities carried out by belligerents against neutral States.

Nevertheless, the traditional law of neutrality, as an institution protecting the right of neutral States to remain outside the war, despite its declining effectiveness, retained it legal validity in this war. That is because belligerent States that waged wars or hostilities against neutral States attempted to justify their actions by asserting that those neutral States had committed violations of neutrality. On the other hand, neutral States condemned the actions of belligerent States as violations of international law, asserting that they had been observing neutrality. In other words, both neutral States and belligerent States shared the idea that a belligerent State may not wage war or hostilities against a neutral State as long as the neutral State observes neutrality. In order to illustrate this point, we shall consider the cases of Norway, the Netherlands and Belgium, which were eventually involved in the war by belligerents despite their wishes to remain neutral.

1.3.1 Norway

The Norwegian government made a declaration of neutrality immediately after the Second World War broke out.[39] Great Britain and Germany, which were at war with each other, promised to respect the neutrality of Norway in this war, providing the other belligerent State respected the Norwegian neutrality and Norway itself maintained neutrality.[40] Despite these promises, the belligerents carried out hostilities in the territory of Norway, and Norway was ultimately involved in the war.

Great Britain was the first to carry out hostilities within the territory of Norway: in the *Altmark* incident of February 1940. The *Altmark* incident refers to the incident in which the British destroyer *Cossack* battled against the *Altmark*, a German Naval Auxiliary, which was passing through the territorial waters of Norway, as the *Cossack* attempted rescue of British prisoners of war on board the *Altmark*. The Norwegian government made "a strong protest against grave violation of Norwegian neutrality" to the British government: The acts of the *Cossack* within Norwegian territorial waters violated Article 2 of the 1907 Hague Convention (XIII) concerning the Rights and Duties of Neutral Powers in Naval War, which forbade belligerent States from committing any act of hostility in the territorial waters of neutral States.[41]

The issue in this incident was whether the passage of the *Altmark* through the territorial waters of Norway was "the mere passage (le simple passage) through its territorial waters of war-ships", as provided for in Article 10 of the 1907 Hague Convention (XIII), and therefore, whether it was the passage by which "[t]he neutrality of a Power is not affected".[42] The *Altmark* originally engaged in the operation of supplying fuel and other materials to the *Admiral Graf Spee*, a German battle cruiser. After the *Graf Spee* had self-destructed in the River Plate (Uruguay) in December 1939,[43] the *Altmark* attempted to return to Germany with approximately 300 British prisoners of war on board. On 14 February 1940, the *Altmark* entered Norwegian territorial waters off the Trondheim while going around the north of Great Britain in order to avoid the English Channel, which was being strictly controlled by the British Navy. It travelled 400 miles through Norwegian territorial waters in the two days before encountering the *Cossack*. In this incident, the issue was whether the passage of approximately 400 miles through Norwegian territorial waters over two days for the purpose of avoiding being seized or attacked by British warships could be considered as "the mere passage" through the territorial waters of a neutral State.

According to the Norwegian government, as the *Altmark* has passed through its territorial waters without stopping even once in a Norwegian port, the rules regarding the period of stay in neutral ports of belligerent warships, which is provided for in Article 12 of the 1907 Hague Convention (XIII), does not apply to this case: The rule applicable in this case is the rule regarding the passage of belligerent warships through the territorial waters of neutral States, which is provided for in Article 10 of the same Convention, but neither the Hague Convention (XIII) nor the Norwegian domestic laws place any limitations on the duration of the passage through the territorial waters of a neutral State. The Norwegian government maintains that the presence of prisoners of war on board the *Altmark* does not affect the nature of the *Altmark*'s passage through Norwegian territorial waters. For these reasons, the Norwegian government concludes that the passage of the *Altmark* through Norwegian territorial waters has not violated the neutrality of Norway, and that Norway, by permitting such passage, has not committed any violation of neutrality.[44]

On the other hand, according to the British government, the *Altmark* used Norwegian territorial waters as "shelter" in order to avoid being attacked or seized by British warships, and Norway was obliged to take necessary measures to prevent such use of its territorial waters. Norway, for example, should have refused the *Altmark* from entering into Norwegian territorial waters. But it did not do so. The British government, therefore, concluded:

152 *The development of the law of neutrality*

> [T]he use made by the *Altmark* of Norwegian territorial waters was not a legitimate exercise of the right of innocent passage, and ought not have been permitted by the Norwegian Government; and that the action of the Norwegian Government in permitting, and, indeed, facilitating, the *Altmark*'s operations, and in making no proper enquiry as to the nature and object of those operations, constituted a failure to observe the obligations of neutrality. In the light of the facts and the above considerations, His Majesty's Government feel that they were fully justified in taking the action which in the circumstances they felt compelled to take.[45]

In this incident, the opinions of the governments of Norway and Great Britain differed as to whether the passage of the *Altmark* through Norwegian territorial waters was a violation of neutrality, and, therefore, whether Norway should have refused such passage in order to maintain neutrality.[46] However, what is crucial is that both governments shared the view that hostilities against a neutral State or within its territory are prohibited as long as the neutral State observes neutrality; on the contrary, there were cases in which hostilities against a neutral State are permitted if the neutral State failed to take the necessary measures to maintain neutrality. That is why it was debated as to whether Norway had taken the measures necessary to maintain neutrality. In other words, the traditional law of neutrality, as an institution guaranteeing the right of neutral States to remain outside the war, functioned as a framework for the negotiations between the two governments in this incident.

The *Altmark* incident changed the German government's perception of Norwegian neutrality. The background to that was the issue of the importation of iron ore from Sweden to Germany via Norway.[47] Germany was dependent on Sweden for the importation of iron ore, which was essential in carrying out the war. But the ports of Bothnia in Sweden, from where it was exported, were frozen during the winter; hence, the iron ore was taken by train to the ice-free port of Narvik in Norway and, after being shipped from the same port, was transported to Germany through Norwegian territorial waters. As long as Norway remained neutral, Norwegian territorial waters was neutral territorial waters, and Great Britain could not seize ships transporting iron ore within neutral Norwegian territorial waters. Germany, therefore, considered the Norwegian neutrality to be beneficial to Germany. However, the *Altmark* incident made clear that Great Britain had the intention to violate the neutrality of Norway and to carry out hostilities in Norwegian territorial waters, and that Norway was unable and unwilling to resist these actions. At least, that was the perception of the German government. The German government, therefore, considered it necessary to occupy Norway before Great Britain would do so, in order to secure the iron ore that was essential for carrying out the war. Germany actually carried out military operations to occupy Norway on 9 April 1940.

The German government presented a memorandum to the Norwegian government and justified the military operations as follows:

The development of the law of neutrality 153

The Nordic States have tolerated the interference (Übergriffen) of Great Britain and France, not only by failing to resist them, but also by not taking any countermeasures (Gegenmaßnahmen) to oppose grave violations of sovereign rights (Hoheitsrechte).

Therefore, the [German] Imperial government is forced to believe that the Norwegian Royal government will continue to take the same attitude toward measures that have already been planned and are yet to be carried out by Great Britain and France. Even if the Norwegian Royal government has the intention to take countermeasures, it is clear to the [German] Imperial government that the military force of Norway is not sufficient to effectively oppose the military operations of Great Britain and France.

In this decisive phase of the struggle for existence (Existenzkampfes) wherein the people of Germany have pushed into by Great Britain and France, the [German] Imperial government cannot tolerate under any circumstances the Scandinavian States being made into regions of war (Kriegsschauplatz) by Great Britain and France, and people of Norway being used either directly or indirectly in the war against Germany.[48]

The "interference" of Great Britain and France and "grave violations of sovereign rights" of Norway, which was referred to in this memorandum, were, according to the German government, the fact that Great Britain and France demanded that Scandinavian States allow the use of their territory "as bases for military operations" in order to attack northern Germany. According to the German government, Norway had thus far tolerated such interference and would probably continue to do so. In sum, the German government asserted that Norway was unwilling and unable to prevent the military use of Norwegian territory by Great Britain and France, and therefore Germany was forced to carry out military operations to occupy Norway in order to prevent the military use of the Norwegian territory by those States.

In this memorandum, the German government took a view that the occupation of the Norwegian territory by the German army was a "defensive measure (Sicherheitsmaßnahmen)" to prevent the occupation of the Norwegian territory by Great Britain and France, which did not create a state of war between Germany and Norway. However, on 24 April 1940, Germany declared that a state of war existed between the two States due to the Norwegian resistance to the German army.[49]

In this war, the belligerent States (Great Britain and Germany) carried out hostilities against Norway, and Germany finally declared war against Norway. However, what is crucial is the fact that both Great Britain and Germany attempted to justify their acts by asserting that Norway had committed violations of neutrality, and that the Norwegian government, on its part, contended that it had maintained neutrality and condemned the acts of Great Britain and Germany as being impermissible under international law. In other words, all three States shared the view that, as long as a neutral State maintains neutrality, belligerent States are prohibited from carrying out hostilities or from declaring

154 *The development of the law of neutrality*

war against the neutral States. The law of neutrality, just as prior to the First World War, functioned as the framework to decide the legality or illegality of the hostilities and wars by belligerent States against neutral States. The Norwegian government, in condemning the hostilities and wars conducted by Great Britain and Germany, invoked its status as a neutral, but did not invoked the Pact of Paris. The significance of this fact will be considered in section 1.3.3.

1.3.2 *The Netherlands and Belgium*

In August 1939, just prior to the outbreak of the Second World War, the German and British governments respectively made promises to the governments of the Netherlands and Belgium to respect the neutrality of the latter States, providing the other belligerent State also respected their neutrality.[50] The governments of the Netherlands and Belgium issued declarations of neutrality as soon as the war broke out, thereby declaring their intention to remain neutral in this war.[51]

However, even before the outbreak of the war, Adolf Hitler had already made plans to occupy the Netherlands and Belgium in case of war with Great Britain and France. According to Hitler's idea, the purpose of the occupation of the Netherland and Belgium was to attack Great Britain from the air bases in these States and to protect the Ruhr.[52] These plans were put into practice on 10 May 1940, when the German army invaded the Netherlands and Belgium and occupied their territories.

The German government presented memorandums with identical content to the governments of the Netherlands and Belgium, which justified the invasion and occupation of both States. The German government pointed out that Great Britain and France had plans to attack Germany from the West by passing through the territories of Belgium and the Netherlands and stated the following in connection to the attitudes of Belgium and the Netherlands with regard to these plans:

> Germany has recognised and respected the integrity (Integrität) of Belgium and the Netherland *on the natural assumption* (*unter der selbstverständlichen Voraussetzung*) that these two States would maintain strict neutrality in the case of the war between Germany on the one hand and Great Britain and France on the other.
>
> Belgium and the Netherlands have not fulfilled these *conditions* (*diese Bedingung*). They have admittedly tried to keep an appearance of maintaining neutrality so far, but in reality, these two States have unilaterally favoured the enemies of Germany and encouraged their intentions (Absichten).[53]

According to the German government, as Belgium and the Netherlands had aided Great Britain and France and had not maintained strict neutrality in this war, the conditions on which Germany was to respect the territorial

The development of the law of neutrality   155

integrity of Belgium and the Netherlands had not been satisfied. The German government alleged, as the proof that Belgium and the Netherlands had not maintained strict neutrality, many facts such as the fact that they had not taken any measures against the violation of their airspace perpetrated by the air forces of Great Britain and France, and the fact that they had provided support for the intelligence gathering activities of Great Britain and France inside Germany.

The German government drew the following conclusion from the alleged failure of Belgium and the Netherlands to maintain strict neutrality:

> The [German] Imperial government, in this struggle for survival into which German people have been forced by Great Britain and France, does not intend to stand idly by watching the attacks carried out by Great Britain and France, nor does it have the intention to ignore the war until it reaches the territory of Germany after passing through Belgium and the Netherlands. Therefore, it has given the German army an order to *guarantee the neutrality* (*Neutralität sicherzustellen*) of these States with all military means.[54]

The German government justified its invasion and occupation of the Netherlands and Belgium as measures to "guarantee the neutrality" of these States on the basis of the alleged failure of both States to satisfy the "conditions" on which Germany would respect the neutrality of these States, that is, the conditions that both States would maintain strict neutrality. To "guarantee neutrality" means to prevent the use of the territory of these States by Great Britain and France for the purpose of military operations against Germany.

Objecting to this assertion, the governments of the Netherlands and Belgium claimed to the German government that they had maintained strict neutrality. The government of the Netherlands presented a verbal note to the German Ministry of Foreign Affairs through the legation in Berlin on 10 May 1940, which asserted:

> There is absolutely no legal justification (Rechtfertigung) for German aggression against the Netherlands. The Netherlands has maintained its neutrality in all earnestness – and the Chancellor of the German Empire has several times solemnly promised not to violate [the neutrality of the Netherlands], particularly in the declaration made on 26 August 1939.
>
> In violation of the basic principles of law and morality, Germany has torn up several hundred years of peaceful and friendly relations with the nationals of the Netherlands.[55]

At the same time as making a protest to the German government,[56] the Belgian government issued a statement to the foreign representatives in Brussels (10 May 1940), contending that Belgium had maintained strict neutrality and condemning the actions of Germany:

156 *The development of the law of neutrality*

> For the duration of this conflict, Belgium has always maintained strict and faithful neutrality ... Just as in August 1914 when Germany violated the neutrality of Belgium secured on the basis of the treaty of 19 April 1839, Germany today has attacked Belgium in opposition to the promises concluded in 1937 and updated in 1939. Just as in 1914, an attack on a neutral State is unjustifiable in itself (injustifiée en soi), and even more unjust as it goes against the promises made.[57]

In sum, there were conflicting views between the government of Germany on the one hand and the governments of the Netherlands and Belgium on the other, as to whether the German invasion and occupation of the Netherlands and Belgium was lawful and whether the Netherlands and Belgium had maintained neutrality. (The governments of the Netherlands and Belgium regarded the German invasion and occupation as war,[58] while the German government denied it as being war.[59]) However, all three States shared the view that the conditions for belligerents to abstain from committing hostilities or making war against neutral States was that the neutral States themselves maintain neutrality: While belligerents were permitted to resort to war against a neutral State that had committed violations of neutrality, war or hostilities against a neutral State that had observed strict neutrality were prohibited. In other words, the law of neutrality, as an institution that provides the framework for determining the legality or illegality of war on the part of belligerents against neutral States, functioned as before. As in the case of Norway, the governments of the Netherlands and Belgium invoked their status as neutrals when condemning the acts of Germany, but the Pact of Paris was not invoked even once. The significance of this fact will be considered below.

1.3.3 Evaluation of the cases

In the cases of Norway, the Netherlands and Belgium, while there was a conflict of views between the belligerents and the neutral States as to whether the neutral States had maintained neutrality, there was a common assumption that belligerent States were not permitted to carry out hostilities or make war against neutral States that were maintaining strict neutrality. In other words, the law of neutrality, as an institution that provides the framework for determining the legality or illegality of war on the part of belligerents against neutral States, still functioned in State practice during the Second World War.

However, as typically demonstrated by the fact that Hitler had made plans to occupy the Netherlands and Belgium prior to the outbreak of the Second World War, the allegation made by the belligerent States that the neutral States had committed violations of neutrality was nothing more than an excuse to justify existing military operations. In the Second World War, belligerent States also carried out hostilities or made war against other neutral States, such as Denmark, Greece, Iceland and Luxembourg.[60] Although the law of neutrality, which protected the legal status of neutral States not to be involved in war,

The development of the law of neutrality 157

retained its legal validity during the Second World War, its effectiveness was largely declining.

Nevertheless, many States relied on the law of neutrality in the Second World War. Forty States issued declarations of neutrality at the beginning of this war.[61] Neutral States such as Norway, the Netherlands and Belgium condemned the military operations carried out against them by belligerent States, by invoking their status as neutrals. The reliance of many States on the law of neutrality seemed to be due to the lack of any other available means of ensuring their peace and security. As seen in sections 1.1 and 1.2 of this chapter, the collective security system of the League of Nations, which was expected to be a more effective means of ensuring peace and security than the law of neutrality in the 1920s, had no longer functioned since the latter half of the 1930s.

These facts show that the law of neutrality served at least some useful functions for a State wishing to remain outside the war. Certainly, the military actions of belligerent States were primarily determined by political, strategic and tactical factors. However, when belligerent States carried out military operations against neutral States, the belligerent States always attempted to justify their actions with reference to international law. Belligerents do not always succeed in justifying their actions, and there are varying degrees of persuasiveness in their justifications. Also, in cases where the justifying argument does not hold up, or in cases where there is a low level of persuasiveness, the belligerent State is condemned for violating international law. The fact that belligerent States have attempted to legally justify their actions even in such extreme situations as war shows that States view allegations of violations of international law as political costs, which they try to avoid to whatever extent possible.[62] Neutral States have invoked the law of neutrality and have condemned the acts of belligerent States as being illegal in order to place limitations on the actions of belligerent States by imposing political costs. In the Second World War, neutral States have relied on the law of neutrality because they have recognised the utility of the law of neutrality as an institution of international law.

As seen in section 1.1 and 1.2 of this chapter, neutral States, which invoked the status of neutrality when condemning the military actions of belligerent States against neutral States during the Second World War, did not invoke the Pact of Paris. What was the reason for this? When the armed forces of a State (a belligerent State in this case) invades or attacks another State (a neutral State in this case) or occupies its territory, these acts would violate the Pact of Paris. In those cases, would it not have been reasonable for neutral States to invoke the Pact of Paris when condemning the actions of belligerent States? Nevertheless, why did these States rely on the law of neutrality when condemning the actions of belligerent States without invoking the Pact of Paris?

One possible explanation for this is that States supported the view denying the legal or obligatory character of the Pact of Paris.[63] Indeed, some writers in the interwar period had denied the obligatory character of the Pact of Paris. The grounds for such a view were: (1) the deficiency of the Pact of Paris in prohibiting war as a means of self-help without providing other means of redress;[64] and

158   *The development of the law of neutrality*

(2) that the Pact of Paris reserved the right of self-defence of contracting States, and in particular, it recognised each State's authority to judge by itself what constituted the right of self-defence.[65] However, it is difficult to say that the views denying the legal or obligatory character of the Pact of Paris were supported by State practice. That is because the Pact of Paris was frequently invoked and applied in the practice of States during the interwar period and the Second World War.[66]

Yet, there remained many uncertainties regarding the interpretation of the Pact of Paris, including the issue of its legal character, and the issue of the extent of the right of self-defence, which was reserved in the Pact. In comparison, the law of neutrality was a long-standing tradition since at least at the end of the eighteenth century, and there existed treaties that had codified its principles and rules (namely, the 1907 Hague Convention (V) respecting the Rights and Duties of Neutral Powers and Persons in Case of War on Land and the Convention (XIII) concerning the Rights and Duties of Neutral Powers in Naval War). In such circumstances, States might have considered that the law of neutrality provided a more reliable basis than the Pact of Paris, as the framework that determined the legality or illegality of wars and hostilities carried out by belligerent States against neutral States. That being so, it was natural that States frequently relied on the law of neutrality without invoking the Pact of Paris.[67]

1.4 Non-reliance of the law of neutrality in the Second World War

As we have seen in the previous section, in the Second World War, many States, such as Norway, the Netherlands and Belgium, relied on the law of neutrality as a means of remaining outside the war and thereby ensuring their peace and security. On the other hand, there were also States that took measures incompatible with neutrality in this war. The typical example of such States was the United States from 1939 to 1941, which provided military assistance to Great Britain, a belligerent in the war. As we will see, the United States had no intention to remain outside the war.

1.4.1 Assistance given to Great Britain by the United States

On 5 September 1939, immediately after the outbreak of the Second World War, the United States government issued a proclamation of neutrality and invoked the Neutrality Act of 1937.[68] The Neutrality Act of 1937 is the statute of the United States, the main content of which is a clause that forbids, in cases where war breaks out between other States, the export of "arms, ammunition or implements of war" from any place in the United States to any belligerent State (commonly known as the "arms embargo clause").[69] "Arms, ammunition or implements of war" exported and transported by sea to a belligerent State are contraband of war, which may be seized and confiscated by the other belligerent. As noted in section 1.4.3 of Chapter 2, in the traditional law of neutrality, private individuals were free to export and transport contraband articles if they

The development of the law of neutrality   159

were prepared for the risk of seizure and confiscation by belligerents, and neutral States were not bound to prohibit or prevent the export and transportation of contraband articles by private individuals. Nevertheless, the United States voluntarily prohibited the export and transport of "arms, ammunition or implements of war" from the United States to belligerent States by the 1937 Neutrality Act. This prohibition was based on the idea that, from the experience of being drawn into the First World War due to the friction with belligerent States regarding issues of maritime commerce, a voluntary prohibition of the export of contraband articles was necessary, even though it was not required by the international law of neutrality, in order to avoid friction with belligerent States and to remain outside the war.[70] In the interwar period, the United States imposed greater restrictions on its own actions than those demanded by the international law of neutrality, in order not to be involved in wars between other States. However, in any event, as long as it was applied impartially to all belligerent States, the voluntary prohibition by a neutral State on the export of contraband of war was permissible under the law of neutrality (see Article 9 of the Hague Convention (V) respecting the Rights and Duties of Neutral Powers and Persons in Case of War on Land). As the Neutrality Act of 1937 prohibited the export of arms, ammunition or implements of war to *any* belligerent State, the application of this law did not violate any rules of the law of neutrality.

Later, however, the United States gradually strengthened its policy of assisting Great Britain.[71] (1) On 4 November 1939, the Neutrality Act of 1937 was revised by the enactment of the Neutrality Act of 1939, which repealed the arms embargo clause,[72] thereby allowing private individuals to export "arms, ammunition or implements of war" from the United States to Great Britain. (2) On 3 September 1940, the United States government announced that it would transfer fifty United States Navy destroyers to Great Britain in exchange for acquiring the right to lease naval and air force bases on British islands in the Caribbean Sea from Great Britain (the so-called the "destroyer deal").[73] (3) Furthermore, on 11 March 1941, the so-called "Lend-Lease Act" was enacted. According to this law, "the President may, from time to time, when he deems it in the interest of national defense, authorize the Secretary of War, the Secretary of the Navy, or the head of any other department or agency of the Government" to "sell, transfer title to, exchange, lease, lend, or otherwise dispose of" any "defense article" – "defense article" includes materials such as weapons, munitions, aircraft, vessels – to "the government of any country whose defense the President deems vital to the defense of the United States".[74] The United States took these three measures not as a belligerent State but as a third State. For example, Robert H. Jackson, Attorney General of the United States, described the enactment of the Lend-Lease Act as "aid short of war", and emphasised that the United States was not in a state of war with any State.[75]

Of these three measures taken by the United States, as regards the revision of the 1937 Neutrality Act by enacting the 1939 Neutrality Law, there were conflicting views about whether the revisions of the neutrality laws after the outbreak of the war were compatible with the status of neutrality, but most writers

160 *The development of the law of neutrality*

were of opinion that such revisions did not constitute violations of neutrality, and the United States government also took such a view.[76] On the contrary, the transfer of fifty destroyers to Great Britain falls under "[t]he supply ... by a neutral Power to a belligerent Power, of war-ships", which a neutral State should abstain from according to Article 6 of the 1907 Hague Convention (XIII) concerning the Rights and Duties of Neutral Powers in Naval War. Also, the selling of or transferring title to "defense articles" including weapons, munitions, aircraft or vessels to belligerent States based on the Lend-Lease Act also fall under Article 6 of the same Convention, and thus acts contrary to neutrality.[77]

These measures taken by the United States government might have given Germany a legal basis for declaring war against the United States. For example, regarding the transfer of destroyers from the United States to Great Britain, Winston Churchill, then Prime Minister of Great Britain, later stated in his memoirs that "[t]he transfer to Great Britain of fifty American warships was a decidedly unneutral act by the United States. It would, according to all the standards of history, have justified the German Government in declaring war upon them".[78] In fact, when Germany declared war against the United States on 11 December 1941, it invoked the "violations of neutrality (Neutralitäts-brüchen)" on the part of the United States as a basis of declaring war.[79]

However, Germany, which declared war against the United States on 11 December 1941, had left "decidedly unneutral act[s] by the United States" for 21 months, as counted from the enactment of the Neutrality Act of 1939, or at least for twelve months, as counted from the transfer of destroyers to Great Britain. Why did Germany not declare war against the United States until December 1941? And, why had the United States, which had considered it necessary to assist Great Britain, not entered the war by itself?[80] In order to answer these questions, it is necessary to understand the basic policies of Germany and the United States in the Second World War.

1.4.2 Political background

The basic policy of Germany in the Second World War was to prevent the entry of the United States into the war.[81] Germany had the experience of being defeated by inviting the entry of the United States in 1917 into the First World War, in addition to the operations two fronts against France and Russia. Based on this experience, Hitler's strategy in the Second World War was to successively defeat the enemies, and he had no intention to bring the United States into the war until victory over Great Britain had been achieved.

The policy taken by Hitler in order to prevent the United States from entering into the war was: first, to utilise the isolationism in the United States; second, to utilise Japan to restrain the United States.

The first policy was to support isolationist groups within the United States and to strengthen isolationism among American people by means of propaganda activities.[82] Isolationism, which had been increased among the American people

The development of the law of neutrality 161

in the 1930s, was still strong after the outbreak of the Second World War, and the United States government was unable to ignore this and enter the war. Passively, the German policy was to prevent American public opinion from shifting from the isolationist to the interventionist viewpoint and supporting entry of the United States in the war. Based on the experience in the First World War in which the German naval attack on American merchant ships triggered the participation of the United States in the war, Germany refrained from attacking American merchant ships so as not to provoke the American people. For that reason, Hitler repeatedly ordered the German navy not to attack American merchant ships.

The second policy taken by Hitler in order to prevent the entry of the United States into the war was to utilise Japan to restrain the United States. More specifically, Hitler attempted to persuade Japan to attack British territory in Southeast Asia, including Singapore, and thereby to restrain the United States.[83] If Japan attacked British territory in Southeast Asia, the position of Great Britain in this war would be conclusively weakened, which would mean that the United States, feeling a sense of isolation, would be deterred from entering the war. Furthermore, the United States would not enter the war, as an attack on British territory in Southeast Asia would be an insufficient justification for Roosevelt in persuading Americans to participate in the war. This policy was planned in December 1940, and an attempt to persuade the Japanese government was made in the first half of 1941. However, contrary to the expectation of the German government, namely, the expectation that Japan would restrain the United States but without declaring war against it, the Japanese government, in fact, not only tried to find a solution to the China problem through the direct negotiations with the United States, but also finally declared war against the United States. As a result, Germany was forced to declare war against the United States based on the Tripartite Pact of 1940 with Japan and Italy, and the policy of utilising Japan to restrain the United States failed completely.

On the other hand, the basic policy of the United States government in the Second World War, and particularly that of President Roosevelt, was to prevent a German victory in the war and to aid Great Britain in order to achieve that.[84] This was because, if Nazi Germany were to be victorious over Great Britain and to rule Europe, it would pose great military, economic and ideological threats to the Unites States.[85] On the basis of this basic policy, "America was obliged to make every effort to prevent Great Britain's defeat – in the extreme case, even to enter the war itself".[86] In fact, it was necessary for the United States to enter the war in order to prevent a German victory, which was recognised by President Roosevelt.

Nevertheless, it was difficult for Roosevelt to guide the United States into the war. As noted above, isolationism was still strong in Congress and among public opinion, which opposed the participation of the United States in the war. Roosevelt could not ignore that, and in the 1940 Presidential elections, he won re-election by pledging that the United States would never enter the war.

In this way, President Roosevelt was in a dilemma: Although he recognised that it was necessary for the United States to enter the war in order to prevent a

162 *The development of the law of neutrality*

German victory, he was bound by public opinion that opposed the entry into the war. In this situation, "Roosevelt was eagerly awaiting an 'accident' in the Atlantic Ocean that would justify the entry of the United States into the war against Germany".[87] An "accident" in this context means an incident in which German Navy submarines might attack American merchant ships or warships. Roosevelt thought that he could invoke such an accident, if it were to occur, to persuade American people to accept the entry of the United States into the war. However, Hitler, seeing through the dilemma of the United States government, ordered the German Navy not to attack any American merchant ships or warships, and did not give the United States the room to enter into the war. Ultimately, Roosevelt's dilemma was resolved by the Japanese declaration of war against the United States, which was followed by the German declaration of war against the United States. It was natural the United States government decided to take up the German declaration of war without hesitation.[88]

1.4.3 Evaluation of the practice of the United States

As seen above, in the early years of the Second World War, the United States provided various kinds of military assistance to Great Britain, which gave Germany a legal basis of declaring war against the United States. Actually, Germany invoked the "violations of neutrality" on the part of the United States as a basis of declaring war on the United States on December 1941. Nevertheless, the United States had provided many kinds of military assistance to Great Britain since the start of the war. This was because the United States government did not wish to avoid, but rather welcomed the German declaration of war on the United States, which would resolve the dilemma of the United States government: the dilemma in which, though it was necessary to enter the war in order to prevent a German victory, the United States was unable to enter the war by itself, due to the isolationism in the country.

The Second World War was not the first time that a third State provided military assistance to a belligerent without entering the war. For example, as seen in section 2.3.2 of Chapter 2, Portugal, in the First World War, provided military assistance to Great Britain without entering in the war until March 1916.

Such practice is by no means contrary to the object and purpose of the law of neutrality. As discussed in Chapter 2, the so-called "duties of neutral States" are the *conditions* to be fulfilled by a State that wishes to remain neutral and remain outside the war, rather than *duties*. The provision of military assistance to a belligerent is regarded as an act equivalent to the "participation in the war". But as the "participation in the war" was not prohibited in international law – at least prior to the First World War, and, thereafter, under certain circumstances – the provision of assistance to a belligerent, which was equivalent to the participation in the war, was not prohibited by international law.[89] In his essay regarding the assistance given to Great Britain by the United States, Edwin Borchard properly points out that the provisions

The development of the law of neutrality   163

of military assistance to a belligerent are "political acts which an independent and sovereign country is free to take".[90] According to Borchard, third States that provide military assistance to a belligerent can not escape "the penalties of unneutrality"[91] or "paying the price of their unneutral acts by being attacked as belligerents",[92] but each sovereign State is free to do such "political acts" and to pay the price of unneutrality.[93]

Some writers in the 1940s began to describe the legal status of States providing assistance to a belligerent without entering the war as "non-belligerency" as opposed to strict neutrality.[94] Such a description has been accepted by writers after the Second World War, and, the practice of the United States in the early years of the Second World War has been treated as one of the main precedents of "non-belligerency".

However, in State practice during the Second World War, the concept of "non-belligerency" was used as a political concept, rather than a legal concept describing the legal status of States providing assistance to a belligerent without entering the war. For example, the United States government, which openly provided many kinds of military assistance to Great Britain, did not describe its status as one of "non-belligerency".[95] On the other hand, for example, Spain, which declared itself as a "neutral" at the outbreak of the Second World War (the declaration of neutrality on 4 September 1939), declared on 13 June 1940 that Spain was in a position of "non-belligerency".[96] Spain took various measures to support Germany, including allowing German submarines to use Spanish ports as a base of supply. However, such measures had started in September 1939, before the declaration of "non-belligerency",[97] and were originally carried out as secret measures.[98] Spain did not use the concept of "non-belligerency" in order to legally justify these measures. The Spanish declaration of "non-belligerency" was issued in order to declare as a political message that Spain was by no means disinterested in the war.[99] Actually, the Spanish government, when it declared non-belligerency, explained that this declaration was not made because "Spain had the intention to depart from an attitude of strict neutrality" but in order to avoid "providing an impression of disinterest".[100]

It is certainly possible to use the term "non-belligerency", regardless of the usage of this term in State practice, as a legal concept describing the legal status of a State providing military assistance to a belligerent without entering the war: It is possible to categorise third States in war into "neutral States", which observe strict neutrality by abstaining from providing assistance to either belligerent, and "non-belligerent States", which deviate from neutrality by providing assistance to a belligerent. However, at the time of the Second World War, and possibly even today as well, there exists no special rule of international law that applies to "non-belligerent States" only. For example, in prize law, vessels are either enemy vessels or neutral vessels, and goods are either enemy goods or neutral goods. There is no category of "non-belligerent vessels" or "non-belligerent goods" as opposed to enemy or neutral vessels and enemy or neutral goods. Therefore, vessels and cargo belonging to a third State providing military assistance to either belligerent without entering the war would be treated either

164 *The development of the law of neutrality*

as neutral vessels and cargo, or as enemy vessels and cargo.[101] The concept of "non-belligerency" seems to be of little legal value unless any special rules applicable to "non-belligerent States" are established. That being so, it may be sufficient to regard a third State which provides military assistance to either belligerent without entering the war as being a neutral State that is not entitled to claim the right to remain neutral.

2 A new conception of neutrality as presented by writers in the interwar period: origins of the confusion that currently exists

As we have seen in the preceding section, the traditional law of neutrality retained its legal validity despite its declining effectiveness during the interwar period and the Second World War. In State practice during this period, the law of neutrality, as before the First World War, was viewed by States as an institution for guaranteeing the right of neutral States to remain outside war on the conditions that they observe strict neutrality.

However, prominent writers in the interwar period presented a new conception of neutrality, which was fundamentally different from the traditional conception of neutrality that originated in the theory presented by eighteenth-century scholars and had been supported by State practice from the end of eighteenth century to the Second World War. The conception of neutrality as presented by writers in the interwar period was different from the traditional conception of neutrality in the following two respects. First, writers in the interwar period contended that the right of States to remain neutral did not exist. Second, they argued that the historical basis of the so-called "duty of impartiality" was the freedom of States to resort to war and the equality of belligerents. This conception of neutrality has been accepted by most scholars after the Second World War, and still remains the prevailing view today.

However, we should not consider this conception as correct just because many scholars have supported it. The thesis of this book is that the new conception of neutrality as presented by prominent scholars in the interwar period was not correct, with reference to the historical development of the law of neutrality. On the other hand, there were a few writers who correctly understand the essential character of the law of neutrality: Edwin M. Borchard (1884–1951), Lassa Oppenheim (1858–1919) and Kisaburo Yokota (1896–1993). We shall first consider their views about the law of neutrality.

2.1 The theory of neutrality of Borchard, Oppenheim and Yokota

As nineteenth-century scholars did, Borchard, Oppenheim and Yokota affirmed the existence of the right of States to remain neutral. Oppenheim, who took the view that "third States ... have no right to demand to remain neutral" in the first edition (1906) and the second edition (1912) of his *International Law*, stated in the third edition (1921) of the same book:

The development of the law of neutrality 165

The doctrine propounded by me in the previous editions of this work, and also by other writers, that third States have no right to demand to be neutral, cannot be upheld in face of the modern development of the institution of neutrality; they have a right to demand that neither belligerent should force them into war.[102]

In other words, Oppenheim changed his view negating the existence of the right to remain neutral, which he had adopted in the first and second editions of *International Law*, and adopted the view affirming its existence.[103] Therefore, according to Oppenheim, for example, "the declaration of war is *ipso facto* a violation of International Law, as when a belligerent declares war upon a neutral State for refusing passage to its troops".[104] Also, Borchard affirmed the existence of the right of States to remain neutral, by stating:

In return for obligations assumed by a neutral, the belligerents undertake to respect his rights as a neutral, *including the right to stay out of the war....* You cannot help one side at the expense of the other and hope to remain neutral or escape of the penalties of unneutrality. You can't have it both ways. If you wish to remain neutral you must respect the obligations of neutrality, know what is neutral and what is not, and display some capacity to handle yourself.[105]

What, then, is the theoretical basis of the right to remain neutral? Oppenheim presented a solution to this question in the third edition of his *International Law*.[106] According to Oppenheim, there are two different cases in which a belligerent State makes war on a neutral State. The first is the case in which a belligerent State makes war on a hitherto neutral State "on account of a dispute not connected with the cause of the war then in progress". Such a war does not constitute "a violation of neutrality". The second is the case in which a belligerent State makes war on a hitherto neutral State "simply because it does not suit the belligerent any longer to recognise its impartial attitude"; for instance, in a case where "a belligerent may desire to march troops through a neutral country, and the neutral will not permit this". War in the second case constitutes "a violation of neutrality". In other words, according to Oppenheim, when State A and State B are at war, State A may resort to war against State C in order to resolve a dispute between A and C. This is a new war that is separate from the causes of the war between States A and B (the first case mentioned above). On the other hand, it is not permissible for State A to involve State C in the war between States A and B based on strategic necessities to perform the war (the second case mentioned above). According to Oppenheim war is a means of resolving disputes or other issues between States,[107] and a State may declare war in order to resolve a dispute with another State, but it is sufficient for that war to be limited to the State with which there is the dispute. It is not permissible for that war to be expanded to neutral States unrelated to the dispute that is the cause of the war. This view is the same as that of de Visscher, which was

166   *The development of the law of neutrality*

considered in section 2.4.4. of Chapter 2. According to them, the personal scope of a war is limited by the "cause of the war", that is, the dispute or issue that causes the war.

As stated by Borchard, a neutral State enjoys "the right to stay out of the war" "[i]n return for obligations assumed by a neutral", and there are obligations that should be observed "[i]f [a State] wish[es] to remain neutral". Therefore, those obligations of neutral States should be referred to as the *conditions* for remaining neutral, rather than as the *duties*. Regarding this point, Yokota stated:

> It seems proper to view them [the impartiality and non-assistance] as the conditions or means of neutrality. They are the conditions in order for neutrality to exist, and the means by which neutrality is practised. In order for neutrality to exist, or to put it another way, in order for a State to be in a position as a neutral State, it is necessary to take an impartial attitude towards both belligerent States, and abstain from providing special assistance to either belligerent State. If a State takes a partial attitude and provides special assistance to a belligerent, the other belligerent would no longer recognise it as a neutral State and treat it as an enemy or a quasi-enemy.[108]

In sum, according to Borchard, Oppenheim and Yokota, neutral States may enjoy the *right to remain neutral* on the *condition* that they take impartial attitudes towards both belligerent States, and abstain from providing special assistance to either belligerent State. The right to remain neutral refers to the "right to demand that neither belligerent should force them into war" (Oppenheim), or "the right to stay out of the war" (Borchard).[109]

On the other hand, a belligerent is permitted to resort to war against a neutral State that does not fulfil the *condition* of enjoying the right to remain neutral. For instance, Borchard states:

> Impartiality is the keynote of neutrality (Oppenheim, 4th ed., 563). If some only could be selected either for the permission or prohibition, neutrality would at once be violated and the country discriminated against would have a legitimate *casus belli*. The discrimination is an unfriendly and hostile act of greatest significance, and against a strong Power might very readily be a prelude to war. It is, indeed, a warlike act, if not itself an act of war.[110]

In other words, by committing acts contrary to neutrality, States would pay "the price of their unneutral acts by being attacked as belligerents.[111]

However, as the impartiality towards and the abstention from providing assistance to belligerents is the *condition* to be fulfilled if a State wishes to remain neutral and outside the war, rather than the *duties*, third States are not prohibited from assisting either belligerent, if they will accept "the penalties of unneutrality" or "the price of their unneutral acts", namely, the price of being involved in the war and becoming a belligerent. Borchard, discussing the provision of assistance by the United States to Great Britain in the early years of the Second World War, observed:

> [A] nation may go to war at any time for any reason it sees fit, taking the necessary consequences of so portentous a step, but that a neutral cannot claim the right to commit acts of belligerency, either under the head of sanctions, helping the victims of aggression, or its own superior virtues; that the acts already committed by the United States are acts of war and cannot be legally explained or excused as "measures short of war"; that the United States is already in a state of limited war and may at any time become a shooting belligerent. These are political acts which an independent and sovereign country is free to take; and this can be done more forthrightly by not invoking the jargon of collective security.[112]

According to Borchard, the provision of assistance to a belligerent by a third State is an act of war, and the other belligerent may declare war against the third State. These are the "penalties" or "price" of unneutral acts. However, accepting such "penalties" or "price" are "political acts which an independent and sovereign country is free to take", and is not prohibited by international law. Yokota also states:

> Seen from this perspective, the fundamental duties of neutrality, that is, the impartiality towards belligerents and the non-assistance to either belligerent are required to be performed as the *conditions* or *means* of ensuring the essence of neutrality, remaining outside the war, and claiming the rights and interests as neutral States. If a State does not wish to ensure the essence of neutrality and to claim the rights and interests as a neutral, the State does not need to fulfil that condition, and does not required to perform the fundamental duties of neutrality (the impartiality towards belligerents and the non-assistance to either belligerent) ... Therefore, as regards non-belligerent States under consideration, if those States do not wish to be in the status of neutrality and do not claim the rights and interests as neutrals, they do not need to observe the duties of neutrality, and the failure to observe these duties cannot be regarded as illegal.[113]

In summary, according to Borchard, Oppenheim and Yokota, the impartiality towards belligerents and the non-assistance to either belligerent are the *conditions* for enjoying the right to remain neutral, rather than the *duties*. Therefore, if a State does not wish to remain neutral and to avoid being involved in the war, it is not required to fulfil this condition. The provision of assistance to a belligerent is an "act of war" against the other belligerent, but it is a "political act which an independent and sovereign country is free to take" and it is not a wrongful act.

The theory of neutrality presented by Borchard, Oppenheim and Yokota is a correct and appropriate understanding of the traditional law of neutrality in view

168 *The development of the law of neutrality*

of its historical development, which we have considered so far in this book. The so-called "duties of neutral States" have been, as correctly understood by those scholars, considered as the *conditions* of enjoying the "right to remain neutral" rather than the duties in State practice and literature since the eighteenth century.

However, as seen below, some prominent scholars in the interwar period presented a new conception of neutrality, which fundamentally differed to that of Borchard, Oppenheim and Yokota, and such a conception has become the prevailing view after the Second World War.

2.2 Origins of the prevailing view after the Second World War

The characteristics of the view that was advanced by prominent scholars in the interwar period and has became the one prevailing after the Second World War are twofold: First, it denies the existence of the right to remain neutral in the law of neutrality and regards such non-existence as self-evident. Second, it considers that the historical basis of the so-called "duty of impartiality" in the traditional law of neutrality was the freedom of States to resort to war and the equality of belligerents.

2.2.1 Denial of the right to remain neutral and its consequences

A PREVALENCE OF THE VIEW DENYING THE RIGHT TO REMAIN
NEUTRAL

As noted in section 2 of Chapter 2, nineteenth-century writers affirmed that neutral States had the right to remain neutral. While writers who denied the existence of the right to remain neutral appeared in the early twentieth century, many writers, such as de Visscher, still affirmed the existence of the right to remain neutral. Also, in the early twentieth century, even those writers who denied the existence of the right to remain neutral were aware that many other writers affirmed its existence. For example, Oppenheim, who denied the existence of the right to remain neutral in the first edition of his *International Law* in 1906, recognised that "many writers assert the existence of such a right", and did never consider its non-existence as self-evident. Furthermore, as seen in section 2.1 of this chapter, Oppenheim revised his view taken in the first and second editions of *International Law* and affirmed the existence of the right to remain neutral in the third of the same book.

However, many writers in the interwar period denied the existence of the right to remain neutral and considered its non-existence as self-evident. For example, Josef L. Kunz, in his book published in 1935, stated:

> According to general international law, as the duty to remain neutral (Pflicht zur Neutralität) does not exist, the right to remain neutral (das Recht auf Neutralität) does not exist. There exists neither the right to be

neutral at the start of the war nor the right to remain neutral throughout the duration of the war.... According to positive general international law, belligerent States have the right to declare war on third States at any time, whether that is at the outbreak of war, or during the war.[114]

The only authorities cited here by Kunz are an article of Hammarskjöld in 1920[115] and an article of Falconbridge in 1919.[116] He neither considered nor cited the articles of de Visscher and the third edition of Oppenheim's *International Law*, which affirmed the existence of the right to remain neutral. Kunz considered the non-existence of the right to remain neutral as self-evident.

The view such as that of Kunz, which considers the non-existence of the right to remain neutral as self-evident, has been accepted by most writers after the Second World War and remains the prevailing view today. For example, Yasuo Ishimoto (1924–2015), in his article published in 1956, quoting the aforementioned book of Kunz, states: "In classical international law, belligerent States were permitted at any time to declare war on third States. Thus, the position of neutral States to remain outside the war was not ultimately under the legal protection."[117] Such a view is supported not only by Ishimoto but also by most contemporary writers.[118]

B A NEW ISSUE RAISED: THE INFLUENCE OF THE OUTLAWRY OF WAR UPON THE LAW OF NEUTRALITY

According to those writers such as Kunz and Ishimoto who deny the existence of the right to remain neutral, the law of neutrality is an institution that imposes one-sided burdens on neutral States. According to writers who affirm the existence of the right to remain neutral, neutral States, in exchange for fulfilling certain conditions (observing the so-called "the duties of neutral States"), may enjoy the right to remain neutral, which is a great benefit for neutral States. In contrast, for those writers such as Kunz and Ishimoto, who deny the existence of such a right, the law of neutrality imposes duties on neutral states but confers no right or benefit to neutral States. Of course, writers such as Kunz and Ishimoto acknowledge that neutral States, so far as remaining neutral, can enjoy various rights known as the "rights of neutrals" such as the territorial inviolability and the freedom for maritime commerce. However, these rights are nothing more than the rights that neutral States have even in times of peace.[119] On the other hand, the duties of neutral States are, as stated by Kunz, "*special* duties (*besondere* Verpflichtungen) that do not exist in times of peace".[120] According to such an understanding, neutrality "means the whole of duties of neutrals (bedeuten sämtlich Pflichten der Neutralen", and neutrals "receive only burdens (nur Lasten erhält)" from the law of neutrality.[121] In other words, from the perspective of these writers, "the law of neutrality is an institution that modifies the international law of peace *in the interest of belligerents*".[122]

Those writers who deny the existence of the right to remain neutral and regard the law of neutrality as an institution that imposed one-sided burdens on

170 *The development of the law of neutrality*

neutral States raise the following issue: Are third States still bound by the law of neutrality under the contemporary international law which has in principle prohibited war? As regards the reason why such an issue is raised, Ishimoto observed: "The law of neutrality, which mainly consisted of the duties of neutral States, was completely compatible with the structure of international law that did not regulate acts of resorting to war itself. Because war was not always illegal, every belligerent could claim greater rights than those in times of peace as against neutral States. If war has become illegal, we cannot explain why an illegal belligerent can claim greater rights than those in times of peace as against neutral States."[123]

This issue was actually debated by writers in the 1930s. There were many writers who argued that third States were not automatically bound by the law of neutrality under the contemporary international law that prohibited war.[124] The foremost of such an argument was the so-called "Budapest Articles of Interpretation", which was adopted by the International Law Association in the 1934 Budapest session. These articles were adopted as a result of discussing the influence of the Pact of Paris on the various institutions of international law, including the law of neutrality. One of these articles provides:

> In the event of a violation the Pact by a resort to armed force or war by one signatory State against another, the other States may, without thereby committing a breach of the Pact or of any rule of International Law,... decline to observe towards the State violating the Pact the duties prescribed by International Law, apart from the Pact, for a neutral in relation to a belligerent.[125]

In other words, as contracting States of the Pact of Paris are released of the duties of neutrality with regard to States violating the Pact, they may provide military assistance to the State being illegally attacked. The ground for this view was that wars in violation of the Pact of Paris were wrongful acts, and wrongful acts cannot produce rights (*ex injuria non jus oritur*) – the rights of belligerent States to demand neutral States to observe the duties of neutrality.[126]

However, not all writers who considered the law of neutrality as an institution imposing one-sided burdens on neutral States supported the view as presented by the Budapest Articles of Interpretation. Kunz himself was one such writer. According to Kunz:

> It is often said that the Pact of Paris has placed war "outside the law" (mis la guerre "hors la loi"). This popular phrase does not correspond to the realities of positive law. War has not been placed outside the law by the Pact of Paris, but contracting States declare the renunciation of it, which is juridically very different thing.[127]

"[T]he *prohibited* war constitutes an internationally wrongful act, but remains nonetheless *war* in the sense of international law, and thus is under the law of war."[128] "The other contracting States have the right to make *war* against the State violating the Pact, but if they do not do so, they are obliged by the law of neutrality."[129] In other words, according to Kunz, the Pact of Paris only regulates the commencement of war, and wars that have started are the same as wars in the former times, and the law of neutrality applies to these wars as before.

C EVALUATION

The conception of neutrality that prevails today, as represented by Kunz and Ishimoto – the view that the right to remain neutral did not exist in the traditional law of neutrality, and belligerent States were free at any time to make war on neutral States, regardless of the acts taken by neutral States – contradicts the historical facts that this book has considered. The idea that States had the right to remain neutral has been supported by writers and the practice of States since the end of the eighteenth century. Also, the conception of neutrality as represented by Kunz and Ishimoto is not consistent with State practice during the interwar period and the Second World War. As seen in section 1 of this chapter, belligerent States resorting to war on neutral States always attempted to justify their actions by alleging that neutral States had committed violations of neutrality, and did never take the view that belligerents were free at any time to resort to war against neutral States.

According to the view taken by many writers such as Kunz and Ishimoto, the law of neutrality is an institution imposing one-sided burdens on neutral States, and an issue arises as to whether neutral States are released from these burdens under the contemporary international law that prohibits war. However, the main thesis of this book is that the view advocated by many writers such as Kunz and Ishimoto, is not correct; rather, the view advanced by Borchard and Yokota, according to which neutral States may enjoy the right to remain neutral in exchange for bearing certain burdens (the so-called the "duties of neutrals"), is a correct understanding of the traditional law of neutrality. From the viewpoint of Borchard, Yokota and the present author, the issue raised by writers such as Ishimoto does not arise: the so-called "duties of neutral States" are the conditions to be fulfilled if States wish to enjoy the right to remain neutral, rather than duties, and States that do not mind being involved in the war do not need to fulfil these conditions. As stated by Borchard, the decision of a States to pay "the price of their unneutral acts", namely, the price of being involved in the war and becoming a belligerent is a "political act which an independent and sovereign country is free to take" and it is not a wrongful act.[130]

2.2.2 New explanations about the so-called "duty of impartiality"

The second characteristic of the view which was advocated by prominent scholars in the interwar period and which has become the prevailing view after the Second World War is: It explains that the historical basis of the so-called "duty of impartiality" in the traditional law of neutrality was the freedom of States to resort to

172 *The development of the law of neutrality*

war and the equality of belligerents. It is not exactly clear who first presented such an explanation. However, what is clear is that such an explanation did not exist in legal literature and State practice prior to the First World War, and that such an explanation did exist in books and articles written by Hearsch Lauterpacht and Carl Schmitt in the interwar period (and the period immediately after the Second World War). The explanations presented by Lauterpacht and Schmitt have influenced the prevailing view after the Second World War.

A LAUTERPACHT

The first edition (1905 and 1906) and second edition (1912) of Oppenheim's *International Law* were written by Oppenheim himself, and, after his death, the third edition (1920 and 1921) was revised and published by Roxburgh, the fourth edition (1926 and 1928) by McNair, and from the fifth (1935 and 1937) to the eighth editions (1955) were revised and published by Lauterpacht. The fifth edition revised by Lauterpacht contained the following statement which did not exist in the previous editions:

> The hardening, in the eighteenth century, of the conception of neutrality in the direction of absolute neutrality was due to the recognition by International Law of the sovereign right of war regardless of its cause. The distinction between just and unjust war was jettisoned, and absolute neutrality was the necessary corollary of that development.[131]

According to Lauterpacht, the traditional law of neutrality, the main content of which was the idea that neutral States were required to take attitudes of strict impartiality towards belligerents, could not have been established under the just war doctrine, which distinguished between just and unjust wars, but was first established under the international law that recognised "the unrestricted right of sovereign States to go to war".[132]

Lauterpacht developed this explanation in more detail in his article of 1936. In this article, he stated:

> At a time when war was a legally recognised process not only for giving effect to rights but also for changing the law, taking sides in any actual war constituted interference in a legal relation permitted or even authorised by law. As such it has been likened to the torts of maintenance and champerty in English law.[133]

According to him, war was a procedure to give effect rights and to change the law in traditional international law: If a State unrelated to this procedure, namely, a neutral State intervened in the procedure between other States in support of one belligerent, it would be the same as the torts of maintenance and champerty, which is prohibited in English law; therefore, it was prohibited in traditional international law.

The development of the law of neutrality   173

Such an explanation about the duties of impartiality presented by Lauterpacht during the interwar period was maintained in his books and articles published after the Second World War. For example, in the seventh edition of Oppenheim's *International Law* (1952), he did not change the abovementioned statement presented in the fifth edition of the same book.[134] He also wrote in his article of 1953: "[U]ntil the First World War, the right to wage war constituted an unlimited prerogative right of sovereign States; no neutral States, therefore, could arrogate to itself the right to pass judgment on the legality of a war and to shape its conduct accordingly."[135]

These books and articles written by Lauterpacht have been often quoted and relied upon as an explanation about the basis of the duty of impartiality in the traditional law of neutrality.[136] In other words, the explanation presented by Lauterpacht regarding the traditional law of neutrality was received as the prevailing view after the Second World War.

B CARL SCHMITT

Carl Schmitt also advanced the view that the traditional law of neutrality as an institution requiring neutral States to take impartial attitudes towards both belligerents could be first established under the international law that denied the just war doctrine and regarded all belligerents as equal. He explained this by using the concepts of "the non-discriminatory concept of war (der nichtdiskriminierende Kriegsbegriff)" and "the non-discriminatory concept of neutrality (der nichtdiskriminierende Neutralitätsbegriff)".

Schmitt presented this view in his *Die Wendung zum diskriminierenden Kriegsbegriff* published in 1938. In this book, which was aimed at critically discussing the design of world order centred on the League of Nations,[137] Schmitt contrasted the traditional "non-discriminatory concept of war" and the "non-discriminatory concept of neutrality" with the "discriminatory concept of war (der diskriminierende Kriegsbegriff)" and the "discriminatory concept of neutrality (der diskriminierende Neutralitätsbegriff)", which appeared during the First World War and thereafter. According to Schmitt, the traditional "non-discriminatory concept of neutrality" was the concept of neutrality that "the non-belligerent States, regardless of the legality or illegality of belligerent parties, were obliged the strictest impartiality".[138] This concept of neutrality was based on the "non-discriminatory concept of war", which did not distinguish between legal and illegal wars.[139] On the other hand, the "discriminatory concept of neutrality", which was adopted by the declaration of Wilson, then President of the United States, on 2 April 1917 and the League of Nations, is a concept that permitted third States to intervene in the war based on the distinction between legal and illegal wars. According to Schmitt, this concept of neutrality is based on the "discriminatory concept of war", which distinguishes between legal and illegal wars.[140]

Schmitt, in his *Der Nomos der Erde* published in 1950, gave a more detailed explanation about the "non-discriminatory concept of war" and the

174   *The development of the law of neutrality*

"non-discriminatory concept of war". This book, while highly regarding the restriction of war based on the concept of "just enemies (*justus hostis*)" in the Public Law of Europe (Jus Publicum Europaeum), argues that the Public Law of Europe collapsed after 1890.[141] In this book, Schmitt explains the relationship between the traditional "non-discriminatory concept of war" and neutrality. According to him, in the religious wars that were carried out in the sixteenth and the seventeenth centuries, the belligerent parties viewed and discriminated each other as "law-breakers and pirates (Verbrecher und Piraten)", and thus those wars had the character of "war of extermination (Vernichtungskrieg)". By contrast, in wars carried out under the modern "Public Law of Europe", the belligerent parties viewed each other as "just enemies (*justus hostis*)", and "war can thereby be viewed as something analogous to a duel (etwas einem Duell Analoges)", by which "a real progress (ein wirklicher Fortschritt)" of "enclosure and control (eine Umgrenzung und Hegung) of European wars" became possible.[142] Also, "the concept of just enemies created room for neutrality of third States in international law".[143] As a result of war being viewed as "something analogous to a duel", "neutral States acted as the impartial witnesses (die unparteiischen Zeugen)".[144] Furthermore, according to Schmitt, the principle of equality of States established in this period contributed to the formation of the concept of neutrality, which is the basis of impartiality towards belligerents: "The legal principle of equality of States makes it is impossible to discriminate between the State that wages a just war and the State that wages a unjust war. To do so would be for a sovereign to be the judge (Richter) of another State, which contravenes the legal equality of sovereigns."[145] In sum, according to Schmitt, the concept of neutrality that demands third States to take impartial attitudes towards belligerents emerged as a result of the introduction the "non-discriminatory concept of war", according to which all belligerents were equal and should not be discriminated by third States.

As recently argued by Masaharu Yanagihara, Schmitt's "non-discriminatory concept of war" is considered as the origin of the term "non-discriminatory concept of war", which is commonly used by Japanese international lawyers.[146] Japanese international lawyers seem to have also accepted Schmitt's idea that the "non-discriminatory concept of neutrality" – the concept of neutrality based on impartiality towards belligerents – and the "non-discriminatory concept of war" – the idea that all belligerent States are viewed as equal – were two sides of the same coin.[147] For example, Takeo Sogawa, in his article "Carl Schmitt and the Transformation of the Legal Concept of War" published in 1953, states that "the discriminatory neutrality is a decisive factor of the discriminatory concept of war, which must be emphasized before all else", and thereby identifies the "structural relationship between neutrality and war".[148] Also, Yasuo Ishimoto, who was probably influenced by Sogawa's 1953 article and, therefore, at least indirectly influenced by Schmitt, stated in his book of 1958: "[T]he non-discriminatory concept of war, not the just war doctrine, was a theory *more* compatible with the law of neutrality."[149] Furthermore, Shigejiro Tabata, in his textbook published in 1955, observed: "[T]he conception of neutrality as

The development of the law of neutrality   175

impartial attitudes towards belligerents ... was intimately connected to the emergence of the so-called non-discriminatory concept of war, in which just and unjust belligerents in war could not be distinguished. In other words, in times of war, third States were not in a position to make a judgement about who was right or wrong, and therefore, it was not appropriate to provide special aid to either party, and both must be treated impartially, which is the point of this conception."[150] These explanations provided by Tabata, Sogawa and Ishimoto have been accepted by many writers in Japan and remains the prevailing view in Japan.[151]

C EVALUATION

According to Lauterpacht and Schmitt, the equality of belligerents (the "non-discriminatory concept of war") was an essential prerequisite to the traditional law of neutrality, a basic principle of which was the strict impartiality towards belligerents: In international law prior to the First World War, in which States had unrestricted freedom to resort to war and all belligerents were viewed as equal, third States were not permitted to make judgement of the justice and injustice of belligerents and were obliged to take impartial attitudes towards all belligerents. Such a view about the traditional law of neutrality has become the prevailing view in Europe and America, where the publications and articles of Lauterpacht were frequently quoted and referred to, and also in Japan, where the publications of Schmitt were quoted and referred to. Such a view is considered almost as common knowledge.

However, such a view regarding the traditional law of neutrality first appeared in the 1930s, and, to the best of the author's knowledge, did not exist before the 1920s. For example, as noted above, when looking at the first seven editions of Oppenheim's *International Law*, the aforementioned statement that Lauterpacht presented in the fifth edition did not exist in any of the first four editions. This means that it was an original idea of Lauterpacht.

However, the view that was presented by Lauterpacht and Schmitt and has been accepted by many contemporary writers has the following two fundamental defects.

First, Lauterpacht and Schmitt understood that the traditional law of neutrality prohibited neutral States from judging the justness and unjustness of belligerents. But this understanding contradicts the historical facts that we have identified in this book. Eighteenth-century scholars, which Lauterpacht and Schmitt had recognised for their significance in the formation of the traditional conception of neutrality, did not insist that the judgement by third States on the justice and injustice of belligerents was prohibited. For instance, Wolff, in his book of 1764, clearly stated: "there is no need that neutral nations should suspend their judgement concerning the justice of the war, although *it may be wiser (consultum)* that they should not express it openly".[152] Vattel also held: even when "they are convinced which party is in the right", States may remain neutral from the perspective of the benefits to the State.[153] Also, as noted in

176 *The development of the law of neutrality*

section 1.4.1 of Chapter 2, in State practice and literature in the nineteenth century, the expression of sympathy by a neutral State towards one of the belligerents was not considered as a violation neutrality. For instance, Bluntschli stated: "A State can have a lively sympathy (ein lebhaftes Mitgefühl) towards a belligerent party and openly express its displeasure (Unwillen) against the other belligerent party, and nevertheless can remain neutral. Mere opinions and expression of opinions about the legality and illegality and about the political conflicts is not an act of war, nor is it the participation in the war."[154] In sum, in the traditional law of neutrality, the judgement by third Sates on the legality and illegality of the war and even the expression of sympathy for a belligerent based on that judgement was neither prohibited nor considered as being contrary to neutrality.

The second defect of the view presented by Lauterpacht and Schmitt is the inability to explain the freedom of third States to enter the war between other States under traditional international law. According to Lauterpacht and Schmitt, the duties of neutral States to take impartial attitudes towards all belligerents and to abstain from providing assistance to either belligerent were based on the idea that the discrimination between the belligerents was prohibited. However, in traditional international law, third States were free at any time to enter the war between other States:[155] Supporting a belligerent by entering the war and discriminating against the other belligerent was not prohibited. In short, the idea that third States should not discriminate between belligerents does not apply to the States that support a belligerent after entering the war. Therefore it is unreasonable to apply this idea only to neutral States that have not yet entered the war. Lauterpacht, Schmitt and any other writers have not answered this question.

Notes

1 Motives of States to remain neutral could be various. In some cases, States might decide to remain neutral in order to gain economic profits of continuing maritime commerce with belligerents: if a State is involved in the war and becomes a belligerent, the merchant vessels and their cargoes belonging to that State are subject to capture as enemy vessels and goods; thus, States might claim the status of neutrality with the primary objective of avoiding such a consequence and enjoying the freedom of maritime commerce. On the other hand, there could be States whose primary objective to remain neutral is to maintain their peace and security rather than to gain economic profits. It is to be noted that, in history, the demand of neutral States to maintain their maritime commerce has often been the cause of conflict with the belligerent States, which in some cases has led to war with the belligerents. See Neff, *Rights and Duties of Neutrals*, 71–72, 75.

2 As discussed in section 2 of Chapter 2, if a third State provided military assistance to a belligerent State on the basis of an alliance treaty, it is a violation of neutrality, and the other belligerent is legally entitled to treat such a third State as an enemy and to wage war against it. However, the other belligerent does not always treat such a State as an enemy. In practice, belligerents sometimes refrain from waging war against third States due to various political, strategic or tactical factors. A State is free to ensure its security by concluding an alliance with other States, if it considers

The development of the law of neutrality 177

alliance as being a more effective means of security than the status of neutrality. For a study on alliance from the perspective of international law, see e.g. Erich, *Über Allianzen und Allianzverhältnisse*; Rehm, "Die völkerrechtliche Stellung des Verbündeten", 118–152.

3 While the choice of a State to remain neutral is a matter of political decision, the right of a State having chosen the neutral status not to be involved in the war and the conditions for enjoying that status are, of course, matters of law.

4 While it is generally understood that the system of collective security appeared after the First World War, some writers view the permanent neutrality that existed in the nineteenth century as being a form of collective security. See Taoka, "Permanent Neutrality in the Classification of Forms of Security", 50–73 [in Japanese].

5 Tabata, *New Lecture on International Law*, 2:206 [in Japanese].

6 See above, note 1 of Introduction.

7 Treaty of Mutual Guarantee between Germany, Belgium, France, Great Britain and Italy, done at Locarno, 16 October 1925, *LNTS* 54 (1926): 290–301.

8 On the relationship between the Covenant of the League of Nations and Neutrality, see e.g. Cohn, "Neutralité et Société des Nations", 153–204; D'Astorg, *La neutralité et son réveil*, 67–93; Graham, "Effect of the League of Nations", 357–377; Obuchi, "The League Covenant and the Concept of Neutrality", 1–15 [in Japanese]; Politis, "La notion de la neutralité", 259–268; Tachi, "The League of Nations and the Relations of Neutrality", 32–41 [in Japanese]; Whitton, "La neutralité et la Société des Nations", 449–567.

9 Paragraph 1, Article 16 of the Covenant of the League of Nations provides that any Member of the League which resorts to war in disregard of its covenants under Articles 12, 13 or 15 "shall *ipso facto* be deemed to have committed an act of war against all other Members of the League". This appears to mean that a state of war is automatically created between the covenant-breaking State and the other member States. However, according to the resolution adopted by the Assembly in 1921: "The unilateral action of the defaulting State cannot create a state of war: it merely entitles the other Members of the League to resort to war or to declare themselves in a state of war with the Covenant-breaking State". Resolutions and Recommendations Adopted on the Reports of the Third Committee: 2. Economic Weapons, adopted on 4 October 1921, League of Nations, *Official Journal Special Supplement*, no. 6 (1921): 24. This resolution, which provides guidelines for the interpretation of the Covenant, does not have binding force on the members of the League. See Tachi, *Treatise on the Covenant of the League of Nations*, 256 [in Japanese]. However, in practice, Article 16 was applied in accordance with this resolution. In cases where Article 16 was applied, a state of war was not automatically created between the covenant-breaking State and the other member States. Thus, there could exist situations where members of the League took sanction measures under Article 16, without becoming belligerents, that is, without resorting to war against the covenant-breaking State. Therefore, the relationship between Article 16 and neutrality was debated.

10 See Article 9 of the Hague Convention (V) respecting the Rights and Duties of Neutral Powers and Persons in case of War on Land 1907.

11 Article 16 of the Covenant does not prohibit Covenant States applying these measures not only to the covenant-breaking State but also to the victim State. However, as the purpose of Article 16 is to place sanctions on the Covenant-breaking State, it is assumed that these measures are to be applied to the Covenant-braking State only. See Obuchi, "The League Covenant and the Concept of Neutrality", 13 [in Japanese].

12 See Whitton, "La neutralité et la Société des Nations", 504.

13 See above, p. 90.

14 The Pact of Paris (General Treaty for the Renunciation of War; The Kellogg–Briand Pact) of 1928, which prohibited "recourse to war for the solution of international

178   *The development of the law of neutrality*

controversies" and war "as an instrument of national policy", contained no provision for sanctions against the violations. General Treaty for the Renunciation of War as an Instrument of National Policy, signed at Paris, 27 August 1928, *LNTS* 94 (1929): 57. Therefore, in wars started in violation of the Pact of Paris, third States were free to remain neutral. In fact, in wars that broke out since the conclusion of the Pact of Paris, there existed Contracting States of the Pact of Paris which declared neutrality. See Wani, "Prohibition of War and Neutrality", 31–46 [in Japanese].

15 See Momose, *Small States*, 37–40, 55–61, 81–105 [in Japanese].

16 For details on how Switzerland joined the League, see Irie, *Collapse of the Versailles System*, 2:622–635 [in Japanese]; Huber, "Die schweizerische Neutralität und der Völkerbund", 80–136.

17 Le Conseil fédéral aux Signatoires des Traités de Paix et aux Etats invités à adhérer à la Société des Nations, 14 janvier 1920, Annexe, Mémorandum, 13 janvier 1920, *DDS* 7(2): 464–467 (doc. 228).

18 Les Délégués du Conseil fédéral à Londres, G. Ador et M. Huber, à la Division des Affaires étrangèeres du Département politique, 13 février 1920, Annexe, Société des Nations, L'accession de la Suisse comme membre de la Société des Nations, Resolution adoptée par le Conseil de la Société des Nations, réuni à Londres, au Palais de St-James, le 13 février 1920, *DDS* 7(2): 511–512 (doc. 247).

19 Decoppet à Calonder, 28. Juli 1919, *DDS* 7(2): 54–55 (doc. 24).

20 Decoppet à Calonder, 28. Juli 1919, Annexe 2, Rapport de la minorité de la Commission de la Défense nationale, Bern, 14./18. Juli 1919, Die Schweiz und der Völkerbund. Militärisches Gutachten, *DDS* 7(2): 66–77 (doc. 24) [italics in the original].

21 Decoppet à Calonder, 28. Juli 1919, Annexe 1, Bericht der Merheit der Landesverteidigungskommission an das eigen. Militärdepartment zuhanden des Bundesrates betreffend die militärischen Folgen des Eintritts der Schweiz in den Völkerbund, Bern, 18. Juli 1919, *DDS* 7(2): 55–66 (doc. 24).

22 Botschaft des Bundesrates an die Bundesversammlung betreffend die Frage des Beitrittes der Schweiz zum Völkerbund (Vom 4. August 1919), *Bundesblatt der schweizerischen Eidgenossenschaft*, Jahrgang 1919, 4. Bd. (1919): 541–680.

23 Momose, *Small States*, 135 [in Japanese; emphasis in the original]. Regarding the effectiveness of the institution of neutrality as a means of ensuring security for third States in the nineteenth century, as well as their political background, and how the rapid decline in the effectiveness of that institution in the First World War led to various small European States participating in the collective security system of the League of Nations, see also, Morgenthau, "Problem of Neutrality", 109–128.

24 Declaration of Neutrality in the Bolivian-Paraguayan War, 13 May 1933 [Argentina], in Deák and Jessup, *Collection*, 1:9–10; Decree No. 22,744, Ordering the Observance of Complete Neutrality in the War between Bolivia and Paraguay, 23 May 1933 [Brazil], in ibid., 1:92–97; Decree No. 458, Declaring the Neutrality of Chile in the War between Bolivia and Paraguay, 13 May 1933, in ibid., 1:357–358; Proclamation of Neutrality in the Bolivian-Paraguayan War, 13 May 1933 [Peru], in ibid., 2:873–874; Decree Proclaiming Neutrality in the War between Bolivia and Paraguay, 12 May 1933 [Uruguay], in ibid., 2:1269.

25 Dinichert à Stucki, 31. Oktober 1935, *DDS* 11:532–533 (doc. 173); The Ambassador in Italy (Long) to the Secretary of State, 10 October 1935, *FRUS 1935*, 1:804.

26 See Cohn, *Neo-Neutrality*, 245; Verzijl, *International Law in Historical Perspective*, Part IX-B, 264.

27 On the return of many States to the traditional neutrality in the late 1930s, see e.g. Hyde, "Belgium and Neutrality", 81–85; Koht, "Neutrality and Peace", 280–289; La Pradelle, "La Belgique retourne à la neutralité", 538–546; Morgenthau, "End of Switzerland's 'Differential' Neutrality", 558–562; Morgenthau, "Resurrection of

The development of the law of neutrality   179

Neutrality in Europe", 473–486; Ténékidès, "La neutralité en son état d'évolution actuelle", 256–285.

28 See Saito, *History of International Politics in the Interwar Period*, 2–3, 195–208 [in Japanese].

29 League of Nations, *Official Journal* 16 (1935): 1225.

30 Oka, *History of International Politics*, 285 [in Japanese].

31 Momose, *Small States*, 158 [in Japanese].

32 League of Nations, *Official Journal Special Supplement*, no. 154 (1936): 19.

33 Conseil Fédéral, Procès-verbal de la séance du 22 février 1938, Annexe, Exposé des Eidgenössischen Politischen Departementes über die Neutralität der Schweiz im Völkerrecht, Bern, 19. February 1938, *DDS* 12:473–483 (doc. 215).

34 Paravicini à Motta, 15 janvier 1938, *DDS* 12:396 (doc. 183); Le Chef du Département politique, G. Motta aux Légations de Suisse à Bruxelles, Bucarest, Varsovie et Stockholm, 27 avril 1938, Annexe, Mémorandum sur la neutralité de la Suisse au sein de la Société des Nations, *DDS* 12:636–639 (doc. 277).

35 Denmark-Finland-Iceland-Norway-Sweden, Declaration regarding Similar Rules of Neutrality, Signed at Stockholm, 27 May 1938, *AJIL Supplement* 32 (1938): 141–163.

36 Bring, "Commentary", 841; Padelford, "New Scandinavian Neutrality Rules", 789–793.

37 Paravicini à Motta, 15 janvier 1938, *DDS* 12:396 (doc. 183).

38 See Gervais, "La pratique de la neutralité", 8.

39 Déclaration de neutralité, No. 111/39, Tokio, le 4 septembre 1939, in *Laws and Regulations of Various States during the War in 1939 and 1940*, ed. the Navy Secretariat of Japan, pt. 1, vol. 2, p. 394.

40 Der Staatssekretär an die Gesantschaften in Oslo, Stockholm und Helsinki, den 1. September 1939, *ADAP*, Ser. D, Bd. 7, Nr. 525; Halifax to Dormer, September 21, 1939, *BDFA*, pt. 2, ser. F, vol. 67, p. 206. Do the belligerent States' promises to respect Norway's neutrality have constitutive or declaratory effects in terms of their duty to respect the neutrality of Norway and abstain from waging war and carrying out hostilities against it? According to the State practice during the Second World War, it was understood that this kind of promise simply had declaratory effects with regard to the belligerent States' duty to respect neutrality. This is because, in State practice, there were no cases in which wars and hostilities were carried out merely because a promise to respect neutrality had not been made. As discussed below, when waging wars and hostilities against neutral States, belligerent States always attempted to justify their acts on the basis that the neutral States had committed violations of neutrality. If the duty to respect neutrality were constituted by promises made by belligerents, belligerents would not have made such promises with regard to States that they needed to attack or occupy for strategic purposes. Despite that, the fact that belligerent States made promises to respect the neutrality of such States indicates that it was not believed that it was unnecessary to respect the neutrality of States which the belligerents had not made promises to respect neutrality.

41 Dormer to Halifax, 17 February 1940, *BDFA*, pt. 3, ser. L, vol. 1, p. 162.

42 While Norway had ratified the Hague Convention (XIII) concerning the Rights and Duties of Neutral Powers in Naval War, Great Britain had not ratified it. Nevertheless, in the *Altmark* incident, both the British government and the Norwegian government made arguments based on the provisions of the Hague Convention (XIII) as reflecting rules of customary international law at the time of this case. See Oppenheim (Lauterpacht ed.), *International Law*, 7th ed., 2:695.

43 The *Admiral Graf Spee* incident, in which the *Graf Spee* self-destructed in the River Plate, includes many interesting issues regarding neutrality. See Tachi, "*Admiral Graf Spee*", 49–74 [in Japanese].

180 *The development of the law of neutrality*

44 Aide-mémoire, 24 February 1940, *BDFA*, pt. 3, ser. L, vol. 1, p. 172; Dormer to Halifax, 26 February 1940, ibid., 176–178.

45 Halifax to Colban, 15 March 1940, *BDFA*, pt. 3, ser. L, vol. 1, pp. 180–186.

46 Views of writers regarding this case are divided. On the one hand, some writers did not view the passage of the *Altmark* through Norwegian territorial waters as violating the neutrality of Norway, and therefore Norway, which allowed this passage, did not perform acts contrary to neutrality. See e.g. Borchard, "Was Norway Delinquent...?" 289–294; Hyde, *International Law*, 3:2339–2340. On the other hand, some writers viewed the 400-mile passage of the *Altmark* into neutral territorial waters over a period of two days with the objective of avoiding attack or seizure by enemy warships as not being "mere passage". Rather, it was viewed as amounting to the use of "neutral ports and waters as a base of naval operations against their adversaries", which was prohibited by Article 5 of the Hague Convention (XIII) concerning the Rights and Duties of Neutral Powers in Naval War, and the majority of writers took this view. According to this view, Norway was, as a neutral State, required to refuse and prevent such a passage, and Great Britain was justified in taking measures of "self-preservation", "auto-protection" or "self-help". See e.g. Bisschop, "*Altmark*", 67–79; MacChesney, "Altmark Incident", 320–343; Oppenheim (Lauterpacht ed.), *International Law*, 6th ed., 2:554–556; Telders, "L'incident de l'Altmark", 90–100; Waldock, "Release of the *Altmark*'s Prisoners", 216–238.

47 See Ørvik, *Decline of Neutrality*, 216–246.

48 Der Reichsaußenminister an den Gesandten in Oslo, den 7. April 1940, [Nebenanlage 1] Memorandum, 9. April 1940, *ADAP*, Ser. D, Bd. 9, Nr. 53.

49 Hackworth, *Digest of International Law*, 6:170.

50 See Der Reichsaußenminister an die Bothschaft in Brüssel, den 25. August 1939, *ADAP*, Ser. D, Bd. 7, Nr. 272; Halifax to Clive, 27 August 1939, *BDFA*, pt. 2, ser. F, vol. 30, p. 305. As regards the significance of promise given by belligerents to respect the neutrality of third States, see note 40 of this chapter.

51 The Declaration of Neutrality by the Dutch Government, in *Laws and Regulations of Various States during the War in 1939 and 1940*, ed. the Navy Secretariat of Japan, pt. 1, vol. 2, p. 251; The Declaration of Neutrality [by the Belgian government], in ibid., 461.

52 See Higgins, "The Netherlands", 125.

53 Memorandum der Reichsregierung an die Königlich Belgische Regierung und die Königlich Niederländische Regierung, den 9. Mai 1940, *ADAP*, Ser. D, Bd. 9, Nr. 214 [italics added].

54 Ibid. [italics added].

55 Verbalnote der Niederländischen Gesandschaft, den 10. Mai 1940, *ADAP*, Ser. D, Bd. 9, Nr. 224.

56 Protestation remise au Gouvernement allemand, le 10 mai 1940 par l'Ambassadeur de Belgique à Berlin, *DDB* 5:515–516.

57 Spaak aux Représentants des Gouvernements étrangeres à Bruxelles, le 10 mai 1940, *DDB* 5:517–518. The promise by Germany in 1937, which is referred to in this document, is printed in Enclosure in Doc. 144 (Spaak to Eden, le 10 Octobre 1937): Declaration by the German Government, *BDFA*, pt. 2, ser. F, vol. 30, p. 228.

58 Der Botschafter in Brüssel an das Auswärtige Amt, den 10. Mai 1940, *ADAP*, Ser. D, Bd. 9, Nr. 221; Der Gesandte in Den Haag an das Auswärtige Amt, den 10. Mai 1940, ibid., Nr. 222; Verbalnote der Niederländischen Gesandschaft, den 10. Mai 1940, ibid., Nr. 224.

59 Memorandum der Reichsregierung an die Königlich Belgische Regierung und die Königlich Niederländische Regierung, den 9. Mai 1940, *ADAP*, Ser. D, Bd. 9, Nr. 214.

The development of the law of neutrality   181

60 See Wylie, *European Neutrals and Non-Belligerents*, 1–237.

61 See above, p. 150.

62 On the "legitimating functions" of international law, see Onuma, "Law and Politics in International Society", 22–24 [in Japanese].

63 On the view denying the legal or obligatory character of the Pact of Paris, see Brownlie, *Use of Force*, 83.

64 See e.g. Taoka, "Value of the Pact of Paris", 32–35 [in Japanese].

65 Morris, "Pact of Paris", 88–91.

66 Onuma, *Prolegomena to the Responsibility for War*, 126 [in Japanese].

67 However, in the post-war military trials at Nuremberg, there were cases in which the hostilities and wars by Germany against neutral States such as Norway, Denmark, Belgium, the Netherlands and Luxembourg were evaluated by reference to the Pact of Paris, rather than the law of neutrality. For instance, in the *Goering* case, the International Military Tribunal at Nuremberg held that German invasions against these States could not be justified as measures of self-defence and were, therefore, aggressive wars in violation of the Pact of Paris. *In re* Goering, Nuremberg, International Military Tribunal, 1 October 1946, *International Law Reports*, ed. Lauterpacht (1946): 208–211.

68 Proclaiming the Neutrality of the United States in the War between Germany and France; Poland; and the United Kingdom, India, Australia and New Zealand, *Department of State Bulletin* 1 (1939): 203–208; Export of Arms, Ammunition, and Implements of War to France; Germany; Poland; and the United Kingdom, India, Australia and New Zealand, ibid., 208–211.

69 Joint Resolution to Amend the Joint Resolution Entitled "Joint Resolution Providing for the Prohibition of the Export of Arms, Ammunition, and Implements of War to Belligerent Countries; the Prohibition of the Transport of Arms, Ammunition, and Implements of War by Vessels of the United States for the Use of Belligerent States; for the Registration and Licensing of Persons Engaged in the Business of Manufacturing, Exporting, or Importing Arms, Ammunition, or Implements of War; and Restricting Travel by American Citizens on Belligerent Ships during War", Approved 31 August 1935, as Amended, 1 May 1937, in Deák and Jessup, *Collection*, 2:1106–1115.

70 Warren, "Troubles of a Neutral", 378. The first statute of the United States that prohibited the export of "weapons, munitions and military equipment" to belligerent States was the Neutrality Act of 1935. This Act ceased to be effective on 29 February 1936, and a new statute was enacted in 1936 (the 1936 Neutrality Act), which then ceased to be effective on the last day of April 1937. Later, another new statute was enacted in 1937 (the 1937 Neutrality Act). The 1937 Neutrality Act was in effect at the time of the outbreak of the Second World War. The Neutrality Acts of 1935, 1936 and 1937 each have different details, but they all retain the clause prohibiting the export of "weapons, munitions and military equipment" to belligerent States (the so-called arms embargo clause). On the Neutrality Laws of the United States in the 1930s, see for example, Deák, "United States Neutrality Acts", 73–114; Dumbauld, "Neutrality Laws of the United States", 267–270; Onuma, *Prolegomena to the Responsibility for War*, 121–127 [in Japanese]; Shinohara, *US International Lawyers in the Interwar Years*, 123–148.

71 For further details, see Onuma, *Prolegomena to the Responsibility for War*, 127–142 [in Japanese].

72 Neutrality Act of 1939, Approved 4 November 1939: Joint Resolution to Preserve the Neutrality and the Peace of the United States and to Secure the Safety of Its Citizens and Their Interests, *AJIL Supplement* 34 (1940): 44–55. The Neutrality Act of 1939 expanded the scope of application of the so-called "Cash and Carry" clause, which had applied to goods other than "arms, ammunition, or implements of war" in the 1937 Neutrality Act, to "any articles or materials" (including "arms,

182 *The development of the law of neutrality*

ammunition, or implements of war"), and enabled the export of weapons, munitions and military equipment from the United States to belligerent States ((a) and (c) of clause 2 of the Neutrality Act of 1939). The "Cash and Carry" clause is a clause which permits the export of goods from the United States to belligerent States on the conditions that those goods are purchased in *cash* within the United States and are *carried* on non-US ships.

73 The British Ambassador to the Secretary of State, 2 September 1940, *Department of State Bulletin* 3 (1940): 199–200; The Secretary of State to the British Ambassador, 2 September 1940, ibid., 200; Message of the President, 3 September 1940, ibid., 201.

74 An Act to Promote the Defense of the United States, Approved 11 March 1941, *AJIL Supplement* 35 (1941): 76–79.

75 Address of Robert H. Jackson, Attorney General of the United States, Inter-American Bar Association, Havana, Cuba, 27 March 1941, *AJIL* 35 (1941): 349.

76 As writes who argued that the revisions of the neutrality laws after the outbreak of the war were incompatible with neutrality, see e.g. Berber, "Die amerikanische Neutralität", 448–452; Eagleton, "Duty of Impartiality", 99–104; Jessup, "Reconsideration of 'Neutrality' Legislation", 556–557. As writers who took the contrary view, see e.g. Fenwick, "Revision of Neutrality Legislation", 728–730; Gundermann, *Die parteiliche Änderung*, 67–139; [Harvard Law School,] "Rights and Duties of Neutral States in Naval and Aerial War", 316–319; Oppenheim (Lauterpacht ed.), *International Law*, 6th ed., 2:534. For the view of the United States government, see Message of the President to the Congress, *Department of State Bulletin* 1 (1939): 275–280; Statement by the Secretary of State, ibid., 280–281.

77 The United States government itself admitted that the Lend-Lease Act was incompatible with the status of neutrality. See Address of Robert H. Jackson, Attorney General of the United States, Inter-American Bar Association, Havana, Cuba, 27 March 1941, *AJIL* 35 (1941): 349; Statements by the Secretary of State before the House Foreign Affairs Committee, 15 January 1941, *Department of State Bulletin* 4 (1941): 90.

On the other hand, regarding the transfer of destroyers to the United Kingdom, the United States government, while admitting the applicability of Article 8 of the 1907 Hague Convention (XIII), maintained that it was compatible with the status of neutrality. See Opinion of the Attorney General, 27 August 1940, *Department of State Bulletin* 3 (1940): 201–207. According to the United States government, warships (including destroyers) are contraband of war, but a neutral government is not obliged to prevent private individuals from exporting contraband articles to belligerent States. A neutral government is bound to prevent private individuals from building, fitting out or arming vessels within its territory, only when the *vessels are intended to be used as men-of-war*. According to the United States government, overage destroyers transferred to the United Kingdom are "clearly not built, armed, or equipped with any such intent or with reasonable cause to believe that they would ever enter the service of a belligerent", and thus the transfer of such destroyers to the United Kingdom is nothing but a normal export of contraband articles and not contrary to the status of neutrality.

However, there was a fundamental flaw in this argument. Certainly, as discussed in section 1.3.3 of Chapter 2, the legal doctrine of intent, according to which the fitting out or arming of vessels that a neutral government should prevent and those that the government was not bound to prevent were distinguished by the *intent* of private individuals engaging in fitting out, arming and sale of vessels, was supported in State practice in the nineteenth century. However, the legal doctrine of intent is a doctrine that applies to the building, fitting out, arming, or exporting of vessels *by private individuals, not by neutral governments*. The supply of warships by a neutral government to a belligerent is regulated not by Article 8 of Hague Convention

The development of the law of neutrality 183

(XIII) concerning the Rights and Duties of Neutral Powers in Naval War, but by Article 6 of the same Convention, which provides that "[t]he supply, in any manner, directly or indirectly, by a neutral Power to a belligerent Power, of war-ships ... is forbidden". That is why the arguments of the United States government regarding the transfer of destroyers to Great Britain were unanimously criticised by writers. See e.g. Briggs, "Neglected Aspects", 569–587; Wright, "Transfer of Destroyers", 680–689; Borchard, "Attorney General's Opinion", 690–697; Yokota, "Transfer of American Destroyers", 73–86 [in Japanese].

78 Churchill, *Second World War*, 2:358.

79 Der Reichsaußenminister an die Botschaft in Washington, den 10. Dezember 1941, *ADAP*, Ser. D, Bd. 13(2), Nr. 572.

80 The second paragraph of the preamble to the Pact of Paris (see above, note 14 of this chapter), which provided that "any signatory Power which shall hereafter seek to promote its national interests by resort to war should be denied the benefits furnished by this Treaty", would have provided a sufficient legal basis for the United States to declare war against Germany. It was perfectly possible to contend that the German invasion of Poland on 1 September 1939 was a violation of the Pact of Paris. In fact, the French government contended so. See Léger a Guariglia, 3 settèmbre 1939, in Ministero degli Affari Esteri, *I documenti diplomatici italiani*, 9a. ser., 1:18. Therefore, the United States government could have argued that it had been released from the duties under the Pact of Paris by virtue of the second paragraph of the preamble to the Pact and recovered the freedom to wage war against Germany.

81 See Trefousse, *Germany and American Neutrality*, 25–27.

82 Ibid., 27, 43–52, 60, 74–77, 120–121, 129–136.

83 Ibid., 91–103, 137–156.

84 Kissinger, *Diplomacy*, 369–393.

85 See Trefousse, *Germany and American Neutrality*, 13–23. From a military perspective, in the nineteenth century and thereafter, it was thought that British naval control over the Atlantic Ocean was a condition necessary for the safety of the American continent, and if that condition remained unfulfilled, the safety of the American continent would be damaged. Economically, it could not be permitted that most of the trading partner States of the United States would fall under the control of Nazi Germany, which opposed the principle of free trade and pursued the policy of economic monopolisation. Ideologically, a victory for Germany meant that fascism would spread, thus endangering democracy.

86 Kissinger, *Diplomacy*, 387.

87 Aruga and Miyazato, *Outline of American Diplomatic History*, 125 [in Japanese].

88 In this regard, Kissinger observes: "By initiating hostilities, the Axis powers had solved Roosevelt's lingering dilemma about how to move the American people into the war. Had Japan focused its attack on Southeast Asia and Hitler not declared war against the United States, Roosevelt's task of steering his people toward his view would have been much more complicated." "Why Hitler thus freed Roosevelt to concentrate America's war effort on the country Roosevelt had always considered to be the principal enemy has never been satisfactorily explained." Kissinger, *Diplomacy*, 392, 393.

89 See above section 2.3 of Chapter 2. The Pact of Paris and the United Nations Charter have restricted the freedom of States to resort to war or use force, and thereby limited the extent to which States may participate in a war or armed conflict. The participation in a war or armed conflict in support of a belligerent that has illegally resorted to war or used armed force is prohibited. However, the participation in a war or armed conflict in support of a lawful belligerent is permissible as a result of exercising the freedom to wage war that is recovered by the second paragraph of the preamble of the Pact of Paris (see above, note 80 of this chapter), or, in the case of the United Nations Charter, as an exercise of the right of collective self-defence

184 *The development of the law of neutrality*

(Article 51). In the Second World War, the United States government, based on the assumption that Great Britain was carrying out a lawful war, provided military assistance to Great Britain, namely an act equivalent to "the participation in the war", which was lawful according to the view of the United States.

90 Borchard, "War, Neutrality and Non-Belligerency", 625.

91 Borchard, "Neutrality", *Yale Law Journal* 48 (1939): 46.

92 Borchard, "War, Neutrality and Non-Belligerency", 622.

93 As we have argued, a third State's military assistance to a belligerent is not prohibited under international law and needs no justification if the third State has no intention to remain neutral. Nevertheless, the United States government attempted to legally justify its military assistance to Great Britain by referring to, for example, the so-called Budapest Articles of Interpretation adopted by the International Law Association in 1934. See Hearings before the House Committee on Foreign Affairs, 77th Congress, 1st sess., on H. Res. 1776 regarding the Lend-Lease Bill, in Hackworth, *Digest of International Law*, 7:680–681; Address of Robert H. Jackson, Attorney General of the United States, Inter-American Bar Association, Havana, Cuba, 27 March 1941, *AJIL* 35 (1941): 348–359. The Budapest Articles of Interpretation, which shall be considered in section 2.2 of this chapter, based on the assumption that a neutral State was *prohibited* in the traditional law of neutrality from providing military assistance to a belligerent, takes a view that third States are no longer bound by the traditional duties of neutrality as a result of the prohibition of war by the Pact of Paris. The thesis of this book is that such an assumption about the traditional law of neutrality is not correct. The United States government was influenced by the view based on such an incorrect assumption. However, there were also some instances where the United States government advanced an argument based on a correct assumption about the law of neutrality. According to this argument, the law of neutrality is a means of ensuring the security of neutral States, providing that a neutral State fulfils certain conditions. However, in view of the circumstances at that time, where Germany did not respect the neutrality of European neutral States such as Norway, the law of neutrality does not serve as a means of security for the United States; rather, providing assistance to Great Britain is a much better policy for the security of the United States. See, for example, Statements by the Secretary of State before the House Foreign Affairs Committee, 15 January 1941, *Department of State Bulletin* 4 (1941): 90.

94 On the concept of "non-belligerency", see Borchard, "War, Neutrality and Non-Belligerency", 618–625; Coudert, "Non-Belligerency in International Law", 143–151; Freytagh-Loringhoven, "Nichtkriegführungen und wohlwollende Neutralität", 332–333; Grewe, "Der Status der Nichtkriegführung", 206–207; Kunz, "Neutrality and the European War", 747–751; Lalive, "Quelques nouvelles tendances de la neutralité", 46–58; Preuss, "Concepts of Neutrality and Non-Belligerency", 97–109; Wilson, " 'Non-Belligerency' ", 121–123; Yokota, "Legal Doctrine of Non-Belligereny, (1) (2)", 545–569, 759–781.

95 Onuma, *Prolegomena to the Responsibility for War*, 144–145 [in Japanese].

96 Hoare to Halifax, 13 June 1940, *BDFA*, pt. 3, ser. F, vol. 13, p. 292.

97 See Hernández-Sandoica and Moradiellos, "Spain and the Second World War", 248. In addition to Spain, States that described their position in the war as being one of "non-belligerency" included Italy, Egypt and Turkey. However, it was not necessarily clear whether these States aided belligerent States in a way that was incompatible with the status of neutrality. At the very least, the concept of "non-belligerency" was not invoked to *legally* justify the provision of assistance to belligerents. For example, Italy referred to its position as "non-belligerency" because, for Mussolini, who felt guilty about not entering the war as an ally of Germany, describing its status as "neutral" would be a disgrace for Italy. Therefore, like the case of Spain, the concept of "non-belligerency" which Italy referred to solely functioned as a

The development of the law of neutrality 185

political concept. See Grob, *Relativity of War and Peace*, 10–11; Rousseau, *Le droit des conflits armés*, 371.

98 See Iiyama, *Battles of Neutral States*, 222 [in Japanese].
99 Spain's interest in this war referred to the hope to acquire British Gibraltar and French North Africa after the war as a return for entering the war on the side of Italy and Germany. In May 1940, Germany occupied France, and Italy entered the war in June of the same year, thus eliminating France's threat on Spain and simultaneously weakening the strength of the British fleet in the Mediterranean Sea. While the Spanish government wished to take this good opportunity to enter the war and to acquire the territories mentioned above, the Spanish economy had been depleted by the Spanish Civil War and participating in another war would be impossible for some time. Therefore, Spain could only enter the war when Germany and Italy were sure of victory. Spain's declaration of "non-belligerency" was made to show that, while in this dilemma, it could not immediately enter the war, but that it had the intention to enter the war in the near future. See Hernández-Sandoica and Moradiellos, "Spain and the Second World War", 249–251.
100 Halifax to Selby, 14 June 1940, *BDFA*, pt. 3, ser. F, vol. 13, p. 293.
101 For example, the Prize Court of Hamburg, in the *Marietta Nomikos* case (1940), without deciding whether there existed a state of war between Germany and Egypt, held that Egypt must be treated as an "enemy" of Germany "for the purpose of prize jurisdiction" "on account of the English domination and military occupation of Egypt". The Marietta Nomikos, Germany, Prize Court of Hamburg, 16 February 1940, *Annual Digest 1943–45*, 568–570.
102 Oppenheim (Roxburgh ed.), *International Law*, 3rd ed., 2:406.
103 Oppenheim died on 7 October 1919, but he had prepared the third edition of *International Law* while he was still alive. Although he died before it was completed, he left behind the manuscripts and documents in preparation for the revisions. The third edition of *International Law* was edited and published by Roxburgh based on these manuscripts and documents, and it includes section that incorporates Oppenheim's revised manuscripts and sections added and amended by Roxburgh where Oppenheim had not revised anything. According to Roxburgh, the section on "the right to remain neutral" (Paragraph 299 of Volume 2) was a revision added by Oppenheim himself. See ibid., vi.
104 Ibid., 79.
105 Borchard, "Neutrality", *Yale Law Journal* 48 (1939): 46 [italics added].
106 Oppenheim (Roxburgh ed.), *International Law*, 3rd ed., 2:417.
107 According to Oppenheim, disputes which may be settled by war include political disputes as well as legal disputes. Ibid., 67, 81–82. In other words, not only wars waged for international delinquencies but also wars waged in order to change rules of international law or treaties were lawful.
108 Yokota, "Legal Doctrine of Non-Belligerency (2)", 771–772 [in Japanese].
109 Borchard, in a joint work with Lage, called this right "the legal right to remain neutral". See Borchard and Lage, *Neutrality for the United States*, 4.
110 Borchard, "Arms Embargo and Neutrality", 294.
111 Borchard, "War, Neutrality and Non-Belligerency", 622.
112 Ibid., 624–625.
113 Yokota, "Legal Doctrine of Non-Belligerency (2)", 774 [in Japanese; italics added].
114 Kunz, *Kriegsrecht und Neutralitätsrecht*, 215.
115 Hammarskjöld, "La neutralité en général", 59.
116 Falconbridge, "Right of a Belligerent to Make War upon a Neutral", 204–212.
117 Ishimoto, "International Organization and Neutrality", 31 [in Japanese]. In this article, Ishimoto cites another article that he has published, in which Kunz's *Kriegsrecht und Neutralitätsrecht* is cited. Ishimoto, "Historical Development of Neutral System (1)", 36 [in Japanese].

186 *The development of the law of neutrality*

118 See above, pp. 5–6.

119 Ishimoto, *Historical Study on the Law of Neutrality*, 20 [in Japanese].

120 Kunz, *Kriegsrecht und Neutralitätsrecht*, 215 [italics in the original].

121 Huber, "Die Fortbildung des Völkerrechts", 586.

122 Ishimoto, *Historical Study on the Law of Neutrality*, 21 [in Japanese; emphasis in the original].

123 Ibid., 21.

124 See e.g. Wright, "Meaning of the Pact of Paris", 59–61; Wright, "Neutrality and Neutral Rights", 83–84; Boye, "Shall a State Which Goes to War in Violation of the Kellog-Briand Pact Have a Belligerent's Rights in respect of Neutrals?" 768–769; [Harvard Law School,] "Rights and Duties of States in Case of Aggression", 823–909.

125 International Law Association, *Report of the Thirty-Eighth Conference Held at Budapest*, 67.

126 Ibid., 13–15, 17.

127 Kunz, "Plus de lois de la guerre?" 43.

128 Kunz, *Kriegsrecht und Neutralitätsrecht*, 5 [italics in the original].

129 Kunz, "Plus de lois de la guerre?" 44 [italics in the original].

130 See note 112 of this chapter and accompanying text.

131 Oppenheim (Lauterpacht ed.), *International Law*, 5th ed., 2:530–531.

132 Ibid., 516.

133 Lauterpacht, "Neutrality and Collective Security", 148. According to *Jowitt's Dictionary of English Law*,

> Maintenance is the giving of assistance or encouragement to one of the parties to a civil action by a person who has neither an interest in the action nor any other motive recognised by the law as justifying his interference. Maintenance includes champerty (q.v.), where the assistance is given in consideration of a promise of part of the proceeds or subject-matter of the suit if it succeeds. At common law until 1967 maintenance was both actionable (as a tort) and indictable, and contracts involving it are still illegal.
>
> Greenberg, *Jowitt's Dictionary of English Law*, 2:1398

134 Oppenheim (Lauterpacht ed.), *International Law*, 7th ed., 2:639, 664.

135 Lauterpacht, "Limits of the Operation of the Law of War", 237.

136 E.g. Bowett, *Self-Defence*, 157; Brownlie, *Use of Force*, 402; Greenwood, "Concept of War", 298; Komarnicki, "Place of Neutrality", 412; Meyrowitz, *Le principe de l'égalité des belligérants*, 370; Tucker, *Law of War and Neutrality at Sea*, 166.

137 On the significance of this book, see Takeshima, *Politics of Carl Schmitt*, 164–169 [in Japanese].

138 Schmitt, *Diskriminierenden Kriegsbegriff*, 34.

139 Ibid., 32, 34, 38.

140 Ibid., 1–2, 38–39, 46, 51.

141 On the significance of this book, see Takeshima, *Politics of Carl Schmitt*, 179–204 [in Japanese].

142 Schmitt, *Der Nomos der Erde*, 112–115.

143 Ibid., 114.

144 Ibid., 115.

145 Ibid., 138–139.

146 Yanagihara, "Idea of Non-Discriminating War", 6–12 [in Japanese].

147 As highlighted by Yanagihara, the idea of Schmitt's *nichtdiskriminierende Neutralitätsbegriff* is completely different to that of the "non-discriminatory conception of war" used by Japanese international lawyers. For Schmitt, the change from the *nichtdiskriminierende Kriegsbegriff* to the *diskriminierende Kriegsbegriff* should be regarded negatively in terms of abandoning the "enclosure and control of war"

The development of the law of neutrality 187

which have been achieved by the non-discriminatory concept of war, whereas for Japanese international lawyers, the change from the "non-discriminatory conception of war" to the "discriminatory conception of war" is viewed as being positive. See Yanagihara, "Idea of Non-Discriminating War", 18–20 [in Japanese]. However, it is fair to say that both Schmitt and Japanese international lawyers share the view that the duty of neutral States to treat belligerent States impartially in the traditional law of neutrality was based on the equality of belligerent States in traditional interantional law.

148 Sogawa, "Carl Schmitt and the Transformation of the Legal Concept of War (I)", 95 [in Japanese].

149 Ishimoto, *Historical Study on the Law of Neutrality*, 18 [in Japanese; emphasis in the original]. On the influence of Sogawa's article on Ishimoto, see Yanagihara, "Idea of Non-Discriminating War", 24 [in Japanese].

150 Tabata, *International Law* (Tokyo: Yushindo, 1955), 2:242 [in Japanese].

151 See e.g. Onuma, *Prolegomena to the Responsibility for War*, 126 [in Japanese]; Onuma, *International Law*, 605 [in Japanese]; Sugihara, *Lectures on Modern International Law*, 461–464 [in Japanese]; Tsutsui, *Encyclopedic Dictionary of International Law*, 240 [in Japanese]; Fujita, *Lectures on International Law*, 2:428 [in Japanese]; Matsui *et al.*, *International Law*, 8, 325–326 [in Japanese]; Mayama, "Non-Belligerency", 732–733 [in Japanese]; Matsuda, "New Guidelines", 49 [in Japanese]; Morikawa, "Neutrality", 219 [in Japanese]; Morikawa, "Acts concerning Japan-US Defence Cooperation", 49 [in Japanese].

152 Wolff, *Jus gentium*, § 674 [italics added].

153 Vattel, *Le droit des gens*, Liv. III, Chap. VII, § 106.

154 Bluntschli, *Das moderne Völkerrecht*, 418.

155 If war is considered as being analogous to a duel and neutral States as being analogous to observers in a duel, as Schmitt explained, neutral States would be prohibited from entering the war, as witnesses (Zeugen) were prohibited from intervening in the duel in support of one of the participants. Nevertheless, Schmitt acknowledges that even in the non-discriminatory concept of war neutral States may "in any time intervene [in the war] by virtue of their sovereign *jus ad bellum*". See Schmitt, *Der Nomos der Erde*, 139.

Conclusion

1 Conclusion of this book

The objective of this book was to identify the essential character of the traditional law of neutrality by reconsidering its historical development from the sixteenth century to 1945. To summarise the conclusion of this book, the traditional law of neutrality was an institution that legally protected the right of neutral States not to be involved in war (the "right to remain neutral"), and the so-called "duties of neutral States" were the *conditions* that neutral States should fulfil if they wished to remain outside the war, rather than the *duties* of neutral States.

The contribution of the conclusion presented by this book as compared to the existing studies is as follows.

First, it has been generally assumed and even regarded as self-evident that belligerent States were free at any time to make war on neutral States, and that neutral States did not have the right not to be involved in war in traditional international law. However, the basis of such an assumption is that, in international law prior to the First World War which recognised the unlimited freedom of States to wage war, belligerent States, as a matter of course, should have had the freedom to declare war on neutral States, which had not been proven by the practice of States or legal literature prior to the First World War. The first contribution of this book is that, based on the detailed historical studies, it has proven the existence of the "right to remain neutral", that is, the right of neutral States not to be involved in war in traditional international law. This book has also identified the basis of this right: The basis of the right of neutral States not to be involved in war was, in State practice from the sixteenth to the eighteenth centuries, agreements between belligerents and third States (neutrality treaties); according to eighteenth-century writers such as Wolff and Vattel, the just war doctrine; and in the period from the nineteenth to the first half of the twentieth centuries, the concept of the causes of war, which limits the personal scope of war.

The second contribution of this book is that it has revised the existing explanation about the so-called "duty of impartiality". It has generally been assumed that neutral States were not permitted to discriminate between belligerents and

Conclusion 189

to assist either belligerent because all belligerents were equal in traditional international law, which permitted the unrestricted freedom of war. However, we cannot find any such explanation in State practice and legal literature prior to the First World War. As we have identified in this book, the reason why neutral States should abstain from providing military assistance to either belligerent was not because the provision of assistance was *prohibited*, but because the provision of assistance was regarded as an act equivalent to the indirect participation in the war, which States should abstain from *if they wished to remain neutral* and *remain outside the war*. On the other hand, the expression of sympathy by a neutral State towards a belligerent was not considered as an act contrary to neutrality because it "is not an act of war, nor is it the participation in the war".[1] In other words, acts contrary to the so-called "duty of impartiality" were not prohibited, but such acts were acts that should be abstained from as the *conditions* for enjoying the right to remain neutral. Therefore, if States did not mind being involved in the war and becoming belligerent States, they were free to undertake acts contrary to neutrality. That is why this book has basically not used the terms "the duty of impartiality" and "the duties of neutral States" and enclosed these terms with quotation marks.

Furthermore, as the third contribution that may be implied by the analysis of this book, it may be considered as revising the existing view regarding the legal status of war in traditional international law. While there remain many uncertainties about the legal status of war in traditional international law, many writers have shared the view that States had the unrestricted freedom to resort to war in traditional international law, particularly in nineteenth-century international law. The most typical examples of those writers are those who have described war in traditional international law as an "extra-legal phenomenon" or phenomenon "outside the law".[2] However, the main thesis of this book is that war by belligerents against neutral States that fulfilled the condition of the right to remain neutral was not free but prohibited in international law even in the period from the nineteenth to the early twentieth centuries, when the just war doctrine had lost its support. War in traditional international law was not an "extra-legal phenomenon" but a means of resolving disputes or issues between States. From this perspective, war had not to be expanded to States unrelated to the dispute or the issue that caused the war, that is, neutral States. In other words, in international society in which there is no central authority for resolving disputes or issues between States, the law of neutrality was an attempt to restrict the personal scope of war to States involved in the dispute or issues.

2 Issues for further research

The objective of this book was to identify the essential character of the traditional law of neutrality by reconsidering its historical development, thereby gaining a perspective that would resolve the various issues regarding the current status of the law of neutrality. While resolving these issues regarding the current

190   *Conclusion*

status of the law of neutrality is a matter for further research, based on the analysis of this book, we can present some guidelines for resolving these issues.

As noted in section 1 of the Introduction, as regards the current status of the law of neutrality, contemporary scholars have debated whether it is *lawful* for a State to take a position of "non-belligerency": "the situation of those States which, while not wishing to enter the conflict on the side of one belligerent, do not, at the same time, choose to be bound by traditional neutrality obligations".[3] While the views of scholars differ as to the legality or illegality of attitudes of "non-belligerency", they have shared some assumptions about the traditional law of neutrality. However, as some of these assumptions have been revised by the analysis of this book, the debates on the current status of the law of neutrality should also be reorganised.

One of the grounds for those writers who affirm the legality of attitudes of "non-belligerency" is that the historical foundation of the "duty of impartiality" was the equality of belligerents as a consequence of the unrestricted freedom of States to resort to war, and that such a basis has disappeared as a result of the outlawry of war. However, as identified in this book, the basis of the so-called "duty of impartiality" in the traditional law of neutrality was not the equality of belligerents. As acts contrary to the "duty of impartiality" were regarded as acts equivalent to "acts of war" or "the participation in the war", a State wishing to remain outside the war should abstain from those acts. But such acts were not prohibited in traditional international law. Certainly, belligerents were equal in traditional international law, where resort to war was not prohibited, but third States were not prohibited from assisting a belligerent either by entering the war or without entering the war. Such assistance should be abstained from *if* a State wished to remain neutral, but those States not wishing to avoid being involved in the war did not need to abstain from those acts. In short, the view that affirms the legality of attitudes of "non-belligerency" in contemporary international law has been based on a mistaken assumption about the historical basis of the traditional law of neutrality.

On the other hand, it is not the case that those writers who deny the legality of attitudes of "non-belligerency" have assumed the correct understanding of the traditional law of neutrality. The ground for this view is the continuing validity of the traditional law of neutrality, in which States that do not take part in a war automatically become neutral States and are bound by the duty of impartiality. However, according to the analysis of this book, in the traditional law of neutrality, acts contrary to the "duty of impartiality" were not prohibited, but such acts should be abstained from if States wished to remain outside the war. In traditional international law, it was not prohibited for third States that did not claim the right to remain neutral to provide military assistance to either belligerent. That being so, we cannot argue that attitudes of "non-belligerency" are illegal, based solely on the continuing validity of the traditional law of neutrality.

Based on the analysis of this book, the issue to be discussed regarding the current status of the law of neutrality is not the legality or illegality of attitudes

Conclusion   191

of "non-belligerency". Attitudes of "non-belligerency", that is, attitudes of States that provide military assistance to a belligerent without entering the war or international armed conflict, which were legal in traditional international law, seem to be still legal in contemporary international law based on the right of collective self-defence (Article 51 of the United Nations Charter). Rather, the issue to be debated is the legal consequences of attitudes of "non-belligerency" as opposed to the status of neutrality: What are the legal advantages of choosing the status of neutrality as compared to taking attitudes of "non-belligerency"? In other words, the issue to be discussed in further research is whether the law of neutrality, which was the institution that legally protected the right of neutral States not to be involved in war, has any legal relevance in contemporary international law.

In the traditional law of neutrality, a belligerent was permitted to "treat as an enemy" a third State violating neutrality; on the contrary, a third State that observed neutrality was legally entitled not to be "treated as an enemy". To be treated as an enemy means being treated as a belligerent. If a hitherto neutral State is treated as an enemy and becomes a belligerent, the following two consequences follow. First, the territory of that State becomes regions of war, in which belligerent States may conduct hostilities (belligerents are not permitted to conduct hostilities in the territory of neutral States). Second, merchant vessels and cargoes of that State become enemy vessels and enemy cargoes, which are subject to seizure and confiscation by belligerents (neutral vessels and cargoes are not subject to seizure and confiscation except in cases of the transportation of the contraband of war, the breaches of blockade, or engaging in unneutral service etc.).

The issue is to what extent the framework of the traditional law of neutrality is applicable in contemporary international law and whether the traditional law of neutrality has any value in contemporary international law. A "non-belligerent" State, which provides military assistance to a belligerent, would be treated as an enemy by the other belligerent if we applied the framework of the traditional law of neutrality. However, the issue is whether the aforementioned two consequences would follow with regard to a non-belligerent State in contemporary international law. As regards the first consequence, in modern international law where the use of forces by States in international relations is prohibited in principle, acts of hostilities or the use of force do not automatically become legal even if "war" breaks out; rather, each act of hostility or the use of force should be evaluated with reference to the justifying grounds of the use of force such as the right of self-defence. In other words, the concept of "war" is legally irrelevant in relation to the principle of the non-use of force.[4] That being so, when evaluating the legality of hostilities conducted by belligerent States against non-belligerent States in contemporary international law, the framework of the traditional law of neutrality seems to have little relevance, and it might be sufficient to apply the framework of the principle of non-use of force and its exceptions (self-defence, etc.). In other words, the law of neutrality, as an institution that legally protects the status of neutral States to remain outside

192 *Conclusion*

the war, might be absorbed into the principle of non-use of force in contemporary international law. However, recalling that, in State practice during the Second World War, the legality of wars and hostilities against neutral States (Norway, the Netherlands, Belgium) by belligerent States (Germany and Great Britain) was debated not relying on the framework of the prohibition of war by the Pact of Paris and the right of self-defence as an exception to that, but relying on the framework of the law of neutrality,[5] there may be room for the law of neutrality to function as a framework for the legal regulation of the use of force by belligerents against third States. On the other hand, as regards the second consequence, the law of neutrality may not be absorbed into the principle of non-use of force. The issue of whether belligerent States (States party to an armed conflict) should treat the vessels and cargoes of non-belligerent States as enemy vessels and cargoes or as neutral vessels and cargoes cannot be resolved by applying the principle of the non-use of force, and thus the traditional law of neutrality still has legal relevance in contemporary international law.[6]

However, the current status and relevance of the law of neutrality in contemporary international law is an issue that must be studied in the future on the basis of the analysis of this book, and on the basis of the detailed examination of State practice after the Second World War.

Notes

1 See above, note 158 of Chapter 2.
2 See e.g. Ishimoto, *Changing Structure of International Law*, 7 [in Japanese]; McNair, "Collective Security", 152; Onuma, *Prolegomena to the Responsibility for War*, 15 [in Japanese]. See also Wright's view cited in note 330 of Chapter 2, according to which war is not a legal institution, but an "unfortunate event", like flood, fire or insurrection in municipal law.
3 Gioia, "Neutrality and Non-Belligerency", 76.
4 See Greenwood, "Concept of War", 301–303. However, as stated in note 14 of Introduction, it is still unclear what legal effects are produced by "war", the "use of force" and "armed conflict" in modern international law.
5 See above, pp. 154, 156, 157–158.
6 It remains still unclear whether States party to an international armed conflict may exercise the right of capture against merchant vessels and cargoes belonging to third States in modern international law, and if so, on what ground. It is also unclear whether neutral vessels and cargoes are treated differently from enemy vessels and cargoes, as in the traditional law of prize. In State practice since the Second World War, however, States party to international armed conflicts have captured merchant vessels and cargoes of third States, and in principle have met no opposition by third States. See Mayama, "Capture of Merchant Ships of the Third States in the Armed Conflicts" [in Japanese].

Bibliography

Unpublished materials

The National Archives (Public Record Office), London.
Foreign Office and Predecessor: Political and Other Departments: General Correspondence before 1906.
FO 7/226.
Foreign Office: Political Departments: General Correspondence from 1906–1966.
FO 371/1883, 2105, 2161, 2164, 2188, 2231, 2278, 2472, 2759.
Foreign Office: Treaty Department and Successors: General Correspondence from 1906.
FO 372/706.

Published materials

Akten zur deutschen auswärtigen Politik 1918–1945. Baden-Baden: Imprimerie Nationale.
American State Papers, Class 1, *Foreign Relations.* 6 vols. Washington: Gales and Seaton, 1833–59. Reprint, Buffalo, New York: William S. Hein & Co., 1998.
Bourne, Kenneth, and D. Cameron Watt, eds. *British Documents on Foreign Affairs: Reports and Papers from the Foreign Office Confidential Print.* Frederick, MD: University Publications of America, 1984–.
Bundesblatt der schweizerischen Eidgenossenschaft. Bern: Stämpfli, 1848–1977.
Churchill, Winston S. *The Second World War.* 6 vols. 3rd ed. London: Cassel & Co., 1950–54.
Commission nationale pour la publication de documents diplomatiques suisses. *Documents diplomatiques suisses: 1848–1945.* 15 tomes. Bern: Benteli, 1979–.
Deák, Francis, and Phillip C. Jessup, eds. *A Collection of Neutrality Laws, Regulations and Treaties of Various Countries.* 2 vols. Washington, DC: Carnegie Endowment for International Peace, 1939. Reprint, Westport, CT: Greenwood Press, 1974.
De Visscher, Ch., et F. Vanlangenhove, éd. *Documents diplomatiques belges, 1920–1940: La politique de sécurité extérieure.* 5 tomes. Bruxelles: Palais des Académies, 1964–66.
Department of State Bulletin. Washington, DC: United States Government Printing Office, 1939–.
Documents of the United Nations Conference on International Organization San Francisco, 1945. 22 vols. London: United Nations Information Organizations, 1945.
Du Mont, J. *Corps universel diplomatique du droit des gens.* 8 tomes. Amsterdam: P. Brunel, R. et J. Wetstein, et G. Smith, Henri Waesberge, et Z. Chatelain, 1726–31.

194 *Bibliography*

Foreign Office. *British and Foreign State Papers.* 170 vols. London: James Ridgway, 1812–1968.

Foreign Relations of the United States. Washington: United States Government Printing Office, 1861–.

Grewe, Wilhelm G., hrsg. *Fontes historiae iuris gentium.* 3 Bde. Berlin: Walter de Gruyter, 1988–95.

Hackworth, Green Haywood. *Digest of International Law.* 8 vols. Washington: Government Printing Office, 1940–44.

Hansard's Parliamentary Debates. London: Printed by T. C. Hansard for Baldwin, Cradock, and Joy.

Lauterpacht, H., ed. *Annual Digest and Reports of Public International Law Cases.* London: Butterworth & Co., 1940–50.

Lauterpacht, H., ed. *International Law Reports.* London: Butterworth & Co., 1950–.

League of Nations. *Official Journal.* London: Harrison, 1920–.

League of Nations. *Official Journal Special Supplement.* London: Harrison & Sons, 1920–.

League of Nations, *Treaty Series: Publication of Treaties and International Engagements Registered with the Secretariat of the League of Nations.* 205 vols. 1920–1946.

Marsden, R. G., ed. *Documents relating to Law and Custom of the Sea.* 2 vols. [London]: Navy Records Society, 1915–16. Reprint, Union, New Jersey: The Lawbook Exchange, 1999.

Martens, Georg Friedrich von. *Recueil de traités d'alliance, de paix, de trève, de neutralité, de commerce, de limites, d'échange etc. et plusieurs autres actes servant à la connaissance des relations etrangères des puissances et états de l'Europe tant dans leur rapport mutuel que dans celui envers les puissances et états dans d'autres parties du globe depuis 1761 jusqu'à présent.* 2e éd. Gottingue: Dieterich, 1817–35.

Ministère des Affaires Étrangères. *Deuxième conférence international de la paix, La Haye 15 Juin–18 Octobre 1907: Actes et documents.* 3 tomes. La Haye: Imprimerie Nationale, 1907.

Ministero degli Affari Esteri, Commissione per la pubblicazione dei documenti diplomatici. *I documenti diplomatici italiani.* Roma: Libreria dello Stato, 1952–.

Ministry of Foreign Affairs of Japan, ed. *Nihon gaiko bunshyo.* [Documents on Japanese Foreign Policy]. Tokyo: Ministry of Foreign Affairs of Japan, 1936–.

Moore, John Bassett. *A Digest of International Law, as Embodied in Diplomatic Discussions, Treaties and Other International Agreements, International Awards, the Decisions of Municipal Courts, and the Writings of Jurists, and Especially in Documents Published and Unpublished, Issued by Presidents and Secretaries of State of the United States, the Opinions of the Attorneys-General, and the Decisions of Courts, Federal and State.* 8 vols. Washington, DC: Government Printing Office, 1906.

Navy Secretariat of Japan, ed. *Shyowa juyonen, jugonenn senso kakkoku kaisen kankei horei.* [Laws and Regulations of Various States during the War in 1939 and 1940] 1940.

Papers relating to the Treaty of Washington. 6 vols. Washington, DC: Government Printing Office, 1872–74.

Pardessus, J. M. *Collection de lois maritimes antérieures au XVIIIe siècle.* 6 tomes. Paris: Imprimerie Royale, 1828–45.

Parry, Clive, ed. *Consolidated Treaty Series.* 231 vols. Dobbs Ferry, New York: Oceana Publications, 1969–81.

Proceedings of the International Naval Conference Held in London, December 1908-February 1909. London: Printed for His Majesty's Stationery Office by Harrison.

Bibliography 195

Samwer, Charles, et Jules Hopf. *Nouveau recueil général de traités et autres actes relatifs aux rapports de droit international: Continuation du grand recueil de G. Fr. de Martens.* 2e sér. Gottingue: Librairie de Dieterich, 1876–1910.

Schiemann, von Theodor, hrsg. *Kaiser Nikolaus im Kampf mit Polen und im Gegensatz zu Frankreich und England 1830–1840.* Berlin: Druck und Verlag von Georg Reimer, 1913.

Schindler, Dietrich, and Jiri Toman, eds. *The Laws of Armed Conflicts: A Collection of Conventions, Resolutions and Other Documents.* 4th ed. Leiden: Martinus Nijhoff, 2004.

Scott, James Brown, ed. *The Proceedings of the Hague Peace Conferences: Translation of the Official Texts: The Conference of 1907.* 3 vols. New York: Oxford University Press, 1920.

United Nations, *Treaty Series: Treaties and International Agreements Registered or Filed and Recorded with the Secretariat of the United Nations.* New York: United Nations, 1946–.

Books and articles (in European languages)

Accioly, Hildebrando. "Guerre et neutralité en face du droit des gens contemporain". Dans *Hommage d'une génération de juristes au président Basdevant*, 1–9. Paris: Éditions A. Pedone, 1960.

Akashi, Kinji. *Cornelius van Bynkershoek: His Role in the History of International Law.* The Hague: Kluwer Law International, 1998.

Albrecht, Erich. *Über Requisitionen von neutralem Privateigentum, insbesondere von Schiffen.* Breslau: J. U. Kern's Verlag, 1912.

Alvarez, Alejandro. *La grande guerre européenne et la neutralité du Chili.* Paris: A. Pedone, 1915.

Baker, Sherston, revised. *Halleck's International Law: Rules Regulating the Intercourse of States in Peace and War.* London: C. Kegan Paul & Co., 1878.

Balladore-Pallieri, Giorgio. *Diritto bellico.* 2a. ed. Padova: CEDAM, 1954.

Bassompierre, A. de. "L'article 10 de la cinquième convention de La Haye". *RDILC*, 3e sér., 4 (1923): 236–246.

Bauslaugh, Robert A. *The Concept of Neutrality in Classical Greece.* Berkeley, CA: University of California Press, 1991.

Baxter, Richard R. "The Legal Consequences of the Unlawful Use of Force under the Charter". *Proceedings of the American Society of International Law* 62 (1968): 68–75.

Belin, J. "La porté de la neutralité américaine". *RGDIP* 43 (1936): 416–436.

Benton, Elbert Jay. *International Law and Diplomacy of the Spanish-American War.* Gloucester, MA: Peter Smith, 1968.

Berber, Friedrich. "Die amerikanische Neutralität im Kriege 1939/1941". *ZaöRV* 11 (1942–43): 445–476.

Berber, Friedrich. *Lehrbuch des Völkerrechts*, Bd. 2, *Kriegsrecht.* München: C. H. Beck, 1962.

Bergbohm, Carl. *Die bewaffnete Neutralität, 1780–1783: Eine Entwicklungsphase des Völkerrechts im Seekrieg.* Berlin: Puttkammer & Mühlbrecht, 1884.

Bernard, Mountague. *A Historical Account of the Neutrality of Great Britain during the American Civil War.* London: Longmans, Green, Reader, and Dyer, 1870.

Bindschedler, Rudolf L. "Die Neutralität im modernen Völkerrecht". *ZaöRV* 17 (1956–57): 1–37.

196 *Bibliography*

Bindschedler, Rudolf L. "Frieden, Krieg und Neutralität im Völkerrecht der Gegenwart". In *Multitudo Legum jus unum: Festschrift für Wilhelm Wengler zu seinem 65. Geburtstag*, herausgegeben von Josef Tittel und den Mitarbeitern des Instituts für internationales und ausländisches Recht an der Freien Universität Berlin, 1:27–49. Berlin: Interrecht, 1973.

Bindschedler, Rudolf L. "Neutrality, Concept and General Rules". In *Encyclopedia of Public International Law*, 3:549–553. Published under the auspices of the Max Planck Institute for Comparative Public Law and International Law under the direction of Rudolf Bernhardt. Amsterdam: North-Holland, 1997.

Bisschop, W. R. "The Altmark". *Transactions of the Grotius Society* 26 (1940): 67–82.

Blankart, Franz A. "Der Neutralitätsbegriff aus logischer Sicht". In *Discordia concors: Festgabe für Edgar Bonjour zu seinem siebzigsten Geburtstag am 21. August 1968*, herausgegeben von Marc Sieber, 605–623. Basel: Helbing & Lichtenhahn, 1968.

Blix, Hans. *Sovereignty, Aggression and Neutrality*. Stockholm: Almqvist & Wiksell, 1970.

Bluntschli, J. C. "Opinion impartiale sur la question de l'Alabama et sur la manière de la résoudre". *RDILC* 2 (1870): 452–485.

Bluntschli, J. C. *Das moderne Völkerrecht der civilisirten Staaten als Rechtsbuch dargestellt*. 2. Aufl. Nördlingen: C. H. Beck, 1872.

Bluntschli, J. C. "Résolutions proposées à l'Institut". *RDILC* 6 (1874): 581.

Boczek, Boleslaw Adam. "Law of Warfare at Sea and Neutrality: Lessons from the Gulf War". *Ocean Development and International Law* 20 (1989): 239–271.

Bodin, Jean. *Les six livres de la république*. Paris: Fayard, 1986.

Boidin, Paul. *La lois de la guerre et les deux conférences de La Haye (1899–1907)*. Paris: A. Pedone, 1908.

Borchard, Edwin. "The Neutrality Claims against Great Britain". *AJIL* 21 (1927): 764–768.

Borchard, Edwin. "Restatement of the Law of Neutrality in Maritime Warfare". *AJIL* 22 (1928): 614–620.

Borchard, Edwin. "The Arms Embargo and Neutrality". *AJIL* 27 (1933): 293–298.

Borchard, Edwin. "Neutral Embargoes and Commercial Treaties". *AJIL* 30 (1936): 501–506.

Borchard, Edwin. "Sanction v. Neutrality". *AJIL* 30 (1936): 91–94.

Borchard, Edwin. " 'Neutrality' and Civil Wars". *AJIL* 31 (1937): 304–306.

Borchard, Edwin. "Neutrality and Unneutrality". *AJIL* 32 (1938): 778–782.

Borchard, Edwin. "The Power to Punish Neutral Volunteers in Enemy Armies". *AJIL* 32 (1938): 535–538.

Borchard, Edwin. "Neutrality". *Yale Law Journal* 48 (1939): 37–53.

Borchard, Edwin. "The Attorney General's Opinion on the Exchange of Destroyers for Naval Bases". *AJIL* 34 (1940): 690–697.

Borchard, Edwin. "Was Norway Delinquent in the Case of the Altmark?" *AJIL* 34 (1940): 289–294.

Borchard, Edwin. "War, Neutrality and Non-Belligerency". *AJIL* 35 (1941): 618–625.

Borchard, Edwin, and Williams Potter Lage. *Neutrality for the United States*. 2nd ed. New Haven, CT: Yale University Press, 1940.

Bothe, Michael. "Neutrality in Naval Warfare: What is Left of Traditional Law?" In *Humanitarian Law of Armed Conflict Challenges Ahead: Essays in Honour of Frits Kalshoven*, edited by Astrid J. M. Delissen and Gerard J. Tanja, 387–405. Dordrecht: Martinus Nijhoff, 1992.

Bibliography 197

Bothe, Michael. "Neutrality at Sea". In *The Gulf War of 1980–1988: The Iran-Iraq War in International Legal Perspective*, edited by Ige F. Dekker and Harry H. G. Post, 205–211. Dordrecht: Martinus Nijhoff, 1992.

Bothe, Michael. "Neutrality, Concept and General Rules". In *The Max Planck Encyclopedia of Public International Law*, edited by Rüdiger Wolfrum, 617–634. Oxford: Oxford University Press, 2012.

Bothe, Michael. "The Law of Neutrality". In *The Handbook of International Humanitarian Law*, 3rd ed., edited by Dieter Fleck, 549–580. Oxford: Oxford University Press, 2013.

Bottié, F. *Essai sur la genèse et l'évolution de la notion de neutralité*. Paris: Les Édition Internationales, 1937.

Bowett, D. W. *Self-Defence in International Law*. Manchester: Manchester University Press, 1958.

Boye, Thorvald. "Shall a State Which Goes to War in Violation of the Kellog-Briand Pact Have a Belligerent's Rights in respect of Neutrals?" *AJIL* 24 (1930): 766–770.

Boye, Thorvald. "Quelques aspects du développement des règles de la neutralité". *RDADI* 64 (1938): 161–228.

Bridge, F. R., and Roger Bullen. *The Great Powers and the European States System 1815–1914*. London: Longman, 1980.

Briggs, Herbert W. "Neglected Aspects of the Destroyers Deal". *AJIL* 34 (1940): 569–587.

Bring, Ove, "Commentary (1938 Stockholm Declaration regarding Similar Rules of Neutrality)". In *The Law of Naval Warfare: A Collection of Agreements and Documents with Commentaries*, edited by N. Ronzitti, 839–843. Dordrecht: Martinus Nijhoff, 1988.

Brown, Philip Marshall. "Malevolent Neutrality". *AJIL* 30 (1936): 88–90.

Brown, Philip Marshall. "Neutrality". *AJIL* 33 (1939): 726–727.

Brown, Sidney H. *Der neutrale Charakter von Schiff und Ladung im Prisenrecht*. Zürich: Art Institut O. Füssli, 1926.

Brownlie, Ian. "Volunteers and the Law of War and Neutrality". *International and Comparative Law Quarterly* 5 (1956): 570–580.

Brownlie, Ian. *International Law and the Use of Force by States*. Oxford: Oxford University Press, 1963.

Bustamante, Antonio S. "The Hague Convention concerning the Rights and Duties of Neutral Powers and Persons in Land Warfare". *AJIL* 2 (1908): 95–120.

Bynkershoek, Cornelius van. *Quaestionum juris publici libri duo*. The Classics of International Law, edited by James Brown Scott. Vol. 1, A Photographic Reproduction of the Edition of 1737, with a List of Errata, and a Portrait of Bynkershoek. Vol. 2, A Translation of the Text, by Tenney Frank, with an Introduction by J. de Louter, and an Index. Oxford: Clarendon Press, 1930.

Calvo, M. Charles. "Examen des trois règles de droit international proposées dans le traité de Washington". *RDILC* 6 (1874): 453–532.

Calvo, M. Charles. *Le droit international théorique et pratique: Précédé d'un exposé historique des progrès de la science du droit des gens*. 6 tomes. 5e éd. Paris: Rousseau, 1896.

Carre, Henri. *Les incidents de neutralité de la Guerre Russo-Japonaise (année 1904): Étude de droit international public*. Paris: H. Charles-Lavauzelle[, 1904?].

Carter, Alice Clare. "The Dutch as Neutrals in the Seven Years' War". *International and Comparative Law Quarterly* 12 (1963): 818–834.

Castrén, Erik. *The Present Law of War and Neutrality*. Helsinki: Suomalaisen Tiedeakatemia, 1954.

198 *Bibliography*

Castrén, Erik. "Neutralität". *Archiv des Völkerrechts* 5 (1955): 21–40.

Castrén, Erik. *Civil War*. Helsinki: Suomalainen Tiedeakatemia, 1966.

Cavaglieri, A. "Belligeranza, neutralità e posizioni giuridiche intermedie". *Rivista di diritto internazionale*, 2. ser., 8 (1919): 58–91, 328–362.

Chadwick, Elizabeth. *Traditional Neutrality Revisited: Law, Theory and Case Studies*. The Hague: Kluwer Law International, 2002.

Chadwick, Elizabeth. "The 'Impossibility' of Maritime Neutrality during World War 1". *Netherlands International Law Review* 54 (2007): 337–360.

Chamberlain, Joseph P. "The Embargo Resolutions and Neutrality". *International Conciliation*, no. 251 (1929): 257–295.

Chaumont, Charles Marie. *La conception américaine de la neutralité: Essai sur le droit international de la neutralité aux États-Unis*. Paris: A. Rousseau, 1936.

Chaumont, Charles Marie. "Nations Unies et neutralité". *RCADI* 89 (1956): 1–59.

Chen, Ti-chiang. *The International Law of Recognition: With Special Reference to Practice in Great Britain and the United States*. London: Stevens, 1951.

Clark, G. N. "Neutral Commerce in the War of the Spanish Succession and the Treaty of Utrecht". *BYIL* 9 (1928): 69–83.

Cohn, Georg. "Neutralité et Société des Nations". Dans *Les origines et la œvres de la Société des Nations*, édité par P. Munch, 2:153–204. Copenhague: Gydendalske Boghandel, 1924.

Cohn, Georg. "The System of Sanctions of Article 16 of the Covenant and the Future Role of Neutrality". In *Collective Security: A Record of the Seventh and Eighth International Studies Conferences*, edited by Maurice Bourquin, 402–403. Paris: International Institute of Intellectual Co-operation, 1936.

Cohn, Georg. *Neo-Neutrality*. Translated by Arthur S. Keller and Einar Jensen. New York: Columbia University Press, 1939.

Colombos, C. John. *A Treatise on the Law of Prize*. 3rd ed. London: Longmans, Green and Co., 1949.

Coudert, Frederic R. "Non-Belligerency in International Law". *Virginia Law Review* 29 (1942): 143–151.

Crichton, V. M. S. "The Pre-War Theory of Neutrality". *BYIL* 9 (1928): 101–111.

Curtis, Roy Emerson. "The Law of Hostile Military Expeditions as Applied by the United States". *AJIL* 8 (1914): 1–37, 224–255.

D'Astorg, Bertrand. *La neutralité et son réveil dans la crise de la S. D. N.* Paris: Recueil Sirey, 1938.

De Visscher, Ch. "De la belligérance dans ses rapports avec la violation de la neutralité". *Transaction of the Grotius Society* 2 (1916): 93–104.

De Visscher, Ch. "Les lois de la guerre et la théorie de la nécessité". *RGDIP* 24 (1917): 74–108.

Deák, Francis. "The United States Neutrality Acts: Theory and Practice". *International Conciliation*, no. 358 (1940): 73–114.

Deák, Francis. "Neutrality Revisited". In *Transnational Law in a Changing Society: Essays in Honor of Philip C. Jessup*, edited by Wolfgang Friedmann, Louis Henkin and Oliver Lisstzyn, 137–154. New York: Columbia University Press, 1972.

Dehn, C. G. "The Problem of Neutrality". *Transactions of the Grotius Society* 31 (1946): 139–149.

Dennis, William Cullen. "The Right of Citizens of Neutral Countries to Sell and Export Arms and Munitions of War to Belligerents". *Annals of the American Academy of Political and Social Science* 60 (1915): 168–182.

Despagnet, Frantz. *Cours de droit international public.* 4e éd. Paris: Recueil Sirey, 1910.

Dickson, Edwin D. "Neutrality and the Munitions Traffic". *Proceedings of the American Society of International Law* 29 (1935): 45–51.

Dickson, John. "Neutrality and Commerce". *Proceedings of the American Society of International Law* 29 (1935): 106–116.

Dinstein, Yoram. "The Laws of Neutrality". *Israel Yearbook on Human Rights* 14 (1984): 80–110.

Dinstein, Yoram. *War, Aggression and Self-Defence.* 5th ed. Cambridge: Cambridge University Press, 2011.

Dinstein, Yoram. *Non-International Armed Conflicts in International Law.* Cambridge: Cambridge University Press, 2014.

Divine, Robert A. *The Illusion of Neutrality.* Chicago, IL: The University of Chicago Press, 1962.

Doehring, Karl. "Neutralität und Gewaltverbot". *Archiv des Völkerrechts* 31 (1993): 193–205.

Doswald-Beck, Louise. "The Legal Validity of Military Intervention by Invitation of the Government". *BYIL* 56 (1985): 189–252.

Drummond, Donald F. *The Passing of American Neutrality.* New York: Greenwood Press, 1968.

Dumbauld, Edward. "Neutrality Laws of the United States". *AJIL* 31 (1937): 258–270.

Duttwyler, von Herbert E. *Der Seekrieg und die Wirtschaftspolitik des neutralen Staates: Eine Betrachtung des Wirtschaftskrieges zur See und seiner Auswirkungen auf die Neutralen von 1939 bis zur Kapitulation Italiens; Mit Nachträgen bis zur Kapitulation Deutschlands; Mit besonderer Berücksichtung der Lage der Schweiz und ihrer Hochseeschiffahrt.* Zürich: Polygraphischer Verlag A.G., 1945.

Eagleton, Clyde. "Neutrality and Neutral Rights following the Pact of Paris for the Renunciation of War". *Proceedings of the American Society of International Law* 24 (1930): 87–95.

Eagleton, Clyde. "Revision of the Neutrality Act". *AJIL* 33 (1939): 119–126.

Eagleton, Clyde. "The Duty of Impartiality on the Part of a Neutral". *AJIL* 34 (1940): 99–104.

Eckhardt, Curt. "Das Neutralitätsgesetz der Vereinigten Staaten von 1937". *ZaöRV* 8 (1938): 231–256.

Einicke, Paul. *Rechte und Pflichten der neutralen Machte im Seekrieg.* Tübingen: J. C. B. Mohr, 1912.

Erich, Rafael. *Über Allianzen und Allianzverhältnisse nach heutigem Völkerrecht.* Hensingfors: Buchdruckerei-Aktingesellschaft Sana, 1907.

Les États neutres européens et la Seconde Guerre mondiale: Colloque international organisé par les Instituts d'histoire des Universités de Neuchâtel et de Berne, sous les auspices du Comité international et de la Commission suisse d'histoire de la Seconde Guerre mondiale, Neuchâtel-Berne, 5–9 septembre 1983. Neuchâtel: Éditions de la Baconniere, 1985.

Eustathiadès, Constantin Th. "La première application en Europe de la reconnaissance de belligérance pendant la guerre d'indépendence de la Grèce". Dans *Recueil d'études de droit international en homage à Paul Guggenheim,* 22–43, Genève, 1968.

Eysinga, W. J. M. van. "Die Niederlande und das Neutralitätsrecht während des Weltkrieges". *Zeitschrift für Völkerrecht* 16 (1931): 603–632.

Fabela, Isidro. *Neutralité.* Paris: Édition A. Pedone, 1949.

Falconbridge, John Delatre. "The Right of a Belligerent to Make War upon a Neutral". *Transactions of the Grotius Society* 4 (1918): 204–212.

200 Bibliography

Feldbæk, Ole. "Eighteenth-Century Danish Neutrality: Its Diplomacy, Economics and Law". *Scandinavian Journal of History* 8 (1983): 3–21.

Fenwick, Charles G. "Neutrality and International Organization". *AJIL* 28 (1934): 334–339.

Fenwick, Charles G. "Neutrality and Responsibility". *AJIL* 29 (1935): 663–665.

Fenwick, Charles G. "The Revision of Neutrality Legislation in Time of Foreign War". *AJIL* 33 (1939): 728–730.

Fenwick, Charles G. *American Neutrality: Trial and Failure.* New York: New York University Press, 1940.

Fenwick, Charles G. "Neutrality on the Defensive". *AJIL* 34 (1940): 697–699.

Fenwick, Charles G. "Is Neutrality Still a Term of International Law?" *AJIL* 63 (1963): 100–102.

Fiore, Pasquale. *Nouveau droit international public suivant les besoins de la civilisation moderne.* Traduite de l'Italien et annotée par Charles Antoine. 3 tomes. 2e éd. Paris: Durand, 1885–86.

Frankenbach, Carl Otto Heinrich. *Die Rechtsstellung von neutralen Staatsangehörigen in kriegführenden Staaten.* Marburg a. L.: Verlag von Adolf Ebel, 1910.

Freytagh-Loringhoven, Axel Fraiherr von. "Nichtkriegführungen und wohlwollende Neutralität". *Zeitschrift der Akademie für deutsches Recht* 7 (1940): 332–333.

Friede, Wilhelm. "Das amerikanische Neutralitätsgesetz von 1937". *ZaöRV* 7 (1937): 769–792.

Funck-Brentano, Th., et Albert Sorel. *Précis du droit des gens.* 2e éd. Paris: Librairie Plon, 1887.

Fujita, Hisakazu. "1856 Paris Declaration respecting Maritime Law". In *The Law of Naval Warfare: A Collection of Agreements and Documents with Commentaries,* edited by N. Ronzitti, 61–75. Leiden: Martinus Nijhoff, 1988.

Gaborit, René. *Questions de neutralité maritime soulevées par la guerre russo-japonaise: L'inviolabilité des eaux neutres, l'asile, le charbonnage en neutres.* Paris: A. Pedone, 1906.

Gabriel, Jürg Martin. *The American Conception of Neutrality after 1941.* Basingstoke: Macmillan Press, 1988.

Gabriel, Jürg Martin. "Die Gegenläufigkeit von Neutralität und humanitären Interventionen". *Schweizerische Zeitschrift für internationales und europäisches Recht* 10 (2000): 219–236.

Galiani, Ferdinando. *De' doveri de' principi neutrali verso i principi guerreggianti, e di questi verso i neutrali, libri due.* Milano: s.n., 1782.

Galina, A. "Das Problem der Neutralität im gegenwärtigen Völkerrecht". In *Gegenwartsprobleme des Völkerrechts,* 154–182. Berlin: VEB Deutscher Zentralverlag, 1962.

Gama, Domicio da. "The Neutrality Rules Adopted by Brazil". *Annals of the American Academy of Political and Social Science* 60 (1915): 147–154.

García-Mora, Manuel R. *International Responsibility for Hostile Acts of Private Persons against Foreign States.* The Hague: Martinus Nijhoff, 1962.

Gardiner, D. A. "The History of Belligerent Rights on the High Seas in the Fourteenth Century". *Law Quarterly Review* 48 (1932): 521–546.

Gareis, Karl. *Institutionen des Völkerrechts.* Giessen: Verlag von Emil Roth, 1888.

Garner, James Wilford. *International Law and the World War.* 2 vols. London: Longmans, Green and Co., 1920.

Garner, James Wilford. "The Pan American Convention on Maritime Neutrality". *AJIL* 26 (1932): 574–579.

Garner, James Wilford. "The United States Neutrality Act of 1937". *AJIL* 31 (1937): 385–397.

Garner, James Wilford. "The United States 'Neutrality' Law of 1937". *BYIL* 19 (1938): 44–66.

Geffcken. "Die Neutralität". In *Handbuch des Völkerrechts: Auf Grundlage europäischer Staatspraxis*, herausgegeben von Franz von Holtzendorff, 4:605–789. Hamburg: J. F. Richter, 1889.

Gentili, Alberico. *Hispanicae advocationis libri dvo*. The Classics of International Law, edited by James Brown Scott. Vol. 1, A Photographic Reproduction of the Edition of 1661, with an Introduction by Frank Frost Abbott, and a List of Errata. Vol. 2, A Translation of the Text, by Frank Frost Abbott, with an Index of Authors Prepared by Arthur Williams. New York: Oxford University Press, 1921.

Gentili, Alberico. *De jure belli libri tres*. The Classics of International Law, edited by James Brown Scott. Vol. 1, A Photographic Reproduction of the Edition of 1612, a List of Errata, and a Photograph of a Monument to Gentili. Vol. 2, A Translation of the Text, by John C. Rolfe, with an Introduction by Coleman Phillipson, and Indexes. Oxford: Clarendon Press, 1933.

Gervais, André. "La pratique de la neutralité dans la Seconde Guerre mondiale". *Die Friedens-Warte* 48 (1948): 4–17.

Giebler, Richard. *Die rechtliche Stellung der Angehörigen neutraler Staaten im Landgebiete der Kriegführenden*. Königshütte O.-S.: Buchdruckerei R. Giebler, 1911.

Ginsburgs, Goerge. "The Soviet Union, the Neutrals and International Law in World War II". *International and Comparative Law Quarterly* 11 (1962): 171–230.

Gioia, Andrea. "Neutrality and Non-Belligerency". In *International Economic Law and Armed Conflict*, edited by Harry H.G. Post, 51–110. Dordrecht: Martinus Nijhoff, 1994.

Gioia, A., and N. Ronzitti. "The Law of Neutrality: Third States' Commercial Rights and Duties". In *The Gulf War of 1980–1988: The Iran-Iraq War in International Legal Perspective*, edited by Ige F. Dekker and Harry H. G. Post, 221–242. Dordrecht: Martinus Nijhoff, 1992.

Goetschel, Laurent. "Neutrality, a Really Dead Concept?" *Cooperation and Conflict* 34 (1999): 113–139.

González, Salvador Rodríguez. "The Neutrality of Honduras and the Question of the Gulf of Fonseca". *AJIL* 10 (1916): 509–542.

Graham, Jr., Malbone Watson. "Neutrality and the World War". *AJIL* 17 (1923): 704–723.

Graham, Jr., Malbone Watson. "The Effect of the League of Nations Covenant on the Theory and Practice of Neutrality". *California Law Review* 15 (1927): 357–377.

Greenberg, Daniel. *Jowitt's Dictionary of English Law*. 2 vols. 3rd ed. London: Sweet & Maxwell, Thomson Reuters, 2015.

Greenwood, Christopher. "The Concept of War in Modern International Law". *International and Comparative Law Quarterly* 36 (1987): 283–306.

Greenwood, Christopher. "The Relationship between *jus ad bellum* and *jus in bello*". *Review of International Studies* 9 (1983): 221–234.

Greenwood, Christopher. "The Applicability of International Humanitarian Law and the Law of Neutrality to the Kosovo Campaign". *Israel Yearbook on Human Rights* 31 (2001): 111–144.

Gregory, Charles Noble. "The Sale of Munitions of War by Neutrals to Belligerents". *Annals of the American Academy of Political and Social Science* 60 (1915): 183–191.

202 *Bibliography*

Gregory, Charles Noble. "Neutrality and the Sale of Arms". *AJIL* 10 (1916): 543–555.

Grewe, Wilhelm G. "Der Status der Nichtkriegführung". *Zeitschrift der Akademie für deutsches Recht* 7 (1940): 206–207.

Grewe, Wilhelm G. "Wirtschaftliche Neutralität". *Zeitschrift der Akademie für deutsches Recht* 7 (1940): 141–144.

Grieve, W. P. "The Present Position of 'Neutral' States". *Transactions of the Grotius Society* 33 (1947): 99–118.

Grewe, Wilhelm G. *Epochen der Völkerrechtsgeschichte.* Baden-Baden: Nomos Verlagsgesellschaft, 1984.

Grob, Fritz. *The Relativity of War and Peace: A Study in Law, History, and Politics.* New Haven: Yale University Press, 1949.

Grotius, Hugo. *De jure belli ac pacis libri tres.* The Classics of International Law, edited by James Brown Scott. Vol. 1, A Photographic Reproduction of the Edition of 1646, with a Portrait of Grotius. Vol. 2, A Translation of the Text, by Francis W. Kelsey, with the Collaboration of Arthur E. R. Boak, Heny A. Sanders, Jesse S. Reeves, and Herbert F. Wright, with an Introduction by James Brown Scott. Oxford: Clarendon Press, 1925.

Guggenheim, Paul. "Der Neutralitätsbegriff im allgemeinen Völkerrecht und in der internationalen Organisation". In *Internationale Festschrift für Alfred Verdross zum 80. Geburtstag,* herausgegeben von René Marcic, Hermann Mosler, Erik Suy, und Karl Zemanek, 119–128. München: Wilhelm Fink Verlag, 1971.

Gundermann, Dietrich. *Die parteiliche Änderung von Neutralitätsgesetzen nach Kriegsausbruch, dargestellt unter bosonderer Berücksichtigung des US Neutrality Act 1939: Ein Beitrag zu Fragen des Neutralitätsrechtes.* Hamburg: Alfred Metzner, 1965.

Guttman, Egon. "The Concept of Neutrality since the Adoption and Ratification of the Hague Neutrality Convention of 1907". *American University International Law Review* 14 (1998): 55–60.

Haase, Joachim. *Wandlung des Neutralitätsbegriffes.* Leipzig: Robert Noske, 1932.

Hackwitz, Gunther v. *Die Neutralität im Luftkriegsrecht.* Stuttgart: Ferdinand Enke, 1927.

Haggenmacher, Peter. *Grotius et la doctrine de la guerre juste.* Paris: Presses Universitaires de France, 1983.

Hägglöf, Gunnar. "A Test of Neutrality: Sweden in the Second World War". *International Affairs* 36 (1960): 153–167.

"The Hague Conventions and the Neutrality of Belgium and Luxemburg". *AJIL* 9 (1915): 959–962.

Hall, William Edward. *The Rights and Duties of Neutrals.* London: Longmans Green, and Co., 1874.

Hall, William Edward. *A Treatise on International Law.* 2nd ed. Oxford: Clarendon Press, 1884.

Halleck, H. W. *Elements of International Law and Laws of War.* Philadelphia, PA: J. B. Lippincott, 1866.

Hambro, Edvard. "Das Neutralitätsrecht der nordischen Staaten". *ZaöRV* 8 (1938): 445–469.

Hamel, A. van. "Can the Netherlands be Neutral?" *Foreign Affairs* 16 (1938): 339–346.

Hammarskjöld, Hj. L. "La neutralité en général: Leçons données à l'Académie de Droit International de La Haye, Août 1923". *Bibliotheca Visseriana Dissertationum Ius Internationale Illustrantium* 3 (1924): 53–141.

Bibliography 203

[Harvard Law School.] "Draft Conventions, with Comment, Prepared by the Research in International Law of the Harvard Law School, II. Rights and Duties of Neutral States in Naval and Aerial War". *AJIL Supplement* 33 (1939): 167–817.

[Harvard Law School.] "Draft Conventions, with Comment, Prepared by the Research in International Law of the Harvard Law School, III. Rights and Duties of States in Case of Aggression". *AJIL Supplement* 33 (1939): 819–909.

Haug, Hans. *Neutralität und Völkergemeinschaft*. Zürich: Polygraphischer Verlag, 1962.

Hautefeuille, L.-B. *Des droits et des devoirs des nations neutres en temps de guerre maritime*. 3 tomes. 3e éd. Paris: Librairie de Guillaumin et Cie, 1868.

Heffter, August Wilhelm. *Das europäische Völkerrecht der Gegenwart*. Berlin: Verlag von E. H. Schroeder, 1844.

Heilborn, Paul. *Rechte und Pflichten der neutralen Staaten: In Bezug auf die während des Krieges auf ihr Gebiet übertretenden Angehörigen einer Armee und das dorthin gebrachte Kriegsmaterial der kriegführenden Parteien*. Berlin: Verlag von Julius Springer, 1888.

Heilborn, Paul. *Das System des Völkerrechts entwickelt aus den völkerrechtlichen Begriffen*. Berlin: Verlag von Julius Springer, 1896.

Heintschel von Heinegg, Wolff. *Seekriegsrecht und Neutralität im Seekrieg*. Berlin: Duncker & Humblot, 1995.

Heintschel von Heinegg, Wolff. "Wider die Mär vom Tode des Neutralitätsrechts". In *Krisensicherung und Humanitärer Schutz: Festschrift für Dieter Fleck*, herausgegeben von Horst Fischer, Ulrike Froissart, Wolff Heintschel von Heinegg, und Chirstian Raap, 221–241. Berlin: Berliner Wissenschafts-Verlag, 2004.

Heintschel von Heinegg, Wolff. " 'Benevolent' Third States in International Armed Conflicts: The Myth of the Irrelevance of the Law of Neutrality". In *International Law and Armed Conflict: Exploring the Faultlines*, edited by Michael N. Schmitt and Jelena Pejic, 543–568. Leiden: M. Nijhoff, 2007.

Heintschel von Heinegg, Wolff. "Neutrality in Cyberspace". In *4th International Conference on Cyber Conflict*, edited by C. Czosseck, R. Ottis, K. Ziolkowski, 35–46. NATO CCD COE Publications, 2012.

Heintschel von Heinegg, Wolff. "The Law of Armed Conflict at Sea". In *The Handbook of International Humanitarian Law*, 3rd ed., edited by Dieter Fleck, 463–547. Oxford: Oxford University Press, 2013.

Heintschel von Heinegg, Wolff. "Territorial Sovereignty and Neutrality in Cyberspace". *International Law Studies* 89 (2013): 123–156.

Helfman, Tara. "Neutrality, the Law of Nations, and the Natural Law Tradition: A Study of the Seven Years' War". *Yale Journal of International Law* 30 (2005): 549–586.

Henkin, Louis. "Force, Intervention, and Neutrality in Contemporary International Law". *Proceedings of the American Society of International Law* 57 (1963): 147–173.

Hernández-Sandoica, Elena, and Enrique Moradiellos. "Spain and the Second World War, 1939-1945". In *European Neutrals and Non-Belligerents during the Second World War*, edited by Neville Wylie, 241–267. Cambridge: Cambridge University Press, 2002.

Hershey, Amos S. *The International Law and Diplomacy of the Russo-Japanese War*. New York: The Macmillan, 1906.

Hershey, Amos S. *The Essentials of International Public Law*. New York: The Macmillan Company, 1912.

Hershey, Amos S. "Neutrality and International Law". *International Journal of Ethics* 26 (1916): 168–176.

Hershey, Amos S. "Some Popular Misconceptions of Neutrality". *AJIL* 10 (1916): 118–121.

204 Bibliography

Higgins, Humphrey. "The Netherlands: Political Antecedents to the German Offensive". In *Survey of International Affairs 1939–1946: The Initial Triumph of the Axis*, edited by Arnold Toynbee and Veronica M. Toynbee, 122–143. London: Oxford University Press, 1958.

Higgins, Pearce A. *The Hague Peace Conferences and Other International Conferences concerning the Laws and Usages of War: Texts of Conventions with Commentaries*. Cambridge: Cambridge University Press, 1909.

Hohfeld, Wesley Newcomb. *Fundamental Legal Conceptions: As Applied in Judicial Reasoning and Other Legal Essays*. Edited by Walter Wheeler Cook. New Haven: Yale University Press, 1923.

Höjer, Torvald. "Der Genesis der schwedischen Neutralität". *Historische Zeitschrift* 186 (1958): 65–79.

Holbraad, Carsten. *Danish Neutrality: A Study in the Foreign Policy of a Small State*. Oxford: Clarendon Press, 1991.

Holland, Thomas Erskine. *Lectures on International Law*. Edited by Thomas Alfred Walker and Wyndham Legh Walker. London: Sweet & Maxwell, 1933.

Hopper, Bruce. "Sweden: A Case Study in Neutrality". *Foreign Affairs* 23 (1945): 435–449.

Horn, Martin. *Die geschichtliche Entwicklung des neuzeitlichen Neutralitätsbegriffes*. Würzburg: Wissenschaftlicher Werke Konrad Triltsch, 1936.

Hostettller, Peter. "Neutrals, Disarming and Internment of Belligerents". In *The Max Planck Encyclopedia of Public International Law*, edited by Rüdiger Wolfrum, 652–653. Oxford: Oxford University Press, 2012.

Hostettller, Peter, and Olivia Danai. "Neutrality in Air Warfare". In *The Max Planck Encyclopedia of Public International Law*, edited by Rüdiger Wolfrum, 634–638. Oxford: Oxford University Press, 2012.

Hostettller, Peter, and Olivia Danai. "Neutrality in Land Warfare". In *The Max Planck Encyclopedia of Public International Law*, edited by Rüdiger Wolfrum, 638–643. Oxford: Oxford University Press, 2012.

Hübner, M. *De la saisie des batimens neutres ou du droit qu'ont les nations belligérantes d'arrêter les navires des pleuples amis*. 2 tomes. La Haye, 1759.

Huber, Max. "Die Fortbildung des Völkerrechts auf dem Gebiete des Prozess- und Landkriegsrechts durch die II. Internationale Friedenskonferenz im Haag 1907". *Jahrbuch des öffentliches Rechts der Gegenwart* 2 (1908): 470–649.

Huber, Max. "Die schweizerische Neutralität und der Völkerbund". Dans *Les origines et l'œvre de la Société des Nations*, édité par P. Munch, 1:68–136. Copenhague: Gyldendalske Boghandel, 1923.

Huber, Max. "Neutralitätsrecht und Neutralitätspolitik". *Schweizerisches Jahrbuch für internationales Recht* 5 (1948): 9–28.

Hufenbecher, Paul. *Die Rechte und Pflichten der neutralen Mächte und Personen im Falle eines Landkriegs: Nach dem V. Abkommen der Zweiten Haager Friedenskonferenz*. Elberfeld: Wuppertaler Akt. Druckerei, 1912.

Hyde, Charles Cheney. "The Hague Convention respecting the Rights and Duties of Neutral Powers in Naval War". *AJIL* 2 (1908): 507–527.

Hyde, Charles Cheney. "International Co-operation for Neutrality". *University of Pennsylvania Law Review* 85 (1936–37): 344–357.

Hyde, Charles Cheney. "Belgium and Neutrality". *AJIL* 31 (1937): 81–85.

Hyde, Charles Cheney. *International Law: Chiefly as Interpreted and Applied by the United States*. 3 vols. 2nd revised ed. Boston: Little, Brown and Company, 1947.

Hyneman, Charles S. "Neutrality during the European Wars of 1792–1815: America's Understanding of Her Obligations". *AJIL* 24 (1930): 279–309.

Hyneman, Charles S. *The First American Neutrality: A Study of the American Understanding of Neutral Obligations during the Years 1792 to 1815*. Urbana, IL: University of Illinois, 1934. Reprint, Philadelphia: Porcupine Press, 1974.

Institut de Droit International. *Annuaire de l'Institut de Droit International* 1 (1877).

International Institute of Humanitarian Law. *San Remo Manual on International Law Applicable to Armed Conflicts at Sea: Prepared by International Lawyers and Naval Experts Convened by the HIIHL*. Cambridge: Cambridge University Press, 1995.

International Law Association. *Report of the Thirty-Eighth Conference Held at Budapest in the Hungarian Academy of Science, 6 to 10 September 1934*. London: The Eastern Press, 1935.

International Law Association. *Report of the Sixty-Seventh Conference Held at Helsinki, Finland, 12 to 17 August 1996*. London, 1996.

Ipsen, Knut. *Völkerrecht*. 6. Aufl. München: C. H. Beck, 2014.

Jennings, R. Y. "The Caroline and McLeod Case". *AJIL* 32 (1938): 82–99.

Jessup, Philip C. "The Birth, Death and Reincarnation of Neutrality". *AJIL* 26 (1932): 789–793.

Jessup, Philip C. "Is Neutrality Essential?" *Proceedings of the American Society of International Law* 27 (1933): 134–142.

Jessup, Philip C. "The New Neutrality Legislation". *AJIL* 29 (1935): 665–670.

Jessup, Philip C. "Toward Further Neutrality Legislation". *AJIL* 30 (1936): 262–265.

Jessup, Philip C. "Neutrality Legislation – 1937". *AJIL* 31 (1937): 306–313.

Jessup, Philip C. "The Reconsideration of 'Neutrality' Legislation in 1939". *AJIL* 33 (1939): 549–557.

Jessup, Philip C. "The 'Neutrality Act of 1939'". *AJIL* 34 (1940): 95–99.

Jessup, Philip C. "Should International Law Recognize an Intermediate Status between Peace and War?" *AJIL* 48 (1954): 98–103.

Jessup, Philip C. *Neutrality, Its History, Economics and Law*. Vol. 4, *Today and Tomorrow*. New York: Columbia University Press, 1936. Reprint, New York: Octagon Books, 1976.

Jessup, Philip C., and Francis Deák. "The Early Development of the Law of Neutral Rights". *Political Science Quarterly* 46 (1931): 481–508.

Jessup, Philip C., and Francis Deák. "The Early Development of the Law of Contraband of War I, II, III". *Political Science Quarterly* 47 (1932): 526–546; 48 (1933): 62–93, 334–358.

Jessup, Philip C., and Francis Deák. *Neutrality, Its History, Economics and Law*. Vol. 1, *The Origins*. New York: Columbia University Press, 1935. Reprint, New York: Octagon Books, 1976.

Johnson, James Turner. *Ideology, Reason, and the Limitation of War: Religious and Secular Concepts, 1200–1740*. Princeton, NJ: Princeton University Press, 1975.

Karsh, Efraim. *Neutrality and Small States*. London: Routledge, 1988.

Kasai, Naoya. "The Laws of War". In *A Normative Approach to War: Peace, War, and Justice in Hugo Grotius*, edited by Yasuaki Onuma, 244–275. Oxford: Clarendon Press, 1993.

Kastenberg, Joshua E. "Non-Intervention and Neutrality in Cyberspace: An Emerging Principle in the National Practice of International Law". *Air Force Law Review* 64 (2009): 43–64.

Kelsen, Hans. *Principles of International Law*. New York: Rinehart & Company, 1952.

206 *Bibliography*

Kelsey, Jeffrey T. G. "Hacking into International Humanitarian Law: The Principles of Distinction and Neutrality in the Age of Cyber Warfare". *Michigan Law Review* 106 (2008): 1427–1451.

Kent, James. *Commentaries on American Law*. 4 vols. New York: O. Halsted, 1826.

Keppler, Kurt. "Die neue Neutralität der Schweiz". *Zeitschrift für öffentliches Recht* 18 (1939): 505–545.

Kissinger, Henry. *Diplomacy*. New York: Simon & Schuster, 1994.

Kleen, Richard. *Lois et usages de la neutralité*. 2 tomes. Paris: A. Chevalier-Marescq, 1898.

Klüber, Jean Louis. *Droit des gens moderne de l'Europe*. Stuttgart: Librairie de J. G. Cotta, 1819.

Knight, S. M. "Neutrality and Neutralization in the Sixteenth Century: Liège". *Journal of Comparative Legislation and International Law*, 3rd series, 2 (1920): 98–104.

Kohler, Joseph. "Notwehr und Neutralität". *Zeitschrift für Völkerrecht* 8 (1914): 576–580.

Koht, Halvdan. "Neutrality and Peace: The View of a Small Power". *Foreign Affairs* 15 (1937): 280–289.

Kolb, Robert. "Origin of the Twin Terms *jus ad bellum/jus in bello*". *International Review of the Red Cross*, no. 320 (1997): 553–562.

Komarnicki, Titus. "The Place of Neutrality in the Modern System of International Law". *RCADI* 80 (1952): 395–510.

Komarnicki, Titus. "The Problem of Neutrality under the United Nations Charter". *Transactions of the Grotius Society* 38 (1953): 77–91.

Köpfer, Josef. *Die Neutralität im Wandel der Erscheinungsformen militärischer Auseinandersetzungen*. München: Bernard & Graefe Verlag für Wehrsesen München, 1975.

Kotzsch, Lothar. *The Concept of War in Contemporary History and International Law*. Genève: Librairie E. Droz, 1956.

Kulsrud, Carl J. *Maritime Neutrality to 1780: A History of the Main Principles Governing Neutrality and Belligerency to 1780*. Boston: Little, Brown, and Co., 1936. Reprint, Union, N. J.: Lawbook Exchange, 2000.

Kunz, Josef L. "Plus de lois de la guerre?" *RGDIP* 41 (1934): 22–57.

Kunz, Josef L. "The Covenant of the League of Nations and Neutrality". *Proceedings of the American Society of International Law* 29 (1935): 36–45.

Kunz, Josef L. *Kriegsrecht und Neutralitätsrecht*. Wien: Verlag von Julius Springer, 1935.

Kunz, Josef L. "Le problème de la neutralité aux États-Unis 1920–1939". *RGDIP* 47 (1940): 66–156.

Kunz, Josef L. "Neutrality and the European War 1939–1940". *Michigan Law Review* 39 (1941): 719–754.

Kussbach, Erich. "L'évolution de la notion de neutralité dans les conflits armés actuels". *Revue de Droit Pénal Militaire et de Droit de la Guerre* 17 (1978): 19–36.

Kussbach, Erich. "Protocol I and Neutral States". *International Review of the Red Cross*, no. 218 (1980): 231–249.

La Pradelle, Paul de. "L'évolution de la neutralité". *Reuve de Droit International* 14 (1934): 197–221.

La Pradelle, Paul de. "La Belgique retourne à la neutralité". *Revue de Droit International* 18 (1936): 538–546.

La Pradelle, Paul de. "The Evolution of Neutrality". In *Collective Security: A Record of the Seventh and Eighth International Studies Conferences*, edited by Maurice Bourquin, 404–412. Paris: International Institute of Intellectual Co-operation, 1936.

Bibliography 207

Lalive, Jean-Flavien. "Quelques nouvelles tendances de la neutralité". *Die Friedens-Warte* 40 (1940): 46–58.

Lammasch, Heinrich. "Unjustifiable War and the Means to Avoid It". *AJIL* 10 (1916): 689–705.

Lauterpacht, H. "The Pact of Paris and the Budapest Articles of Interpretation". *Transactions of the Grotius Society* 20 (1935): 178–202.

Lauterpacht, H. "Neutrality and Collective Security". *Politica* 2 (1936): 133–155.

Lauterpacht, H. "Neutrality and the Covenant of the League". In *Collective Security: A Record of the Seventh and Eighth International Studies Conferences*, edited by Maurice Bourquin, 412–418. Paris: International Institute of Intellectual Co-operation, 1936.

Lauterpacht, H. *Recognition in International Law*. Cambridge: Cambridge University Press, 1948.

Lauterpacht, H. "The Limits of the Operation of the Law of War". *BYIL* 30 (1953): 206–243.

Lawrence, T. J. *The Principles of International Law*. London: Macmillan and Co., 1895.

Lawrence, T. J. *War and Neutrality in the Far East*. London: Macmillan and Co., 1904.

Leistikow, Gunnar. "Denmark's Precarious Neutrality". *Foreign Affairs* 17 (1939): 611–617.

Leite, Joaquim da Costa. "Neutrality by Agreement: Portugal and the British Alliance in World War II". *American University International Law Review* 14 (1998): 185–199.

Leonhard, Alan T., ed. *Neutrality: Changing Concepts and Practices*. Lanham, MD: University Press of America, 1998.

Leontiades, Leonidas. "Die Neutralität Griechenlands während des Weltkrieges". *ZaöRV* 2 (1931): 120–170.

Lévy, Roger. "French Neutrality during the Sino-Japanese Hostilities". *Pacific Affairs* 11 (1938): 433–446.

Lieblich, Eliav. *International Law and Civil Wars: Intervention and Consent*. London: Routledge, 2013.

Lifschütz, Alex. "Die Neutralität". *Niemeyers Zeitschrift für internationales Recht* 27 (1918): 40–124.

Liszt, Franz v. *Das Völkerrecht systematisch dargestellt*. Berlin: Verlag von O. Haering, 1898.

Lorimer, James. *The Institutes of the Law of Nations: A Treatise of the Jural Relations of Separate Political Communities*. 2 vols. Edinburgh: Blackwood, 1883–84.

MacChesney, Brunson. "The Altmark Incident and Modern Warfare: 'Innocent Passage' in Wartime and the Right of Belligerent to Use Force to Redress Neutrality Violations". *Northwestern University Law Review* 52 (1957): 320–343.

Machiavelli, Niccol. *Il principe*. Introduzione e note di Federico Chabod: a cura di Luigi Firpo. 11a ed. Torino: Giulio Einaudi, 1979.

Madariaga, Isabel de. *Britain, Russia, and the Armed Neutrality of 1780: Sir James Harris's Mission to St. Petersburg during the American Revolution*. London: Hollis & Carter, 1962.

Maffert, S. *L'évolution de la neutralité de 1914 à la guerre de 1939*. Paris: Édition A. Pedone, 1943.

Manning, W. M. Oke. *Commentaries on the Law of Nations*. London: S. Sweet, 1839.

Marquina, Antonio. "The Spanish Neutrality during the Second World War". *American University International Law Review* 14 (1998): 171–184.

Martens, George Fréderic de. *Précis du droit des gens moderne de l'Europe*. Nouvelle edition. Éditée par Ch. Vergé. Paris: Guillaumin, 1858.

208 Bibliography

Martens, George Fréderic de. *Précis du droit des gens moderne de l'Europe fondé sur les traité et l'usage.* 2e éd. Gottingue: Librairie de Dieterich, 1801.

Martens, George Fréderic de. *Summary of the Law of Nations, Founded on the Treaties and Customs of the Modern Nations of Europe.* Translated by William Cobbett. Originally published in Latin as: *Primae lineae juris gentium Europaearum practici.* Philadelphia: T. Bradford, 1795. Reprint, Littleton, Colo.: F. B. Rothman, 1986.

Mathieu, Beltran. "The Neutrality of Chile during the European War". *AJIL* 14 (1920): 319–342.

McNair, Arnold D. "Collective Security". *BYIL* 17 (1936): 150–164.

McNair, Lord, selected and annoted. *International Law Opinions.* 3 vols. Cambridge: Cambridge University Press, 1956.

McNair, Lord, and A. D. Watts. *Legal Effects of War.* 4th ed. Cambridge: Cambridge University Press, 1966.

McNeil, John H. "Neutral Rights and Maritime Sanctions: The Effects of Two Gulf Wars". *Virginia Journal of International Law* 31 (1991): 631–643.

Mehr, Farhang. "Neutrality in the Gulf War". *Ocean Development and International Law* 20 (1989): 105–106.

Meyer, Alex. *Das Neutralitätsrecht im Luftkriege: Eine kritische Studie auf Grund der von der Haager Juristenkommission (11. Dez. 1922/19. Feb. 1923) aufgestellten Entwürfe.* Berlin: Carl Heymanns Verlag, 1931.

Meyrowitz, Henri. *Le principe de l'égalité des belligérants devant le droit de la guerre.* Paris: A. Pedone, 1970.

Michel, Nicolas. "Le statut juridique de la neutralité suisse à l'épreuve du conflit du Kosovo". *Schweizerische Zeitschrift für internationales und europäisches Recht* 10 (2000): 197–218.

Miele, Alberto. *L'estraneità ai conflitti armati: Secondo il diritto internazionale.* 2 volumi. Padova: CEDAM, 1970.

Minear, Larry. "The Theory and Practice of Neutrality: Some Thoughts on the Tensions". *Revue Internationale de la Croix-Rouge* 81, no 833 (1999): 63–71.

Morgenthau, Hans J. "The End of Switzerland's 'Differential' Neutrality". *AJIL* 32 (1938): 558–562.

Morgenthau, Hans J. "The Resurrection of Neutrality in Europe". *American Political Science Review* 33 (1939): 473–486.

Morgenthau, Hans J. "The Problem of Neutrality". *University of Kansas City Law Review* 7 (1940): 109–128.

Morgenthau, Hans J. "Neutrality and Neutralism". In Hans J. Morgenthau, *Dilemmas of Politics,* 185–209. Chicago: University of Chicago Press, 1958.

Morris, Roland S. "The Pact of Paris for the Renunciation of War: Its Meanings and Effect in International Law". *Proceedings of the American Society of International Law* 23 (1929): 88–109.

Morrissey, Alice M. "The United States and the Rights of Neutrals, 1917–1918". *AJIL* 31 (1937): 17–30.

Neff, Stephen C. *The Rights and Duties of Neutrals: A General History.* Manchester: Manchester University Press, 2000.

Neff, Stephen C. *War and the Law of Nations: A General History.* Cambridge: Cambridge University Press, 2005.

Norton, Patrick M. "Between the Ideology and the Reality: The Shadow of the Law of Neutrality". *Harvard International Law Journal* 17 (1976): 249–311.

Nussbaum, Arthur. "Just War: A Legal Concept?" *Michigan Law Review* 42 (1943): 453–479.

Nys, Ernest. "Notes sur la neutralité". *RDILC*, 2c sér., 2 (1900): 461–498, 583–617; 3 (1901): 15–49.

Nys, Ernest. "Traités de subside et troupes auxiliaires dans l'ancien droit: Politique des subsides; Emprunts émis au profit d'états belligérants sur les marchés neutres". *RDILC*, 2e sér., 15 (1913): 173–196.

Ochsner, Richard. *Der Transit von Personen und Gütern durch ein neutrales Land im Falle des Landkrieges.* Polygraphischer Verlag A.G. Zürich, 1948.

Oeter, Stefan. "Ursprünge der Neutralität: Die Herausbildung des Instituts der Neutralität im Völkerrecht der frühen Neuzeit". *ZaöRV* 48 (1988): 447–488.

Oeter, Stefan. *Neutralität und Waffenhandel.* Berlin: Springer, 1992.

Ogley, Roderick. *The Theory and Practice of Neutrality in the Twentieth Century.* London: Routledge & K. Paul, 1970.

Onuma, Yasuaki. "War". In *A Normative Approach to War: Peace, War, and Justice in Hugo Grotius,* edited by Yasuaki Onuma, 57–121. Oxford: Clarendon Press, 1993.

Oppenheim, L. *International Law: A Treatise.* 2 vols. London: Longmans, Green, and Co., 1905–06.

Oppenheim, L. *International Law: A Treatise.* 2 vols. 2nd ed. London: Longmans, Green and Co., 1912.

Oppenheim, L. *International Law: A Treatise.* Edited by Ronald F. Roxburgh. 2 vols. 3rd ed. London: Longmans, Green and Co., 1920–21.

Oppenheim, L. *International Law: A Treatise.* Edited by Arnold D. McNair. 2 vols. 4th ed. London: Longmans, Green and Co., 1926, 1928.

Oppenheim, L. *International Law: A Treatise.* Edited by H. Lauterpacht. 2 vols. 5th ed. London: Longmans, Green and Co., 1935, 1937.

Oppenheim, L. *International Law: A Treatise.* Edited by H. Lauterpacht. 2 vols. 6th ed. London: Longmans, Green and Co., 1940, 1944.

Oppenheim, L. *International Law: A Treatise.* Edited by H. Lauterpacht. 2 vols. 7th ed. London: Longmans, Green and Co., 1948, 1952.

Ortolan, M. Théodore. *Règles internationales et diplomatie de la mer.* 2 tomes. 4e éd. Paris: H. Plon, 1864.

Ørvik, Nils. *The Decline of Neutrality 1914–1941: With Special Reference to the United States and the Northern Neutrals.* 2nd ed. Plymouth: Frank Cass & Co., 1971.

Ottolenghi, Giuseppe. *Il rapporto di neutralità.* Torino: Unione Tipografico-Editrice Torinese, 1907.

Packard, Jerrold M. *Neither Friend nor Foe: The European Neutrals in World War II.* New York: Fire World Publishing, 1992.

Padelford, Norman J. "The New Scandinavian Neutrality Rules". *AJIL* 32 (1938): 789–793.

Padelford, Norman J. "Neutrality, Belligerency, and the Panama Canal". *AJIL* 35 (1941): 55–89.

Pares, Richard. *Colonial Blockade and Neutral Rights 1739–1763.* Oxford: Clarendon Press, 1938. Reprint, Philadelphia: Porcupine Press, 1975.

Pelloux, Robert. "L'embargo sur les exportations d'armes et l'évolution de l'idée de neutralité". *RGDIP* 41 (1934): 58–75.

Petrochilos, Georgios C. "The Relevance of the Concepts of War and Armed Conflict to the Law of Neutrality". *Vanderbilt Journal of Transnational Law* 31 (1998): 575–615.

210   Bibliography

Phillimore, George Grenville. "The Future Law of Neutrality". *Transactions of the Grotius Society* 4 (1918): 43–70.

Phillimore, Robert. *Commentaries upon International Law.* 4 vols. London: William G. Benning and Co., Law Booksellers, 1854–61.

Phillips, W. Alison, and Arthur H. Reede. *Neutrality, Its History, Economics and Law.* Vol. 2, *The Napoleonic Period.* New York: Columbia University Press, 1936. Reprint, New York: Octagon Books, 1976.

Piédelièvre, R. *Précis de droit international public ou droit des gens.* 2 tomes. Paris: Cotillon, F. Pichon, Successeur, 1895.

Pieper, Ulrike. *Neutralität von Staaten.* Frankfurt am Main: Peter Lang, 1997.

Politakis, George P. "Variations on a Myth: Neutrality and the Arms Trade". *German Yearbook of International Law* 35 (1992): 435–506.

Politakis, George P. "From Action Stations to Action: U.S. Naval Deployment, 'Non-Belligerency', and 'Defensive Reprisals' in the Final Year of the Iran-Iraq War". *Ocean Development and International Law* 25 (1994): 31–60.

Politakis, George P. *Modern Aspects of the Laws of Naval Warfare and Maritime Neutrality.* London: Kegan Paul International, 1998.

Politis, Nicolas. "La notion de la neutralité et la Société des Nations". *Scientia* 44 (1928): 259–268.

Politis, Nicolas. *Neutralité et la paix.* Paris: Librairie Hachette, 1935.

Pradier-Fodéré, P. *Traité de droit international public européen et américain: Suivant les progrès de la science et de la pratique contemporaines.* 8 tomes. Paris: A. Pedone, Editeur, 1885–1906.

Preuss, Lawrence. "The Concepts of Neutrality and Non-Belligerency". *Annals of the American Academy of Political and Social Science* 218 (1941): 97–109.

Pyke, H. Reason. *The Law of Contraband of War.* Oxford: Clarendon Press, 1915.

Raymond, Gregory A. "Neutrality Norms and the Balance of Power". *Cooperation and Conflict* 32 (1997): 123–146.

Rehm, Hermann. "Die völkerrechtliche Stellung des Verbündeten". *Niemeyers Zeitschrift für internationales Recht* 26 (1916): 118–152.

Reid, Gilbert. "The Neutrality of China". *Yale Law Journal* 25 (1915): 122–128.

Rivier, Alphons. *Principes du droit des gens.* 2 tomes. Paris: Librairie nouvelle de droit et de jurisprudence Arthur Rousseau, 1896.

Roach, J. Ashley. "Neutrality in Naval Warfare". In *The Max Planck Encyclopedia of Public International Law*, edited by Rüdiger Wolfrum, 643–648. Oxford: Oxford University Press, 2012.

Rolin-Jaequemyns, M. G. "Les trois règles de Washington". *RDILC* 6 (1874): 561–569.

Ronzitti, Natalino. "The Crisis of the Traditional Law Regulating International Armed Conflicts at Sea and the Need for its Revision". In *The Law of Naval Warfare: A Commentary on the Relevant Agreements and Documents*, edited by N. Ronzitti, 26–32. Dordrecht: Martinus Nijhoff, 1988.

Ronzitti, Natalino. "Le droit humanitaire applicable aux conflits armés en mer". *RCADI* 121 (1993): 9–196.

Ronzitti, Natalino. *Diritto internazionale dei conflitti armati.* 2a. ed. Torino: G. Giappichelli Editore, 2001.

Ronzitti, Natalino. "Italy's Non-belligerency during the Iraqi War". In *International Responsibility Today: Essays in Memory of Oscar Schacter*, edited by Maurizio Ragazzi, 197–207. Leiden: Martinus Nijhoff, 2005.

Bibliography 211

Roth, Brad R. *Governmental Illegitimacy in International Law.* Oxford: Oxford University Press, 1999.

Rougier, Antoine. *Les guerres civiles et le droit des gens.* Paris: L. Larose, 1903.

Rousseau, Charles. *Le droit des conflits armés.* Paris: Éditions A. Pedone, 1983.

Roxburgh, R. F. "Changes in the Conception of Neutrality". *Journal of Comparative Legislation and International Law*, 3rd ser., 1 (1919): 17–24.

Royen, W. P. J. A. van. *Analyse du problème de la neutralité au cours de l'évolution du droit des gens.* La Haye: Martinus Nijhoff, 1938.

Russell, Frederick H. *The Just War in the Middle Ages.* Cambridge: Cambridge University Press, 1975.

Russo, Jr., Francis V. "Neutrality at Sea in Transition: State Practice in the Gulf War as Emerging International Customary Law". *Ocean Development and International Law* 19 (1988): 381–399.

Sadiford, Roberto. "Das italienische Krieg- und Neutralitätsgesetz". *ZaöRV* 9 (1939): 605–619.

Sanborn, Frederic Rochwell. *Origins of the Early English Maritime and Commercial Law.* New York: The Century Co., 1930.

Sauser-Hall, Georges. *Des belligérants internés chez les neutres en cas de guerre terrestre.* Genève: Georg & Cie, Libraires-Éditeurs, 1910.

Schätzel, Walter. "Neutralität". *Die Friedens-Warte* 53 (1955): 28–36.

Schaub, Adrian R. *Neutralität und Kollektive Sicherheit: Gegenüberstellung zweier unvereinbarer Verhaltenskonzepte in bewaffneten Konflikten und Thesen zu einem zeit- und völkerrechtsgemässen modus vivendi.* Basel: Helbing & Lichtenhahn, 1995.

Schaub, Adrian R. "Aktuelle Aspekte der Neutralität". *Schweizerische Zeitschrift für internationales und europäisches Recht* 6 (1996): 353–371.

Scheuner, Ulrich. *Die Neutralität im heutigen Völkerrecht.* Köln: Westdeutscher Verlag, 1969.

Schindler, Dietrich. "La neutralité suisse de 1920 à 1938". *RDILC*, 3e sér., 19 (1938): 433–472.

Schindler, Dietrich. "Die schweizerische Neutralität 1920–1938". *ZaöRV* 8 (1938): 413–444.

Schindler, Dietrich. "Aspects contemporains de la neutralité". *RCADI* 121 (1967): 221–321.

Schindler, Dietrich. "Der 'Kriegszustand' im Völkerrecht der Gegenwart". In *Um Recht und Freiheit: Festschrift für Friedrich Auust Freiherr von der Heydte zur Vollendung des 70. Lebensjahres*, herausgegeben von Heinrich Kipp, Franz Mayer, und Armin Steinkamm, 555–576. Berlin: Duncker & Humblot, 1977.

Schindler, Dietrich. "L'emploi de la force par un État belligérant sur le territoire d'un État non belligérant". In *Estudios de derecho internacional: Homenaje al profesor Miaja de la Muela*, 2:847–864. Madrid: Editorial Tecnos, 1979.

Schindler, Dietrich. "State of War, Belligerency, Armed Conflict". In *The New Humanitarian Law of Armed Conflict*, edited by Antonio Cassese, 3–20. Napoli: Editoriale scientifica, 1979.

Schindler, Dietrich. "Probleme des humanitären Völkerrechts und der Neutralität im Golfkonflikt 1990/91". *Schweizerische Zeitschrift für internationales und europäisches Recht* 1 (1991): 3–23.

Schindler, Dietrich. "Kollektive Sicherheit der Vereinten Nationen und dauernde Neutralität der Schweiz". *Schweizerische Zeitschrift für internationales und europäisches Recht* 2 (1992): 435–479.

212 Bibliography

Schindler, Dietrich. "Transformations in the Law of Neutrality since 1945". In *Humanitarian Law of Armed Conflict Challenges Ahead: Essays in Honour of Frits Kalshoven*, edited by Astrid J. M. Delissen and Gerard J. Tanja, 367–386. Dordrecht: Martinus Nijhoff, 1992.

Schindler, Dietrich. "Neutrality and Morality: Developments in Switzerland and in the International Community". *American University International Law Review* 14 (1998): 155–170.

Schlüter, Ferdinand. "Kelloggpakt und Neutralitätsrecht". *ZaöRV* 11 (1942–43): 24–32.

Schmalz, Geheimen Rath. *Das europäische Völkerrecht*. Berlin: Duncker und Humblot, 1817.

Schmitt, Carl. *Die Wendung zum diskriminierenden Kriegsbegriff*. München: Duncker u. Humbolt, 1938.

Schmitt, Carl. *Der Nomos der Erde im Völkerrecht des Jus Publicum Europaeum*. Köln: Greven Verlag, 1950.

Schmitz, Ernst. "Das Neutralitätsgesetz der Vereinigten Staaten von 1939". *Zeitschrift der Akademie für deutsches Recht* 6 (1939): 667–669.

Scholz, Franz. *Drahtlose Telegraphie unde Neutralität*. Berlin: Verlag von Franz Vahlen, 1905.

Schopfer, Sidney. *Le principe juridique de la neutralité et son évolution dans l'histoire du droit de la guerre*. Lausanne: Librairie F. Rouge, 1894.

Schwarzenberger, Georg. "The 'Aid Britain' Bill and the Law of Neutrality". *Transactions of the Grotius Society* 27 (1941): 1–29.

Scott, James Brown. "Proposed Amendments to the Neutrality Laws of the United States". *AJIL* 10 (1916): 602–609.

Scott, James Brown. "Foreign Enlistment in the United States". *AJIL* 12 (1918): 172–174.

Scott, James Brown. "The Neutrality of the Good Neighbor". *Proceedings of the American Society of International Law* 29 (1935): 1–11.

Scott, James Brown. "Neutrality of the United States". *AJIL* 29 (1935): 644–652.

Seger, Paul. "The Law of Neutrality". In *The Oxford Handbook of International Law in Armed Conflict*, edited by Andrew Clapham and Paola Gaeta, 248–270. Oxford: Oxford University Press, 2014.

Seidl-Hohenveldern, Ignaz. "Befreiungskriege und Neutralität". In *Studi in onore di Manlio Udina*, 1:645–661. Milano: A. Giuffrè, 1975.

Seidl-Hohenveldern, Ignaz. "Der Begriff der Neutralität in den bewaffneten Konflikten der Gegenwart". In *Um Recht und Freiheit: Festschrift für Friedrich August Freiherr von der Heydte zur Vollendung des 70. Lebensjahres*, herausgegeben von Heinrich Kipp, Franz Mayer, und Armin Steinkamm, 593–613. Berlin: Duncker & Humbolt, 1977.

Sersic, Maja. "Neutrality in International Armed Conflicts at Sea". In *International Law: New Actors, New Concepts Continuing Dilemmas: Liber Amicorum Božidar Bakotić*, edited by Budislav Vukas and Trpimir M. Šošić, 583–593. Leiden: Martinus Nijhoff, 2010.

Shinohara, Hatsue. *US International Lawyers in the Interwar Years: A Forgotten Crusade*. Cambridge: Cambridge University Press, 2012.

Skubiszewski, K. "Use of Force by States, Collective Security, Law of War and Neutrality". In *Manuals of Public International Law*, edited by Max Srřrensen, 739–843. New York: St. Martin's Press, 1968.

Stark, Francis R. *The Abolition of Privateering and the Declaration of Paris*. New York: AMS Press, 1967.

Bibliography 213

Steiger, Heinhard, und Michael Schweitzer. "Neutralität". In *Geschichtliche Grund-begriffe: Historisches Lexikon zur politisch-sozialen Sprache in Deutschland*, herausgegeben von Otto Brunner, Werner Conze, und Reinhart Koselleck, 4:315–370. Stuttgart: Klett-Cotta, 1972–97.

Steiner, George A. "Italian War and Neutrality Legislation". *AJIL* 33 (1939): 151–157.

Stimson, Henry L. "Neutrality and War Prevention". *Proceedings of the American Society of International Law* 29 (1935): 121–129.

Stone, Julius. *Legal Controls of International Conflict: A Treatise on the Dynamics of Disputes- and War-Law*. New York: Rinehart & Company, 1954.

Strisower, Leo. "Die Geschichte des Neutralitätsgedankens". *Zeitschrift für öffentliches Recht* 5 (1926): 184–204.

Suárez, Francisco. *Selections from Three Works of Francisco Suárez, S. J.: De legibus, ac deo legislatore*, 1612, *Defensio fidei catholicae, et apostolicae adversus anglicanae sectae errores*, 1613, *De triplici virtute theologica, fide, spe, et charitate*, 1621. The Classics of International Law, edited by James Brown Scott. Vol. 1, The Photographic Reproduction of the Selections from the Original Editions, a List of Errata, and a Portrait of Suárez. Vol. 2, An English Version of the Texts, Prepared by Gwladys L. Williams, Ammi Brown, and John Waldron, with Certain revisions by Henry Davis, S. J.; together with an Introduction by James Brown Scott, an Analytical Table of Contents, Indexes, and a Portrait of Suárez. Oxford: Clarendon Press, 1944.

Taoka, Ryoichi. *The Right of Self-defence in International Law*. Osaka: The Institute of Legal Study, Osaka University of Economics and Law, 1978.

Taubenfeld, Howard J. "International Action and Neutrality". *AJIL* 47 (1953): 377–396.

Telders, B. M. "L'incident de l'Altmark". *RGDIP* 48·49 (1941–45): 90–100.

Ténékidès, C. G. "La neutralité en son état d'évolution actuelle". *RDILC* 20 (1939): 256–285.

Textor, Johann Wolfgang. *Synopsis juris gentium*. The Classics of International Law, edited by Ludwig von Bar. Vol. 1, Reproduction of the First Edition, with Introduction by Ludwig von Bar, and List of Errata. Vol. 2, A Translation of the Text, by John Pawley Bate, with Index of Authors Cited. Washington: Carnegie Institution of Washington, 1916.

Theutenberg, Von Bo Johnson. "Die schwedische Neutralität vor dem Hintergrund der modernen Waffentechnologie". *German Yearbook of International Law* 29 (1986): 382–416.

Thomae Aquinatis, S. *Summa theologiae*. Cura et studio Sac. Petri Caramello. 3 vols. Torino: Marietti, 1952–56.

Thomas, Charles Marion. *American Neutrality in 1793: A Study in Cabinet Government*. New York: Columbia University Press, 1931.

Thonier, André. *De la contrebande de guerre: Étude de droit international*. Bordeaux: Imprimerie G. Gounouilhou, 1904.

Torrelli, Maurice. "La neutralité en question". *RGDIP* 96 (1992): 7–43.

Trefousse, H. L. *Germany and American Neutrality 1939–1941*. New York: Bookman Associates, 1951.

Truyol y Serra, Antonio. "Zur Entstehungsgeschichte der Neutralitätslehre im neuzeitlichen Staats- und Völkerrechtsdenken: Boteros 'Discorso della neutralità' in seiner Beziehung zur Neutralitätslehre bei Macchiavelli und Bodin". *Österreichische Zeitschrift für öffentliches Recht* 8 (1957–58): 449–460.

Tucker, Robert W. *The Law of War and Neutrality at Sea*. Washington, DC: United States Government Printing Office, 1957.

214 *Bibliography*

Turlington, Edgar. *Neutrality, Its History, Economics and Law*. Vol. 3, *The World War Period*. New York: Columbia University Press, 1936. Reprint, New York: Octagon Books, 1976.

Twiss, Travers. *The Law of Nations Considered as Independent Political Communities: On the Rights and Duties of Nations in Time of War*. 2nd ed. Oxford: The Clarendon Press, 1875.

Ullmann, E. von. *Völkerrecht*. Tübingen: Verlag von J. C. B. Mohr (P. Siebeck), 1908.

Vagts, Detlev F. "Neutrality Law in World War II". *Cardozo Law Review* 20 (1998): 459–482.

Vagts, Detlev F. "The Traditional Legal Concept of Neutrality in a Changing Environment". *American University International Law Review* 14 (1998): 83–102.

Vanderpol, Alfred. *La doctrine scolastique du droit de guerre*. Paris: A. Pedone, 1919.

Vattel, E. de. *Le droit des gens, ou principes de la loi naturelle appliqués à la conduite et aux affaires des nations et souverains*. The Classics of International Law, edited by James Brown Scott. Vol. 1, Photographic Reproduction of the Book I and Book II of First Edition (1758), with an Introduction by Albert de Lapradelle. Vol. 2, Photographic Reproduction of the Book III and IV of the First Edition (1758). Vol. 3, Translation of the Edition of 1758 (by Charles G. Fenwick), with an Introduction by Albert de Lapradelle. Washington, DC: The Carnegie Institution of Washington, 1916.

Verdross, Alfred von. *Völkerrecht*. Berlin: Verlag von Julius Springer, 1937.

Verdross, Alfred von. "La neutralité dans le cadre de l'O. N. U., particulièrement celle de la république d'autriche". *RGDIP* 60 (1957): 177–192.

Verdross, Alfred von. "Neutrality within the Framework of the United Nations Organization". In *Symbolae Verzijl*, 410–418. La Haye: M. Nijhoff, 1958.

Verraes, Fernand. *Les lois de la guerre et la neutralité*. 2 tomes. Bruxelles: Oscar Schepens & Cie, Éditeurs, 1906.

Verzijl, J. H. W. *International Law in Historical Perspective*. Part IX-B, *The Law of Neutrality*. Leyden: Sijtohoff & Noordhoff, 1979.

Victoria, Francisci de. *De indis et de ivre belli relectiones*. The Classics of International Law, edited by Ernest Nys. Washington: Carnegie Institution of Washington, 1917.

Waddell, D. A. G. "British Neutrality and Spanish-American Independence: The Problem of Foreign Enlistment". *Journal of Latin American Studies* 19 (1987): 1–18.

Waldkirch, E. v., und Ernst Vanselow. *Neutralitätsrecht*. Stuttgart: W. Kohlhammer, 1936.

Waldock, C. H. M. "The Release of the *Altmark*'s Prisoners". *BYIL* 24 (1947): 216–238.

Walker, Thomas Alfred. *The Science of International Law*. London: C. J. and Sons, 1893.

Walker, Wyndham Legh. "Recognition of Belligerency and Grant of Belligerent Rights". *Transactions of the Grotius Society* 23 (1937): 177–219.

Warren, Charles. "What are the Rights of Neutrals Now, in Practice?" *Proceedings of the American Society of International Law* 27 (1933): 128–134.

Warren, Charles. "Troubles of a Neutral". *Foreign Affairs* 12 (1934): 377–394.

Waultrin, René. "La neutralité scandinave". *RGDIP* 11 (1904): 5–42.

Weiss, André. *The Violation by Germany of the Neutrality of Belgium and Luxemburg*. Paris: Librairie Armand Colin, 1915.

Westlake, John. *International Law*. Part II, *War*. 2nd ed. Cambridge: Cambridge University Press, 1913.

Wheaton, Henry. *Elements of International Law*. The Classics of International Law: The Literal Reproduction of the Edition of 1866 by Richard Henry Dana, Jr., edited, with notes by George Grafton Wilson. Oxford: Clarendon Press, 1936.

Bibliography   215

Wheaton, Henry. *Elements of International Law: With a Sketch of the History of the Science.* Philadelphia, PA: Carey, Lea & Blanchard, 1836. Reprint, Union, New Jersey: The Lawbook Exchange, 2002.

Wheeler, Gerald John. *Foreign Enlistment Act, 1870, 33 & 34 Vict. c. 90., with Notes of the Leading Cases on This and the American Act.* London: Eyre & Spottiswoode, 1896.

Whitton, John B. "La neutralité et la Société des Nations". *RCADI* 17 (1927): 449–571.

Williams, Jr., Walter L. "Neutrality in Modern Armed Conflicts: A Survey of the Developing Law". *Military Law Review* 90 (1980): 9–48.

Wilson, George Grafton. "War and Neutrality". *AJIL* 27 (1933): 725–726.

Wilson, George Grafton. "The Law of Neutrality and the Policy of Keeping Out of War". *AJIL* 34 (1940): 89.

Wilson, Robert R. "Neutrality of Eire". *AJIL* 34 (1940): 125–127.

Wilson, Robert R. "Escaped Prisoners of War in Neutral Jurisdiction". *AJIL* 35 (1941): 519–523.

Wilson, Robert R. " 'Non-Belligerency' in relation to the Terminology of Neutrality". *AJIL* 35 (1941): 121–123.

Wilson, Robert R. "Questions relating to Irish Neutrality". *AJIL* 36 (1942): 288–291.

Wilson, Robert R. "Some Current Questions relating to Neutrality". *AJIL* 37 (1943): 651–656.

Wiswall, Jr., F. L. "Neutrality, the Rights of Shipping and the Use of Force in the Persian Gulf". *Virginia Journal of International Law* 31 (1991): 619–629.

Wolff, Christian. *Jus gentium methodo scientifica pertractatum.* The Classics of International Law, edited by James Brown Scott. Vol. 1, The Photographic Reproduction of the Edition of 1764 with an Introduction by Dr. Otfried Nippold, a List of Errata, and a Portrait of Wolff. Vol. 2, A Translation of the Text, by Joseph H. Drake, with a Translation (by Francis J. Hemelt) of the Introduction by Otfried Nippold, an Index, and a Portrait of Wolff. Oxford: Clarendon Press, 1934.

Wolff, Hans-Jürgen. *Kriegserklärung und Kriegszustand nach klassischem Völkerrecht: Mit einem Beitrag zu den Gründen für eine Gleichbehandlung Kriegführender.* Berlin: Duncker & Humblot, 1990.

Woolsey, L. H. "Neutral Persons and Property on the High Seas in Time of War". *Proceedings of the American Society of International Law* 29 (1935): 72–80.

Woolsey, L. H. "The Fallacies of Neutrality". *AJIL* 30 (1936): 256–262.

Woolsey, L. H. "Government Traffic in Contraband". *AJIL* 34 (1940): 498–503.

Woolsey, L. H. "Taking of Foreign Ships in American Ports". *AJIL* 35 (1941): 497–506.

Woolsey, Theodore D. *Introduction to the Study of International Law: Designed as an Aid in Teaching, and in Historical Studies.* 5th ed. New York: Charles Scribner's Sons, 1878.

Woolsey, Theodore D. "Les trois règles de Washington". *RDILC*, VI (1874), 559–560.

Wrange, Pål. "Neutrality, Impartiality and Our Responsibility to Uphold International Law". In *Law at War: The Law as It Was and the Law as It Should Be: Liber Amicorum Ove Bring*, edited by Ola Engdahl and Pål Wrange. 273–292. Leiden: Martinus Nijhoff, 2008.

Wright, Quincy. "The Destruction of Neutral Property on Enemy Vessels". *AJIL* 11 (1917): 358–379.

Wright, Quincy. "Changes in the Conception of War". *AJIL* 18 (1924): 755–767.

Wright, Quincy. "The Future of Neutrality". *International Conciliation*, no. 242 (1928): 353–372.

216 *Bibliography*

Wright, Quincy. "Neutrality and Neutral Rights following the Pact of Paris for the Renunciation of War". *Proceedings of the American Society of International Law* 24 (1930): 77–87.

Wright, Quincy. "The Meaning of the Pact of Paris". *AJIL* 27 (1933): 39–61.

Wright, Quincy. "The Power to Declare Neutrality under American Law". *AJIL* 34 (1940): 302–310.

Wright, Quincy. "The Present Status of Neutrality". *AJIL* 34 (1940): 391–414.

Wright, Quincy. "Rights and Duties under International Law as Affected by the United States Neutrality Act and the Resolutions of Panama". *AJIL* 34 (1940): 238–248.

Wright, Quincy. "The Transfer of Destroyers to Great Britain". *AJIL* 34 (1940): 680–689.

Wright, Quincy. "The Lend-Lease Bill and International Law". *AJIL* 35 (1941): 305–315.

Wright, Quincy. "Repeal of the Neutrality Act". *AJIL* 36 (1942): 8–23.

Wright, Quincy. "The Outlawry of War and the Law of War". *AJIL* 47 (1953): 365–376.

Wylie, Neville, ed. *European Neutrals and Non-Belligerents during the Second World War.* Cambridge: Cambridge University Press, 2002.

Zemanek, Karl. "Ändert sich das völkerrechtliche Neutralitätsrecht und mit ihm die österreichische Neutralität?" *Österreichische Juristen-Zeitung* 47 (1992): 177–182.

Zemanek, Karl. "Neutralität und Aussenhandel". In *Um Recht und Freiheit: Festschrift für Friedrich August Freiherr von der Heydte zur Vollendung des 70. Lebensjahres*, herausgegeben von Heinrich Kipp, Franz Mayer, und Armin Steinkamm, 759–774. Berlin: Duncker & Humbolt, 1977.

Zemanek, Karl. "Wirtschaftliche Neutralität". *Juristische Blätter* 81 (1959): 249–251.

Books and articles (in Japanese)

Akashi, Kinji. "Junana seiki Oranda no churitsu tsusyo seisaku: Bainkerusufuku riron no kensyo". [The Dutch Policy on Neutral Commerce in the 17th Century: An Examination of Bynkershoek's Theory]. *Kaiho dai kenkyu hokoku (ho bungaku kei)* [Report of Japan Maritime Safety Academy (The Law and Literature Section)] 38, no. 1–2, part 1 (1992): 101–123.

Arai, Kyo. "Iran Iraku senso ni okeru kaijo keizai sen: Sono kokusaiho jo no imi". [Maritime Economic Warfare in the Iran-Iraq War: An International Law Perspective]. *Kyoto Gakuen Hogaku* [Kyoto Gakuen Law Review] no. 2–3 (1999): 387–431.

Aruga, Tadashi, and Seigen Miyazato, eds. *Gaisetsu Amerika gaiko shi: Taigai ishiki to taigai seisaku no hensen* [An Outline of American Diplomatic History: The Transitions of an External Perception and Foreign Policy]. New ed. Tokyo: Yuhikaku, 1998.

Bothe, Michael. "Jus in bello o meguru shomondai (naisen no buryoku funsoho, churitsu hoki no genjo to kongo)". [Issues related to "jus in bello" (Laws applicable to internal armed conflicts) (Law of Neutrality)]. In *Kokusai jindoho ni kansuru semina hokokusho* [Seminar on International Humanitarian Law Report], 62–74. [Ministry of Foreign Affairs], 2000.

Fujita, Hisakazu. *Kokusaiho kogi II: Jinken, heiwa* [Lectures on International Law, Vol. 2, Human Rights and Peace]. Tokyo: University of Tokyo Press, 1994.

Fujita, Hisakazu. *Kokusai jindoho* [International Humanitarian Law]. 2nd ed. Tokyo: Yushindo kobunsha, 2003.

Iiyama, Yukinobu. *Churitu-koku no tatakai.* [Battles of Neutral States]. Tokyo: Kojinsya, 2005.

Irie, Keishiro. *Verusaiyu taisei no hokai* [The Collapse of the Versailles System]. 3 vols. Tokyo: Kyoei shobo, 1943–44.

Bibliography 217

Ishimoto, Yasuo. "Churitsu seido no seiritsu katei (1)(2)". [Historical Development of Neutrality System]. *Kokusaiho Gaiko Zassi* [Journal of International Law and Diplomacy] 51, no. 5 (1952): 31–61; 52, no. 3 (1953) 63–88.

Ishimoto, Yasuo. "Kokusai-soshiki to churitsu". [International Organization and Neutrality]. *Kokusaiho Gaiko Zassi* [Journal of International Law and Diplomacy] 55, no. 1 (1956): 27–56.

Ishimoto, Yasuo. *Churitsu seido no shiteki kenkyu* [A Historical Study on the Law of Neutrality]. Tokyo: Yuhikaku, 1958.

Ishimoto, Yasuo. "Kokusai rengo to churitsu". [The United Nations and Neutrality]. In *Kokusai rengo no kenkyu: Taoka Ryoichi Sensei Kanreki Kinen Ronbun-syu* [Studies on the United Nations: Essays in Honour of Professor Taoka Ryoichi for His Sixtieth Birthday], edited by Shigejiro Tabata, 1:66–87. Tokyo: Yuhikaku, 1962.

Ishimoto, Yasuo. "Senso to gendai kokusaiho". [War and Modern International law]. In *Iwanami koza Gendaiho 12: Gendaiho to kokusaisyakai* [Iwanami Lectures on Modern Law 12: Modern Law and International Society], edited by Yuichi Takano, 71–108. Tokyo: Iwanami shoten, 1965.

Ishimoto, Yasuo. "Kosenken to senji kokusaiho: Seifu toben no kento". ["Right of Belligerency" and International Law of War with Particular Reference to Art. 9 of Japanese Constitution]. *Jochi Hogaku Ronshu* [Sophia Law Review] 29 no. 2–3 (1986): 33–69.

Ishimoto, Yasuo. *Kokusaiho no kozo-tenkan* [The Changing Structure of International Law]. Tokyo: Yushindo, 1998.

Isomura, Eiji. "Kokuren kensho ga churitsuho ni ataeta eikyo". [The Effects on the Law of Neutrality of the UN Charter]. *Seinan gakuin daigaku daigakuin Hogaku kenkyu ronshu* [Seinan Gakuin University Graduate School Graduate Studies in Law], no. 23 (2005): 21–37.

Ito, Fujio. "Keibatsu senso no kannen to sono riron no keisei ni tsuite: Kokusaiho gakusetsu shi no kenkyu". [Idea of *Bellum Vindicativum* and Formation of its Theory: A Study of the History of the Law of Nations]. *Hobun Ronso* [A Quarterly Journal of Law and Literature], no. 3 (1952): 1–20.

Ito, Fujio. *Suaresu no kokusaiho riron* [Suárez' Theory of International Law]. Yuhikaku, 1957.

Ito, Fujio. "Jieiken no hoshi". [Legal History of the Right of Self-Defence]. *Kokusaiho Gaiko Zassi* [Journal of International Law and Diplomacy] 59, no. 1–2 (1960): 28–55.

Ito, Fujio. *Vitoria no kokusaiho riron: Kokusaiho gakusetsu shi no kenkyu* [Vitoria's Theory of International Law: A Study on the History of International Law Theories]. Tokyo: Yuhikaku, 1965.

The Japan Institute of International Affairs. *Churitsu shugi no kenkyu* [Studies on Neutralism]. 2 vols. Tokyo: The Japan Institute of International Affairs, 1961.

Kasai, Naoya. "Gurotiusu ni okeru senso to shokokumin no ho: Seitosei to gohosei no kosaku". [Some Observation on Grotian Conception of *jus gentium*]. *Kokusaiho Gaiko Zassi* [Journal of International Law and Diplomacy] 83, no. 1 (1984): 31–63.

Kawakami, Keiitsu. "Dasutorugu churitsu keisei no rekishiteki-seijiteki danmen". [The Historical and Political Aspects of the Formation of Neutrality in D'Astorg]. *Kansai daigaku kenkyu ronshu (Horitsu-seiji hen)* [Kansai University Research Journal (Law and Politics)] no. 11 (1941): 47–73.

Kawakami, Keiitsu. "Genzai ni okeru churitsu no chii". [The Present Status of Neutrality]. *Koho Zasshi* [Journal of Public Law] 7, no. 1 (1941): 37–59.

Kinshichi, Norio. *Porutogaru shi* [Portuguese History]. An enlarged ed. Tokyo: Sairyusha, 2003.

218 Bibliography

Komori, Teruo. "Kokusaihogaku ni okeru dentoteki churitsu to gendai no churitsu". [Traditional Neutrality and Modern Neutrality in International Law Thories]. *Kokusai mondai* [International Affairs], no. 213 (1977): 14–37.

Komori, Teruo. "Gendai ni okeru churitsu hoki no dato kiban: Churitsuteki chii ni okeru kohei gensoku no igi to seitosei o chusin toshite". [The Validating Grounds of the Law of Neutrality at Present]. In *Buryoku funso no kokusaiho* [International Law of Armed Conflict], edited by Shinya Murase and Akira Mayama, 85–118. Tokyo: Toshindo, 2004.

Kotani, Tsuruji. "Senso to churitsu tono kankei". [The Relationship between War and Neutrality]. *Gaiko Jiho* [Revue Diplomatique] no. 896 (1942): 20–38.

Matsuda, Takeo. "Shin gaidorain shuhen jitai sochi hoan no kokusaihoteki kento". [Analysis of the Bill concerning the New Guidelines and Perilous Situations in Areas Surrounding Japan from an International Law Perspective]. *Horitsu jiho* 71, no. 1 (1999): 46–50.

Matsui, Yoshiro, Haruo Saburi, Shigeki Sakamoto, Kaoru Obata, Takeo Matsuda, Norio Tanaka, Izumi Okada, and Kimio Yakushiji. *Kokusaiho* [International Law]. 5th ed. Tokyo: Yuhikaku, 2007.

Matsukuma, Kiyoshi. "Konsorato deru mare". [Consolato del mare]. In *Kokusai kankei ho jiten* [Encyclopedia of International Law], 2nd ed., edited by Japanese Society of International Law, 401. Tokyo: Sanseido, 2005.

Mayama, Akira. "Dainijitaisen go no buryokufunso niokeru daisangoku sempaku no hokaku (1) (2)". [Capture of Merchant Ships of the Third States in the Armed Conflicts after W. W. II. (1) (2)]. *Hogakuronso* [Kyoto Law Review] 118, no. 1 (1985): 68–96; 119, no. 3 (1986): 75–94.

Mayama, Akira. "Kai jo keizai sen ni okeru churitsu hoki no tekiyo ni tsuite". [The Application of the Law of Neutrality in Economic Warfare at Sea]. *Sekaiho nempo* [Yearbook of World Law] 8 (1988): 17–31.

Mayama, Akira. "Nichi-Bei boei kyoryoku notameno shishin to senpaku no kensa". [The Guidelines for U.S.-Japan Defence Cooperation and Inspection of Ships]. *Boei ho kenkyu* [Defense Law Studies] no. 22 (1998): 109–137.

Mayama, Akira. "Kai jo churitsu to koho chiiki shien". [Maritime Neutrality and Logistic Support]. *Jurisuto* [Jurist], no. 1279 (2004): 20–30.

Mayama, Akira. "Hi kosen jotai". [Non-Belligerency]. In *Kokusai kankei ho jiten* [Encyclopedia of International Law], 2nd ed., edited by Japanese Society of International Law, 732–733. Sanseido, 2005.

Momose, Hiroshi. *Shokoku: Rekishi ni miru rinen to genjitsu* [Small States: The Ideal and Reality in History]. Tokyo: Iwanami shoten, 1988.

Mori, Tadashi. *Jieiken no kisou: Kokuren kensho ni itaru rekishiteki tenkai* [The Right of Self-Defence in International Law: From the *Caroline* Incident to the United Nations Charter]. Tokyo: University of Tokyo Press, 2009.

Morikawa, Koichi. "Kokusaiho kara mita shin Nichi-Bei boeikyoryoku kanrenho tou". [Acts concerning Japan-US Defence Cooperation from an International Law Perspective]. *Jurisuto* [Jurist], no. 1160 (1999): 44–52.

Morikawa, Koichi. "Buryokukogeki jitai kaijoyuso kiseiho to kokusaiho". [Maritime Transportation Act and International Law]. *Jurisuto* [Jurist], no. 1279 (2004): 11–19.

Morikawa, Koichi. "Churitsu: Kokuren taisei to churitsu wa ryoritsu suruka". [Neutrality: Is Neutrality Compatible with the United Nations System?]. In *Kokusaiho kiwado* [Keywords of International Law]. 2nd ed., edited by Naoya Okuwaki and Akira Kotera, 218–221. Tokyo: Yuhikaku, 2006.

Bibliography 219

Morita, Keiko. "Buryoku funso no daisangoku ni taisuru buryoku koshi no seitosei". [Host States Face Legal Consequences of Armed Conflict: Neutrality Violation or Armed Attack?]. *Boei Kenkyusho kiyo* [*NIDS Security Studies*] 7, no. 2–3 (2005): 137–156.

Morita, Keiko. "Buryoku funso ji no daisangoku ryoiki shiyo no kiketsu: Buryoku kogeki eno gaitosei no kanten kara". [The Legitimate Use of Force against Non-Belligent States in Armed Conflict]. *Boei Kenkyusho kiyo* [NIDS Security Studies] 8, no. 2 (2006): 137–156.

Naruse, Osamu, Yamada Kingo, and Seiji Kimura, eds. *Sekai rekishi taikei Doitsushi 1: Senshi-1648 nen* [An Outline of German History I: From Prehistoric Times to 1648]. Tokyo: Yamakawa shuppansya, 1997.

Nishi, Taira. "Senso gainen no tenkan towa nanika: nijusseiki no Oshu kokusaiho rironkatachi no senso to heiwa no ho". [What is the Turn of the Concept of War?; The Law of War and Peace of International Legal Theorists in the Mid-twentieth Century]. *Kokusaiho Gaiko Zassi* [Journal of International Law and Diplomacy] 104, no. 4 (2006): 63–90.

Obuchi, Niemon. "Renmei kiyaku to churitsu gainen". [The League Covenant and the Concept of Neutrality]. *Ho to Keizai* [Law and Economy] 9, no. 6 (1938): 1–15.

Oka, Yoshitake. *Kokusai seiji shi* [History of International Politics]. Tokyo: Iwanami shoten, 1955.

Onuma, Yasuaki. *Senso sekinin ron josetsu* [Prolegomena to the Responsibility for War]. Tokyo: University of Tokyo Press, 1975.

Onuma, Yasuaki. "Kokusai shakai ni okeru ho to seiji". [Law and Politics in International Society]. In *Nihon to kokusaiho no hyakunen*, I [A Hundred Years of Japan and International Law I], edited by the Japanese Society of International Law, 1–34. Tokyo: Sanseido, 2001.

Onuma, Yasuaki. *Kokusaiho* [International Law]. Tokyo: Toshindo, 2005.

Osawa, Akira. "Kokusaiho chitsujo ni okeru seisai to churitsu (1)-(4)". [Sanction and Neutrality in the System of International Law]. *Kokusaiho Gaiko Zassi* [Journal of International Law and Diplomacy] 37, no. 4 (1938): 1–29; no. 5: 74–97; no. 7: 1–30; no. 8: 36–70.

Osawa, Akira. "Kokusai funso to churitsu no gainen". [International Disputes and the Concept of Neutrality]. In *Nomura kyoju kanreki shukuga: Koho seiji ronsyu* [Essays in Honour of Professor Nomura for His Sixtieth Birthday: A Collection of Essays on Public Law and Politics], edited by Toru Gyobu, 697–764. Tokyo: Yuhikaku, 1938.

Osawa, Akira. "Churitsu gainen no hensen". [The Transitions of the Concept of Neutrality]. *Horitsu jiho* 11, no. 11 (1939): 1059–1964.

Ota, Yoshiki. *Gurotiusu no kokusai-seiji shiso: Shuken-kokka chitsujo no keisei* [Political Thought of Hugo Grotius: Emergence of Modern International System and the Idea of Sovereign State]. Kyoto: Minerva shobo, 2003.

Saito, Takashi. *Senkanki kokusai-seiji shi* [History of International Politics in the Interwar Period]. Tokyo: Iwanami shoten, 1978.

Shinobu, Junpei. *Senji-kokusaiho kogi* [Lectures on International Law in Times of War]. 4 vols. [Tokyo:] Maruzen, 1941.

Sogawa, Takeo. "Karu Shumitto ni okeru 'senso kannen no tenkan' ni tsuite (1)". [Carl Schmitt and the Transformation of the Legal Concept of War (I)]. *Hogaku* [Journal of Law and Political Science] 17, no. 2 (1953): 74–101.

Sugihara, Takane. "Kindai kokusaiho no hokihansei ni kansuru ichikosatsu: Senso no ichizuke tono kankei ni oite". [The Legal Character of Modern International Law: With

220 Bibliography

Particular Reference to the Legal Status of War]. In *Kokusai shakai no ho kozo: Sono rekishi to genjo* [The Legal Structure of International Society: Its History and the Present], edited by Haruyuki Yamate and Shigeru Kozai, 89–116. Tokyo: Toshindo, 2003.

Sugihara, Takane, Chiyuki Mizukami, Tomohito Usuki, Atsushi Yoshii, Nobuyuki Kato, and Akira Takada. *Gendai kokusaiho kogi* [Lectures on Modern International Law]. 5th ed. Tokyo: Yuhikaku, 2012.

Tabata, Shigejiro. *Kokusaiho* [International Law]. 2 vols. Tokyo: Yushindo, 1954–55.

Tabata, Shigejiro. *Kokusaiho shinko* [A New Lecture on International Law]. 2 vols. Tokyo: Toshindo, 1990–91.

Tachi, Sakutaro. "Kokusai renmei to churitsu kankei". [The League of Nations and the Relations of Neutrality]. *Kokka Gakkai Zasshi* [Journal of the Association of Political and Social Sciences] 34, no. 7 (1920): 32–41.

Tachi, Sakutaro. *Senji kokusaiho ron* [A Treatise on International Law in Times of War]. Tokyo: Nihon hyoronsha, 1931.

Tachi, Sakutaro. *Kokusai renmei kiyaku ron* [A Treatise on the Covenant of the League of Nations]. Tokyo: Kokusai renmei kyokai, 1932.

Tachi, Sakutaro. "Amerikagasshukoku sin churitsu ho yogi (1) (2)". [The Essentials of the US Neutrality Act of 1937]. *Kokusaiho Gaiko Zassi* [Journal of International Law and Diplomacy] 36, no. 8 (1937): 1–30; no. 9: 1–26.

Tachi, Sakutaro. "Kokusaiho jo no senji churitsu". [Wartime Neutrality in International Law]. In *Genjitsu kokusaiho syomondai* [Practical Problems of International Law], by Sakutaro Tachi, 77–129. Tokyo: Iwanami shoten, 1937.

Tachi, Sakutaro. "Adomiraru grafu shupe go jiken". ["Admiral Graf Spee" Affair]. *Kokusaiho Gaiko Zassi* [Journal of International Law and Diplomacy] 39, no. 7 (1940): 49–74.

Tachi, Sakutaro. "Kokusaiho jo no churitsu no kako, genzai oyobi shorai". [The Past, Present and Future of Neutrality in International Law]. *Kokka Shiken* 14, no. 4 (1942): 21–41.

Takano, Yuichi. *Kokusaiho gairon* [An Outline of International Law]. 2nd ed. 2 vols. Tokyo: Kobundo, 1986.

Takeshima, Hiroyuki. *Karu Shumitto no seiji: 'Kindai' eno hangyaku* [The Politics of Carl Schmitt: Revolts against the "Modern"]. Tokyo: Fukosha, 2002.

Tanaka, Tadashi. "Buryoku kisei ho no kihon kozo". [The Basic Structure of International Law Governing the Use of Force]. In *Gendai kokusaiho no shihyo* [Basic Principles of Modern International Law], 2nd ed., by Shinya Murase, Naoya Okuwaki, Terumi Furukawa and Tadashi Tanaka, 263–334. Tokyo: Yuhikaku, 1994.

Taoka, Ryoichi. "Fusen jyoyaku no igi". [The Value of the Pact of Paris]. *Hogaku* [Journal of Law and Political Science] 1, no. 2 (1932): 1–35.

Taoka, Ryoichi. "Churitsu no gogi ni tsuite". [The Meaning of the Term Neutrality]. *Koho Zasshi* [Journal of Public Law] 1, no. 12 (1935): 45–56.

Taoka, Ryoichi. "Churitsu koku yori kosen koku eno kokuki yushutsu to hagu jusan go joyaku hachi jo tono kankei". [Export of Aircrafts from Neutral States to Belligerent States and its Relationship with Article 8 of the Hague Convention XIII]. *Hogaku* [Journal of Law and Political Science] 6, no. 6 (1937): 46–61.

Taoka, Ryoichi. "Churitsu ryoiki to kosen koku gun yo kokuki". [Belligerent Military Aircrafts in the Territories of Neutral States]. *Hogakuronso* [Kyoto Law Review] 31, no. 3 (1937): 314–347.

Taoka, Ryoichi. "Kokusai churitsuho to beikoku churitsuho". [The International Law of Neutrality and the Neutrality Acts of the United States]. In *Sasaki hakase kanreki kinen: Kokka oyobi horitsu no riron* [Essays in Honour of Dr Sasaki for His Sixtieth Birthday: Theory of State and Law], edited by Tokuji Tamura, 215–235. Tokyo: Yuhikaku, 1938.

Taoka, Ryoichi. *Kokusaihogaku taiko* [An Outline of International Law]. 2 vols. Tokyo: Ganshodo shoten, 1938–39.

Taoka, Ryoichi. "Anzen hosho no bunrui ni okeru eisei churitsu no chii". [The Status of Permanent Neutrality in the Classification of Forms of Security]. *Hotetsugaku shikiho* [Philosophy of Law Quarterly], no. 6 (1950): 50–73.

Taoka, Ryoichi. *Eisei churitsu to Nihon no anzen hosho* [Permanent Neutrality and Japan's Security]. Tokyo: Yuhikaku, 1950.

Taoka, Ryoichi. *Kokusaiho III* [International Law III]. New ed. Tokyo: Yuhikaku, 1973.

Tsuji, Kenji. "Gentei churitsu ron: Jukyuseiki zenhanki no churitsu riron". [The Qualified Neutrality: The Leading Theory of Neutrality in the First Period of 19th Century]. *Saga daigaku Keizai Ronshu* [Saga University Economic Review] 26, no. 2 (1993): 177–201.

Tsutsui, Wakamizu. *Gendai kokusaiho ron: Kokusaiho ni okeru daisan jotai* [A Treatise on Modern International Law: The Intermediate Status in International Law]. Tokyo: University of Tokyo Press, 1972.

Tsutsui, Wakamizu. *Senso to ho* [War and Law]. 2nd ed. Tokyo: University of Tokyo Press, 1976.

Tsutsui, Wakamizu, ed. *Kokusaiho jiten* [Encyclopedic Dictionary of International Law]. Tokyo: Yuhikaku, 1998.

Unemura, Shigeru. *Ei-Bei ni okeru kokusaiho to kokunaiho no kankei* [The Relationship between International Law and Municipal Law in Anglo-American Law]. Kyoto: Horitsu bunka sha, 1969.

Wani, Kentaro. "Churitsu seido ni taisuru senso ihoka no eikyo: Senkan ki oyobi dainiji taisenchu no gakusetsu·kokka jikko no kento". [Prohibition of War and Neutrality: Doctrine and State Practice 1919–1945]. *Kokusai kankei ron kenkyu* [Studies on International Relations] 18 (2002): 27–54.

Wani, Kentaro. "'Churitsu' kannen no kigen: Juroku kara juhasseiki ni okeru 'churitsu'". [The Origin of the Conception of Neutrality]. *Kokusai kankei ron kenkyu* [Studies on International Relations] 22 (2004): 97–123.

Wani, Kentaro. "Dentoteki churitsu seido no seiritsu: Juhasseiki kara nijusseiki syoto ni okeru churitsu". [The Evolution of the Institution of Neutrality 1793–1919]. *Kokusai kankei ron kenkyu* [Studies on International Relations] 24 (2005): 29–57.

Wani, Kentaro. "Kaijohokaku ho no seitoka konkyo: Rondonsengen (1909) izen no gakusetsu, kokkajikko no kento". [The Legal Foundations of Prize Law in Traditional International Law]. *Kokusaiho Gaiko Zassi* [Journal of International Law and Diplomacy] 113, no. 4 (2015): 45–70.

Yamauchi, Susumu. *Ryakudatsu no ho kannen shi: Chu-kinsei Yoroppa no hito, senso, ho* [A History of Legal Conception of Looting: Man, War, and Law in Medieval and Early Modern Europe]. Tokyo: University of Tokyo Press, 1993.

Yanagihara, Masaharu. "Funso kaiketsu hoshiki no hitotsu toshite no senso no ichizuke ni kansuru ichi kosatsu". [War as a Means of Settlement of International Disputes]. In *Oda Shigeru sensei koki shukuga: Funso kaiketsu no kokusaiho* [Dispute Settlement in International Law: Essays in Honour of Judge Shigeru Oda for His Seventieth Birthday], edited by Takane Sugihara, 2–22. Tokyo: Sanseido, 1997.

222 Bibliography

Yanagihara, Masaharu. *Vorufu no kokusaiho riron* [The Theory of International Law of Christian Wolff]. Tokyo: Yuhikaku, 1998.

Yanagihara, Masaharu. "Iwayuru 'musabetsu senso kan' to senso no ihoka: Karu Shumitto no gakusetsu wo tegakari toshite". [The So-called "Idea of Non-Discriminating War" and the Outlawry of War: In Relation with the Doctrine of Carl Schimitt]. *Sekaiho nempo* [Yearbook of World Law] 20 (2001): 3–29.

Yokota, Kisaburo. "Amerika churitsuho no kenkyu: Tokuni sono jissaiteki kino ni tsuite". [A Study on the Neutrality Acts of the United States: Particularly their Practical Functions]. In *Nakamura Shingo hakase tsuito kinen: Jikyoku kankei kokusaiho gaiko ronbunshu* [Essays in Memory of Dr. Nakamura Shingo: Essays on the Current Issues of International Law and Diplomacy], edited by Masao Ichimata and Zengo Ohira, 299–332. Tokyo: Ganshodo shoten, 1940.

Yokota, Kisaburo. "Amerika no hi-churitsuteki churitsu". [Unneutral Neutraity of the United States]. *Gaiko Jiho* [Revue Diplomatique], no. 870 (1941): 1–9.

Yokota, Kisaburo. "Amerika no kuchikukan joto". [On the Transfer of American Destroyers]. *Kokusaiho Gaiko Zassi* [Journal of International Law and Diplomacy] 40, no. 2 (1941): 73–86.

Yokota, Kisaburo. "Hi kosen jyotai no hori (1)(2)". [The Legal Doctrine of Non-Belligerency (1) (2)]. *Hogaku Kyokai Zasshi* [Journal of the Jurisprudence Association] 60, no. 4 (1942): 545–569; no. 5: 759–781.

Yokota, Kisaburo. *Kaiyo no jiyu* [The Freedom of the Sea]. Tokyo: Iwanami shoten, 1944.

Yokota, Kisaburo. *Anzen hosho no mondai* [Problems of Security]. Tokyo: Keiso shobo, 1949.

Index

act of war 8, 78, 85, 88, 102, 105–7, 117, 134n244, 134n246, 166–7, 176, 189–90
Admiral Graf Spee, the 151, 179n43
alliance 85–7, 107–8, 141–2, 176n2
Altmark case 132n218, 150–2, 179n42, 180n46
American Civil War 63, 79, 92
American War of Independence (1775–83) 122n3
angary, the right of 15n34
animus belligerendi 138n302
armed conflict 1–3, 13n14, 183n89, 192n4
Armed Neutrality 42

Belgian neutrality, the German violation of 8–10, 115–16, 147
Belgium 144, 149; during the Second World War 154–8, 181n67, 192; in the Franco–Prussian War 130n186; permanent neutrality of 9, 133n225
belligerency, recognition of 64–8, 72–3
belligerent rights 6, 15n33, 15n34, 67, 89–90, 130n176
blockade 7, 14n23, 40–1, 43, 67, 89, 104, 144, 191
Bluntschli, J.C. 85–6, 106, 137n280, 176
Bodin, Jean 44
Borchard, Edwin 162–8, 171
Budapest Articles of Interpretation 170, 184n93
Bynkershoek, Cornelius van 26, 31, 34, 49n97, 50n113, 51n135, 51n138, 55

Canadian Rebellion (Insurrection) (1837–8) 71, 115, 125n106
capture at sea 39–42, 82–3, 88–9, 104, 130n174, 192n6

Caroline incident 115, 125n106
casus belli 101, 132n215, 134n244, 166
cause of war 62, 82, 84, 112, 117–21, 165–6, 188
Cavaglieri, A. 113, 117
Chaco War 148
champerty 172, 186n133
China: in the First World War 115, 139; in the Russo-Japanese War 115
civil war 59–60, 62, 64–71
collective security 12n11, 141–2, 145, 147–50, 157, 177n4
collective self-denfence 13n18, 183n89, 191
commercial adventure 75–8, 87
Consolato del mare 41–2, 52n144, 52n150
contraband of war 6–7, 14n23, 40–3, 52n150, 75, 77, 81–3, 87–90, 95, 104, 117, 129n167, 158–9, 182n77, 191
Cuban War of Independence, the Second (1895–8) 72
cyber warfare 2

Danish Fleet incident (1807) 115–16
de Visscher, Charles 10, 113, 118–20, 140n329, 140n330
declaration of neutrality 55, 63–5, 67, 74, 107, 109, 148; *see also* Table of national legislations
declaration of war 63, 108, 135n246, 138n302
due diligence 80–1, 128n143, 132n207
duties of a neutral State 6, 106–7, 113–14, 117–18, 129n174, 169–71, 188–9
duty of abstention 7
duty of acquiescence 6, 89, 130n176
duty of impartiality 3–8, 168, 171–5, 188–90
duty of non-discrimination 7

224 *Index*

duty of prevention 7
duty to remain neutral 5, 14n30, 113, 168

enemy character 15n36, 41–2
equality of belligerents 3, 6–7, 172, 174–5, 190
ex injuria non jus oritur 170

Falklands/Malvinas Conflict 3
Fiore, Pasquale 86, 107–8
fitting out and arming of vessels 56, 58, 60, 62, 64, 74–83, 98, 128n143, 132n207, 182n77
Franco–Prussian War (1870–1) 63, 130n186, 130n189
free ships free goods, the doctrine of 41–2, 52n150
freedom of (maritime) commerce 3, 6, 39–43, 104, 137n296, 169; *see also* neutral commerce
French Revolutionary Wars 55–6, 121

Gareis, Karl 106–7, 134n246
Gentilis, Albericus 27–8
Germany: declaration of war against Portugal (1916) 110; declaration of war against the United States (1942) 162; violation of Belgian neutrality *see* Belgian neutrality, the German violation of
Greece in the First World War 115, 138n309
Greek War of Independence 65
Grewe, Wilhelm G. 10, 17, 22
Grotius Hugo 27–30, 44, 53n158, 53n159

Hague Peace Conference (1899), the First 93–4
Hague Peace Conference (1907), the Second 1, 91, 93–102
Hall, William Edward 88
Halleck, H.W. 112, 137n280
Hautefeuille, L.-B. 104
Heilborn, Paul 139n319
Heintschel von Heinegg, Wolff 8
Hershey, Amos S. 55, 112–13, 119–20, 140n329, 140n330
Hitler, Adolf 154, 156, 160–2, 183n88
Hohfeld, Wesley Newcomb 130
hostile infection, the doctrine of 41
Hübner, Martin 26, 30, 33, 48n83, 55

imperfect neutrality *see* qualified neutrality

injuria (injure; injury) 27, 30–1, 35–6
innocent passage 90, 152
Institut de Droit International 83
International Law Association's "Helsinki Principles on Maritime Neutrality" (1996) 14n23
intervention 138n302
Iran–Iraq War (1980–8) 2–3
Ishimoto, Yasuo 6, 43, 169–71, 174–5
isolationism 160–2
Italo–Ethiopian War, the (1935–6) 148

Japan: in the First World War 115, 139n310; in the Second World War 160–2
jus ad bellum 1, 35, 134n233, 187n155
jus in bello 1, 134n233
just cause of war 27, 30–1, 35–9, 50n97, 111–12
just war doctrine 7, 23–4, 27–31, 35–7, 39, 44, 49n97, 111–12, 118, 172–3, 188; the decline of 112–13
just war, the obligation to assist a belligerent waging a 28, 37–9

Kleen, Richard 86, 106, 112
Klüber, Jean Louis 112, 137n280
Korea in the Russo-Japanese War (1904–5) 115, 138n309, 140n328
Kunz, Josef L. 14n30, 168–71

Lauterpacht, H. 7, 172–3, 175–6
Law Officers of the Crown 79, 81, 127n132
legal doctrine of intent 77–8, 182n77
letters of marque 63, 122n8
letters of neutrality 19, 21–2, 26, 46n29
Lifschütz, Alex 117–18

Machiavelli, Niccolò 44n7
McNair, Arnold D. (Lord) 14n30, 65, 172
maintenance, torts of 172, 186n133
Manchurian Conflict (1931) 148
Martens, George Fréderic de 55, 85, 103
Meyrowitz, Henry 8
Miele, Alberto 10, 17–18, 22–3, 55
military assistance to a belligerent 3–4, 84; without entering the war 108–10, 162–3
military expeditions 59, 68–74, 78, 81–4, 88, 102–3, 105

NATO bombing against Yugoslavia (1999) 2

Netherlands: during the Second World War 154–8, 192; in the eighteenth century 21, 23; in the interwar period 144, 149
neutral asylum 91–2, 95–6, 130n189
neutral character 15n36
neutral commerce 39–40, 42, 53n156; *see also* freedom of (maritime) commerce
neutral persons 96–7
neutral ports *see* warships
neutral waters *see* warships
neutralis 18–19, 28–30, 50n113
neutralitas 18–19, 28, 30, 48n83, 50n113, 51n138
neutrality laws 55, 60, 63–4, 72–4, 84, 121n3, 149, 159, 182n76; *see also* Table of national legislations
neutrality treaties 10–11, 17–32, 55; *see also* Table of treaties
non-belligerency 3–5, 163–4, 184n97, 185n99, 190–1
non-discriminatory conception of war 3, 5, 7, 14n20, 174, 186n147
non-intervention, the principle of 65
non-use of force, the principle of 2, 191–2
Norway 144, 149; during the Second World War 150–4, 156–8, 192

Oeter, Stefan 10, 17, 22, 26
Oppenheim, L. 68, 112, 114, 117, 119–20, 139n312, 164–9, 172

pacific blockade 138n302, 144
passage of troops through the land territory of a neutral State 90, 92, 95
permanent neutrality 5, 9, 133n225, 134n231, 177n4
Phillimore, Robert 86
Poland: the insurrection in 1831 66–7; invasion by Germany (1939) 150
Portugal: civil war in 1828 69 (*see also* Terceira affair); in the First World War 109–10, 162
Pradier-Fodéré, P. 108
prerogative *see* royal prerogative
prisoners of war 31, 67, 130n189; escaped prisoners of war 91, 96; internment by a neutral State 91, 96; in the *Altmark* case 150–1
privateering 56–8, 63, 77–8, 122n8
prize, bringing in a neural port 90, 100
prize law 4, 14n23, 15n36, 24, 104, 163

qualified neutrality 50n109, 85–7

recognition of belligerency *see* belligerency, recognition of
region of war 104, 134n229, 191
reprisals 138n302
requisition 15n34, 97, 110
right to remain neutral 5–6, 55, 102–5, 164–8, 188; the conditions for 105–8; the theoretical basis of 117–21; the view denying the existence of 112–18, 168–71
rights of a neutral State 6, 89–90, 104, 113, 137n296, 169
Rivier, Alphons 105, 113, 129n157, 134n231
Roosevelt, Franklin 161–2, 183n88
royal prerogative 62–3, 123n40, 128n143
rules of Washington 80–3, 128n143, 132n207
Russo-Japanese War (1904–5) 115, 140n328

San Remo Manual on International Law Applicable to Armed Conflicts at Sea 14n23
Schmitt, Carl 173–6
self-defence 115–16, 125n106, 138n299, 138n302, 138n308, 158, 181n67, 183n89, 191–2; *see also* collective self-denfence
self-preservation 116, 119, 125n106, 138n299, 138n308, 180n46
sick and wounded, passage through the territory of neutral States 90–1, 95, 130n186, 131n194
Sogawa, Takeo 174–5
sovereignty 82, 101, 103, 105, 114
Suárez, Francisco 23, 27, 29, 48n69
Switzerland 144, 149; in the Franco–Prussian War (1870–1) 130n189; in the Napoleonic Wars 115, 139n310; participation in the League of Nations 145–8; permanent neutrality of 133n225
sympathy, the expression of, by a neutral State 85, 105–6, 129n157, 176, 189

Tabata, Shigejiro 7, 174–5
Terceira affair 68–71
territorial inviolability 3, 6, 9–10, 94, 104, 113, 125n106, 137n296, 138n299, 145

226 *Index*

Textor, Johann Wolfgang 23–4, 46n40, 48n83
Thirty Years' War (1618–48) 19, 23, 25
Thomas Aquinas 27
three rules of Washington *see* rules of Washington

Ullmann, E. von 106–7
United States: assistance to Great Britain in the Second World War 158–64; in the French Revolutionary Wars 55–6, 121n3; the transfer of destroyers to Great Britain (destroyers deal) 159–60, 182n77
unneutral service (hostile assistance) 7

Vattel, Emer de 26, 30–5, 37–9, 48n83, 49n93, 50n108, 50n109, 151n138, 55, 65–7, 89, 111–12, 175, 188
Versailles system 148
Vitoria, Francisco de 23, 27, 29, 53n158
violation of neutrality 98, 107–8, 110–11, 115–16, 136n279, 150–2, 156, 160, 162, 165, 179n40
voluntary law of nations 31, 49n93

Walker, William 72
war: the concept of 13n14, 137n280, 138n302, 191–2; the freedom of States to resort to 3–8, 23–4, 47n45, 112, 142, 164, 168, 175, 188–90; the outlawry of 3, 169, 190
wars of independence of Spanish America in 1810s 59–60, 65
warships: in the territorial waters of neutral States 92–3, 98–100; the length (period) of stay in a neutral port 92, 99; passage of the territorial waters of neutral States 92, 99, 151–2, 180n46; repair in neutral ports 92, 99; replenishment of supply of material in neutral ports 92, 99
Westlake, John 78, 102
Westphalia, the peace of 26
Wheaton, Henry 65–6, 112
Wolff, Christian 18, 21, 23, 26, 30–9, 46n34, 48n83, 49n93, 111, 175, 188
Wright, Quincy 140n330

Yokota, Kisaburo 164, 166–8, 171